THE
CAMBRIDGE
GUIDE TO
Asian Theatre

EDITED BY
James R. Brandon

ADVISORY EDITOR
Martin Banham

CAMBRIDGE
UNIVERSITY PRESS

PUBLISHED BY THE PRESS SYNDICATE OF THE UNIVERSITY OF CAMBRIDGE
The Pitt Building, Trumpington Street, Cambridge, United Kingdom

CAMBRIDGE UNIVERSITY PRESS
The Edinburgh Building, Cambridge CB2 2RU, UK
40 West 20th Street, New York, NY 10011–4211, USA
477 Williamstown Road, Port Melbourne, VIC 3207, Australia
Ruiz de Alarcón 13, 28014 Madrid, Spain
Dock House, The Waterfront, Cape Town 8001, South Africa

http://www.cambridge.org

© Cambridge University Press 1993

First published 1993
Paperback edition 1997
Reprinted 1999, 2000, 2002 (twice), 2005

Printed in the United Kingdom at the University Press, Cambridge

Typeset in Swift 9.5/11.5 (KS)

A catalogue record for this book is available from the British Library

Library of Congress Cataloguing in Publication data
Cambridge guide to Asian theatre/edited by James R. Brandon;
advisory editor, Martin Banham
p.   cm.
Includes bibliographical references and index.
1. Theater Asia Dictionaries. 2. Performing arts Asia Dictionaries.
I. Brandon, James R.   II. Banham, Martin.
PN2860.C35   1993
792′.095 dc20   93-22340   CIP

ISBN 0 521 58822 7 paperback

Contents

Contributors

James R. Brandon
University of Hawai'i at Manoa
Introduction, Japan (traditional theatre)

Oh-kon Cho
State University of New York, College of Brockport
Korea

Kathy Foley
University of California, Santa Cruz
Burma, Cambodia, Indonesia, Laos, Malaysia, Oceania,
Philippines, Thailand, Vietnam (traditional theatre)

David G. Goodman
University of Illinois at Urbana-Champaign
Japan (modern theatre)

Krishen Jit
University of Malaya
Indonesia, Malaysia, Philippines, Singapore,
Thailand, Vietnam (modern theatre)

Colin Mackerras
Griffith University
China

Farley Richmond
State University of New York, Stony Brook
Bangladesh, India, Nepal, Pakistan, Sri Lanka

A. C. Scott
University of Wisconsin-Madison
China

Daniel S. P. Yang
University of Colorado, Boulder; Hong Kong Repertory Theatre
Hong Kong, Taiwan

Toni Shapiro has provided additional material
on the current situation in Cambodia.

EDITOR'S PREFACE

When *The Cambridge Guide to World Theatre* was published in 1988, it was immediately recognized as an indispensable reference work in theatre. One of its great values was its ecumenical placing of European, North and South American, African, Arab, Oceanic and Asian theatres side-by-side and page-by-page throughout that substantial volume. It made a forceful statement that Euro-American theatres could no longer be the standard by which other theatres of the world were to be judged. Each culture produces its own forms of performance, which must be understood within its own cultural and historical contexts, not as a shadow of, or in comparison (usually invidious) to, a Western 'norm' which is assumed to be superior. I was happy to have been invited by Martin Banham, editor of *The Cambridge Guide to World Theatre*, to be editorial consultant for Asia and Oceania and to suggest writings for that work.

I was even more pleased when Cambridge University Press proposed that the Asian materials from *The Cambridge Guide to World Theatre* be presented in this separate volume. A smaller volume dedicated to theatre in Asia and Oceania would be convenient for students and scholars specializing in Asian or Pacific theatre. What is more, it opened the opportunity to revise and improve what were already excellent articles.

The book is designed to provide, within the space constraints of a single volume, an overall description of the theatre that evolved in Asia and the Pacific over the course of 2000 years, and of the performances that exist in this region today. The articles are written by specialists in one or more areas and cover the theatre of Asia and the Pacific from China in the north to Indonesia in the south, and from Pakistan in the west to Polynesia in the east. Regional similarities and common themes are discussed in the Oceania entry, which covers Melanesia, Micronesia and Polynesia, and in the general Introduction. The bulk of the book consists of 19 national, that is country, chapters (i.e. Cambodia, India, China). Each consists of a major country article covering the historical development and current status of theatre. If information is abundant and the theatre complex, this is followed by cross-indexed, genre entries that describe repertory and performance characteristics of important theatre forms in greater detail. A group of artist entries is included for most countries, giving information about important playwrights, actors, and directors of the past and present. Finally, a select bibliography of major writings in English concludes the country chapter.

Countries are arranged alphabetically, as are genre names and artist names within each entry; this, we believe, will help the interested reader find specific information. In general we follow current national configurations, so that Tibet, for example, is included as a part of China, while Hong Kong and Taiwan are country entries. There are two exceptions: the separate nations of North and South Korea are covered in one entry, and the numerous island nations of the South Pacific are grouped together in the Oceania article.

Nine leading scholars of the theatre in Asia and the Pacific have contributed either whole or partial country entries in this book. Regrettably A. C. Scott died during the time he was writing the major article on Chinese theatre for *The Cambridge Guide to World Theatre*; the China entries were completed by Colin Mackerras. For the present volume, authors have revised their entries, often extensively. Each has added recent information about current performances and has expanded coverage of areas previously underrepresented. Toni Shapiro, conducting research in theatre in Phnom Penh, has contributed current data for Cambodia. Cambridge University Press has expanded the size of this volume in order to accommodate some 100 newly-written genre and artist entries. Finally, the bibliographies have been updated and new photographs have been selected to illustrate the theatre forms.

All the entries are cross-referenced, so that a word in small capitals (or italic small capitals for words that would normally be in italic) indicates that a separate entry exists under that word.

My warmest thanks go to Sarah Stanton, editor at Cambridge University Press, for providing generous and steadfast support throughout the complex editing process, and to Caroline Bundy for seeing the manuscript through to publication. I also want to thank Elizabeth Casper for her efficient editorial assistance, in particular for the South Asian entries. Finally, I send a grateful Hawai'ian *mahalo* to Martin Banham, the farsighted visionary who conceived of this series of encyclopedias of world theatre.

JAMES R. BRANDON
Honolulu 1993

INTRODUCTION

Perhaps 25,000 theatre troupes perform traditional and modern plays in the enormous geographic area of the Asian mainland and the adjoining islands of the western Pacific Ocean. In fact, no one knows the full extent of performing arts among the two billion people who live in some 40 nation-states within the region. There are too many performers, too many remote regions, and there is too much daily change for anyone to know for certain. What is known, is that theatrical arts in Asian and Pacific-island cultures are ancient, highly developed, rich almost beyond imagining in their diversity, and very much alive today for large segments of the population.

From Pakistan in the west to the Hawai'ian Islands in the east, and from China in the north to Indonesia in the south, the theatrical arts have evolved into as many as 700–800 distinct forms or genres. Each is clearly different from neighbouring theatre forms. Each reflects the unique language, religious views, social structures and daily lives of the people – artists and audiences – who have created it. Each is distinguishable by its own constellation of music, movement, acting style and staging conventions, and by dramatic content and form. Even to the relatively uninitiated observer, KYŌGEN comedies in Japan stand apart from KABUKI or from BUNRAKU, also from Japan, and they are artistic and cultural worlds away from Indonesian LUDRUK, BHAVAI in India or Beijing opera in China, forms which also feature comic elements. The distinctiveness of each country's theatre forms and their historical development will be described in detail in the chapters that follow, each chapter contributed by a specialist author (or authors) and devoted to a single country.

At the same time, shared features link genres within and between countries. We can even, with considerable caution, identify interregional and even pan-Asian-Pacific traditions and patterns of performance. In this chapter I will suggest some of the major commonalities among theatre forms in Asia and the Pacific islands that arose from centuries, even millennia, of interrelationships, and from similarity of race and ethnicity, of religion, of politics, of language or of literary traditions.

Four major geographic (and cultural) regions may be identified within this vast sweep of land and ocean. South Asia, which encompasses the present nation-states of Bangladesh, India, Nepal, Pakistan and Sri Lanka, is the home of Hinduism and Buddhism, the source of dramatic themes from the epics, the *Ramayana* and the *Mahabharata*, and mother to a pervasive and multifaceted classical dance tradition. The outpouring of fecund detail, a baroque love of brilliant theatrical display and the vibrant use of colour, emotion and rhythm in performance mark South Asian forms.

China, Hong Kong, Taiwan, Japan and Korea comprise East Asia. They share cultures based on Confucian civil ethics, systems of imperial rule and Buddhist philosophy. The Chinese writing system of calligraphic characters was adopted in all these areas, and in the process Chinese literature and Chinese arts of brush painting, music and dance were introduced as well. In East Asia a spirit of decorum and restraint, and a concern for structural simplicity and clarity, are apparent in the performing arts.

The countries of Southeast Asia – Burma, Cambodia, Indonesia, Laos, Malaysia, the Philippines, Singapore, Thailand and Vietnam – have welcomed religions, literature and dance from both South and East Asia, and fused these with rich indigenous performance traditions. Malay peoples settled Indonesia, Malaysia, southern Thailand, Singapore and the Philippines, and these countries share many theatre traits in common. Related Chinese-influenced musics are heard in theatres in northern Burma and hero, Amir Hamza, appears in BANGSAWAN in Malaysia and, in Indonesia, the world's most populous Muslim nation, in KETOPRAK and WAYANG golek. Muslim and Christian influences contend in Philippine KOMEDYA, and Christian biblical stories and later mediaeval romances are dramatized in Sri Lankan PASKU, Indian CAVITTU NATAKAM, and Philippine SENAKULO.

However, it should not be imagined that this dramatic material travels intact and unaltered from one culture to another. Just as Japanese Buddhism is different from Chinese Buddhism (to say nothing of Sri Lankan Buddhism), Chinese stories dramatized in Korea and Japan are greatly altered and acquire a local flavour. One of Asia's ur-myths tells of a celestial bird-maiden who, captured by a mortal, escapes to heaven by dancing in her angel's feathers: this basic story acquires an aesthetic expression in the The Angel Robe (Hagoromo) in Japanese theatre, while the conflicting human and sacred views are fundamental in Manora in Thai, Burmese and Malaysian drama.

The Hindu Ramayana contains one of the world's great mythic motifs: the withdrawal of the hero, Rama, from affairs of the world, initiation through asceticism and the gaining of spiritual power (mana, sakti), and return to temporal rule. In various forms, this philosophic–political quest theme occurs in dramas far beyond India. It is found in Thai LAKON FAI NAI and LIKAY, in Indonesian and Malaysian WAYANG and in Cambodian LAKON BASSAK in varied guises. When Rama himself appears on the Javanese or Balinese stage he is localized into a Javanese or Balinese king; in Buddhist Burma, Thailand and Cambodia, Rama is portrayed as Buddha in a former life. Events in the Chinese 'Three Kingdoms' stories are known not just in Chinese theatre forms, but are dramatized in Vietnam, Japan and Korea as well. The legend, originating in India, of the one-horned wizard who traps the rain gods and brings drought to the world, is dramatized in China and in Japan in NŌ, KYŌGEN, and KABUKI.

Historical intermixture of genres

Asian and Pacific performance styles and content have been carried by performers to neighbouring countries often over periods of time, resulting in performance similarities among cultures. Dancers, actors and musicians either carried their performance skills to foreign countries, or, conversely, learned performance skills while abroad and then brought them home. We don't know which of these two processes occurred but, a millennium ago, Indian-style dance became known to performers far beyond that country's boundaries. It fused with local dance styles, creating numerous related dance forms, among them, Indonesian LEGONG and WAYANG ORANG, Cambodian LAKON KABACH BORAN, Thai LAKON FAI NAI and Malaysian MAK YONG.

Javanese shadow-puppet performers carried their theatre to neighbouring Malaysia, Cambodia and Bali (perhaps Indian shadow players came to Southeast Asia earlier). Korean and Japanese artists learned masked dances at the Chinese court in the early Tang dynasty (618–907), returned home and transplanted the Chinese performing style to their own courts, in the process establishing in Korea kiak and in Japan BUGAKU and gigaku. The theatre music of Vietnam shows inescapable affinities with that of Okinawa, and of Taiwan and the Philippines as well, resulting from hundreds of years of small-scale artistic exchange along seafaring routes of trade. During national wars between Vietnam and China (11th–13th centuries), and among Cambodia, Thailand and Burma (15th–18th centuries), entire court troupes were captured as booty. As a result there are significant intermixtures of theatre forms and performance styles among these countries.

Finally, Western entrepreneurs and colonial administrations brought popular forms of Western music, dance and theatre into India, the Philippines and Japan beginning in the 16th century, and into other countries somewhat later. From these and later European and American contacts stem such urban popular entertainments as bodabil (vaudeville) in the Philippines, urban professional melodrama in Calcutta and Bombay, and all-female operetta, takarazuka, in Japan. In the early decades of the 20th century, Chinese and Korean students studying in Japan discovered Western melodrama and serious drama through Japanese productions and translations. By the time of World War II, a considerable number of Asian playwrights, directors and actors had travelled to Europe and the United States, learning Western spoken drama and realistic theatre. With Ibsen and Stanislavski as their inspiration, they returned to create a modern, serious, realistic drama in their own countries. English-language theatre became strongly established in Singapore and the Philippines, and, to a lesser extent, Hong Kong, Malaysia and Burma, all areas under long-lasting British or American colonization. Concurrently, traditional Asian artists were performing on tour in the West for the first time. Artists of the European avant-garde were able to see *Mei Lanfang, kabuki*, and Cambodian and Balinese dance troupes. Brecht, Artaud and Meyerhold were deeply influenced and artists in other fields as well – Eisenstein, Rodin, Loie Fuller, Isadora Duncan and others – responded to the vividly 'exotic other' of these epochal performances in the early decades of the 20th century.

In the nearly 50 years following the end of World War II, theatrical interchange between Asia–Oceania and Europe–America has become established as a continuous process of mutual interaction, so that recent developments in theatre anywhere in the world are quickly known to at least some theatre practitioners in every country of this area. Happenings, absurdism, deconstructionism and multiculturalism echo in theatre practice here as well as in the West. Concurrently, Western actors, dancers, musicians, directors and playwrights are seriously

American actor, James Grant Benton, performs a standard *kabuki* acting pattern (*kata*) in *Narukami the Thundergod*, Asian Theatre Program, University of Hawaii (1973), directed by James R. Brandon.

studying the performance forms of Asia and Oceania, often gaining considerable mastery in them.

Performance training and transmission

A two-step process of performance preparation indicates the nature of most Asian traditional theatre. The process is centred in the actor, for the actor is the source and repository of most performance information. In many forms there are strong dramatic texts, written by elite, or at least knowledgeable, specialist playwrights, that exemplify local literary standards and forms. But in other genres the centrality of the actor extends to script composition: the actor may be a playwright, or improvise dialogue and, in some cases, song lyrics during performance. In order to function at this high technical level, the first task of the actor (dancer or musician) is to become proficient in the artistic and performance 'codes', the artistic languages, of the theatre form. One does not begin by training to 'act'; one begins by training to be a skilled 'artist'. The Indian *kathakali* actor spends his childhood forming his body into a pliable instrument for the leaps and whirls of dance, the eye, mouth and cheek movements expressive of emotion and the 600 hand gestures (*hasta, mudra*) that he must flawlessly execute when on stage enacting a role. ZEAMI, writing in 15th-century Japan, said the actor should spend from the age of seven to seventeen mastering the 'two arts' (*nikyoku*) of chanting and dance before seriously studying role-playing, that is, 'acting'. The Indonesian or Malaysian puppeteer learns the 100-plus battle movements of the shadow puppets. The *gamelan* musician who accompanies Javanese theatre learns 120 melodies and the Thai theatre musician learns 200–300 tunes, any one of which may be called for in performance. The Beijing opera student masters scores of movement techniques – 'water sleeve' (*shuixiu*) gestures, tumbling and acrobatics in the fighting arts (*wushu*) – and, at least in the past, carried out demanding vocal exercises outdoors at 5 a.m. summer and winter before the stone 'sounding board' of a city wall.

Second, and only after this firm artistic base has been laid, the actor learns to enact roles in plays. He or she acts within a generic role-type that has been developed by earlier generations of performers within the artistic codes and the subject matter of the theatrical form. Young male hero, older male authority figure, young woman, older woman, villain (often 'foreign' or an ogre, demon, or *jin*, a creature outside the human realm) and clown are roles found in most traditional theatre forms. A performance, then, is one momentary arrangement of pre-known elements, one in a series of performances which are rather like the changing patterns of a kaleidoscope. Performances are examples of an existing artistic form much more than they are the 'production of a play'. The 'play is *not* the thing'; the genre, the art form is. To put together a traditional performance does not require the special outside vision of a director, as we in Western theatre expect (except perhaps when a long-unstaged play is revived). Actors, dancers and musicians are themselves the source of knowledge of how to perform and they are capable of working as a self-directing ensemble.

In part because the musical, dance and voice technique is so highly developed, and so demanding, in Asian and Oceanic performance, systems for transmitting performance knowledge to the next generation are vital to genres' survival. The most common method of professional training is for a pupil to apprentice him- or herself to a master and learn by assisting, watching and receiving informal instruction over an extended period, perhaps a lifetime. The art may be passed from father to son (ICHIKAWA DANJŪRŌ is a 12th-generation *kabuki* actor), or within hereditary clans (Indian *KUTIYATTAM*). These master–pupil relationships are strongly formalized in India, Thailand and especially Japan, with severe penalties exacted on a disciple who abandons a teacher. In some cases a master may take a group of students and train them together in a school (in Hawai'i called *hālau*, 'temple', indicating the sacred nature of performance transmission). Today numerous formal academies also exist to teach young performers of Chinese opera, Indian classical dance, Indonesian, Thai, and Cambodian dance dramas, Korean *sandae-gŭk*, and other forms. They have formalized curricula, large classes, multiple teachers, and are for a fixed number of years. In Japan, training for *kabuki* and

bunraku is now offered in both systems because the master–disciple system could not produce enough actors quickly enough. Most governments in Asia today either run or subsidize academy training.

Unlike text-based Western drama, which can be transmitted by published books and stored for centuries, the art of traditional performance resides in the body of the living performer-teacher. Hence the critical nature of training: if even one generation fails to learn, a theatre genre will be lost irrevocably.

Song, dance, masks, puppetry

It is often said that all Asian performance is 'dance'. This is true in the sense that all acting follows well-defined movement codes, and that every stage movement is carefully controlled. Beyond this, there are numerous theatre genres that fuse choreographed stage movement (steps, turns, stamps, jumps, hand and arm gestures, facial expression) with rhythmic music, and often with sung lyrics as well. The dance is a major structural component in the dramatic composition and story-telling of many forms. Formal set dances, with opening, development and conclusion, and specific placement within the play structure, are easily recognizable. There is good reason to call such performances 'dance dramas'.

Other forms can be said to be built around song. In these, sung lyrics are the major component of dramatic structure, and the 'actor' is required to have developed exceptional vocal skill. For convenience, we often call these forms 'operas' in English, for example, Korean *P'ANSORI*, Indonesian *ARJA*, Chinese *KUNQU*, Taiwanese *GOZAI XI*, Indian *KHYAL*.

Actors in scores of genres wear masks, the mask's transformative power allowing the performer to wholly transcend self and portray gods, spirits of the dead, demons, mythological figures and animals as well as ordinary humans. Certainly the beyond-human worlds that are evoked in Indonesian *TOPENG*, Indian *chhau*, Cambodian *LAKON KAWL*, Japanese *BUGAKU*, and various Sri Lankan, Tibetan and Nepalese forms, relate closely to the defining nature of the powerful masks that are worn.

A unique feature of theatre in Asia is the

immense importance of puppetry, especially shadow theatre. Doll- or marionette-puppet theatre is known in almost every country of Asia (India, Pakistan, Burma, Indonesia, China, Korea and Japan). Vietnam boasts a unique form of puppetry performed on the surface of a lake (MUÁ RÔI NUOC). Dozens of varieties of leather shadow-play are seen throughout the arc beginning with India in the west, and running through Malaysia, Thailand, Cambodia, Indonesia and the Philippines to the south, and into China in the east. Probably doll figures were originally connected to animistic beliefs and they served as totemic representatives of a clan, while flickering shadows cast on a white screen allowed the shades of the spirit world to manifest themselves before human audiences. Puppets, devoid of mortality, were the ideal representatives for our human performative communication with the sacred realm. Among Asian puppet forms are some of the most sophisticated literary and theatre arts in the world (Japan, BUNRAKU, Indonesia, WAYANG kulit, for example). A 5-ft-tall shadow puppet of Thailand or Cambodia shows an entire scene with multiple characters in tableau. Puppet performance is steeped in ethical and spiritual ambience. Throughout Asia puppet theatre forms have served as progenitors and models for the later development of human theatre forms. Nowhere in Asia is this medium a 'child's' theatre.

When we use the English term opera, mask, dance or puppet to characterize a performance we of course do a disservice by simplifying. Our common use of such terms is perhaps necessary, but it should not obscure the reality that most theatre forms in Asia are interwoven fabrics of music, dance and acting, and after that perhaps also of masks or puppetry: the Chinese opera 'singer' speaks, dances and does acrobatics as well as sing; the nō 'dancer' chants, speaks and sings as well as dances. In an Indonesian 'shadow'-theatre performance, a spectator is treated to the puppeteer's singing, spoken dialogue and chanted narrative, to orchestral music accompanied by female and male choral singing, to sound effects and to colourful puppet figures, as well as the 'shadows' on the screen. Most Asian theatre is 'total theatre' in which all performance aspects are fused into a single form. The nature of each form is largely dependent upon the particular balance among its many components and constituent parts, what element is emphasized and what element is subordinated. (Kyōgen in Japan, primarily a prose dialogue form, is the rare exception that only occasionally uses masks or orchestral musical accompaniment.)

In contrast, in the history of Western performing arts we see an ever-increasing specialization via performance medium. The arts have been separated from each other, so concert music (orchestral music without lyrics), ballet or modern dance (dance with orchestral music), and spoken drama (speech without music, dance, or song) have become totally separate performance genres in Western culture. Drama is still largely equated with literature. In spite of a century of polemics against this limitation, we remain preoccupied with content and meaning, that is, with literary and intellectual concerns, when we consider theatre. Western musical comedy and opera, which might seem exceptions, only prove the strength of this critical bias. Because these forms are not text-based it is common to set them outside the boundaries of 'legitimate' drama, ghettoizing them to the status of 'other'.

Artistic 'codes'

Understanding and appreciating Asian–Pacific theatre requires knowledge of performance, and theatre is equated with performance not literature. All the theatrical means of expression are accorded value. In its diversity and richness of

The 'Pine Room' scene in *The Forty-Seven Loyal Retainers (Kanadehon Chūshingura)*, in *bunraku* performance, National Theatre of Japan, Tokyo.

performance practice, theatre in Asia–Oceania has increasingly become a stimulus and model in the West, as it has to such contemporary theatre figures as Jerzy Grotowski, Peter Brook, Ariane Mnouchkine, David Henry Hwang and Peter Sellars.

Artistic codes reinforce the centrality of the genre, as opposed to the (Western) centrality of the individual piece being performed. The great performers in this region are like jazz musicians, who, steeped in the structural system of the music, are the source of creation. Also, although all structures are inherently confining, and therefore limiting, they also provide the base from which the great artist goes on to create new compositions.

It would be incorrect to assume these performance codes are matters merely of technique. Meaning adheres to them in several dimensions. In the broadest sense, the actor functions in a way parallel to the ritualist: an agent responsible in the aesthetic-symbolic sphere for precisely replicating received artistic forms, just as the priest is responsible in the sacred-symbolic sphere for correctly replicating received ritual forms. Hence, the need for the traditional actor to devote every fibre of his being to the forms of the art. This does not mean that performance is religious; it means that the actor's focus is almost never the self, but the genre. What is often called by Western observers an 'actor's theatre' is in fact an 'acting theatre' with the focus on the larger aesthetic of received structures and not on the individual actor.

Codes suggest a world larger than the specific world of the characters in a single play. The codes encompass all the plays in the repertory (or at least subgroups within the repertory). Characters as 'types' are larger than a single individual and speak for groups or classes of people. (We accept this concept in representative government, politically, but it is harder for us to see the value of this in our arts.)

The discipline and control shown by the performer promotes within the performance a sense of order and knowability. This could be connected to reification through story line of stasis within societies. It communicates to the audience, if only on the subliminal level, the values of control and discipline in the individual.

Codes create 'stylization' in performance, a term that connotes something superficial, precious, and probably not serious, in much Western discourse. But art means artifice in a positive way: something artificial, something man-made, as opposed to occurring in nature. Plato was wrong, art is not false: art's function in human society is that its stage 'artifices' symbolically interpret our human and social condition in structured and elliptical ways. The artistic codes of music, dance, song, narrative, costuming, masking and the like in Asia and the Pacific are lenses through which human life is refracted into patterns unique to each genre. This is no simple mirror to nature, but a process much more artistically elaborate and symbolically complex.

Theatre's medium is the actor's living body; the actor represents another. Theatre is the only art form humans have devised which is based on transformation of the artist (actor) into a symbolic other. Transformation is socially important in societies where humans commune with the sacred realm in performance and codes play an important part of this enabling process. The most complete transformations occur in possession or trance, states in which the performer is understood to wholly lose conscious power over his or her actions on stage. Because the actor's body has undergone lengthy artistic discipline, a performer is enabled to undergo extreme states of transformation, becoming with relative ease a supernatural serpent in a Chinese opera, a demonic figure of rage in *kathakali* performance, or the witch figure of Rangda in Balinese *barong*. Pivotal *kabuki* scenes show the theatrical transformation of a human being into a god, demon or beast, via costume and makeup change. Such enactments would be difficult if not impossible to achieve within a realistic-based theatre, not because the transformation would strain audience credibility, but because the untrained actor is physically and mentally incapable of sustaining the suprahuman physical demands which extreme states of transformation require. Gender transformations are common – actresses portraying male characters in Indonesia, Cambodia, Thailand, China; actors playing female characters in India, China and Japan. These transformations are filtered through, and supported by, the strong artistic codes assigned to gender portrayal.

In the development of Asia and Oceania's many masked theatre forms, we can see a powerful impulse toward transformation of an extreme kind. The vivid makeup styles of red, green, black and white that evolved in *kathakali*, in *kabuki* and in Chinese opera, perform the same theatrical function of supporting a violent transformation of actor into a wholly different character. It is commonly said that 'an actor can play any role' in *kabuki*, because command of artistic codes allows *any* transformation, irrespective of actor personality or 'ability'.

Transformation is a socially dangerous event. In traditional societies that prize highly the maintenance of social stability, theatre is suspect (at the same time that it also promotes stability). The actor-artist, shaman-like, has the power to transform, if only symbolically, into a god or evil demon on stage before the community, and he, too, is suspect. The Asian performer has often been feared for being social misfit, outcast, wanderer in an agricultural society. To the extent that theatre as a social institution is based on the actor's transformative function, theatre is suspect in all societies and all ages. From a social perspective, puppet representation is 'safe' – the inanimate puppet can portray a god with a good deal less danger than can a human actor. It may be that realism was so readily accepted by Western societies in part because the dangerously liminal aspect of transformation virtually disappeared in plays about daily life and acting was rationally explained as a internal psychological task of the actor (not a public action).

Aesthetics and structure

There is no single Asian–Oceanic aesthetic of theatre nor is there a single structural pattern, but rather numerous, even opposing, aesthetics and structures. For example, Indian theatre's comprehensive *rasa-bhava* aesthetic, described by the writer BHARATA MUNI, is based on congruences. It is an elaborate and specific system to help the performer identify the means of expression that are most appropriate to convey one or more of the basic human emotions (gentle words and caressing gestures to convey love, for exam-

ple). The locus of the aesthetic effect, *rasa*, is in the mind and heart of the spectator. Quite different from this is the *in-yō (yin-yang)* principle of light-and-dark which ZEAMI recommends should regulate a *nō* actor's performance. He advised doing the unexpected in order to surprise the audience, to pique their interest : if it is a night performance, do a bright, lively play; if your competitor has just scored a success with brilliant dancing, emphasize the beauty of chant in your performance. The opposition, and balancing, is a property of the performance itself and rests directly with the performer. Different aims of performance are summed up in two expressions: in India a theatre-goer is 'one who sees' the play, while in China an audience goes to 'hear theatre'. Other examples could be given to illustrate that there is great variety within the hundreds of genres and language groups being considered later. Again it is important to repeat: 'Asia' and 'Oceania' are only words to identify conveniently broad geographic areas that encompass richly variant arts.

Performances are structured in time in sophisticated ways. The longest time cycle I am aware of is a Papua New Guinea dance play that extends over a decade. Many seasonal performances are timed to match annual celebrations of planting and harvesting, of the new year and summer solstice. A day's programme will almost always follow a well-known structural order: a 3-part structure in Indonesian *wayang*, in which musical pitch rises through the 9-hour evening performance (among other features), or, to cite another well-known example, a 4-part structure in Japanese *kabuki*, in which scenes are arranged so the audience will experience, in sequence over the 4–6-hour performance, strong, slow formality, languid elegance, lively casualness and colourful, rhythmic action. By custom, performance is usually limited to certain hours (this may be in part restriction, in part preference). Time may be structured in cyclical terms. In Javanese dance and music, it is said the audience should be unaware of any beginning or end points, and should be carried along by continuous movement and sound representing the neverending cycle of life. An all-day *kabuki* play will conclude on an interesting tableau, cutting off the conclusion of the story. Within a performance, refined concepts of timing, dynamics and temporal flow regulate the actor and supporting musicians and singers in their interactions. One of the most famous of these is *jo-ha-kyū*, literally, 'opening-breaking (apart)-speeding up', which is easily observable in the continual tempo changes that occur in dance moment by moment and in song phrase by phrase throughout a *nō* performance. Spontaneity is achieved through the delicate balance between actor and music: the idea that in sophisticated performance movements should be slightly off the beat is widespread. Contrary to standard Western analyses of theatre, these structural systems organize performance elements – rhythm, emotional tone, volume, colour, mass, intensity, speed – to the exclusion, total or partial, of content.

The present situation

A truly remarkable number of traditional theatre forms, some over 1000 years old, continue being performed for Asian and Pacific audiences today. But other theatre genres have been lost. If the historical continuity of theatre in the region is impressive, it is also true that change occurs without cease. Audience tastes, economic circumstances and social values change, and as long as human bodies are the carriers of the tradition, changes must occur in plays, performance style and 'codes' of performance. The rate of change is

also being profoundly influenced by the increasing interrelatedness of nations and people.

Two opposing currents swirl and push against each other. I do not believe there ever will be such a thing as one global village, but intercultural mixing of theatres is occurring at an unprecedented rate today. Asian and Oceanic artists regularly tour abroad and attend international symposia and conferences, absorbing the latest in world theatre happenings. Pacific governments are proud to host international and regional theatre festivals. And everywhere tourism is expanding exponentially. The walls that only a few decades ago still separated genre from genre, and culture from culture, are falling rapidly. And the impact of international television, via satellite and video-cassette, is increasingly important and apparent.

The opposing current is an intense pride in one's self and one's culture, often with a concomitant aversion to the import of foreign culture and arts. Not very long ago local intellectuals might have accepted Western theatre theories which held that Sanskrit drama was an inferior form of drama because it did not achieve 'tragedy', and *nō* was not even drama, since it was not based on 'dramatic conflict'. But no longer. In a replay of the early-20th-century polemic stance that 'Western science' must not contaminate 'national spirit', many want to accept Western political and economic systems while simultane-

A modern stage comedy starring the popular comedian, Fujima Kambei, as a working class hero, Nakaza Theatre, Osaka (1972).

ously preserving local cultural values. In modern theatre this originally meant taking the dramatic structure of realist drama and realistic methods of acting and staging, and filling that structure with the content of Asian and Pacific social and political situations. Local playwrights wrote about contemporary local situations and often met with audience indifference. Actors, performing translations of Ibsen, Shaw or Chekhov, were called on to ape the behaviour and dress of Norwegians, Englishmen and Russians – leading to the nickname 'red haired' drama. (In India and Southeast Asia, characters and scenes were localized for popular, non-elite audiences, to avoid the foreign stigma.) The sense of ambivalence toward melding Western and indigenous elements is most apparent in modern theatre, but it underlies many policies and strategies found in traditional theatre as well.

Conclusion

Throughout Asia and Oceania, governments and broadly-based social and artistic organizations seek to preserve and invigorate traditional, indigenous theatre forms that reflect their cultural legacy. The challenge of radio, film and television for audiences is daunting. Foreign, mainly Western, films are extremely popular and on video-cassette are widely sold in most countries. Major efforts to provide local theatre subsidies, to build national theatre complexes, and to establish training institutions to assure transmission to the next generation of performers are a part of most government development plans. Similarly, avant-garde playwrights and directors have sought since the 1960s and 70s to return to traditional performing 'roots' in their search for new theatre forms that reflect each cultural and national identity. Their assertion of artistic and cultural independence often grows from the deliberate rejection of Western realist theatre imported over the past century. Realism in any case does not interest most Asian audiences for it

lacks the vital theatricality of familiar traditional forms. Burgeoning economies provide audiences in many countries with the means to support artistic pursuits. And so traditional revival and radical experiments in form and content are two contrasting and significant features of theatre at present. It is not strange that theatre today should exhibit the *in-yō* dialectic of opposites balanced within the whole, for old and new are inescapable aspects of the contemporary Asia–Oceania circumstance. Cultures and nations throughout the world are interrelated. Innumerable interrelationships exist among theatres and theatre forms not only within Asia and the Pacific Ocean, but with theatres and nations outside the region. Inescapably, the performers of Asia and of Oceania are becoming responsible not just to their local audiences but also to audiences around the world.

Bibliography

E. Barba and N. Savarese, *A Dictionary of Theatre Anthropology*, tr. R. Fowler, London and New York, 1991; F. Bowers, *Theatre in the East: A Survey of Asian Dance and Drama*, New York, 1956; J. R. Brandon, *Theatre in Southeast Asia*, Cambridge, Mass., 1967, *Brandon's Guide to Theater in Asia*, Honolulu, 1976, and (ed.), *The Performing Arts in Asia*, Paris, 1971, *Traditional Asian Plays*, New York, 1972; V. R. Irwin (ed.), *Four Classical Asian Plays in Modern Translation*, Harmondsworth, 1972; E. T. Kirby, *Ur-Drama: The Origins of Theatre*, New York, 1975; M. R. Malkin, *Traditional and Folk Puppets of the World*, Cranbury, N.J., 1978; M. T. Osman (ed.), *Traditional Drama and Music of Southeast Asia*, Kuala Lumpur, 1974; L. C. Pronko, *Theater East and West: Perspectives Toward a Total Theater*, Berkeley, Calif., 1974 (1967); A. C. Scott, *The Theatre in Asia*, New York, 1972; J. Tilakasiri, *The Puppet Theatre of Asia*, Colombo, 1968; Tokyo National Research Institute of Cultural Properties (ed.), *Masked Performances in Asia*, Tokyo, 1987; H. W. Wells, *The Classical Drama of the Orient*, New York, 1965; G. L. Anderson (ed.), *The Genius of the Oriental Theatre*, New York, 1966, and (ed.), *Masterpieces of the Orient*, New York, 1961.

BANGLADESH

Bangladesh was created in 1971 as an independent state from former East Pakistan. The population is predominantly Muslim, sharing this heritage with Pakistanis, while being ethnically and linguistically Bengali, thus sharing a common culture with the Bengali people of northeastern India. This linguistic and cultural tie has been a determining factor in the development of the theatre: Bangladesh theatre is intimately linked to the history of theatre in the whole Bengali-speaking region, including the state of West Bengal in India. Peasants form the majority of the Bengali population both in Bangladesh and West Bengal. Consequently, Bengali-language JATRA troupes (see India) have long enjoyed popularity among villagers throughout the region and have generally been able to cross from one country into the other while touring. Jatra is therefore an exceptional example in Asia of a theatre form that can be considered the 'joint' cultural property of two nations.

Urban theatre had modest beginnings during the 19th century in Dacca, the present capital of Bangladesh, expressing the concerns of the small but growing middle class of urban, intellectual Bengalis. Syed Abul Hasain wrote one prose and one musical play espousing the unity of Hindu and Muslim Bengalis. Until the partition of India and Pakistan in 1947, artists and writers in Dacca and Calcutta shared the ideas and common concerns of Bengali art and culture. After partition and the establishment of Muslim East Pakistan, amateur groups in Dacca broke the conventional prohibition against women on stage and began mounting 'co-acted' modern plays in 1950–51. In the 1950s and 60s the Drama Circle at Dacca University organized numerous amateur productions, and it hosted performances by the famous Bohorupee modern-drama troupe from Calcutta. Beginning in the 1960s the Bangla Academy established an annual Drama Season, which subsidized new productions, sponsored playwriting competitions and brought in troupes from England and the United States, thus opening their theatre to world influences. These influences are apparent in Sayeed Ahmed's *Kalbela* and *Milepost*, which echo Samuel Beckett. Strindberg's The father was staged in the style of local *jatra*, showing a maturing of theatre in this Muslim culture.

As the struggle for an independent Bangladesh grew stronger, many urban theatre people were motivated to work for liberation through their plays. Dramas were written on the theme of the repression of the Bengali people and their plight. In the late 1960s this struggle moved from the theatre halls to the streets and theatre people helped coalesce public support for the independence movement.

A new era was ushered in after independence, in which groups of young players have struggled to establish artistic roots in the community and survive economically. Among the groups founded in the 1970s are Aranyak, Bahubachan, Nagorik, Theatre, Dacca Drama, Padatik, Dacca Padatik, and Kathak. In smaller urban centres other groups have sprung up in recent years. All the groups share common concerns through affiliation with the Bangladesh Centre of the International Theatre Institute.

Bibliography

A. R. Z. Hyder, 'A Small House Beside a Highway: A Play for Television with an Essay, Development of Drama and Theatre in East Pakistan', MFA thesis, Univ. of Hawaii, 1968.

BURMA (MYANMAR)

This Southeast Asian country borders on India, Bangladesh, China, Laos and Thailand; the country is 600 miles by 800 miles in its major land area with a thin strip running another 500 miles down the Malay peninsula. The population of 41 million is composed of hill people and lowlanders. Though music and dance are important among the hill groups, drama is historically a development of the lowland areas where the Burmese predominate. The Burmese speak a Tibeto-Burman language and have adopted cultural patterns from the ethnically related Pyu and Mon who established themselves in the area prior to Burmese migration from Tibet. From the Pyu they learned Theraveda Buddhism, a belief system which, mixed with animist elements, has contributed to performance practice in terms of aesthetics, performance occasions and plot patterns. The recorded history of the Burmese begins with the founding of the kingdom of Pagan in the 11th century.

Though Indian, Chinese and Tibetan influences are evident in the music and repertoire, general Southeast Asian features underlie performance: the assertion that human performance is modelled on the puppet theatre, the function of the clown, set character types, such as the refined hero who clashes with an ogrely villain, and the dramatic structure that moves from court to the wilderness. Written records are rare and theatrical practice is passed orally from teacher to student in training and performance. Four categories can be distinguished: (1) animistic performance; (2) Buddhist theatre; (3) court dance drama; (4) popular performance.

Animistic performance

Until the late 1700s, dance and music seem more significant for human performers than drama in the context of animist performance. Traditionally, the Burmese believe in spirits called *nat*, which, alongside place spirits, include the spirits of

Classical court dance in which hunters holding bows approach the stags who are clearly indicated by their deer headdresses.

heroes, ancestors and even criminals. Throughout Burma, 37 major *nat* are honoured, and female and male transvestite spirit-mediums, *nat kadaw*, ('spirit wives'), enter trance to manifest them during festivals or in private seances for divination. Set songs are used to summon specific spirits. The mediums dance till possessed, then speak in the voice of the possessing spirit. Male mediums are more common than female at present. Shamanic patterns of sickness accompanying the call to the medium role are the norm.

The jerky movements of the ecstatic *nat* dances have perhaps contributed to the percussive nature of Burmese theatrical dance. This aesthetic is ancient, as is attested by the poem of a Tang dynasty official who saw Pyu performers at the Chinese court in AD 802. The twirls and leaps, the costume crowns and the sound of gongs described by him would be appropriate to a contemporary performance. Trance performances may have established the aesthetic, and NAT PWE ('spirit shows') may have provided the early format for drama activities, for legend claims that in the 1400s two outcast princes became the first secular performers by emulating seances of female mediums.

NAT PWE and ANYEIN PWE are two major genres still performed today with roots in trance traditions. In *nat pwe* a group of mediums dress in theatrical garb: the chief medium in the costume of a prince, a junior medium in a princess's costume. *Anyein pwe* features a female singer-dancer and a pair of clowns who perform while she rests, or joke with her. The form may be a secularization of the female trance tradition. The performance structure relates to *nat* dancing: the opening piece of all traditional drama is a *nat* dance executed by a female performer. The low status traditionally accorded to actors may have been accentuated by the animistic association: *nat* mediums hold a devalued position in the Buddhist society.

Buddhist theatre

Some Burmese scholars hold that the first dramas presented were of *Jataka* stories, that is tales presenting prior lives of the Buddha. By being reconceived as stories of incarnations of the historical Buddha, plots and tales from older and indigenous sources were incorporated into this tradition as well. NIBHATKHIN were religious plays on *Jataka*

themes. Scenes were presented on cart stages which stopped in various parts of the town. Aside from *nat pwe*, these were probably the main dramatic presentations in the period prior to 1752. Stories were derived from HAWSA, the story-telling tradition of Burma, in which a reciter told *Jataka* tales. When enacted as *nibhatkhin*, plays included a clown character (*lubyet*) who served the prince and added satirical comment. Like all Southeast Asian clowns, the *lubyet* of today is free to break the story frame as he improvises on any topic. Though he may have come to the *nibhatkhin* from earlier genres, he became ensconced in the Buddhist theatre and associated with the *Jataka* tradition. Because *Jataka* were important themes, classical drama as a whole was called ZAT PWE (literally, '*Jataka* show') and the name was retained even after the repertoire widened to include historical episodes and legends.

Tradition relates that the now rare puppet show, YOKTHE PWE, became the first non-devotional format for the presentation of *Jataka*, and that the repertoire and movements of the marionettes were later emulated by human dancers. Puppet performances of *Jataka* stories were common in the reign of King Bowpaya (1782–1819) when a court minister assigned to oversee theatrical activities gave the form considerable support. Some scholars think puppetry may only have been developed in this era, under the influence of Siamese puppeteers. But the use of marionettes (the complex princess puppet could have had 60 strings), rather than shadow figures like Thai NANG *yai* puppet theatre, and distinctively Burmese pre-play scenes may be evidence to support the Burmese oral tradition of this form's indigenous origin.

Court dance drama

The human dance drama emerged under Thai influence. Scholars believe the major impetus was the capture of the Siamese capital of Ayutthya in 1767 by troops of the Burmese King Hsinbyushin. Siamese court dancers and musicians were taken into exile where they helped develop the indigenous Burmese theatre. Performers modified Siamese dance style, musical instrumentation and plot materials in creating the new art. The relatively high status of these captured performers as compared to *nat* dancers, and the sudden increase in court support of the arts helped raise the status

Artists

Po Sein (1882–1952)
Noted actor. Born Maung Thaik to actor San Dun and dancer Daw Shwe Yoke, he was instrumental in modernizing Burmese performance by incorporating traditional dance and orchestral practice with Western-inspired wing and drop scenery, electrical lighting and a raised stage. He expanded the repertoire to include additional *Jataka* stories about previous lives of the Buddha. *Shin-Thu Dain*, the story of a son who enters the monkhood against his mother's wishes, is an example. During the 1930s he toured the country by riverboat with a troupe of 180 including a chorus line of Anglo-Burmese women. He married a number of wives including the noted actress Kyin Yone who became mother to Maung Khe (Kenneth) Sein who took over the company upon his father's death. He was officially honoured by the government in 1919, and his work raised the status of all performers.

U Kyin U (?–1853)
Playwright who lived in Sinbaungwe and Ava in the first half of the 19th century. He was associated with a group of professional actors and wrote his plays in outline form. His work, as chronicled in the reign of King Mindon, included six plays, three of which are currently extant. *Mahaw* tells the story of Mahaw, a previous incarnation of the Buddha. The son of a rich noble, he becomes a shrewd prime minister who saves his king from a death plot by sending his parrot as a spy to the court of a rival king. *Dewagonban*, literally, 'god-demon', is the son of a king who is brought up by an ogress. He goes through numerous adventures with his betrothed and brother before realizing his true heritage. *Parpahein* explores the intricacies of royal succession. The prince of the title retires from the world to become a hermit. Intrigue, mistaken identity and melodramatic turns of plot characterize this author's work.

U Pon Nya (1807–66)
Playwright. A poet-monk in the court of King Mindon, he was known for the lyricism of his writing. As an astrologer he gave advice to two rebelling princes, leading to his imprisonment. Shortly thereafter he was secretly executed, reportedly for romantic involvement with the wives of his jailor. His plays take their titles from the name of the hero or his occupation: *Pauduma*, *The Water Seller*, *Wizaya*, *Kanthala*, and *Waythandaya*. *Pauduma* tells of the travails of a banished prince who, after bleeding himself to quench his wife's thirst, is attacked and left for dead by the woman so she can marry a limbless criminal. A rebuke to the wives of the king for taking other lovers, this piece was badly received by the female audience. *Wizaya*, based on Singhalese history, tells of an outlaw prince who founds a Buddhist kingdom in Sri Lanka (Ceylon). *Kawthala* is a mythical story in which the hero Kawthala becomes a tree god. *Waythandaya* is based on a *Jataka* story about the generous prince of the title, who gives away even his own children. *The Water Seller* tells how a poor water seller is made crown prince for his integrity, but, realizing the corruption of court, opts to become a hermit. Satires of courtly mores and intrigues are always apparent in his work.

of performance and performers as a whole.

The Thai female group dances probably became the basis for the *yein* Burmese group court dance. Thai mask dance KHON with its *Ramayana* repertoire became the model for the Burmese court mask dance, ZAT GYI. The Burmese, in borrowing the Vishnavite religious epic, considered the hero Rama as a previous incarnation of the Buddha. As in Thai court performance, professional dancers and courtiers mingled in the cast, and ornate costumes and crown-like headdresses adorned the performers who mimed the actions while narrators and chorus sang the text to musical accompaniment.

Soon new texts were introduced: a minister, Myawaddi, created a version of the Panji story called *Inaung* which, like its Thai model titled *Inao*, dwells on the amorous exploits of that Indonesian

Classical court forms

Classical court forms include female dance drama (*LAKON KABACH BORAN*), shadow play (*NANG SBEK THOM*), and mask dance drama (*LAKON KHOL*). Indigenous, Indian and Indonesian influences were probably important in the creation of these arts a millennium ago, but the current forms are close to Thailand's *LAKON FAI NAI, NANG yai* and *KHON*, respectively. The term *lakon* (also spelled *lakhon*) means 'play' or 'drama' in both Khmer and Thai. Research has yet to clarify whether Thai shadow play and masked dance were, like the female dance form, first developed in Cambodia. The confusion on this question is exacerbated by the fact that the current Cambodian variants on the ancient arts are only about 150 years old, and were influenced by Thai models in the 19th century.

Indigenous elements probably contributed to the ritual importance of performance in Khmer courts. As early as the 7th century, dance was a feature of the funeral rites of kings – a court tradition continued into this century. A palace dance-ritual, a weekly ceremonial salutation to teachers and spirits, was thought to promote good luck. More elaborate ceremonies might be staged to promote rain and fertility, *buong suong* ('paying respect to heavenly spirits') performances were enacted to promote rain and for other ritual purposes. Such rites show the link between performance and communication with the supernatural common in Southeast Asia.

Indian influence shows in the popularity of the *Ramayana* in the repertoire and the primary importance of female dancers. The preference for *Ramayana* materials results from Vaishnavite influence which may have come via Indonesia or Bengal. The Indian temple dancers (*devadasi*), who were ritually married to temple idols and, in Vaishnavite practice, became associated with god-kings, probably formed a model for the Khmer court dancers. The references to female dancers in Cambodia begin as early as AD 611 when there are reports of female dancers being dedicated to Hindu temples. The practice of dedicating performers to temples was continued after Buddhism became the state religion, and the practice was most popular in the reign of Jayavarman VII (1181–?1219) when over 3000 dancers were in residence.

Indonesian practices are believed to have been introduced in 802 when Jayavarman II, the founder of the Khmer kingdom and of the *devaraja* ('god-king') cult, reportedly returned from Sriwijaya, a kingdom in the Malay archipelago. The fact that the major Khmer court arts all have clear counterparts in the Malay world bolsters the belief in this venerable connection. The Javanese semiritual court dance (*BEDAYA*), puppet-derived forms (*WAYANG*), and the mask dance (*TOPENG*) are, like the Khmer court arts, modern versions of ancient forms that linked the ruler with the world of ancestors and spirits, ensuring him godlike power.

Similarly, the Cambodian *pinpeat* orchestra shares many structural features with the *gamelan* ensembles indigenous to the Malay world, probably as a result of borrowing in past ages. It is, however, difficult to prove when and how this interchange occurred, for trade contacts with the Malay Archipelago and Malaysian mainland have persisted over many centuries.

The exact nature of ancient Khmer performance is obscure. Some scholars feel that non-dramatic dances by large groups of women were part of the repertoire. Couple dances by women impersonating a prince and a princess appear ancient as well. One 13th-century inscription, cited by Cravath, indicates that a *Jataka* (Buddhist birth-story) was played by female performers, but such reference to dance drama is rare in the Angkor period. Written evidence for shadow play and masked dance is completely lacking. This leads some scholars to feel that narrative drama was not highly developed during the Angkor period. Indeed, to the present, genres that are thought to be the oldest female dance forms of the Malay and Indonesian courts are largely non-dramatic. It is possible that the common dramatic repertoire of Khmer and Thai performance largely evolved in the more secular environment of the Thai courts after Angkor's decline beginning in 1431. Many of the tales currently in the repertoire may first have come from Thai sources.

Information concerning Khmer court arts is scant from the 15th century to the mid 19th century, when, according to the oral tradition, King ANG DUONG directed a reformation of the arts. The practice of court performers prior to that time is said to have been close to village dance, as in *ayay*, described above. The King, who had spent time in the Thai court, directed that the movement, especially of male dancers, be made more rounded and less jerky. Elbows that were held stiffly at shoulder level were lowered. Meanwhile, costumes were modelled on those of the Thai court. Whether these refinements were, as Cambodian oral tradition reports, a return to the past or the expropriation of Thai models can be debated. The innovations do, however, explain the close similarities between Khmer and Thai arts in the present era. Current performance of female dance drama, puppetry, and mask dance derives from this period.

The *lakon kabach boran*, the dance of the palace ladies, is the most important of the court arts. The performers were wives, concubines or relatives of the ruler. A new troupe would normally be organized at the beginning of each ruler's reign, under the direction of a matron appointed by the king. The women would be trained for a single role – male, female, monkey or ogre – according to their body type. Prior to the last generation, men would not be allowed to appear with the ladies. Exceptions to this rule were the man who played

A large leather puppet of *nang sbek thom*, incised to show a *Reamker* tableau: rejoicing in his victory, the monkey Ankut holds aloft the severed head of Indrajit, son of the demon king Ravana.

the hermit role and had certain ritual functions in training and graduating dancers, and the men who played clown roles (cf. Thailand, *lakon fai nai*, and Malaysia, MAK YONG). Floor patterns in the female dance tend toward circles and lines, and the hand gestures are, like most Southeast Asian systems, abstract or pantomimic rather than the gesture language of Indian *mudras*.

The repertoire of the female court dance, which came to be known in the West as the Royal Cambodian Ballet, is currently composed of about 60 *robam* ('pure dance pieces') and 40 *roeung* ('dance dramas'). In the dance dramas, actresses mime the action as an offstage chorus of female singers delivers the text to *pinpeat* musical accompaniment. The stories performed include episodes from the *Reamker*, the Cambodian version of the *Ramayana*, the Javanese *Panji* cycle, the tale of *Anrudh* (a grandson of Krishna), *Jataka* stories including the tale of the bird-woman, *Manora*, and the conch prince, *Preah Sang*, and local legends. The tales typically focus on the struggle of the noble hero with an ogrely villain for the love of a woman. An episode of great popularity is the story of *Sovann Macha*, a fish queen who is courted by Hanuman, the monkey general leading Rama's troops. The artists trained and performed in the palace, dancing when required by the king, and commoners would not normally be allowed to view presentations. But the traditional system has been modified considerably in the last generations.

The history of the dance in the last 100 years is an abstract of the struggle for royal autonomy during the colonial era. The kings strove to maintain the female dance during the French protectorate, inaugurated in 1863, but found the allowances accorded the monarch were not sufficient to support the 500-dancer entourage of former times. By 1904, 100 dancers remained and about half accompanied King Sisowath to Europe to perform at the Marseilles exhibition in 1906. European acclaim followed, but the decay in numbers continued as dancers left the palace to go to school or marry. Frenchmen like George Groslier, who as Art Director of the colony pleaded for support for the troupe, became significant in fostering the dance. In 1928 the Palace administration and French proponents agreed to place the troupe under the University of Fine Arts (École des Beaux Arts). During the 1930s the French authorities gave support to a non-court troupe organized by a former dancer, Say Sangvann, whose dancers, unlike the royal troupe, were willing to appear in French salons. It was a sign of the times that dance was taught and performed outside the palace. The magico-religious significance of the art as a symbol of the potent ruler were on the wane, and kings were forced to quibble about allowances for dance costumes with French civil servants.

Yet the politics of the period were, in a sense, reflective of the tradition of female dance in Cambodia – he who controlled the dance controlled the nation. When the ruler was no longer powerful enough to support his dancers and prevent performance outside the palace, his arts were expropriated by the new rulers, the French.

The former queen mother, KOSSAMAK, was instrumental in a renaissance of the court troupe, which flourished during the reign of her son, Prince Norodom Sihanouk (1922–), who ascended the throne in 1941 and reigned until he was set aside by the Lon Nol government in 1970. She regained control of the dance and effectively revamped the programme, venues and costuming. The queen mother made the royal dancers a significant feature in the emerging culture politics of modern Cambodia.

In the 1960s Sihanouk's daughter Bopha Devi was the major dancer in the group, and, following Kossamak's innovations, the Royal Cambodian Ballet performed at capitals around the world on cultural missions and for visiting heads of state in Cambodia. The 254 members of the troupe (2 male dance teachers, 17 female dance teachers, 6 prime dancers, 25 corps de ballet, 160 pupils, 30 dressers, costumers, jewellery persons and makeup artists, 10 singers, and 4 male clowns) in 1962 show that in this era *lakon kabach boran* was again an important attribute of the Khmer king's power.

Of lesser significance to the Khmer court were the two male forms, the shadow play and the masked dance. *Nang sbek thom* shadow play involves 10 manipulators dancing with large leather panels portraying multiperson scenes of the *Ramayana* story in front of and behind a white screen, while a narrator tells the story to *pinpeat* musical accompaniment. In addition to providing entertainment and edification, some performances might be done to promote rain or cure epidemics. A single troupe was operating in Siam Reap in the early 1970s, and

the form had considerable support during the late 1980s from CHHENG PHON, Minister of Culture. The form can be compared to the Thai *nang yai*, and the curative powers of performance, the use of a percussive orchestra and the strategy of depicting heroic action in a theatre of character types make it analogous to the *wayang* tradition of Indonesia and Malaysia. The mask dance *lakon khol* is believed to have developed from the shadow play, as puppeteers exchanged their leather panels for masks and crown headdresses. The footwork of the dancers is derived from the dance of the puppet manipulators, and the dramatic and musical repertoire correspond to the shadow theatre.

In the early 1970s Prince Sihanouk was deposed, and in the following 20 years the court arts were attenuated. After the advent of the Khmer Rouge government in 1975 many dancers fled the country or were killed. With the takeover of the country in 1979 by a Vietnamese-backed government, classical dance experienced some resurgence. Performers adapted lyrics to express themes relevant to the current socialist government. Outside of Cambodia training continued in refugee camps in Thailand, and what had been a palace prerogative began thus to reach a new part of the Khmer population. But as Khmer have moved overseas, the art has been difficult to maintain, since the expatriates' life in Western society makes it virtually impossible to maintain the kind of daily, intensive rehearsal needed for the dance to flourish. In Paris a group operates under Bopha Devi's direction and a Maryland-based group in the United States toured that nation in 1984.

Modern popular forms

Cambodian popular forms borrow from foreign genres adapting the performances to suit Khmer tastes. Arts like *yike, lakon bassac, ayang*, and spoken drama have this mixed heritage.

Yike developed in response to tours by Malay BANGSAWAN troupes in the late 19th century. The art also parallels LIKAY of Thailand in its mixture of classical and modern features. The introduction of wing-and-drop scenery, the rough approximation of classical dance used for entrances and exits, the humorous burlesques of classical legends and the introduction of new plots coupled with witty improvisation by performers, helped *yike* gain wide popularity among the populace. Performances were even staged at court.

Lakon bassac combines elements borrowed from Vietnamese theatre with indigenous techniques. The form developed in the 19th century in the Bassac river region in Vietnam, where Khmer peoples live, and spread to Cambodia. It mixes traditional Cambodian features and elements of the Chinese-influenced Vietnamese theatre. Brandon notes that *pinpeat* music may play in one scene and a Chinese two-stringed fiddle in the next; while one costume will seem fit for a classical Khmer dance, the next may resemble a Chinese opera outfit.

A third popular form is *ayang* (or *nang kalun*), a shadow-puppet theatre related to the *nang talung* of Thailand. Both the Khmer and Thai shadow genres derive from the Indonesian/Malay *wayang* tradition, but *ayang* is unusual in its use of multiple puppeteers. Stories from the *Reamker* and *Jataka* tradition can be presented, and the buffoonery of the clown endears the form to the peasant audience.

A final form that has developed in the 20th century is spoken Western drama, based on French models. Prince Sihanouk himself wrote and produced plays in this genre. The fate and the future of all Khmer performance art awaits the stabilization of the country.

The current situation: 1980s–1990s

When performers returned to Phnom Penh to re-establish the performing arts after the fall of the Khmer Rouge regime in 1979, they discovered that nearly 90 per cent of their professional colleagues (dancers, musicians, actors and playwrights) had perished during the four years of murderous Khmer Rouge rule or had fled overseas. Virtually all documents on performance – libraries and photographs – had been destroyed. Current efforts, guided by former Minister of Culture Chheng Phon, are directed to rebuilding shattered professional troupes and to recruiting and training a new generation to replace the nation's appalling artistic loss. The National Department of Arts, Ministry of Culture, under the direction of Pich Tum Kravel, actor and playwright, and Hang Sot, musician, operates two theatres in Phnom Penh, the Bassac and Chatomuk. Ten professional theatrical troupes are supported by the Department, including

---

Artists

Ang Duong (1796–1859)
Khmer ruler credited with ushering in the modern era of Cambodian court dance by modifying Khmer traditions of the last century. He accepted Thai practice in costume, repertoire and movement in that era. Movement became more refined and the major court genres (*LAKON KHOL, LAKON KABACH BORAN, NANG SBEK THOM*) were defined during his time.

Chheng Phon
A major adviser and teacher of those resucitating Cambodian theatre since the genocide of the Khmer Rouge regime ended in 1979. Actor and classical dancer, he was director of the National Conservatory of Performing Arts and then Minister of Culture in the 1960s. By 1992 he was one of a mere handful of senior artists and theatre teachers alive who were capable of passing on traditional theatre to young performers.

Kossamak (?1903–75)
Queen mother instrumental in the renaissance of the female court dance, *LAKON KABACH BORAN*, during the reign of her son, Norodum Sihanouk (r.1941–70). She introduced boys to play monkey roles. She made the royal dancers a significant feature of the cultural diplomacy of modern Cambodia. She streamlined the typical performance to fit the short time-period a modern, Western audience finds appropriate. Instead of long dramas, excerpts became the norm and a presentation typically included a group dance, a short dance-drama selection, and a group dance as a finale. During the queen mother's administration of the troupe, performances were frequently staged at Angkor and abroad as well as in the palace. She commissioned sets of costumes modelled on the carvings in Angkor temples, thus moving away from Thai models and returning to earlier Khmer styles.

troupes devoted to *lakon khol, lakon mahori, nang sbek thom, yike, lakon bassac,* modern drama, and *apee,* a newly revived genre that mixes *yike* and classical dance. The Department's *lakon kabach boran* troupe, to which many former members of the Royal Ballet now belong, performs its classical dance-drama repertory for state occasions, ceremonies and festivals as in the past, as well as for tourists and the general public. It has toured abroad, to England and Italy (1990) and Thailand and Hong Kong (1992). To stimulate professional and amateur groups, the Department sponsors yearly festivals in Phnom Penh. The Municipality of Phnom Penh supports three professional troupes: dance, modern drama, and *lakon bassac.*

Young performers are trained in classical performance (classical dance drama, *lakon bassac, yike* and shadow puppetry) at the University of Fine Arts as well as in Khmer folk dance and in modern drama. The dean of the Faculty of Choreographic Arts, Proeung Chhieng, and the chief instructor in the Department of Classical Dance, Mme Chea Samy, are former stars of the Royal Ballet, representing two of the last links with Cambodia's great prewar dance-drama traditions. Students perform in their own theatre and in a rehearsal hall (modelled on the Chan Chhaya Pavilion in the Royal Palace) on the university campus, and have toured with their teachers to India, Japan, eastern Europe and the United States.

Modern spoken drama (*lakon ciet,* 'national drama', or *lakon niyey,* 'spoken drama') began in 1949 with adaptations of short French plays. The National School of Theatre, directed by Peau Yuleng, and its modern drama troupe were established in the 1950s and through the 1960s was extremely active. Training focused on the Stanislavski technique. The national troupe toured with great success through the country, eventually developing into three troupes. A major playwright of spoken drama was Hang Thun Hak, affectionately known as the 'second Molière'. There was a conscious effort to educate society and build national culture through spoken drama. In 1964–5 the school and troupes became incorporated into the University of Fine Arts. In 1975 all modern theatre activity ceased when the Khmer Rouge evacuated the cities and made its violent attempt to radically alter Khmer culture and society.

Spoken drama is extremely popular with contemporary audiences. In 1992, in addition to the three Phnom Penh troupes affiliated with the government institutions mentioned above, professional troupes are found in Kandal, Takeo, Prey

Open-sided rehearsal hall and performance pavilion for *lakon kabach boran,* located in the Grand Palace, Phnom Penh, in 1972.

Veng and Svay Rieng provinces. The Voice of the People radio station has its own modern drama troupe that regularly broadcasts original spoken dramas. Contemporary dramas explore tensions in society – between rich and poor, between the powerful and the powerless – the consequences of these tensions, and ways in which people either overcome their material and moral dilemmas, or are defeated by them and learn to suffer with dignity. Pring Sakon, a famous actor teaching at the University of Fine Arts, combines Western and Khmer theatrical forms, following Chheng Phon's belief that 'modern isn't foreign'.

All provincial seats have a theatre, many with resident companies. In 1992 several hundred amateur troupes existed, both in the capital and throughout the country. Most specialize in popular *lakon bassac*, while those in Kampot and Takeo provinces are famous for *yike*. Recently, as video tapes have become the preferred form of entertainment at festivals and ceremonies, the number of amateur troupes has declined.

Genres

Lakon kabach boran

Classical female dance practised by ladies of the court. Dancers were trained to undertake a single role type – refined male, refined female, monkey or ogre. The only males in a troupe were older teachers and ritual specialists who played hermit and clown roles. The repertory consists of ritual dances, abstract dances (*robom*), and dance dramas (*roeung*) which recount episodes from major epics like the stories of Rama, Inao (the Indonesian Prince Panji) and Anrudh (a grandson of Krishna), or Buddhist *Jataka* stories.

In the dance dramas, actresses mime the action as an offstage chorus of female singers delivers the text to *pinpeat* musical accompaniment. This ensemble customarily includes *samphor* (horizontal drum), *skor thom* (a pair of barrel drums), *kong touch* and *kong thom* (gong chimes), *roneat ek* and *roneat thung* (high- and low-pitched xylophones), *sralai* (oboe), and *ching* (pair of small cymbals). A traditional performance might last for four days with the tale continuing over two four-hour periods each day. Shorter programmes mixing short dramatic episodes and abstract group dances have become the norm since the 1940s.

Lakon khol

Masked, male pantomimed dance drama narrated by two storytellers to *pinpeat* musical accompaniment. It corresponds to Thai KHON and was developed in the courts, with its movement and stories based on the older shadow play NANG SBEK THOM. The epic of the hero Rama (*Reamker*) was favoured story material. Strict iconography of characters characterizes the masks and the specific character can be read from the face and headdress by an observer trained in the genre.

Nang sbek thom

The shadow play in which 10 dancers display large leather panels portraying multiperson scenes in front of and behind a white screen 30 ft long and 10 ft high while two narrators tell the *Reamker* epic to *pinpeat* orchestral accompaniment. The now rare form, which was sometimes done for curative purposes or rainmaking as well as entertainment and edification, shares style and repertoire with the dance drama (*LAKON KHOL*). The 150 panels, which are about $4\frac{1}{2}$ft high, usually show multiple characters in a scene.

Bibliography

J. R. Brandon, *Theatre in Southeast Asia*, Cambridge, Mass., 1967; J. Brunet, *Nang Sbek*, Berlin, 1969, and 'Nang Sbek', in *World of Music*, 9, 4, 1968; E. Blumenthal, 'Cambodia's Royal Dance', in *Natural History*, Apr. 1989, and 'The Court Ballet: Cambodia's Loveliest Jewel', in *Cultural Survival*, Summer 1990; G. Coedes, *The Indianized States of Southeast Asia*, ed. W. Vella, tr. S. Cowing, Honolulu, 1968; P. Cravath, 'Earth in Flower', PhD thesis, Univ. of Hawaii, 1985, and 'The Ritual Origins of the Classical Dance Drama of Cambodia', in *Asian Theatre Journal*, 3, 2, 1986; B. Groslier, 'Danse et musique sous les rois d'Angkor', in *Felicitation Volumes of Southeast Asian Studies Presented to His Highness Dhaninivat Kromamun Bidyalabh Bridhyakorn*, vol. 2, Bangkok, 1965, and *Danseuses cambodgiennes anciennes et modernes*, Paris; A. Leclère, *Le théâtre cambodgien*, Paris, 1911; *Royal Cambodian Ballet*, Phnom Penh, 1963; Chan Moly Sam, *Khmer Court Dance*, Newington, Conn., 1987; Chan Moly Sam and Sam Ang Sam, *Khmer Folk Dance*, Newington, Conn., 1987; S. Thierry, *Les danses sacrées*, Paris, 1963; Tran Quang Thai, 'Kampuchea', in *New Grove Dictionary of Music and Musicians*, ed. S. Sadie, New York, 1980; X. Zarina, 'Royal Cambodian Dancers', in *Classical Dances of the Orient*, New York, 1967.

CHINA

Theatre has been and remains an omnipresent force in the social life of the Chinese. It is first described by a single ambiguous term, *xi*, which originally designated play, games and acrobatics. The name is still current but retains a connotation of plurality as an umbrella word covering a host of theatrical entertainments. When the Chinese speak of theatre specifically they use the names of the musical and dialectal forms which animate their numerous regional dramatic styles. These constitute the corpus of theatre in a national sense. A varying length of tradition lies behind them. Some, like the rice-planting song of northern China, persist as simple forms of song and gestural expression with an uncomplicated musical accompaniment. Other styles practised within the orbit of more sophisticated urban areas, developed as the transmitters of polished theatrical form. Three seminal events mark the long time-span such progress involved. The rise of *ZAJU* theatre in the 13th century set precedents for structured stage practices which endured. The flowering of the *KUNQU* in the 16th century ushered in a theatre of lyrical elegance and scholarly playwrights, while the domination of the Beijing theatre style in the 19th century proclaimed the triumph of an aesthetic for the man in the street.

Chinese traditional theatre is a presentational, secular style of performance essentially musical and choreographic in its basic structure. Synthesis of forms and variety of offering are operative factors. Categorized archetypal character roles predominate, each having its particular formalized speech and movement techniques together with a distinctive makeup and costume style.

The composition of a dramatic text and its interpretation by the actor are conditioned by an ordered arrangement of song, narrative and declamation. Their structural basis results from the dual relationship between musical sound and the spoken word arising from the homonymic nature of the Chinese language. Because of the pitch variations, or tones, which differentiate the meanings of otherwise identically sounding words in Chinese, the sound pattern accruing from the formal organization of rhythm has acquired a particular literary significance. The number of syllables and tonal patterns contained by a line of text became a first element of verse and song composition for the traditional drama. Metrical pattern and rhyme schemes were given priority by the old Chinese dramatist in devising his text. Rhyme tables classifying words with the same tonal movement were the tools of his craft. The playwright did not set words to music; he sought appropriate words to match the auditory permutations of his lines and stanzas. Because of this, there has been handed down an extensive repertoire of tunes, that is to say metrical arrangements having their separate tonal patterns and rhyme schemes, which can be used over and over again in relation to specific emotional situations. Because of this also, the stage musician can command stereotyped styles embodying fixed metrical patterns which complement the tonal–rhythmic format of a play text as stipulated by the dramatist. Dialect naturally affects a compositional style so dependent on auditory effects. The melodic differences resulting from dialectal usage in regional dramatic forms were broadly classified as northern and southern styles by the Chinese in the past. A complex history of borrowing and cross-fusion between the two divisions brought about the musical genres which identify major theatrical styles such as those of Suzhou or Beijing.

Antecedents of theatre

Performance goes back to the earliest times in China. Shamanistic rituals from many centuries before the time of Christ probably involved a com-

bination of song, dance, gesture and costume. The performing arts functioned also as entertainment. An example is shown in a wall painting in a tomb excavated in the early 1960s in Mixian, central Henan Province, dating from about AD 200. It shows a large-scale banquet, probably hosted by the main tomb occupant when alive. A series of small-scale performances is taking place between two long rows of guests. There are dancers, jugglers, plate-spinners and musicians.

The Tang dynasty (618–907) witnessed a climax in the political power and culture of mediaeval China, with many quite developed forerunners of theatre already in existence. An example is the 'adjutant plays' (*canjun xi*), which were comic skits. They included dialogue, string and wind and perhaps percussion instruments as musical accompaniment, and role categories. Both actors and actresses took part, and sometimes there were three roles or even more. Puppet shows were not new to the Tang, but certainly flourished then and were popular in the marketplaces of the cities. The Emperor Minghuang (r. 713-56) loved to watch puppet shows in the inner palace. The 20th-century scholar Sun Kaidi has argued that drama in China imitates and derives from puppets. The arts of the story-tellers were also highly developed by that time. The late-Tang-period poet Li Shangyin records how story-tellers would expound the deeds and wars of the heroes of the Three Kingdoms period (220–65 BC). These were later to be a major arm of the content of all popular Chinese theatre. It was already quite common for entertainers to mount high platforms or stages so that they could better be seen by their audiences. Religious impulses, from shamanism, Taoism, and Buddhism, remain important in many regional 'minority' theatres in outlying areas today, including TIBETAN DRAMA.

Origins of theatre

The Song dynasty ruled all China from 960 to 1127 and southern China until 1279. Meanwhile the Jin dynasty, ruled by the Jurchen people, ancestors of the Manchus, seized the Northern Song capital of Kaifeng in 1126, forcing the Song to relocate their centre of government to Hangzhou in the south.

The Song dynasty is notable for the rise of commerce, together with a class to organize it, and the growth of cities. In this more urbanized environment China's first fully developed theatres arose. Called *goulan* (literally, 'hook balustrades'), they were contained within amusement centres termed *wazi* ('tiles') or *washe* ('tile booths'). The largest amusement centre in early 12th-century Kaifeng held 50 theatres or even more, and the grandest theatre could accommodate several thousand people. They were covered, not open-air, structures and so not subject to the vagaries of the weather. All classes of people frequented them.

In the north such performances were termed *zaju* ('various plays') or, under the Jin dynasty, *yuanben*, and included dancing, acrobatics, the core play, comic patter and a musical conclusion. The terms *zaju* or *yuanben* refer also to the core playlet, which was short and funny and might concern a love affair or satirize officialdom. Apart from a musician, these plays needed actors for four or five characters. Role categories included clown (*fujing*) and jester (*fumo*). Masks were probably used for supernatural roles, and makeup was common.

In the south a new style arose from early in the 12th century: 'southern drama' (*nanxi*). Its place of origin was Wenzhou in southern Zhejiang Province. Its music was based partly on folk songs and it may also have been influenced by Indian drama. The seven role categories of southern drama are the foundations on which most later Chinese theatre has built. *Sheng* and *dan* were respectively the principal male and female characters, *mo* and *wai* secondary male, and *tie* secondary female roles. *Jing* were strong male characters and *chou*, according to Xu Wei (1521–93), had a 'face daubed with black powder and was very ugly'. The *jing* and *chou* roles were frequently interchangeable. In contrast to the *zaju*, all characters sang.

The plays of southern drama were longer and had more complex story lines than earlier performances and in this sense they may be taken as the first stage of a fully developed Chinese drama. The great majority appear to have been love comedies. The two most famous, *Chaste Woman Zhao* (*Zhao zhennü*) and *Wang Kui Renounces Guiying* (*Wang Kui fu Guiying*), deal with unfaithful scholar-lovers who come to a bad end. Most scripts are anonymous, many having been written by 'writing societies'.

The first great age of Chinese theatre

In 1234 the Mongols conquered the Jin and in 1279 the Southern Song armies, and established the

Brick carvings of c. 1279 showing the costumed actors of the Yuan dynasty *zaju*.

Yuan dynasty (1279–1368). After the Mongol conquest of the south, southern drama lost popularity, although it did revive in the middle of the 14th century not long before the fall of the Mongol Yuan dynasty (1368). The form of theatre which replaced it over the intervening century was *zaju*, marking the first great age of Chinese theatre. The apex of Yuan *zaju* was probably reached in the reign of Kublai Khan (1260–94), the man who reunited north and south China.

The texts of just over 160 *zaju* dramas survive. They are contained in two collections, the more important of them entitled *Selection of Yuan Songs* (*Yuanqu xuan*, 1615) collected and edited by Zang Maoxun. They deal with romance, courtesans, friendships between men, tyrannical rulers or rebels, recluses or supernatural beings. Many focus on politics or war, including the heroes of the Three Kingdoms period. Others centre around law cases, the main judge being the famous historical figure Bao Zheng (999–1062), known for his harshness but canonized in Yuan theatre for his benevolence and fairness. Quite a few end sadly or with the death of the leading positive character.

Dramatists were mainly Han Chinese (but also included Uygurs, Mongols and others). They were minor officials, entertainers and traders, not in general men of high social status. It has been suggested, by Chung-wen Shih among others, that Mongol rule blocked off opportunities for educated Han Chinese to enter the bureaucracy, through such measures as the suspension of the civil-service examinations (not reinstated until 1315), and that playwriting was an outlet for their literary talents.

The four most famous *zaju* dramatists are GUAN HANQING, Bai Pu (1226–after 1306), Ma Zhiyuan (1250–c.1325), and Zheng Guangzu (died c.1320). Bai Pu came from an official family which had been torn apart by the Mongol invasion. A Jin loyalist, he refused an offer of service in the Mongol court. He wrote at least 16 dramas, of which three are still extant. His best known play is *Rain on the Paulownia Tree (Wutong yu)* about the doomed love of the Tang Emperor Minghuang for his favourite concubine Yang Guifei, among the most popular stories in Chinese literature.

No musical scores of Yuan dramas have survived. Possibly they were never used much, since the music could be transmitted from teacher to disciple. In any case Yuan drama music appears to have died out during the following Ming dynasty (1368–1644). Musical accompaniment was mainly by stringed instruments, especially the four-string plucked lute (*pipa*). The famous wall painting of a scene from a Yuan *zaju* performance, dated 1324 and found in a temple in Shanxi Province, shows no string players, but does include a player of the side-blown flute (*dizi*), and a clapper player, as well as a drum.

The main role categories of *zaju* are *mo* (male), *dan* (female), *jing* (villain), and *chou* (clown). A play has one male lead and one female character and a number of subsidiary characters. The categorization is similar but not identical to that of the earlier southern drama. The costuming shown in the 1324 mural is colourful and fairly complex. Two characters have heavy black makeup on their eyebrows and white around the eyes. Several male characters are bearded, one with highly stylized whiskers. The mural shows a tiled stage, heavy backdrop painted with two elaborate pictures, but no stage properties.

Performers of either sex acted male or female roles. The heading of the 1324 mural informs us that a certain famous actress 'Elegance of Zhongdu performed here', while the main character depicted, the one presumably played by the named female star, is male. Actresses may well have dominated Yuan theatre. Certainly we know much more about them than the actors because Xia Tingzhi (1316-after 1368) wrote a work called *Green Bower Collection (Qinglou ji)* which is a set of biographies of actresses of the 13th and first half of the 14th centuries. Prostitutes as well as performers, they were wooed, sometimes even married, by high-ranking ministers, generals and literary figures. Although Mongol rulers were initially favourably disposed to the acting profession, one of them later issued a ban on teaching or performing *zaju* and damned such entertainments as lewd. Probably few people took any notice of such an edict, but in general performers held a very low social status.

Why was it that this new theatrical tradition should blossom so suddenly into the magnificent body of art which Yuan *zaju* appears to have been? After all, Han Chinese scholars blocked from the bureaucracy might more easily have turned to other branches of art. James Crump suggests the Jurchen people of the Jin dynasty were accomplished singers and dancers. Other component parts of theatre – acrobatics, pantomime, music, farce – were already flourishing and there was no shortage of good stories in Chinese literature and history. Yuan *zaju* represents the synthesis of several strong existing traditions. The Mongols became acculturated and 'welcomed the dramas which were shaped by music probably already familiar to them and which incorporated the less sophisticated arts that had always delighted them'. It was such processes, he concludes, from which 'the golden age of Yuan drama began'.

The revival of southern drama: marvel dramas

Under the last of the Mongol emperors Shundi (1333-68), the dormant southern drama revived. The term used to refer to the form was one which had been in use to describe stories or novellas during the Tang dynasty: *chuanqi*, literally 'trans-mitting the marvellous'.

The first of these 'marvel dramas' was *The Story of the Lute (Pipa ji)* by Gao Ming. It is based on the same story as *Chaste Woman Zhao*, namely the abandonment by the 2nd-century writer and scholar Cai Yong of his newly-wed wife Zhao Wuniang. However, Gao Ming has altered the characterization to portray Cai in a positive light. In place of his bad end, Gao has him reunited with Zhao, redeemed and rewarded. Zhu Yuanzhang (r. 1368-99), founder of the Ming dynasty, was an admirer of Gao and his play. When Zhu had become the Hongwu Emperor, he urged all noble families to possess a copy and he ordered his actors to perform *The Story of the Lute* every day. Regretting the lack of stringed accompaniment, he commanded members of his Academy of Music to rectify the weakness, so Liu Gao rearranged the orchestra adding the 15-string zither (*zheng*) and 4-string lute (*pipa*).

In the late Yuan and early Ming periods, the 'four great marvel plays' appeared: *The Story of the Thorn Hairpin (Jingchai ji)*, *The Moon Prayer Pavilion (Baiyue ting)*, *The Story of the White Rabbit (Baitu ji)*, and *The Story of Killing a Dog (Shagou ji)*. The first two concern scholars who leave behind their faithful wives to sit for the examinations, do brilliantly in them and are reunited with their beloveds. The marvel dramas have romantic themes, with scholars and beauties in central roles, and lack the warlike content of *zaju* drama.

A prologue, sometimes found in earlier southern dramas, always introduces the action of marvel dramas. It explains the story and announces the title of the play. Sometimes, as in *The Story of the Lute*, it explains the moral as well. Marvel dramas, at least in Ming editions, are divided into scenes, whereas earlier southern dramas were apparently performed without breaks. Yet a basic continuity of style, form and performance connects southern and marvel drama.

The decline of *zaju*

The rise of the marvel drama did not at first negatively affect *zaju*. On the contrary, the early Ming dynasty was a prolific period for *zaju* and quality was also good. Major authors of this period include Zhu Quan (1378-1448) and Zhu Youdun (1379-1439). Zhu Quan was the 17th son of the Hongwu Emperor Zhu Yuanzhang. He wrote twelve *zaju* dramas of which two survive. He also either wrote, or had written, a work entitled *Great Peace Table of Correct Sounds (Taihe zhengyin pu)*, which not only lists the titles of 689 *zaju* plays written from the Yuan period to his own time, but also gives titles of 335 *zaju* melodies arranged into 12 modes, each with poems illustrating the appropriate tonal patterns. Zhu Youdun, a grandson of the Hongwu Emperor, wrote over 30 *zaju* plays, all extant, many dealing with religious subjects, and in which women, either prostitutes or saints, are given prominence.

Xu Wei was a somewhat later dramatist, an eccentric best known for *Four Howls of the Ape (Sisheng yuan)*, which in fact consists of four *zaju* plays. Xu's plays were unconventional in two ways. Firstly, in several of them he departed from the rule that *zaju* should have four acts and a wedge. He was not the first to write a one-act *zaju* drama, but he also wrote two-act and five-act plays, signalling the collapse of the rigid *zaju* structure. Secondly, Xu Wei combined northern and southern music. Again, he was not the first to do this, but his experiment led on quite soon to an even more radical departure from *zaju* tradition when Wang Daokun (1525–93) used only southern music in writing *zaju*. The break was very important because it meant the abandonment of a type of music which had imposed a quite clear northern stamp on the drama.

Thereafter, *zaju* sharply declined in popularity. By the time the Ming dynasy fell in 1644, *zaju* was no longer performed at all and it survives only as a genre of literature.

The southern theatre of the educated

At the time *zaju* was declining, various local dramas rose to prominence, their differences, region to region, revealed in dialect, and especially music. One southern city with a particularly rich musical tradition was Haiyan, a major trading port in Zhejiang Province. The 'music of Haiyan' (*haiyan qiang*) had long flourished as a local form of southern drama. Xu Wei claims that in his own day it was 'in use' in four parts of Zhejiang Province, and it appears to have spread even further afield, including Jiangsu Province and even Beijing, later in the 16th century. Dramas using Haiyan music were probably accompanied by percussion instruments only, but the singing was soft and melodi-

ous. Role categories followed the normal patterns of southern drama. The audience came mainly from the educated classes, rich families and officials. By the end of the 17th century, this earlier form of Haiyan music had died out as an independent style. However, Xu Wei lists it among those musical traditions absorbed into *kunqu*, that drama form which by the end of the Ming dynasty was monopolizing the affections of educated theatre-lovers.

Credit for the creation of *kunqu* is often given to WEI LIANGFU, a 16th-century musician and actor. Wei adapted various familiar musical styles, including not only *haiyan qiang* but also *zaju, yiyang qiang* and the local music of Kunshan, to a new form which was called the 'music of Kunshan' (*kunshan qiang*), now known as *kunqu*. It was Wei's achievement to impose those main musical features which to this day make *kunqu* instantly identifiable. These are a slow-moving melismatic rhythmic melody, and an orchestration dominated by the flute and including the four-string lute and wind organ (*sheng*). The language of the libretti was classical, with many unexplained literary allusions. Stage motions tended to be slow and action sparse. The overall effect was melodious, delicate, refined and even melancholy. *Kunqu* quickly came to be known as 'elegant drama'. Its language and style closed it off from the masses, whose theatre was known, by contrast, as 'flower drama', a term covering most styles other than *kunqu*.

Role categories in *kunqu* closely followed those of marvel dramas. Companies took over stories from preceding styles, especially marvel dramas and *zaju*. Many early pieces had 40 or 50 scenes, like the marvel dramas from which they had been adopted. Performance might require three days and nights. By the 17th century the practice of performing a single scene became the norm. The most famous *kunqu* dramatists were Liang Chenyu, TANG XIANZU, HONG SHENG and KONG SHANGREN.

Kunqu eventually spread throughout most of China, in part transmitted by officials who loved the elevated style. They sponsored their own private companies and took the actors with them when posted to various cities around the country. Of many famous professional companies, the Jixiu of Suzhou is worth special mention. It was formed in 1784 to provide entertainment for the Manchu Qianlong Emperor (r. 1736–96) during his visit to the south in that year. Its members were drawn from among all the best actors of the cities of the Lower Yangzi Valley. It stayed together after the emperor's departure and survived until 1827.

The Hongwu Emperor of the Ming dynasty had founded a eunuch agency in 1390 to provide court entertainment, including theatre. Initially the favoured form was *zaju* but the court was happy to follow the fashion of the upper classes and patronize *kunqu* from the 16th century on. Early in his reign the Qianlong Emperor set up an organization to control court theatre. An official, Zhang Zhao (1691–1745), wrote five lengthy and highly moralistic dramas for the imperial theatre, including *Golden Statutes for Encouraging Goodness* (*Quanshan jinke*) about Mulian's saving his mother from hell. The Manchu Prince Yinlu (1695–1767), an uncle of Qianlong's, adapted the stories of the Three Kingdoms to compile the play *Annals of the Tripod* (*Dingzhi chunqiu*). During their heyday in the 18th century the court companies contained well over 1000 actors, including eunuchs and well-known artists, especially from the south.

Popular theatre; yiyang qiang

Originally a mass form of theatre, *zaju* had been taken over by the educated elite by the 16th century. At about the same time, new forms of popular theatre began to emerge and prosper, numbering by the 20th century some 350 styles. The great majority were popular in one or more localities, some major ones in whole provinces. Many belong to the *yiyang qiang* system of musical theatre.

Yiyang is a place name in eastern Jiangxi Province. Southern drama and *zaju* were heard there about the 13th century and melodies from these combined with local folk music to form the 'music of Yiyang' (*yiyang qiang*). In the 16th century it spread to other places, including the capital at Beijing, and Jiangsu, Anhui, Hunan, Fujian, Guangxi and Guangdong Provinces, and by the middle of the 17th century as far as the southwestern province of Sichuan. Its role categories and stories were similar to those of southern and marvel dramas. Since *yiyang qiang* was popular drama, normally scripts were not written down and only a few texts of the various forms survive from the 16th century. From them it is clear that the libretti were adapted from marvel dramas, and performed in single short scenes.

Several features of the *yiyang qiang* styles are noteworthy. Short sections in colloquial language were added to an original classical text. Thus, a literary allusion to a classical poem might be supplemented by a full recitation of the poem. An educated audience could be expected to recognize a literary allusion, but the ordinary masses who made up the audiences would need to have it pointed out. These added passages, *gundiao* (literally, 'rolling tunes'), could be either sung or, despite their name, spoken. One very important corollary of the *gundiao* was that libretti were much longer than for a corresponding *kunqu* and performances were often of excerpted scenes, rather than whole dramas. Moreover, as the well-known 17th-century drama theorist LI YU put it, 'characters are many but sounds are few'. What he meant was that, in strong contrast to the melismatic *kunqu*, the music of Yiyang was syllabic. It was also rather fast-moving on the whole.

A second feature, which applied to all popular theatre in China, was that these plays used local dialect. The ordinary people did not normally understand the 'official words' of the music of Haiyan or of the bureaucrats who had composed them.

A third feature was the 'helping' or offstage chorus (*bangqiang*). Apparently adopted from earlier southern drama, it is not found in Ming or Qing period drama systems other than the music of Yiyang. Li Yu writes that 'one person would start singing and then several would take up the tune'. The offstage chorus is still a strong feature in contemporary music-of-Yiyang styles, such as Sichuan opera (*CHUANJU*). The practice of a chorus accompanying solo singers in folksongs is extremely ancient in China. It probably arose because instrumental accompaniment was impossible for people at work in the fields and 'labour songs' have always been a normal category of folksong. *Yiyang qiang* styles, like southern drama before them, lacked the accompaniment of string or wind instruments and had only percussion.

The initial net effect of these features was to irritate the refined members of the educated classes, who used terms like 'bawl' to describe the singing of the music of Yiyang. Such contempt did not prevent the rapid and extensive spread of this mass drama, and in any case began to abate in the course of time. By the 18th century there were in Beijing six famous companies devoted to 'capital music drama' (*jing qiang*), which belonged to the music-of-Yiyang systems. Chief of these was the Great Company of the Princely Mansions, indicating that members of the aristocracy were patronizing this popular theatre.

Popular theatre, clapper opera

Another important system of popular theatre styles is 'clapper opera' (*bangzi qiang*). A tune identified as belonging to clapper opera is noted in Shaanxi in the 16th century. The music of this system was initially prevalent only in northern China and today is known in almost all the provinces north of the Yangzi River. By the late 18th century there was a thriving clapper-opera tradition in Sichuan, and it was even popular in the lower Yangzi Valley in places like Suzhou and Yangzhou. Merchants and bankers from Shaanxi and Shanxi, who traded all over the country, may well have brought with them private actors who could perform it.

As its name implies, the chief characteristic linking the styles of the clapper-opera system is the use of the clapper, a datewood block struck with a stick, to beat out the rhythm. In contrast to *kunqu*, the clapper opera emphasizes rhythmic change. In most styles there are eight different rhythms, the main one termed 'one beat, three eyes' (*yiban sanyan*) which corresponds to quick, common time (4/4) in Western music. In sung sections, the dominant poetic structure is seven- or ten-character couplets. Another characteristic of its music is the dominance of stringed instruments. The scholar Li Tiaoyuan (1734–1803) writes that the four-string plucked moon-guitar (*yueqin*) 'responds to the clapper in rhythm which is either hurried or slow', and all clapper styles feature a two-string bowed instrument.

A flourishing clapper opera attracted the attention of scholar-official Yan Changming (1731–87) who wrote that thirty-six famous companies were in operation in Xi'an, Shaanxi's capital, in the 1780s. The most distinguished was called Shuangsai. At the same time, a group of actors of female roles (*dan*) from Sichuan, led by Wei Changsheng (1744–1802), were captivating Beijing audiences with their clapper-opera performances. They probably arrived to take part in the Qianlong Emperor's 70th-birthday celebrations in 1780 and stayed until 1785 when the court prohibited their performances as obscene. In this short time they exercised a tremendous influence on the theatre of the capital and many elements of their art were later absorbed into Beijing opera. Among his innovations, Wei Changsheng wore a false foot beneath his foot and tied to the leg with cotton bandage, enabling him to imitate the gait of a woman with bound feet. Clapper actors were popular not only among the masses, but even among the educated elite.

Popular theatre: the pihuang system

Ten years later, a new group of actors came to Beijing to take part in the celebrations for the Qianlong Emperor's 80th birthday in 1790. These actors were members of companies from Anhui Province and their style of performance belonged to the *pihuang* musical system. Since this was the first time *pihuang* had been heard in the capital, the event is usually regarded as the birth of 'Beijing opera' (See *JINGXI* and *PIHUANG XI*).

Pihuang is actually a combination of two styles, *xipi* and *erhuang*, each of which remains identifiable and separately designated. Both styles can be varied greatly in their rhythm, melody and feeling. A.C. Scott wrote in 1957 that in general *erhuang* 'is used for more serious occasions' in Beijing opera, while *xipi* 'is, on the whole, happy and spirited in feeling'. Each style includes 'counter' (*fan*) tunes which 'are used for sad and tragic occasions'.

Of several theories advanced to explain the origin of *erhuang*, the most likely is that the term is a derivative of Yihuang, the place in Jiangxi Province where the style began. The style was adopted in Anhui Province and became far more popular there than in its original home. *Xipi* was a southern offshoot of clapper opera which spread to Hubei and other provinces from its northern roots in Shaanxi and Shanxi. From the 18th century the two styles became inseparable, their association perhaps beginning in Anhui. Together they spread to all the southern provinces and to Beijing. They formed at least 20 important styles, including not only Beijing opera but also Anhui opera (*huiju*), Hubei opera (*hanju*), Guangdong opera (*YUEJU*), and Jiangxi opera (*ganju*). They also form part of such forms as Sichuan opera (*chuanju*), and Yunnan opera (*dianju*).

Although each regional opera form in *pihuang*

style has its own special points, such as the use of the local dialect and the influence of local folk music, they share many characteristics in common. These include several probably inherited from clapper opera: the use of seven- or ten-character couplets in the libretti, emphasis on rhythmic change, and, with the exception of a very few styles, the domination of the accompanying orchestra by a two-string bowed fiddle.

The actor Gao Yueguan (c. 1770–?1830) is mainly credited with introducing *pihuang* music to Beijing. He and his followers were *dan* performers and early Beijing opera flourished on a kind of slave trade in which parents in Jiangsu and Anhui provinces sold sons to entrepreneurs who took them to Beijing to be trained for the stage. Within a short time after 1790, the 'Four Great Anhui Companies' established themselves as pre-eminent: Spring Stage (Chuntai), Three Celebrations (Sanqing), Four Joys (Sixi) and Harmonious Spring (Hechun). The Spring Stage company continued in the capital for 110 years, and only disbanded in 1900 when the Boxer uprising resulted in the burning down of the theatres of Beijing.

In the 1830s yet another wave of actors, this time from Hubei Province, entered Beijing. From this time Beijing opera changes substantially from an art in which *dan* actors and civil items were dominant, to an art that emphasized *sheng* actors and military plays. The most famous actors of 19th-century Beijing were all *sheng*: CHENG CHANGGENG, Yu Sansheng (1802–66), and Zhang Erkui (1814–64).

In 1860, the court for the first time brought in Beijing-opera actors from the city to perform. The initial experiment was short-lived, but revived by the Empress Dowager Cixi in 1884 to celebrate her 50th birthday. She was an avid enthusiast of the Beijing opera and ensured a continuing flow of fine actors from the city to the imperial court.

The growth of regional theatre in the Ming and Qing periods was paralleled by a similar expansion in local story-telling forms. The music, instruments and dialect varied from place to place, but on the whole the stories were constant and like those of the dramas. *Pingtan*, popular in and near Suzhou, Jiangsu Province, was a particularly well-known story-telling form.

Society, stage and stage arts during the Ming and Qing periods

Theatre in the Ming (1368–1644) and Qing (1644–1911) dynasties was very much a part of the people's lives. Performances accompanied popular festivals and marked prayers to the gods for good harvests in the spring or thanksgiving in autumn. Rich families held performances to accompany sacrifices to their ancestors or banquets for their guests. Theatre was also tightly related to commerce. Temple or other fairs included performances which crowds watched between or even during business transactions. The government treated such occasions with suspicion. Authorities believed that large gatherings of people provided opportunities for political sedition and the planning of rebellion, or for sexual immorality: 'men and women mix unrestrainedly' is a phrase found constantly in the sources describing large crowds of people gathered to watch drama. Many edicts restricted or banned certain plays or practices associated with the theatre.

There was great variety in sites of performance. The permanent, covered, commercial theatres

Peasant theatre in the Qing dynasty as depicted in a painting by Liu Langchan in 1875.

(*goulan*) of earlier centuries tended to go out of fashion. Some temples and guild halls had permanent stages, but otherwise a temporary stage was constructed as required. The marketplace also provided a convenient venue, even without a stage. Performances given during private banquets of the rich needed no stage, only an empty carpeted space near the banqueting tables. A very high-ranking or rich family might have a permanent stage constructed in its mansion. In Beijing a few of these were given over to the public as teahouse-theatres. The entry of Wei Changsheng and his clapper-opera actors led to the repair of these buildings and the construction of others. The period covering the end of the 18th and all of the 19th century was the high point of the traditional teahouse-theatre in Beijing. The best were concentrated in one part of town, just outside the main wall separating the residential areas of the masses from that part of the city where the officials and imperial court lived.

The stage itself was very simple. There was a curtain at the back but none at the front. Several records of Ming-dynasty plays describe elaborate scenery and stage properties, but these are exceptional cases. The norm was a nearly bare stage with no scenery and very simple or no properties.

The simplicity of the stage was balanced by the complexity and symbolism of the actors' art. Manners of walking, differing from character to character, hand gestures and the use of the fingers were all highly stylized and told the audience the nature and behaviour of the character. Costuming and makeup were extremely elaborate and expressive. Even their minor aspects assumed great theatrical significance, an example being the delicate way characters manipulate the very long and loose 'water' sleeves. Although it is not possible to trace the origins of all aspects of the performance of Chinese theatre, it is likely that 'water'-sleeve dance techniques were an artistic skill before the time of Christ. There was undoubtedly change during the Ming and Qing periods, and it took the direction of refining performance techniques and the arts of the stage, making them more complicated and integrating them better into the totality of theatre.

Makeup is a very ancient feature of the Chinese performing arts. In theatre it appears originally to have been simple. Only one of the characters in the 1324 wall-painting has makeup over an area more extensive than that around the eyes. From early Ming times makeup became more complicated and the practice became established of painting the whole face of *jing* characters with a coloured design to show moral or other qualities. Pictures dating from the Ming dynasty show that both in early *kunqu* and *yiyang qiang* dramas the faces of the *jing* characters were fully painted. Red indicated loyalty and patriotism in generals, black honesty, and so on. The complex painted face became a major feature of Beijing opera, where some of the colours hold essentially the same significance as in Ming times.

For many centuries acrobatics have been a major form of entertainment in China. Tumbling, somersaults, and other gymnastics appear to have featured in military plays of Yuan *zaju*, and they became well integrated into the performance of *yiyang qiang* dramas and later popular theatre forms, especially Beijing opera. Military scenes climax in an acrobatics display, with rapid and numerous cartwheels, somersaults and finely timed throwing, kicking back and catching of spears and swords. It is notable that through the Ming period acrobatics were not incorporated into southern drama. Instead Ming-period *kunqu* emphasized the synthesis and synchronization of song and dance movements. In the clapper-opera system actors were allowed to sing while not dancing and *vice versa*, thus breaking this unity. This process probably emerged late in the 18th or early in the 19th century. The change, added to the earlier absorption of acrobatics, made for greater variety and liveliness in the stage movements of the popular theatre forms than in *kunqu*.

Performers in the Ming and Qing periods

The troupes in the Ming and Qing dynasties were basically of two kinds: private and professional. Private troupes belonged to individual rich families and the members were drawn from among their servants or house-slaves. They could give private entertainment to the family or perform for invited guests. The majority of such troupes specialized in *kunqu* drama, but by the 18th century we find cases of private companies performing popular regional styles, an example being the Spring Stage company in Yangzhou, Jiangsu

Teahouse-theatre of the late 19th or early 20th century.

Province, which belonged to the rich salt merchant Jiang Chun (1725–93).

Professional troupes named in the sources were concentrated in particular cities and periods, especially Beijing in the 18th and 19th centuries. The normal pattern was for professional companies to go wandering throughout the countryside in certain seasons of the year, especially before sowing and after the harvest had been reaped. They would stay at a particular place a few days, present a festival and then move on. They financed their activities by sending representatives from door to door collecting, the records claim sometimes extorting, money. Only the best companies were semipermanent. The majority disbanded and reformed themselves from year to year, and the turnover of actors was substantial.

Acting companies of the time were usually either all-male, or all-female, mostly the former. Therefore many actors excelled in women's roles, many actresses in men's. Among professional women's *kunqu* companies, one type was composed of female prostitutes. Several patrons have left behind records of their admiration for the beauty and artistic skills of these women. Their bound feet made the gymnastic movements of military dramas impossible on the stage, as well as preventing them from moving away from their home base.

Training procedures were initially very rudimentary. Examples can be found from both the Ming and Qing periods of actors who in effect taught themselves the necessary skills by sheer determination. The normal procedure was for troupe managers to apprentice or buy small boys and have them taught the trade on a master–disciple basis. The practice reached a high point late in the 18th and in the first half of the 19th century and supplied Beijing opera companies with a virtually limitless number of actors. The main companies in Beijing ran special training schools (*keban*) that taught the slave-boys the necessary arts.

Performers held a very low status in society, one symbol of this being edicts forbidding them to sit for official examinations, the main gateway to the bureaucracy. Edicts of 1369 and 1652 were extended in 1770 to include actors' sons and grandsons. Actors were despised as vagabonds because they wandered about. Some members of the official classes were quite happy to take advantage of the sexual favours offered by performers, but still despised them as immoral. Not only were actresses prostitutes, among actors homosexuality was widespread. A 19th-century law forbade government officials to visit female prostitutes, and as a result the boy actors became effective substitutes. The excellence of mature stars after about 1780, especially in Beijing, raised actors' status slightly, but in general the social position of the acting profession remained extremely low well into the 20th century.

Traditional theatre in the 20th century

Beijing-style theatre continued to dominate the traditional stage through the first half of the 20th century. It retained an unequalled appeal on a national scale and had an enormous following among the ordinary public. This successful transition in an age of cultural iconoclasm was possible because of a particularly talented body of actors. They bore the artistic integrity of the old theatrical tradition forward while adjusting to social change. A towering figure was Beijing-born MEI LANFANG. His artistry and breadth of perception helped the old theatre attain a new pinnacle of public esteem. Not the least of Mei's achievements was his success in international cultural relations resulting from his tours to America and Russia in the 1930s. He stirred Western thinking to new aesthetic insights on theatre. Bertolt Brecht and V. E. Meyerhold were among those who admired, and were deeply influenced by seeing Mei's performances.

Two major reforms were accomplished in the professional world of Mei Lanfang and his peers during the 1920s and 30s. An improved system of training and education for theatre apprentices was introduced and actresses began to achieve professional emancipation. A first attempt at improved training conditions was the founding in 1903 of the Xiliancheng (later renamed the Fuliancheng) School in Beijing. Some of China's greatest Beijing actors graduated from this institution. Boys only were accepted; admitted at the age of seven they were taken on contract for a seven-year period. They lived in, and tuition, board and lodging were free. In return, the school demanded complete professional control, including an obligation to perform in public to fill the school's coffers. It was a hard life demanding meticulous standards and intensive application but it represented a clear advance on older methods when boys could be victimized by unscrupulous individuals.

A revolutionary step came in 1930 when Li Yuying founded a co-educational conservatory for dramatic training in Beijing. The actor CHENG YANQIU was appointed principal. Cheng was highly regarded both for his stage talents and personal integrity. In 1932 Cheng was sent to Europe for a year on behalf of the school to study drama and opera. The first of its kind to admit both sexes on an equal basis, the school provided a general edu-

cation simultaneously with professional training. An ambitious syllabus was taught by special tutors. Professionals were in charge of theatrical training. Although only one class graduated, it set the pattern that today's training methods follow. In 1934 a School for Experimental Drama was founded by Wang Bozheng at Jinan in Shandong. It aimed to develop a new national theatre form based on traditional methods while drawing scientifically on Western methods when required. A four-year course was set up with one year devoted to empirical experiment. In 1937 all of these schools were closed by the War of Resistance against Japan.

The professional rise of the actress in the 1920s and 30s overcame long-standing prejudices. Women were all but excluded from the theatre both as performers and spectators during the 19th century. In the early 1900s one or two all-women troupes were active in Beijing and Shanghai. They performed at private gatherings and were not allowed into theatres. By 1920 women were performing at several Beijing theatres but never alongside actors. During the 1920s Wang Yaoqing (1881–1954), a teacher of Mei Lanfang, and Mei himself ignored old prejudices and took female pupils, a hitherto unknown practice.

In 1928 the actresses Xue Yanqin (1906–86) and Xin Yanqiu (1911–) appeared on the stage of the Great Theatre (Da Xiyuan) in Shanghai with male actors. From the age of eight Xue had studied women's roles, combat techniques and *kunqu* in Beijing under Jin Guorui and later Zhang Cailin. From 1930 through a long acting career Xue appeared regularly with mixed casts, doing much to enhance the theatrical prestige of the actress. In 1960 she assumed a teaching post with the Beijing School of Dramatic Art. Xin Yanqiu studied with Mei Lanfang and Wang Yaoqing. When she began performing with Cheng Yanqiu, she took that famous actor's professional name. Xue and Xin were the vanguard of a galaxy of accomplished women artists who rose to prominence in the prewar years and brought new lustre to traditional theatre.

The rise of the modern theatre

The 20th century began with a movement to create a new theatre inspired by Western example. The old theatre became a target for change. The Western impact on 19th-century China resulted in many young intellectuals being sent abroad to study. Thousands went to Japan where progressive modernization had followed the Meiji Restoration of 1868. Japan was geographically and culturally closer to China than the West. The synthesis of tradition with modernity they found there made cultural adjustment easier. Intellectuals who returned from Japan became a major influence on the early development of modern Chinese theatre.

In 1907 a Chinese group in Tokyo founded the Spring Willow Dramatic Society. Assisted by the Japanese actor Fujisawa Asajirō, who ran an acting school (see Japan, SHINPA), they staged a version of Camille (Chahua nü) by Alexandre Dumas fils in February 1907. The play appealed to the Chinese because the heroine's plight mirrored the rigidity of their own marital conventions and suitably echoed their own social protest.

A five-act adaptation of Uncle Tom's Cabin followed in June. Entitled The Black Slave's Cry to Heaven (Heinu yutian lu) it was staged at the Hongo Theatre in Tokyo where shinpa, an early westernized Japanese genre, was featured. The play's action was expanded with extraneous interludes to please Chinese tastes. A curtain and scenery added novelty of effect. Harriet Beecher Stowe's story was well received for it offered a melodramatic vehicle for protest against racial discrimination from which the Chinese too suffered.

Both productions used translations by Lin Shu, who first put Shakespeare into Chinese, and were performed by all-male casts. Hybrids, they nevertheless offered a substitute for the old song-declamation form and the beginning of a new genre, eventually to be named HUAJU, spoken drama.

Shanghai became the centre for early experiments in the new Western form. The Spring Sun Society under Wang Zhongsheng (d. 1911), who had studied in Japan, staged The Black Slave's Cry to Heaven in 1907. Lu Jingruo (1885–1915), also returned from Japan, organized the New Drama Association in 1912. In 1914 Lu revived the Spring Willow Dramatic Society which produced Camille, among other productions, in a commercial theatre. Stage expertise was slight in these years, and old theatre conventions remained, including female impersonation.

The years 1915–19 marked a turning point. A Western-educated generation was agitating for cul-tural change. In 1916 the American-educated scholar, Hu Shi (1891-1962), spearheaded a movement to replace classical language – understood only by an educated elite – with a standardized vernacular intelligible to all. New journals supporting the New Culture Movement proliferated. Drama ignored by the old literati became recognized as a mouthpiece for social reform. New Youth, a monthly edited by Chen Duxiu (1879–1942), devoted an issue in 1918 to Henrik Ibsen whose work was discussed as an example to follow. In May 1919 students protested in Beijing against the surrender of Chinese sovereignty that was proposed at the Paris Peace Conference, and when the Treaty of Versailles formalized the proposals to China's detriment, national outrage forced the Chinese government to refuse to sign. The new intelligentsia closed ranks in affirming an era of definitive cultural change called the May 4th Movement.

Succeeding events brought new impetus to change in the theatre. In 1921 Gu Jiachen founded the Shanghai Dramatic Association which became a forceful sponsor of new drama. Two of its outstanding members were OUYANG YUQIAN and Hong Shen (1892–1955), stage director-playwright-teacher-film director. The latter studied in America from 1916 to 1922 and aroused controversy on his return by refusing to countenance men playing women's roles. Endorsed by conservative public opinion, this convention remained a barrier to developing a naturalistic acting style. Hong Shen defied long-standing prejudice by recruiting actresses from the more open-minded women of the universities and the Shanghai film world.

In 1921 Ouyang and Hong joined forces with TIAN HAN to found the Creation Society in Shanghai. The first issue of its journal Creation Quarterly in 1922, contained Tian Han's play A Night at a Coffeehouse (Jiafei dian zhi yiye) which became an immediate theatrical cause célèbre. The Society toured productions throughout the country until, in 1923, it was dissolved by government order. Although it was short-lived, the Society was influential in introducing broad audiences to modern theatre.

In the 1930s, the Japanese military threat compounded by the Nationalist–Communist political feud overshadowed intellectual life. People in literature and the arts responded to a new political awareness. In 1931 the League of Left Wing Dramatists was formed. Tian Han and Hong Shen became active members. Plays written and produced to portray current political–social problems were vigorously promoted in schools and factories. The Japanese attack on Shanghai in 1932 intensified theatrical protest, to which the Nationalist government responded with a campaign of repression, forcing leftist theatre underground. Tian Han and other League members were arrested as a deterrent.

The Chinese Communist Party (CCP) began organizing theatre for political action soon after the party's establishment in 1921. In 1931 the Chinese Soviet Republic was declared with its capital at Ruijin. Performers were recruited locally and provided with dramatic training, political education, their food, clothing and a subsistence pittance. Troupes trained at the CCP school in Ruijin were then attached to army units for service in rural territory and the front line. This work culminated in the organization of a Workers and Peasants Dramatic Society. Song, dance and mime were indispensable to appeal to audiences whose sole concept of theatre was provided by traditional opera. An extensive dramatic network functioned on this basis and contributed to establishing a permanent theatre-training school at the CCP wartime base in Yan'an.

Advocacy of drama as a factor in social education was also manifest on the National side. In 1932, Xiong Foxi (1900–65), a playwright-teacher-producer who had studied theatre in America, was invited by the National Association for Advancement of Mass Education to initiate a theatre project in the rural district of Dingxian, Hebei Province. Living among the peasant community provided him with authentic material for writing and producing plays with local people as actors. Within three years the troupe was staging self-supporting productions which attracted considerable notice. The Japanese invasion forced Xiong to lead his group to unoccupied west China. There, as the Farmers Resistance Dramatic Corps, they performed to mass audiences.

Political tensions notwithstanding, the 1930s witnessed the rise of a socially conscious theatre given credibility by the commitment of its practitioners. New dramatists were at work to capitalize on this advance, at times working in film with its

emotive capacity for evoking human values and national sentiment. Tian Han, Ouyang Yuqian and Hong Shen all turned to film as advisers, directors and scenario writers. A complementary and continuing relationship was established between the modern stage movement and the film studios. Xia Yan (1900–95), Japan-returned dramatist and scenario writer, was representative of this trend. His two early stage plays Under a Shanghai Roof (Shanghai wuyan xia) and Sai Jinhua were considered major contributions to the modern repertoire. The first portrayed the alienation and suffering of tenement dwellers in a great city. The second concerned a celebrated Chinese courtesan, one of whose alliances was with Count Alfred von Waldersee, the German commander of the allied forces which occupied Beijing to relieve the Boxer siege in 1900.

Arguably the most important playwright of this period was Cao Yu, a graduate in Western literature from a Beijing university. His first play, Thunderstorm (Leiyu), directed by Hong Shen and Ouyang Yuqian in 1935 for the Fudan University Dramatic Club, Shanghai, was an immediate success. Cao Yu had studied Greek drama and admired Eugene O'Neill and Anton Chekhov, influences discernible in this play with its dark commentary on the Chinese family system and the social degradation it caused. Credibility of characterization and realistic dialogue, allied to an intuitive sense of theatre, stamped this play as a breakthrough for indigenous dialogue drama. Cao Yu's second play Sunrise (Richu) portrayed the corruptive power of materialism and won him a literary prize. Wilderness (Yuanye), Metamorphosis (Shuibian), Peking Man (Beijing ren) and Family (Jia) followed, establishing him as a dramatist of social conscience.

Thunderstorm was taken throughout the country by The China Travelling Dramatic Troupe, founded in Shanghai in 1934 by Tang Huaiqiu. His goal was a modern repertory theatre on a financially viable basis. A co-operative unit, they achieved a homogeneous quality in their acting. Thunderstorm broke all box-office records for modern theatre and this was followed by Hong Shen's equally successful Lady Windermere's Fan. The troupe's aim seemed close to realization when in 1937 war intervened. They moved their base to Hong Kong for a brief period, but that too fell to the Japanese at the end of 1941.

In December 1937 theatre leaders, including Tian Han, met in Hankou to organize the National Dramatic Association to Resist the Enemy, an umbrella for all wartime theatrical activities. In February 1938 Tian Han became director of the government's Cultural Work Committee and head of the Propaganda Section, and a zealous censorship was applied to all dramatic activity. Henceforward modern theatre was subordinated to national propaganda needs. A call for resistance united theatre people as never before. Itinerant by vocation, they responded with travelling troupes to take propagandist theatre to the rural masses. Nationalists and Communists shared a common concept if with divergent ideological intent.

The rapid advance of the invading forces drove the Nationalist government to set up their capital at Chongqing, Sichuan Province. Universities and major educational organizations followed them, together with those prominent in every field of the arts. The emotional climate was typified by the manifesto of Xiong Foxi for his theatre students in west China: 'Cultivate modern drama with an artist's passion and a soldier's discipline to aid China's spiritual regeneration.'

Students of the co-educational Nanjing National Academy of Dramatic Art, founded in 1935 and evacuated to Chongqing, made their professional debut staging street plays and 'living newspapers'. A favoured technique entailed actors anonymously entering teahouses and drawing an audience by seemingly spontaneous dialogues on current affairs. Lack of permanent stages and technical equipment in wartime territory did not deter the hundreds of itinerant troupes. Academics and literary men frequently joined forces with professionals. Urban intellectuals and the rural population shared a new direct relationship as the result of dramatic activities.

Tian Han, official spokesman for theatre in wartime, encouraged these trends as a healthy portent for the future. He adapted such traditional Beijing-opera favourites as *The White Snake* (*Baishe zhuan*) for modern production. Criticized at the time, his version became standard after the war. Ouyang Yuqian worked closely with Tian Han during those years, leading a troupe that toured patriotic plays. Hong Shen ran a theatrical troupe and taught film and drama in the universities. It was a time of shared skills and commitments.

Xia Yan's plays successfully caught the public's mood. Typical was *City of Sorrows* (*Choucheng ji*) satirizing life in Japanese-occupied territory. *Put down Your Whip* (*Fangxia nide bianzi*) denounced Japanese aggression and was outstanding among the mass of propaganda pieces being produced. Cao Yu, in contrast, wrote nothing after his adaptation in 1941 of Ba Jin's novel *Family*. Xiong Foxi became disillusioned with government censorship policy after serving as head of the Sichuan Provincial College of Dramatic Arts. He left for Guilin in the southwest where he engaged in writing and editorial work until 1945.

Wartime Chongqing saw the germination of a national dance movement resulting from the work of Dai Ailian (1916–), a Trinidad-born Chinese danseuse. After studying ballet in England, patriotic motives led her to wartime China. While teaching in Chongqing she began studying local folk and minority nationality dances. With a team of pupil assistants she travelled to outlying areas researching and notating choreographic techniques, eventually forming her own company. Her pioneering work then prepared the way for organized dance education in China later.

The tangential ingredients of narrative, song and descriptive gesture in folk dance embodied primal elements of Chinese theatrical communication. They appealed directly to the uncomplicated emotive responses of peasant audiences. Both Nationalists and Communists sought to profit from this factor in their wartime sensitivity to folk tradition. The Communists were the more uncompromising. The artistic criteria of folk genres were subordinated to theories of proletarian drama created to eliminate the aesthetic 'elitism' of the old theatre.

Following the Long March of 1934–5 the Communists set up their base in the loessic caves at Yan'an in northern Shaanxi Province. There in May 1942 Mao Zedong gave his 'Talks at the Yan'an Forum on Literature and Art'. In them he expounded his Marxist manifesto destined to become the bible of all Chinese cultural endeavour. He spoke at the Lu Xun Art Institute which trained troupes to adapt old folk-performance methods to new content.

One such ancient form much utilized by the Communists was the *yangge* rice-planting song. Originally *yangge* referred to simple rhythmic steps danced to a chant and percussion while planting the rice fields. When Communist troops entered the big cities in 1949 they were preceded by files of dancers performing this simple work form as a victory theme. In time *yangge* was applied collectively to various other types of performances that were developed from it.

During the 19th century the style of *yangge* prevalent in Dingxian, Hebei Province, gradually became elaborated as village performance: 20 to 30 dancers performed with a leader, male and female characters confronted each other with a question –response narrative followed by singing and dance movements extended with representational gesture. Elemental themes from village life and ethics were introduced. A comic character frequently added the necessary touch of earthy humour. Drum, gong, flute and cymbals provided musical accompaniment.

Two scholars, Li Jinghuan and Zhang Shiwen, conducted a government-sponsored field project on the Dingxian style in 1932, afterwards publishing an anthology of plays. It was this genre of performance the Communists found so adaptable and were quick to develop for their needs. *Yangge* troupes proliferated. More than 30 of them staged performances at the 1944 Yan'an spring festival. Their repertoire included a play called *The White-Haired Girl* (*Baimao nü*).

Reputedly of ballad-recitative origin and based on some actual facts, the play had undergone collective revisions prior to the 1944 presentation. In 1945 a new five-act version was prepared with a script and lyrics by He Jingzhi (1924–) and Ding Yi (1921–). Music based on authentic folk sources was composed for it by Ma Ke (1918–76) and five colleagues. Being directed against abusive social practices long familiar to village tenant farmers, it became a theatrical symbol of the revolutionary cause and was constantly performed in the late 1940s and 1950s. The fusion of song, music, chorus work and ordinary speech allied to a contemporary setting set *The White-Haired Girl* apart from either traditional Chinese or modern Western stage practices, though both had clearly offered some inspiration. It appealed to an audience for whom theatre without song and music was inconceivable and dialogue drama in the Western vein meaningless in the context of their lifestyle. *The White-Haired Girl* was the first full-length representative of a new

national genre named *GEJU*, song drama. Flexible in subject matter and musical form it was contemporary but adaptable to regional traditions. It was one solution to finding a middle way between past and present, a long-standing problem of Chinese theatre.

Re-establishment of the Nationalist capital at Nanjing in May 1946 followed Japan's defeat in 1945. In 1946 full-scale civil war broke out as the CCP began its drive for ultimate power. Crippling inflation led to economic chaos and social disintegration. The plight of the universities was desperate, the mood of intellectuals despair.

In 1946 Xiong Foxi became head of the Shanghai Municipal Experimental School of Dramatic Art. Sharing the premises of a local museum and primary school. Xiong's faith in theatre was matched by that of his students and staff. Combining classroom study with working experience they sustained a continuing series of performances for the public in spite of neglible government support. Tian Han, Cao Yu and Hong Shen all taught there after the war. Xia Yen had given up playwriting for film work and Ouyang Yuqian was working for Hong Kong film studios. Dai Ailian, the dancer, another guest of the United States during this period, returned to set up her own school in Shanghai. In 1949 when the Nationalist government left for Taiwan these key artists stayed on to work under the new government. It was a decision which was shared by a large proportion of people prominent in both traditional and modern theatre circles.

The People's Republic 1949-91: policy and theory

On 1 October 1949 the Chinese Communist Party (CCP) established the People's Republic of China (PRC) under its Chairman Mao Zedong. In 1966 Mao launched his radical Cultural Revolution in an attempt to preserve revolutionary purity. With his death in September 1976 and the fall of the radical 'gang of four' the following month, economic modernization soon assumed top priority in China's policy, and in 1981 both the Cultural Revolution and Mao's leadership from 1958 on were largely discredited.

Attitudes towards theatre reflect overall CCP policy, which means that there have been substantial changes from period to period. However, at no time has the CCP believed it should relax its concern with theatre activities altogether. As a result, the fact of censorship has been consistent, even though the extent has varied enormously.

Until 1981, the basic CCP policy and theory of theatre (and other arts) were those Mao advanced in his 'Talks at the Yan'an Forum on Literature and Art'. Mao declared there that theatre reflected society but also influenced it as a means of propaganda, whether it intended to or not. He held all theatre as representing the interests of one class or another and advocated that it should oppose the bourgeoisie and favour the masses of workers, peasants and soldiers. Elsewhere, Mao pushed for the critical assimilation of traditional and foreign theatres.

In July 1950 the new government's Ministry of Culture set up a Drama Reform Committee to determine precisely how practice in the theatre should be brought into line with theory. Among traditional music dramas it retained those which emphasized Chinese patriotism, peasant rebellion or heroism, equality between the sexes, or the political prominence of women. Newly arranged dramas on historical themes were expected to emphasize similar topics. On the other hand, many items considered 'feudal' and siding with the rich against the poor were banned. While the mannerisms, costumes and other aspects of the traditional actor's craft were retained, reform demanded the abolition of some 'unhealthy' usages. No people's hero should be shown in a position which humiliated him before a feudal person such as a monk. Kowtowing and the 'false foot' devised by Wei Changsheng were banned. The Great Leap Forward of 1958 gave strong emphasis to dramas of all forms on contemporary themes, but did not discourage traditional themes. Throughout the 1950s and early 1960s, although the theories of Stanislavski were dominant in spoken-drama circles, those of Bertolt Brecht also had a following, led by Huang Zuoling of the Shanghai People's Art Theatre.

At a meeting of heads of CCP Cultural Bureaux held in April 1963, Mao's wife Jiang Qing had a circular distributed calling for 'the suspension of the performance of ghost plays', by which she meant any traditional music drama or newly arranged historical item. In mid 1964 a Festival of Beijing Opera on Contemporary Themes was held, sig-

nalling the near total disappearance of all such 'ghost plays' from the stage for 13 years. In February 1966 Jiang Qing held a forum on 'Literature and Art in the Armed Forces' which laid down the line on theatre demanded during the Cultural Revolution (1966–76). It followed Mao's ideas closely in its emphasis on class and class struggle and the mass line, but placed an extreme interpretation on them. Thus 'critical assimilation' of tradition meant retention of little more than the name Beijing opera. All content must praise the revolution and the CCP directly, almost all the traditional content, mannerisms and costumes were banned as espousing feudal ideas and class interests. The Forum also pushed the notion of a 'model' drama, one which encapsulated perfectly all the Cultural Revolution's theory of theatre. Over the following years a small number of these 'models' was devised, and professional drama companies were allowed to perform more or less nothing else. One of the main features of the 'models' was their characterization, which portrayed the heroes as faultless, and the villains as without redeeming features.

Jiang Qing was the leader of the 'gang of four' and it was not long after their fall that the Cultural Revolution's theatre theory was discredited. In May 1977 several scenes of a newly arranged historical drama were restaged in Beijing. Early the following year the main power-holder of the new leadership, Deng Xiaoping, gave explicit approval for the revival of traditional music dramas and these began to trickle back, very quickly becoming a veritable torrent which, as of the mid-90s, shows no signs of subsiding. Love-stories and patriotic dramas, as well as those about peasant rebels, again received encouragement and the theme of righted injustice set in the dynastic past became a useful propaganda weapon on behalf of legal reform. Humour again became a dominant part of the Chinese regional drama, and entertainment was accepted as a main purpose of theatre.

The main linchpin in the CCP's theatre policy is the need for variety. The range of form and content continued to broaden until 1989, on the whole with CCP approval. Up till 1989 attempts to hold back this trend towards liberalization, such as the Campaign against Spiritual Pollution in 1983, proved short-lived. In 1982 Mao's 'Talks at the Yan'an Forum' were partly discredited. In theory, theatre should still serve the interests of the 'people' but the emphasis on its use as a propaganda weapon for socialism tended increasingly to weaken. As a result, modern dramas ignoring the role of the CCP in society, and those advocating no solution for its ills, became common. Psychological drama became popular among the urban intelligentsia. The theories of acting and theatre of Bertolt Brecht increased in influence especially among younger playwrights. Since 1979 various forms of foreign theatre have received CCP sponsorship, not only performed by foreign companies in the original language, but also by local troupes and translated into Chinese.

The crisis of 1989, which climaxed in the bloody Tiananmen Square incident in Beijing on 4 June, exercised a highly detrimental effect on modern forms of drama because it placed a clamp on new experiments and ideas in theatre which could be construed as non-supportive of the CCP. In the period following the crisis, the man with chief responsibility for literature and the arts was Li Ruihuan. In a major speech made on 10 January 1990 he emphasized the magnificence of Chinese tradition and called for the critical absorption of foreign cultures. He summarized the relationship between art and politics as follows: 'We do not require literature and art to be directly subordinate to temporary and specific political tasks. At the same time, this does not mean that literature and art can deviate from serving socialism.' Certainly there would be no return to the policies of the Cultural Revolution, when literature and art were indeed directly subservient to political tasks. At the same time, Li's position implied a strong tendency to glorify the Chinese 'nation' through theatre and other arts.

As a result government support for traditional music drama and plays set in the distant past grew noticeably at the expense of those dramas or drama forms focused on modern history or contemporary society. In 1990, the 200th anniversary of the entry of the Anhui companies into Beijing in 1790, a major stage along the path of development of the Beijing opera, was celebrated enthusiastically throughout China. By way of climax, a festival featuring traditional music dramas was held in Beijing attended by Li Ruihuan and Jiang Zemin, CCP Secretary-General.

Form, performance

The main forms of theatre in China since 1949 are traditional music drama, newly arranged historical drama (XINBIAN LISHI JU), spoken drama (huaju), song drama (geju), dance drama (WUJU) and ballet. There are about 350 regional styles of traditional music drama, as explained in the sections on imperial China. The content is always from the distant past. As in the past, stage properties are simple, there is no scenery, but costumes and makeup are elaborate, mannerisms, posture and body movements stylized. An evening's entertainment will normally feature three or four short items. Reform and censorship have removed certain items and passages, but this is the form least affected by the modern age. 'Newly arranged historical dramas' are traditional in most aspects of style, but as the name suggests, are created by contemporary writers and performers. In addition, scores of amateur and professional puppetry troupes perpetuate various regional traditions of puppet play (kuilei xi), shadow play (piying xi), and rod-puppet play (zhangtou kuilei) performance.

Among Westernized forms, the most important is spoken drama (huaju). Only of this form can it be said, in the 1980s, that most items are set in the present or even since 1949. The best representative writer before the Cultural Revolution was LAO SHE. Spoken drama in the 1980s showed inventiveness and innovation and the most outside, mainly Western, influence. Social commentary remained strong, but among avant-garde playwrights, propaganda of the type favoured by the CCP became less and less direct, more and more subdued. Individualism and feminism are hallmarks of contemporary female playwrights such as Bai Fengxi (1934–). Directors have experimented with techniques new to China, for example, variation in the colour and intensity of stage-lighting to show emotional or psychological atmospheres or qualities. Spoken dramas of the PRC normally use elaborate scenery and stage properties and in urban theatres the act curtain is drawn to mark beginning, end or intermission. However, since 1982, a few plays have adopted extremely simple stage properties, and abandoned scenery and the curtain altogether. Body movements and postures are realistic, not stylized as in traditional music drama. But whereas the plays with heavy propaganda content tended to show ideal characters through rather stilted, even stereotypical, movements and postures, natural style became more popular in the 1980s to portray characters who themselves conform less to images laid down as good, mediocre or bad by the CCP.

The introduction of Western ballet is due principally to Soviet influence. Before 1966, ballet meant mainly items of classical European repertoire, especially *Swan Lake*. The 'model' dramas of Jiang Qing included two ballets: *The White-Haired Girl* and *The Red Detachment of Women* (*Hongse niangzi jun*). Since 1976, these items have disappeared as ballets and classical works have returned. At the same time, Chinese artists are making very tentative steps towards creating their own national ballet, including composing new works and training ballet dancers. However, no high priority is given to this form, and it is most unlikely ever to gain great popularity in China outside a small urban intellectual elite.

Illustrative pieces

Of all newly arranged historical dramas, none is more famous than *The White Snake* (*Baishe zhuan*). Originally a folk story about a white snake that turns into a beautiful woman, it underwent numerous adaptations, including a *kunqu* version by an anonymous playwright in the 18th century. Tian Han, one of the PRC's most famous dramatists, adapted it as a Beijing opera, completing the work in 1953. A monk in the *kunqu* is a positive character who succeeds in curbing the power of the wicked snake, but Tian Han has changed the characterization to present him as evil, the snake turned woman as positive. Even though an element of magic is preserved, the item thus advocates a positive role for women.

The theme of patriotism supplements advocacy of equality for women in *Women Generals of the Yang Family* (*Yangmen nüjiang*), arranged as a Beijing opera in 1960 by Lü Ruiming on the basis of a late-Ming novel and a Yangzhou music drama entitled *Centenarian Takes Command* (*Baisui guashuai*). Like all others on traditional themes, this item was banned during the Cultural Revolution. However it was revived in 1978. It is set in the 11th century. A centenarian dowager surnamed Yang persuades the women of her family to resist an enemy aggressing from the north, and their forces win the final victory.

One regional drama on a modern theme is *The Story of the Red Lantern* (*Hongdeng ji*), which features three generations of Communist heroes and their struggle against a Japanese general during the War of Resistance against Japan. The representatives of the two elder generations are killed by the general, but the youngest lives to fight victoriously against him. The item was adapted into a Beijing opera by the playwright-director Ajia (1907–95) and performed at the 1964 Festival of Beijing Opera on Contemporary Themes. It was taken over by Jiang Qing and recognized as one of her model dramas from 1970 on. The characterization was made starker to emphasize the class struggle; Western instruments were added to the accompanying orchestra and the music made more staccato to express the heroism of the Communists better. The item was revived in the festival of December 1990 and January 1991 to mark the 200th anniversary of the entry of the Anhui companies into Beijing. That this was not a sign of a Cultural Revolutionary revival was demonstrated by the fact that the form chosen was Ajia's, with Jiang Qing being accused of having seized the item through an act of robbery.

In the 1980s several spoken dramas and newly arranged historical music dramas appeared on the subject of Li Shimin, one of China's greatest emperors (r. 626–49). He was the second ruler of the Tang dynasty and held the imperial title of Taizong, and so is known also as Tang Taizong. One of the music dramas is the Beijing opera *Tang Taizong*, arranged by Li Lun. It deals with Li Shimin's success in winning over a Turkish invader through mediation and popular support, not force, thus securing national unity. The incident which forms the core of the drama is historical, but the characterization and plot are adapted to advocate political lessons appropriate to the present. An item to be premiered after the 1989 crisis was *Painting Dragons and Filling in Eyes* (*Hualong dianjing*) by Sun Yuexia and others. Set in 627 it portrays Li Shimin as a kind of 'people's emperor' and an example for the Chinese nation and concerns his search for good officials and suppression of corruption. In the 1980s the best writer of newly arranged historical music drama was probably WEI MINGLUN.

More modern national heroes portrayed on the stage since the late 1970s are revolutionaries such as Mao Zedong and Zhou Enlai. In 1981, the 70th anniversary of the overthrow of the last dynasty by

Sun Yatsen and his followers was the occasion for several spoken dramas about him. His wife Song Qingling, who died in 1981, figures prominently in them. The first of the plays was *Sun Yatsen's London Encounter with Danger (Sun Zhongshan Lundun mengan ji)*. Its focus was Sun's arrest by the Chinese legation in 1896 and later release through the efforts of his former teacher, the British doctor Sir James Cantlie. This enables the playwright, Li Peijian, to emphasize not only the courage and unselfishness of Sun, but also the power and wisdom of the British people, represented by Cantlie and others, and Sun's good relations with his 'foreign friends'. The play is unusual in China, even in the 1980s, in being set in a foreign country.

Sites of performance, audiences

Theatre performances can take place in a variety of sites in China, including workers' or rural clubs, a

The Changyin Ge (Joyful Sounds Pagoda), a three-tiered stage in the Imperial Palaces of Beijing, site of the former imperial court.

marketplace or any open space. Street theatre is common only on special occasions such as festivals. In the cities and towns, cinemas are readily used as theatres for live performances. A major theatre encyclopedia published in Beijing in 1983 stated that there were 891 theatres in China in 1949 and 2227 in 1957. It claimed that 'after 1958 [we] continued to build quite a few new theatres' but gave no figures. In the main cities there are a few large theatres, of special note being one opened in Beijing in 1984 which has a 600-square-metre stage able to hold 1000 performers.

Most theatres built since 1949 follow a somewhat stark Soviet architectural style, both internally and externally. In sharp contrast to the teahouse-theatres of the 19th century, the audience is expected to concentrate fully on the performance, and sits in rows facing one side of the stage. In the case of musical items, the text is projected beside the stage to facilitate comprehension. The seats are rarely padded. The large 1984 Beijing theatre has a stage with rising and revolving platforms, a stereo sound system, lamps, spotlights and curtains all controlled by computer, the first of its kind in China.

Some companies own their own theatre. Those not so fortunate negotiate with a local government Bureau of Culture, which co-ordinates the timetables of the various troupes and theatres. Tours are planned through an annual meeting organized by the central Ministry of Culture. In a few parts of China there are special theatres for balladeers or storytellers. Here people sip tea and listen to stories sung out by one or several performers, accompanied by musical instruments. However, in most cases storytellers perform by themselves in parks or squares.

Performances are advertised partly through the local press. Theatres announce forthcoming items and performances through bills in the foyer. Most important of all, advertisements are stuck on special billboards, poles or any free space along the streets or in the markets. This is especially necessary in small towns or villages which lack their own newspaper. Tickets for professional performances are cheap and entry to amateur ones often free. Simple printed programmes are very cheap. Full houses are quite common, especially for good and well performed pieces, but companies frequently complain of low attendances, and nearly empty theatres are distressingly common in provincial centres.

Those involved with the traditional and the newly arranged historical music drama have become very worried over the defection of young people from their audiences. Possibly the gap in performance of over a decade during the Cultural Revolution dealt a crippling blow to youth's interest in such theatre. It was excluded from their education and cultural life for so long that by the time of its revival they simply did not understand it and saw no reason why they should make the effort. In the 1980s and 90s, audiences at urban performances of traditional music dramas are mainly over 40 years of age, with men outnumbering women two or more to one. The same problem affects the countryside, but is not nearly so pronounced there.

Young theatre-goers prefer the spoken drama because they can understand it and it has more to say of relevance to their own lives. However, since the mid 1980s even spoken-drama troupes have been finding it increasingly difficult to make ends meet and to attract large audiences. The form of entertainment which is more and more attracting the largest audience is not theatre, but television. The State Statistical Bureau's 1995 communiqué on the previous year's economy and society declared that there were 764 television stations and 1123 television transmitting and relay stations. Television is available not only in the cities but to very large and increasing areas of the countryside. Ironically the screen does support all drama forms in the sense that both traditional and modern music-dramas and spoken dramas are shown both on television and in the cinema, but the fact is of little comfort to the average performer.

Audiences at traditional music dramas tend to be noisy, possibly in part a reflection of their incomplete understanding of what is happening, but those at spoken drama are quiet. Applause is reserved mainly for notes held an unusual length of time or an excellent acrobatics display. Even very good troupes are lucky to elicit more than a patter at the conclusion of the performance.

The performer

The State Statistical Bureau announced in March 1996 that the number of full professional performing-arts troupes in China in 1995 was 2690. The

The renowned Beijing Opera actor, Wang Yaoqing (1881-1954), in a military *dan* (*wudan*) role in *Qipan Mountain* (*Qipan shan*).

number of troupes in 1950 was 1676 and in 1965 it was 3458, but it had fallen to 2514 by 1971 as a result of the policies of the Cultural Revolution. The year with the highest figure was 1980, with 3533 troupes, but the trend during the 1980s and 1990s was downwards.

The nationalization of professional troupes began in the mid 1950s and was completed during the Cultural Revolution. After the fall of the 'gang of four' the process was reversed and in the early 1980s reform directed towards free enterprise began to be introduced even in state companies. Under the new system, state subsidies to troupes are reduced and the troupe keeps a larger portion of its box-office earnings. Box-office earnings thus assume far greater importance. This aims to 'break the iron rice bowl' and in theory improves quality

Artists

Cao Yu (1910–)

Dramatist (Wan Jiabao). Born in Hubei he gradu-ated in Western literature from Qinghua University, Beijing, and at one time taught at the National Academy of Dramatic Art, Nanjing. In 1934 he published the four-act play *Thunderstorm* (*Leiyu*) which received instant acclaim. Its involved plot covers a single day's events set against the menace of a gathering storm. A tangled history of seduction revealed through the interrelationships of a wealthy industrialist's house-hold ends in tragedy when incest is exposed as a conse-quence of a misalliance. Five other plays written within the next six years include *Sunrise* (*Richu*) and *Wilderness* (*Yuanye*), which, with *Thunderstorm*, form the trilogy that consti-tutes his major achievement. Their theme is the decadence of Chinese prewar society. During the war Cao Yu taught at Fudan University and in 1946 observed theatre in the United States with the play-wright–novelist LAO SHE.

In the 1950s he held a number of cultural and administrative posts in the new government and served on the presid-ium of a conference of writers, artists and theatre people called by the CCP. Soon he came under fire for bourgeois thinking and he remained creatively inactive until his propagan-dist play *Bright Skies* (*Minglang de tian*) was staged at the Beijing People's Art Theatre in 1956. Cao Yu became a CCP member in 1957 when there was a drive to recruit older intellectuals. In 1966 he was seized from his home at night and sent to a reform school in the country. He was rehabilitated like his fellow intellectuals after 1976 and recognized as a father figure of the modern theatre. Reverting to historical themes in 1961, *The Gall and the Sword* (*Dan jian pian*) takes as its theme the wars between the two ancient kingdoms of Wu and Yue in the 5th century BC. The play has an ideological implica-tion in its eulogizing of the people. In 1979 his full trilogy was revived to an enthusiastic recep-tion. From the late 1970s he was concerned with the experimental use of conventions from traditional theatre for historical themes.

Cheng Changgeng (c. 1812–80), the famous Beijing Opera actor of old male roles (*laosheng*): from a picture by Shen Rongpu.

Cheng Changgeng (c. 1812–80)

Actor of old male (*laosheng*) roles in JINGXI. Born in Anhui he moved to Beijing in child-hood and first studied acting under his maternal uncle. Cheng rose to become leader of the Three Celebrations, one of the four major acting companies in the capital. He was outstanding in male roles portraying great statesmen and warriors, and his style of acting was influential on later performers. A man of great personal integrity and dignity he was well regarded at court.

Cheng Yanqiu (1904–58)

Actor in JINGXI. Born in Beijing the son of an impoverished Manchu family, he studied both *jingxi* and KUNQU tech-niques under leading teachers. Specializing in women's roles (*dan*), he rose to professional recognition as one of the 'four great famous *dan*' (*sida mingdan*). MEI LANFANG, Shang Xiaoyun (1900–76) and Xun Huisheng (1900–68) were the other three. Cheng developed an individual style of vocalization and was noted for grace and skill in acting. An influential teacher, in the 1930s he directed the new Academy of Dramatic Art in Beijing and under the PRC spent his last years training a new generation of actors. He played in one film made expressly to record his technical expertise.

Gao Xingjian (1940–)

Writer of HUAJU and drama theorist. Influenced by Western, especially French, ideas he was the most innovative and challenging of the younger playwrights during the 1980s in terms of concept, performance and style. Graduating from the Beijing Foreign Languages Institute in 1962, he visited France in 1979 and after several further visits took up residence there. A highly prolific writer, he is best known for three spoken dramas from the first half of the 1980s: *Warning Signal (Juedui xinhao)*, *Bus Stop (Chezhan)* and *Wild Man (Yeren)*. *Warning Signal* is about unemployed youth. The main character Blackie, intends to take part in a train robbery to get the money he needs to marry, but in the end turns against his accomplice and kills him. Like most other spoken dramas of the time, it is really about serious social problems in Chinese society – unemployment and juvenile delinquency. What is unusual is the play's symbolism and that it offers no solutions. Blackie's murder of his intended accomplice is shown as a redemptive not a criminal act. He is an antihero of a kind virtually unique in China in 1982. *Bus Stop* concerns characters waiting in vain at a bus stop and expressing their memories, disappointments and aspirations, inviting comparison with Beckett's *Waiting for Godot*. It is a didactic play with a clear message in favour of forward movement. In *Wild Man,* Gao not only adopts contemporary notions of total theatre, but returns to the traditional style of drama in which singing, recitation, dance/movement and acting are combined in a total performance. The item has many messages, among which preservation of the environment is foremost.

Guan Hanqing

Dramatist, active in the second half of the 13th century, regarded as the foremost Yuan dynasty ZAJU playwright. During celebrations of his 700th anniversary in 1958, tribute was paid to his affinity with the everyday life of his times. Of his presumed 63 plays, 18 are extant. *Injustice to Dou E (Dou E yuan)* is constantly performed in China and known in the West in translation. Its theme concerns the tragic fate of a young woman wrongly executed as the victim of false witness and a corrupt official. Her innocence is established by cosmic intervention. The emotional vigour of the characterization and an expressive lyrical style exemplify the formative contribution Guan made to early drama.

Guo Moruo (1892–1978)

Dramatist, poet and historian from Sichuan province. In 1921 he was among the leaders of the Creation Society, spawned by the May 4th Movement of 1919. He lived in Japan as a student 1923–26 and again 1928–37. He played a prominent role in the resistance in Shanghai during World War II. Under the PRC he was given numerous government and cultural posts and was one of the very few artists and intellectuals to remain in favour during the decade of the Cultural Revolution.

A strong fighter for women's rights, this issue dominates much of his prodigious literary output. Among his early spoken dramas (written in 1923), *Wang Zhaojun* and *Zhuo Wenjun* , named after their respective heroines, present intelligent and defiant historical women of the distant past, whom Guo intended as positive models for his own times. In his last play, produced in 1962, *Wu Zetian*, the title role is the only woman in Chinese history ever to become emperor (r. 684–705). The play praises both her and the concept that women should occupy high political positions. One of Guo's most productive periods was during the war against Japan. A representative play from those years is *Qu Yuan* (1942), which is about the famous poet of that name of the 3rd and 4th centuries BC and his struggle against tyrannical rulers of his time.

Hong Sheng (1645–1704)

KUNQU dramatist. In Beijing, where he was appointed to the Imperial Academy, he made a reputation as a poet and playwright. His masterpiece *The Palace of Eternal Youth (Changsheng dian*, 1688) came to the notice of the Kangxi Emperor (r. 1662–1723) and thereafter was performed frequently before court society. The plot concerns the love affair of the Tang Emperor Minghuang (r. 713–56) and his favourite concubine Yang Guifei. The theme has been a constant inspiration to poets and dramatists and Hong's play is still regarded as one of China's greatest lyric dramas. In 1689 Hong was dismissed from the Academy for a breach of court etiquette. He spent his remaining days in poverty.

Hou Baolin (1917–92)

Veteran exponent of *xiangsheng*, a story-telling genre involving comic dialogue, wisecracks and mimicry. Hou was born in Beijing, was apprenticed to a street singer, joined a troupe of street entertainers skilled in reciting complete plays from the Beijing repertoire and eventually was accepted as an apprentice by the *xiangsheng* guild. He performed in Beijing and Tianjin and rose to fame partnered by Guo Qiru as his stage foil. He was denounced during the Cultural Revolution but survived to become a national-celebrity. He is a master of improvisation and has a keen sense of characterization through dialect. Hou remains unsurpassed in the art of taking the audience by surprise, the essence of comic genius on the stage.

Kong Shangren (1648–1718)

Kunqu playwright. A descendant of Confucius in the 64th generation and an authority on ancient rites and music, his *The Peach Blossom Fan* (*Taohua shan*, 1699), a 40-scene play written in southern style, is considered a masterpiece of poetic composition. It records the treachery and intrigue which facilitated the Manchu overthrow of the Ming dynasty in 1644. Characters are based on historical personages and its love story is one of the greatest in Chinese literature. The play won immediate popularity but resulted in the playwright's dismissal from office by the Manchu authorities. Kong was considered one of the two great playwrights of his day, the second being HONG SHENG.

Lao She (1899–1966)

Dramatist and novelist of Manchu nationality (pseudonym of Shu Qingchun). Born and edu-cated in Beijing, he left for England in 1924 and taught at the London School of Oriental Studies. He lived in the the United States (1946–49) and, on his return to China, wrote *HUAJU* plays and participated in literary committees and organizations under the new PRC government. His 1950 play *Dragon Beard Ditch* (*Longxu gou*) about the successful rehabilitation of a Beijing slum area earned him the title of People's Artist. In 1957 he published the highly regarded *Teahouse* (*Chaguan*), a three-act, slice-of-life naturalist drama. In it he demonstrates his knowledge and love of the old Beijing institution of the teahouse, his sensitivity to the disintegration of society in the half-century separating 1898 and 1949 and his skilful command of colloquial language. He is perhaps best known for his novel, *Camel Xiangzi*, plagiarized in English as *Rickshaw Boy*, a tragic story of corruption of the innocent. He drowned himself in 1966 following ill treatment by Red Guards during the Cultural Revolution.

Li Yu (1611–80)

Dramatist, drama theorist and director. He trained and directed a theatre troupe of actresses, travelling round the country to perform at homes of high officials. He was a talented and versatile playwright and director. His work reveals a profound knowledge of stage practices and dramatic composition based on first-hand experience. In a rare book on Chinese dramatic theory, *A Temporary Lodge for My Leisure Thoughts* (*Xianqing ouji*, 1671) Li described his own theatre practice in detail and rejected the stigma laid upon theatre by officials and scholars.

Mei Lanfang (1894–1961)

JINGXI star actor and teacher. Born into a traditional Beijing opera family he was trained in women's roles (*dan*) like his father and grandfather before him. He was idolized by the theatregoing public. He created new dance plays based on historical literary themes that gave new dimensions to the repertoire. He innovated roles in which song, dance and combat techniques were combined in solo performance. Mei was active in breaking down prejudices against women and many actresses became his disciples. He collaborated with theatre scholar and adviser-impresario-playwright Qi Rushan (1876–1962). Mei refused to perform during the Japanese occupation of China, remaining secluded in Shanghai. After 1949 he was active on the stage and in teaching, carrying out an extremely heavy programme urged upon him by the new government. His former home in Beijing has been made into a commemorative museum in honour of his achievements.

Ouyang Yuqian (1889–1962)

Modern drama actor, director, theatre educator and dramatist. As a student in Japan in 1907 he acted in *The Black Slave's Cry to Heaven* (*Heinu yutian lu*) and hence took part in the origins of HUAJU. Over a long career he wrote 40 modern plays, directed 50, and adapted or revised some 50 dramas in traditional style. An excellent JINGXI performer of female roles, he was deeply engaged in integrating Chinese tradition with foreign influences. One instance of this was his *Pan Jinlian* (1928). First written as a spoken drama, it was also performed as a Beijing opera, Ouyang Yuqian himself playing the leading female role, Pan Jinlian. Ouyang portrayed an intelligent, passionate rebel against conventional morality.

Tang Xianzu (1550–1616)

KUNQU dramatist. In 1598 Tang abandoned an official career and became a romantic, individualistic playwright. In contrast to his contemporary and rival Shen Jing (1553–1610), who adhered strictly to the traditional forms of metrical composition, Tang sidestepped the rigid rules of orthodox metrical usage in favour of a free, sensual use of diction and poetic expression. Tang's major work is a quartet of plays with a dream motif of which *The Peony Pavilion* (*Mudan ting*) in 55 scenes, is famous for its poetic excellence. The theme of romantic love expounded in a supernatural context has great emotional impact. Excerpts from this play are constantly performed on the traditional stage.

Tian Han (1898–1968)

Dramatist. After study in Japan (1916–22), Tian helped found the literary Creation Society (1921) in Shanghai. In 1928 he was one of the organizers of the left-wing Southern Society (1928) and by 1932 had joined the CCP. When the PRC was established he was appointed to head the Drama Reform Committee under the Ministry of Culture (1950).

Tian Han wrote 24 dramas in traditional style, such as *The White Snake* (*Bai she zhuan*), and some 60 works in the modern genres, HUAJU and GEJU. Representative of his early left-wing period is *Moonlight Serenade of 1932* (*Yijiusanernian de yueguang qu*) about a bus-workers' strike against foreign capitalists that focuses on the class struggle.

Tian's best known spoken drama, *Guan Hanqing* (1958), was chosen to represent the 700th anniversary of the great dramatist GUAN HANQING. The drama portrays Guan as a people's artist and fighter against tyranny, and revolves around Guan's composition of his famous play *Injustice to Dou E* (*Dou E yuan*). His last work was the tragic Beijing opera *Xie Yaohuan* (1961), named after the heroine, an official in the reign of Empress Wu Zetian. Tian died during the Cultural Revolution, one of numerous artists and intellectuals to come under fire from radical Maoists. In its early stages he had been branded one of the 'four villains' of the cultural world: *Guan Hanqing* was denounced and *Injustice to Dou E* was attacked as a 'poisonous weed' by the *People's Daily*.

Wei Liangfu (active 1522–73)

Musician and creator of the present KUNQU musical form. In Jiangsu Province he carried out innovative research on the musical modes which flourished in that southern area. Their principal differences lay in a dialectical usage which affected the rhythm and tempo of song and speech forms. He synthesized modal elements and refined articulation and vocalization so as to match speech tones with tempo and pitch, thereby creating the mellifluous, somewhat plaintive, singing to flute accompaniment which characterizes *kunqu* drama. Wei was assisted in his research by Zhang Yetang, an authority on the northern modal repertoire.

Wei Minglun (1941–)

Writer of Sichuan opera (*CHUANJU*) who achieved a great reputation as an innovative dramatist during the 1980s. His *The Scholar of Bashan* (*Bashan xiucai*), set in 19th-century Sichuan, concerns a scholar who seeks and obtains redress for an unprovoked massacre of the people of Bashan, but dies poisoned by a court official. *Pan Jinlian*, described in the title as 'a Sichuan opera of the absurd', recasts the story of Pan Jinlian, traditionally known as a murderer of one of her husbands and a nymphomaniac. Wei's play lays the blame for Pan Jinlian's crimes and excesses on the evils of China's patriarchal society and on the oppression of women. One strand of the drama relates Pan's fall into vice, a second shows her trial set in the PRC. The action leaps across time and cultures, and char-acters include such divergent women as Empress Wu Zetian, a contemporary Chinese female judge and Tolstoy's Anna Karenina. *Pan Jinlian* has been praised for its relevance to Chinese theatre and to Chinese society of the 1980s.

Yu Zhenfei (1902–92)

Actor in *KUNQU* and *JINGXI*. He was born at Suzhou, the son of Yu Zonghai – an erudite *kunqu* authority – under whom he had his first-lessons at the age of six. After apprenticeship under both *kunqu* and *jingxi* master actors, he quickly became acclaimed for the perfection of his interpretations of the young scholar-hero (*xiaosheng*) in *jingxi*, regularly partnering MEI LANFANG. Through a long professional career Yu has also worked indefatigably to preserve *kunqu*, training a new generation of performers at the Shanghai Municipal Academy of Dramatic Art in the 1950s until his work was disrupted by the Cultural Revolution. He is an accomplished flute (*dizi*) player as well as singer and actor, and the author of a treatise on *kunqu* acting.

because it intensifies competition among actors. Now the possibility of dismissal becomes quite real for lazy or incompetent members. Above all, inequalities increase greatly because performers with big roles in successful plays can earn substantial sums from box-office returns, in addition to their salary, and thus become rich by Chinese standards quite quickly. Social benefits for members of state professional troupes are quite good.

Immediately after coming to power, the CCP abolished the training system of the past and instituted the principle that potential performers should receive a general as well as theatrical education in order to wipe out illiteracy. The training of almost all traditional music-drama students was suspended during the Cultural Revolution and then revived after 1976. Most professional companies run schools through which to recruit, train and educate new performers. For traditional music drama, especially Beijing opera, the main national school is the Chinese Music Drama Institute (Zhongguo Xiqu Xueyuan), set up in 1950. It now has five departments: Beijing-opera performance, music, directing, dramaturgy and stagecraft. Between 1956 and 1982 the institution produced some 1300 graduates.

Entry into training schools at all levels is through highly competitive examination: about 5 per cent of applicants gain admission. There is still a strong bias in favour of males, the rationale being that casts require more men.

CCP policy is to train women to sing female roles and men to sing male. In 1951 Premier Zhou Enlai told the famous *dan* actor Zhang Chunqiu: 'up to you the male *dan*, and that's the end'. If this policy is continued, in time women will perform all *dan* roles, but it appears that a handful of female impersonators are being trained, so the art may not die after all.

The social status of performers has risen greatly under CCP rule. Among the reasons for this are the elimination of the social discrimination which previously afflicted them, a highly organized recruitment and training system, an improved standard of living, and the government's high evaluation of 'art workers' as a profession. There are, however, still strong gradations in the status of performers: stars may be among the most influential and respected members of society, while ordinary performers live in serious poverty and social disregard.

Since the earliest days of its existence the CCP has strongly encouraged amateur artists who, it considered, could assist its propaganda work among the masses to an extent even greater than professionals. The slogan pushed was 'small in scale, rich in variety' (*xiaoxing duoyang*), meaning that long or complicated pieces requiring extensive training or elaborate and expensive costumes should be avoided. The spoken drama, simple songs and dances, or balladry items, were greatly preferred to traditional music drama. The Cultural Revolution gave great priority to 'mass amateur propaganda troupes' and for several years in the late 1960s they were more or less the only source of China's theatrical life.

Since the late 1970s amateur troupes have declined markedly. To fill their place semiprofessional troupes have arisen everywhere in China, especially in the countryside where fully professional theatre is less accessible than in the cities. Peasants form troupes on their own initiative and only the most talented and skilled local performers are chosen. They spend most of the year as peasants, and during the slack season they go around performing, mainly traditional regional music dramas. The reward is financial, for although the performers do not receive salaries, they are paid out of box-office returns according to their contribution to the particular drama. Even if they perform in the street and there is no box-office, they are quite likely to be thrown tips from the audience. In 1983 there were about 3000 semiprofessional troupes in the single province of Anhui, and the number was still rising.

Conclusion

Clearly the period since 1978 has brought enormous changes to the Chinese theatre in all respects. A major feature of society in general and the theatre in particular is a dichotomous impulse towards modernization on the one hand and a traditionalist revival on the other. The major thrust is still socialist in that content tends to reflect social-ist society and many fully professional troupes remain state-owned. However, despite a reversal from mid-1989 to the beginning of 1992 due to the 1989 Tiananmen Square crisis, the overall direction of change since 1978 has been towards greater variety and liberalism in terms of form and content, and free enterprise in organization, with ideology reflecting nationalism more strongly than Marxism-Leninism. Experience in other countries suggests that economic modernization affects traditional arts adversely. Despite the current enthusiasm in China for traditional music drama as an example of its national arts, the same could easily happen there in the next few decades.

Genres

Chuanju (Sichuan opera).

The form of music drama found in Sichuan, China's most populous province, and one of the most important of the country's regional styles. It grew out of five different musical and theatrical styles that originally were independent, four belonging to the main systems of Chinese theatre and introduced from outside the province. The earliest of these, *gaoqiang*, came into Sichuan around the 17th century. A variant of the 'music-of-Yiyang' drama, it featured an offstage chorus. Slightly later, clapper opera, known in Sichuan as *tanqiang* ('strum music'), was introduced from Shaanxi to the north. Next *huqin qiang* ('music of the *huqin*'), a variant of the PIHUANG system, introduced the two-string *huqin* instrument. Aristocratic KUNQU was popular with the officials of Sichuan. The one form native to Sichuan was *dengxi* ('lantern theatre'), a folk style based on local mask dances of village shamans.

Early in the 20th century, the theatre was reformed and the five styles began to be performed on the same stage and were regarded as a unity, though every item still retained its style of origin in its music. The first teahouse-theatres were introduced into Sichuan's cities. Probably the greatest of the reformers was Kang Zilin (1870–1931), a fine actor, teacher and leader of the famous Three Celebrations (Sanqing) Company (est. 1912). Apart from the decade of the Cultural Revolution, Sichuan opera has flourished under the Communists, especially since 1978. The Sichuan Province Chuanju Research

Institute holds the texts of over 2000 plays, most of which follow stories familiar from the literature and theatre of China as a whole.

In performance, stagecraft, costuming and makeup, Sichuan opera is essentially similar to other Chinese regional styles, including Beijing opera, though some of its stage arts are distinctive. For instance, Kang Zilin devised a kick in which the foot, touching the middle of the lower forehead for a split second, leaves the image of a third eye there, a breathtaking technique still practised in Sichuan. Makeup styles are also somewhat different: the painted-face character (*jing*), is restricted to four colours – black, red, white and grey – rather than the many colours used in Beijing opera, and grey rather than green and gold identifies a supernatural being.

Geju (song drama)

In broad usage *geju* can include Western operas. Usually it refers to modern opera, created under CCP influence, that combines Chinese and Western techniques. The orchestra contains mainly Western instruments, with an admixture of Chinese traditional instruments. Melodies are Chinese in flavour, but strongly influenced by Western musical structure and harmonic principles. Complex scenery is used, and costumes and stage mannerisms, postures and gestures tend to be realistic, although retaining the influence of traditional theatre. A single item usually occupies a full evening, but the practice of combining key scenes from several pieces into a programme is not unknown.

The first important song drama was *The White-Haired Girl* (*Baimao nü*). A peasant girl raped by a tyrannical landlord flees to a mountain cave where her hair turns white from her privations. After a rumour of a white-haired spirit haunting the countryside spreads, Communist troops discover the truth. She is reunited with her former suitor and the landlord is publicly sentenced. *The White-Haired Girl* was premiered in April 1945 in Yan'an in conjunction with the Seventh Congress of the CCP and became exceptionally popular. Another example is *Red Guards on Hong Lake* (*Honghu chiwei dui*), about the CCP's revolutionary struggle against the Guomindang in 1930.

Creating new song dramas was encouraged in the 1950s and early 1960s, but they were totally suppressed in the decade of the Cultural Revolution that followed. *The White-Haired Girl* was adapted as a ballet, emphasizing the class struggle, and then revived in Beijing in the original song drama form in 1977. *Red Guards on Hong Lake* was also revived shortly after the fall of the 'gang of four'. Although new song dramas have continued to be written, they have not been large in number, and the song drama tends as a form to lack inventiveness and innovation.

Huaju

The generic term for dialogue plays in Western style. Literally 'spoken drama' or 'speech drama'. *Huaju* had its tentative debut in the first decade of this century. Early inhibiting factors were public prejudice against women on the stage and an inability to dispense with old acting conventions. Since it appealed primarily to Western-educated intellectuals at first it offered no vital challenge to the mass appeal of the old theatre in the countryside. Even today, spoken drama is largely a theatre of the great cities.

The period 1915–19 was one of intellectual revolt against the old Chinese social–cultural order. Sweeping language reforms were introduced. Western literature, including drama, was being read and translated. Ibsen made a powerful impression and taught the intellectuals to use theatre as an art of social protest. In the 1930s actresses were accepted on stage and talented writers and directors returned to China with Western experience. The powerful realism of CAO YU's plays, beginning with *Thunderstorm* (*Leiyu*) in 1935, suggested a strong new direction. The Japanese invasion of China forced artists in new directions.

The war years were marked by the subservience of theatre to patriotic and party propaganda on both the Guomindang and CCP sides. In the event *huaju* remained the poor relation of theatre after the war, the prerogative of school and university drama clubs until the foundation of the PRC in 1949.

The Central Drama Institute, set up in Beijing in 1950, trained actors, directors and set designers for *huaju*. Sino-Soviet relations were then at their zenith and Russian advisers and teachers presided over the modern theatre scene, so that Stanislavski's theories inform the work of many Chinese actors and directors today. During the Cultural Revolution (1966–76) Jiang Qing denounced Stanislavski as bourgeois, along with virtually all spoken dramas performed in China since 1949. Companies were disbanded, their members dispersed and training institutions closed.

Following Jiang's downfall in 1976, Stanislavski has been rehabilitated, training facilities re-organized and companies reformed. A younger generation of playwrights, of whom the most significant is probably GAO XINGJIAN, has increasingly broken away from stereotypes in terms of content, performance and style.

In 1979 a spate of spoken dramas attacked official corruption in contemporary society. *If I Were Real* (*Ruguo wo shi zhende*) by Sha Yexin and others, about a young man who gains great privileges by pretending to be the son of a high army officer, gained considerable attention in the West. *Power versus Law* (*Quan yu fa*) by Xing Yixun (c. 1940–) denounced the widespread seizure of privileges by CCP officials for themselves and their families. The central theme shows the law, supported by the good CCP leader and the people, victorious over corrupt officials, thus attacking individuals, not the party itself.

The necessity of law is a strong theme also in *Fifteen Cases of Divorce* (*Shiwu lihun an*, 1983) by Liu Shugang (c. 1941–), which probes the causes of divorce in contemporary China. The same two performers play the 15 couples suing for divorce. It introduced non-realistic staging techniques considered unusual in a Stanislavskian theatre: no curtain, changing costumes on stage, the use of mime, and symbolic use of properties.

A Friend Comes in a Time of Stress (*Fengyu guren lai*, 1983) by feminist playwright Bai Fengxi (1934–), concerns a brilliant young mathematician who wins a scholarship to go to West Germany, but is pressured by her mother-in-law to withdraw in favour of her husband who has applied for the same scholarship. In refusing to yield to sexist blandishments the heroine appeals for a strong role for women in the professions, calling attention to the fact that professional competition between married couples is frequent in China.

Gouerye's Nirvana (*Gouerye niepan*), about an old peasant whose lifelong ambition is to own his own land, shows his misery and frustration under the rule both of the Guomindang and the CCP. The hero's 'nirvana' is a state between death and life in which he can reflect upon his life. Offering no solutions, the play is characteristic of plays prior to the mid 1989 political crisis: billed as a 'tragicomedy', its overall impact is pessimistic and gloomy.

Much attention has been given to Western drama in recent decades. Arthur Miller's *Death of a Salesman* was directed by Miller and the forward-looking actor-director Ying Ruocheng (1929–) in 1983 at the Beijing People's Art Theatre. In 1986 Ying Ruocheng was co-director of Peter Shaffer's *Amadeus* under the title *The Favoured Son of God* (*Shangdi de chonger*). The year 1986 also saw a major Shakespeare festival in Beijing and in several other cities.

Jingxi

Drama (*xi*) of the Chinese capital (*jing*), that is Beijing; therefore commonly 'Beijing opera' in English (earlier, 'Peking opera'). Also known as *jingju*. In Chinese theatre circles it is more specifically known as '*pihuang* drama' (*PIHUANG XI*), after the name of the musical system used in performance. In 1790 Anhui troupes visiting Beijing for the Qianlong Emperor's birthday celebrations staged innovatory performances incorporating the *pihuang* musical modes. They made a great impact and a new style of performance was born.

By the early 19th century *jingxi* dominated the Beijing stage and eventually usurped the national popularity of KUNQU. Brought to maturity in the venue of the stage connoisseurs and enthusiastically patronized by the court, it flourished along an axis defined by the traditional bastion of Beijing and the westernized sophistication of Shanghai. *Jingxi* achieved international recognition when MEI LANFANG toured America and Russia in the 1930s. For most of its history it has remained an adored national entertainment .

The great success of *jingxi* is due in part to a style which is neither too complicated nor precious. Plays, derived from historical epics and romantic novels of China's past, are familiar to everybody. Play texts are largely anonymous, being revisions made by actors from earlier *kunqu* and *zaju* to suit their performance skills. The repertory divides into civil (*wen*) or military (*wu*) plays, and into serious plays (*daxi*, 'great play') or comic plays (*xiaoxi*, 'small play') on the basis of character type and story content. An actor specializes in one of four role types: male (*sheng*), female (*dan*), painted-face (*jing*), or clown (*chou*), and more specifically in a subtype, for example old male (*laosheng*), old woman (*laodan*) or scholar lover (*xiaosheng*). Specific skills in speaking (*nianbai*), song (*chang*), and acrobatics characterize each role type.

In traditional performance the stage was essentially bare. Elaborate costumes and makeup identify role types and major characters. The orchestra was seated onstage and was aurally and visually integrated with the actors. Written music was not used. The music's two principal styles, *erhuang* and *xipi*, contain a number of metrical arrangements defined in terms of accented and unaccented beats within a measure. The leader of the orchestra uses a pair of wooden clappers manipulated rather like castanets and a hardwood drum with a skin head to beat out the measures. Singing is accompanied by a bowed two-string instrument, *huqin*, which has a florid, rippling line characterized by vibrato and glissando effects. Brass gongs and cymbals mark entrances, exits and emotional climaxes, and are particularly evident in the brilliant acrobatic and dance passages which highlight *jingxi* performance.

Singing is used to express human emotions and psychological reactions accentuated by musical rhythms conveying mood. Role types are vocally identified by pitch, volume and enunciation. Rhyme patterns are created from a system of 13-character groupings which provide a compositional key for the dramatist. The rhyme sounds themselves contain elements from the dialects of Anhui, Sichuan and Hubei. Stanzas of four lines rhyming alternately are standard for monologues and dialogue. Rhyme and melismatic effects serve a vital euphonic function in the actor's vocalization.

Kunqu

The early musical style which gave rise to a theatre genre of the same name. *Kunqu* originated in the Kunshan area dominated by the town of Suzhou in Jiangsu province. The singer-composer WEI LIANGFU and his collaborators transformed the original music into a more refined and sophisticated style by drawing upon other current southern regional modes. Liang Chenyu, who had worked with Wei, composed *Washing the Silk Yarn* (*Huansha ji*), widely acclaimed as the debut of this literary-musical genre. Early developments in stage performance became manifest in two schools of thought concerning dramatic composition. One led by Shen Jing (1553–1610), a theorist first and playwright second, sought to codify a theory of prosody in relation to rhyme, tone and their correlation with the sung text. The second was dominated by playwright TANG XIANZU who advocated poetic licence and free rein to the imagination at the expense of rigid musical theory. *Kunqu* became the preoccupation of scholarly writers during the 17th and 18th centuries.

In its elemental form *kunqu* is performed as chamber music accompanied by a seven-holed horizontal bamboo flute (*dizi*), wooden clappers and a small hardwood drum slung on a tripod. On stage, stringed and percussion instruments are added and singing is synthesized with dance, gesture, song and speech. Monody and monologue are common devices. The pitches of the seven-holed flute, a key instrument in *kunqu*, set the tonics for keys and modalities which animate the versification and general structure of a play. Solo song passages are characterized by extremely intricate ornamentation and lengthy melismatic effects. Dance movements have great fluency of line extended through airy control of sleeve movements. Plays emphasize romantic love.

Kunqu began to lose ground in the late 18th century and by the end of the 19th century it had been superseded in popularity by the more robust theatricality of *PIHUANG*-style theatre, which nonetheless drew upon the older form. Some revival of *kunqu* has been seen in this century. In the 1920s a school was set up in Shanghai that produced talented performers, some of whom are teachers today. Excellent young performers have been trained since 1961 at the Shanghai School of Dramatic Art under the leadership of YU ZHENFEI. *Kunqu* troupes have performed in the United States and Europe on several occasions, their repertoire including the widely acclaimed fusion production, *Kunqu Macbeth* (1987).

Pihuang xi

Drama (*xi*) using the *pihuang* musical system. *Pihuang* is a telescoping of *xipi* and *erhuang*, two musical styles with a complex history and controversial orgin, quite likely in Hubei and Jiangxi Provinces respectively. In 1790 performers from Anhui brought the *pihuang* musical style to Beijing where it became very popular. *Pihuang* style has been freely adapted in many regions, as well as Beijing, forming the musical basis of numerous opera forms. Beijing opera (*JINGXI*) and Guangdong opera (*YUEJU*) are important types of *pihuang xi*.

Tibetan drama

A form of theatre popular in the Tibetan Autonomous Region and among other Tibetan communities, including those in Sichuan, Qinghai and Yunnan Provinces of China, and in India. Among the theatres of China's current minority nationalities it is the oldest and most important.

The origins of a real and developed drama in Tibet go back to the Buddhist monk Tang-ston rgyal-po (flourished 15th century), who formed a company of singers and dancers in which performers impersonated characters in stories based on Buddhist sutras. Only after the 17th century did Tibetan drama gradually split from religious ritual.

Tibetan drama is an integrated art form in which singing, dialogue, dance, acrobatics, mime and extremely colourful costumes all play a part. Musical accompaniment is confined to percussion instruments, drum and cymbal, and a chorus. Makeup is simple, but masks are an important feature. Traditionally Tibetan drama is performed with simple properties in a square, a temple or any open space, spectators on three or all four sides of the action. A favourite venue even now is the old Summer Palace of the Dalai Lama in Lhasa. A large tent is put up and the audience sits round the area where the drama is performed.

There are three sections of a Tibetan drama. The first is the prologue, a masked dance which among other functions explains the plot. Then comes the core, the drama itself. Finally a farewell blessing is given, used by the company to seek donations from the audience.

The heroine Mu Guiying is the most important of the women generals of the Yang family and features in many music-dramas.

Tibetan drama was, and to some extent remains, an oral tradition. Many items were not written down and varied greatly from troupe to troupe and time to time. Over a dozen survive today. They concern Tibetan history and mythology, kings, queens and beautiful women. Several are based on Indian literary works. The characterization tends to be stark, with the positive and negative characters clearly delineated. The elements of love, magic, religion and comedy are strong. Most of the dramas were long and performed in the daytime only, extending over one or several days.

A well-known and popular play is *The Historical Drama of King Srong-btsan sgam-po*. The great Tibetan king of the title, an actual historical figure (d. AD 650), sends an ambassador to China to seek marriage with the Princess Wencheng. With great ingenuity the ambassador performs difficult tasks set him by the Chinese emperor and wins the bride for his king . In contemporary China the story is considered to promote 'the unity of the nationalities'.

In the past performers held a very low social status. Usually men played female roles. Fully professional companies existed, but most were semiprofessional, their members being mainly male peasants serving overlords and acting only part of the year. In late summer each year 12 famous troupes were selected from among these semiprofessional folk groups to gather in Lhasa for a competitive drama season.

The Tibetan Drama Troupe of Tibet was set up in Lhasa in 1960 just after the 1959 rebellion against Chinese rule. It offers mainly traditional pieces in two- to three-hour performances. In line with PRC policy, the pieces are 'reformed', but they retain their traditional dance, costumes, singing style, offstage chorus and masked dance of the prologue, as well as the main elements of the older stories. Reformed performances by the Tibetan Drama Troupe of Tibet use an orchestra much enlarged to include wind and string instruments, not only Tibetan, but also Han Chinese and Western, and are staged in a theatre with properties and scenery. The troupe also performs 'unreformed' traditional items at festival time at the old Summer Palace of the Dalai Lama. In Tibet in the 1990s there are also numerous semi-amateur folk troupes, which perform traditional dramas completely unchanged from the past, except that women play female roles. The custom of gathering troupes in Lhasa for a summer festival was revived in 1984 and it is now again an annual event, opening with the exposition of the Buddha picture at the great 'Bras-spungs Monastery just outside Lhasa.

There have been occasional attempts since 1960 to adapt propaganda themes to Tibetan drama. On the whole the Tibetan people have not welcomed these experiments. In 1987, 1988 and 1989 there were demonstrations in Lhasa in favour of Tibetan independence, which were suppressed by the Chinese government and in the last year led to the imposition of martial law in Lhasa for over one year. The impact of these troubles on drama has been a return to an emphasis on unreformed traditional drama at the expense of reformed, let alone modern items. However, drama continues to play a major role in the social and cultural life of the Tibetan people.

There is a Tibetan Institute of Performing Arts in Dharamsala in the northern Punjab, India, which studies and performs the traditional Tibetan drama.

Wuju (dance drama)

A modern form of drama incorporating Chinese folk dance and Western ballet techniques. *Wuju* instrumentation combines Western and Chinese instruments. Harmonic structure tends to follow Western rules while melodies are characteristically Chinese in flavour. The first large-scale *wuju* drama was *The Precious Lotus Lamp* (*Baolian deng*, 1957). Set in the mythical past, it is a fantasy about a goddess who comes to earth and falls in love with a mortal (see also Thailand, NORA). After being suppressed during the Cultural Revolution *wuju* regained popularity immediately after the fall of the 'gang of four'. In Shanghai in 1977, *The Small Sword Society* (*Xiaodao hui*) praised the 19th-century rebel movement of the title. Many dance dramas feature stories, dance movements and musical elements from China's minority nationalities.

None is better known, either in China or outside, than *Tales of the Silk Road* (*Silu huayu*), created in 1977 by members of the Gansu Song and Dance Ensemble and since then frequently revived. The plot is set in the Tang dynasty and concerns a slave-dancer who is taken to Persia by a rich merchant of that country to escape an evil magistrate. The ending sees the magistrate punished and happy relations between Persia and China. What is distinctive about the piece is that the costumes and many of the dance movements derive from postures shown in Tang-dynasty wall paintings in the Dunhuang caves in Gansu Province. The music, a mixture of styles and melodies, attempts to capture the atmosphere of mediaeval China and Persia. Other important productions of the 1980s include several based on the classical novel *A Dream of Red Mansions* (*Honglou meng*) and one adapted from Tang Xianzu's *The Peony Pavilion*.

Xinbian lishi ju (newly arranged historical drama)

A branch of drama in one of China's numerous regional styles in which the story is set before the 20th century. The term applies almost exclusively to those dramas written under the influence of the CCP.

Music is composed especially for each play following the melodic patterns and texture of the particular regional style of which it is representative. Costumes and makeup take their style from traditional theatre, with variations. On the other hand, there are complex scenery and stage properties and the tendency is for the drama to last a full evening. There is usually a definite structure in the plot, which rises to a climax and conclusion. Normally the plot is set in the dynastic past, and, despite the term 'historical drama', may be based on a mythological story rather than historical fact. There is considerable room for a political message and the great majority of 'newly arranged historical dramas' carry a clear ideological viewpoint. Since 1978 the quantity of dramas written in this form has been greater than for any other, with more and more themes and stories being dug up from the vastness of Chinese history and mythology. In the early days of the PRC, dramas in this category tended to give centre stage to representatives of the masses, including peasant rebels, oppressed women and patriots. In the 1980s and 90s class struggle has been downgraded as an ideological factor generally, including in dramatic characterization, and as a result emperors and scholars can be presented in the favourable light of having made a contribution to the Chinese nation.

Yueju (Guangdong opera)

Yue (another name for Guangdong) *ju* (drama) is the regional form of music drama of Guangdong Province. It is popular also in southern Guangxi, Hong Kong and Macao and among those overseas Chinese communities of North America, Australia and elsewhere whose ancestors came from Guangdong.

Guangdong opera belongs basically to the PIHUANG system of music drama, although the two styles, *erhuang* and *xipi*, have been much changed under the influence of local music.

Cantonese folksongs, *kunqu* and other tunes have been absorbed. Accompanying instruments include the end-blown flute and double-reeded *suona* as well as strings and percussion. Western violin and saxophone were added in the 1920s and remain in use today. There is a certain mellifluousness in the texture of many of the singers' voices, as well as in the accompanying orchestra.

There are basically ten role-categories. Male characters are termed *mo* or *sheng*. In contrast to most contemporary styles of Chinese music drama, the latter is not normally the main role. Other roles are painted-face (*jing*), female (*dan*), and clown (*chou*), whose face is not painted white around the eyes, as are clowns in other opera forms.

The first famous actor of Guangdong opera was Zhang Wu in the 18th century. He came from Hubei Province, where *pihuang* music was practised, so perhaps he was the person who introdused the style to Guangdong. Zhang Wu settled

A county official as a *chou* character, showing the typical white patch on the face, the headgear, whiskers and red garment.

in Foshan, took on students, established a troupe and founded the Qionghua Guildhall for actors. Later influxes of actors of *pihuang* music, from Anhui and Hunan Provinces, strengthened that system's impact on Guangdong opera.

In 1854 the well-known actor Li Wenmao (d. 1861) collected three armies and rebelled against the government in support of the Taiping uprising (1851–64). When the rebellion was defeated, Guangdong opera also was proscribed for being subversive. The Qionghua Guildhall was destroyed and thereafter the centre of a revived Guangdong opera was Guangzhou.

Because Guangdong is adjacent to the British colony of Hong Kong, Guangdong opera has been more subject to foreign influences, especially the film, than any other form of Chinese music drama. Early in this century urban actors began to experiment with more naturalistic movements and gestures, to discard traditional embroidered costumes in favour of the more realistic costumes being used in the spoken drama and film, and to use scenery on the stage. Some new operas were explicitly political in their content, such as one in praise of the female anti-Manchu revolutionary Qiu Jin, who was beheaded in 1907.

Except for the Cultural Revolution decade (1966–76), Guangdong Opera has done well under the PRC. The state-run Guangdong Provincial Guangdong Opera Company was established in 1958. There has been a tendency to return to traditional usage in some aspects of stagecraft such as costuming, movements and gestures.

Yueju (Shaoxing opera)

A style of drama (*ju*) of the Yue region, the ancient state corresponding approximately to Zhejiang Province; usually termed Shaoxing opera or Sheng County theatre in English after its place of origin, Sheng County in Shaoxing, east Zhejiang Province. It was formed in the 20th century, outside of any of the major musical systems of local Chinese drama, by peasant balladeers singing folksongs who joined into small drama troupes. Musical accompaniment was through percussion or chorus.

In 1916 the actor Wang Jinshui brought Shaoxing opera to Shanghai. He and others greatly expanded its scope by absorbing melodies from other local styles of eastern Zhejiang, adding string and other instruments to the accompanying orchestra and expanding the available rhythmic structures. In 1923 a training school for girls was set up in Sheng County and from 1928 all-female companies prospered in Shanghai competing with male companies. By the mid 1930s virtually all performers of Shaoxing opera were female.

As a result romantic love stories are the strong point of Shaoxing opera and military scenes and acrobatics are totally absent. The most famous of the early stories, retaining its popularity today, tells of the love between Liang Shanbo and Zhu Yingtai: they elope, die under tragic circumstances and are transformed into butterflies, hence the name by which the piece is often known in English, *The Butterfly Lovers*.

Under the leadership of actresses like Yuan Xuefen (1922–) staging was reformed in the 1940s. Lighting and scenery were extensively used in traditional and 'newly arranged historical' (*yueju*) music dramas. A soft style of costuming was created that combined influences from JINGXI and historical HUAJU. Designs for female costumes copied old pictures of beautiful women, and soft colours and crepes and georgette replaced bright satins, to accord more closely to *yueju*'s romantic style.

The government of the PRC has generally encouraged Shaoxing opera, allowed its traditional romantic repertory, while urging mixed male and female troupes. Major professional performances use an orchestra that includes some Western instruments, especially the violoncello to provide a stronger bass to the music. Actors now perform some male roles, especially evil ones, but actresses still predominate and in particular play the important scholar-lover (*xiaosheng*) roles.

Zaju (variety play)

Generic term for a style of entertainment in which dance, song, monologue, balladry and farcical skits were given an integrated presentation. Archetypal roles developed within *zaju* are the basis of later divisions. The genre attained significant form in both north and south China in the 12th century, and reached its creative peak during the Yuan dynasty (1234–1368). Beijing opera of modern times may be regarded as a legitimate descendant.

Zaju plays in the Yuan period were comparatively simple in form and followed the rules of prosody, rhyme and metre fundamental to all Chinese lyrical composition. In general a play had four acts plus a 'wedge'. Each act was given a long suite of single-stanza lyrics in one musical mode, the mode changing for each act. The wedge, which was a self-contained scene, allowed the dramatist a certain flexibility. It had a single song sequence with one or two stanzas only and could be situated at the beginning of the play or between any two acts.

Only the leading performer, whether male or female, sang. Ancillary performers carried on the dialogue and action between the singing as well as enforcing the comic pace. The music of Yuan-period plays has been lost and knowledge of stage practices must rely almost entirely on the playscripts. The richly diverse Yuan drama was a thriving popular entertainment catering to all levels of society.

Bibliography

GENERAL: W. Dolby (tr.), *Eight Chinese Plays from the Thirteenth Century to the Present*, New York, 1978, and *A History of Chinese Drama*, London, 1976; E. M. Gunn (ed.), *Twentieth-Century Chinese Drama An Anthology*, Bloomington, Ind., 1983; Tao-Ching Hsü, *The Chinese Conception of the Theatre*, Seattle and London, 1985; C. Mackerras, *Chinese Drama, A Historical Survey*, Beijing, 1990, (ed.), *Chinese Theatre from its Origins to the Present Day*, Honolulu, 1983, 1988, *The Chinese Theatre in Modern Times from 1840 to the Present Day*, London, 1975, and *The Rise of the Peking Opera 1770-1870, Social Aspects of the Theatre in Manchu China*, Oxford, 1972; A. C. Scott (tr. and ed.), *Traditional Chinese Plays*, 3 vols., Madison, 1967, 1969, 1975; S. H. West, *Vaudeville and Narrative: Aspects of Chin Theatre*, Wiesbaden, 1977; E. Wichmann, *Listening to Theatre, The Aural Dimension of Beijing Opera*, Honolulu, 1991.

ZAJU: J. I. Crump, *Chinese Theatre in the Days of Kublai Khan*, Tucson, Ariz., 1980; D. R. Johnson, *Yuan Music Dramas: Studies in Prosody and Structure and a Complete Catalogue of Northern Arias in the Dramatic Style*, Ann Arbor, Mich., 1980; Ching-Hsi Perng, *Double Jeopardy: A Critique of Seven Yüan Courtroom Dramas*, Ann Arbor, Mich., 1978; Shih Chung-wen, *The Golden Age of Chinese Drama: Yuan Tsa-chü*, Princeton, N.J., 1976.

KUNQU: E. Henry, *Chinese Amusement, The Lively Plays of Li Yü*, Hamden, Conn., 1980; J. Huang Hung, *Ming Drama*, Taipei, 1966.

BEIJING OPERA (*JINGXI*): A. C. Scott, *Actors are Madmen, Notebook of a Theatregoer in China*, Madison, 1982, *The Classical Theatre of China*, London, 1957, and *Mei Lanfang, Leader of the Pear Garden*, Hong Kong, 1959; Wu Zuguang, Huang Zuolin and Mei Shaowu, *Peking Opera and Mei Lanfang, A Guide to China's Traditional Theatre and the Art of its Great Master*, Beijing, 1981; C. S. L. Zung, *Secrets of the Chinese Drama: A Complete Explanatory Guide to Actions and Symbols as Seen in the Performance of Chinese Drama*, New York, 1964.

REGIONAL AND FOLK DRAMA: B. Yung, *Cantonese Opera: Performance as a Creative Process*, Cambridge, 1989.

THE PEOPLE'S REPUBLIC: B. S. McDougall (ed.), *Popular Chinese Literature and Performing Arts in the People's Republic of China 1949-1979*, Berkeley, Calif., 1984; C. Mackerras, *The Performing Arts in Contemporary China*, London, 1981; W. J. and R. I. Meserve (eds.), *Modern Drama from Communist China*, New York, 1970; Peking Opera Troupe of Shanghai, *Taking Tiger Mountain by Strategy: A Modern Revolutionary Peking Opera*, Peking, 1971; J. Riley and E. Unterrieder (eds.), *Haishi Zou Hao, Chinese Poetry, Drama and Literature of the 1980s*, Bonn, 1989; C. Tung and C. Mackerras (eds.), *Drama in the People's Republic of China*, Albany, 1987; R. G. Wagner, *The Contemporary Chinese Historical Drama, Four Studies*, Berkeley, Calif., 1990.

HONG KONG

Hong Kong is a British colony on the south coast of China with a population of 5.6 million people, 98 per cent of whom are Chinese. Most come from neighbouring Guangdong Province in China and speak the Cantonese dialect. After the Communist takeover of mainland China in 1949, many refugees came to Hong Kong. These mainlanders plus British, Americans, Europeans, Australians, Indians, Japanese and Portuguese have made Hong Kong a true melting pot of Eastern and Western cultures. Drama and theatre in Hong Kong also reflect this mixture.

The traditional theatre form in Hong Kong is YUEJU, or Cantonese opera, a regional drama of South China whose basic style of stage presentation is related to the more renowned and refined Beijing opera (see China, JINGXI). The great difference is the use of the Cantonese dialect, which affects the style of singing and rhythmic emphasis. Just as Cantonese is a regional dialect, so the theatre there is related to, but different from, its parent form. Cantonese opera in China's Guangdong region (see China, YUEJU (Guangdong opera)) is usually considered inferior to Beijing opera in artistic quality and technical sophistication. The Hong Kong version of Cantonese opera reflects the influence of novelties introduced in performance before the 1960s, which removed the art considerably from its original, characteristically Chinese atmosphere. Its music is often called 'yellow music', meaning that it is mock classical and bears the same relationship to the art that the 'yellow press' has to respectable journalism. Arias, regardless of their classical base, came to contain a note of sentimentality and softness, and tunes were even danceable in a westernized ballroom way. Western instruments became part of the traditional theatre orchestra. Costumes were vulgarized, with sparkling sequins to keep the show glittering. Realistic settings, alien to classical Chinese theatre, showed everything from castle walls to gardens, temples, and palaces. Stylized gestures and movement patterns were still employed, though often sloppily rendered. Such debasement of the traditional art gave the Cantonese theatre of Hong Kong a bad reputation until very recently. At the present time, forward-looking theatre artists are returning Cantonese opera to higher standards, so it will be the equal of other major regional Chinese theatres.

Living side-by-side with the Cantonese opera is Western-style modern Chinese drama, HUAJU or 'spoken drama'. English is an accepted and popular language in Hong Kong; hence one strand of Western-style theatre consists of productions in the English language, almost always mounted by British and American actors for the foreign expatriate audience. The other and more important strand consists of Chinese-language productions staged by local theatre groups and by visiting mainland companies whose audience is the vast majority of the Hong Kong populace. The first known Western-style drama performance was staged in 1844 by British soldiers and their families stationed in Hong Kong. In 1911 two local amateur theatre groups were formed, staging Chinese plays such as *Zhuang Zi Testing His Wife's Virtue* (*Zhang Zi shiqi*) and *Flesh for the Debt of Gold* (*Jinchai roushang*, possibly an adaptation of *The Merchant of Venice*). It is notable that these productions of spoken dramas were mounted only four years after the first Chinese production of Western plays, *La Dame aux camélias* and *Uncle Tom's Cabin*, by students of the Spring Willow Society in Tokyo (see China).

During the period of the Sino-Japanese War prior to Japanese occupation (1937–42), patriotic Hong Kong youths popularized spoken drama. Over 200 amateur groups staged some 300 productions for patriotic causes. A great number of these plays were original one-acts with anti-Japanese themes. Performances were given in school gyms or classrooms, and sometimes at street corners, or at sports fields following a sporting event. The most popular play of that period was *Lay Down Your Whip (Fangxia nide bienzi)*, an agit-prop piece about the suffering of Chinese people caused by the Japanese invasions of their homeland. To avoid persecution, many theatre workers burnt their mimeographed scripts just prior to Japanese military occupation in 1942. Thus most of the original plays written in this period were lost.

After the war Hong Kong modern drama came to life again. Many standard works of Chinese dramatists were staged, such as *Thunderstorm (Lei yu)*, *Family (Jia)*, and *Sunrise (Ri chu)*, by CAO YU (see China). Three professional theatre companies from the mainland also took residence in Hong Kong after the war and staged large-scale productions. *Sorrows of the Noble Family (Jumen yuan)*, *The Story of Ah-Q (Ah-Q jengjuan)*, *The Wedding March (Jiehun jinxinqu)*, *Girls Apartment (Nuzi gongyu)*, *Hell on Earth (Renjian diyu*, adapted from Gorky's *The Lower Depths)*, and *The Imperial Inspector (Qinchai daqeng*, adapted from Gogol's *The Inspector General)* were their most frequently staged plays.

In the 1950s and 60s local dramatists wrote works of considerable maturity and sophistication. Three playwrights deserve mention. Perhaps the most respected theatre worker in Hong Kong was Hu Chun-bin, who wrote *Li Bo the Poet (Li Bo)* and *Dream of the Red Chamber (Honglou meng*, adapted from the famous Chinese novel of the same title). S. I. Hsiung (1903–91) was noted for his adaptation of classical Chinese plays into spoken dramas, such as *Lady Precious Stream* and *The West Chamber*. The English version of the former had been a London and Broadway hit in the 1930s, which made Hsiung a celebrity in the English-speaking world. Yao Hsin-nung, trained at Yale Drama School, was the youngest of the three. Besides being a playwright and stage director, he was a film producer and a scriptwriter in Shanghai and Hong Kong in the 1940s and 50s. His realistic social drama, *The Poor Man's Alley (Quongjen xiang)*, became a hit on the mainland and in Hong Kong during the postwar era.

The contemporary situation

The most important development on the contemporary Hong Kong theatre scene was the establishment in 1977 of the professional Hong Kong Repertory Theatre devoted to spoken drama. Founded and strongly subsidized by the Urban Council, its performances in Cantonese dialect and occasionally in Mandarin are seen in the two new theatres of the Hong Kong Cultural Centre and in various venues in the territory. In 1991, under the

The Hong Kong Repertory Theatre production of Sha Yexin's *Christ, Confucius, John Lennon of the Beatles*, 1991, directed by Daniel S. P. Yang.

artistic directorship of Daniel S. P. Yang (1936–), former director of the Colorado Shakespeare Festival, it staged eight productions totalling 120 performances, its repertory representing a unique balance of Chinese, Western, and Hong-Kong-written plays. As part of its services to the community, it offers educational theatre programmes and sponsors an annual Drama Festival.

Other leading theatre companies in contemporary Hong Kong are the Chung Ying Theatre Company, the Exploration Theatre, and the Carlsberg Wanchai Theatre Company. Chung Ying is a bilingual professional theatre company formed in 1979 with funding first from the British Council then from the Hong Kong government. Its charter was to do English-language theatre-in-education in schools and community centres, and occasionally in larger theatre venues as well. Its original company was British, but now consists of Hong Kong Chinese. Before 1985, Chung Ying actors performed mostly in Cantonese, and occasionally joined guest British actors in English-language productions. Now their productions are almost entirely in Cantonese. The Exploration Theatre (Hak Heng Fong) is a semiprofessional company composed of theatre graduates of the Hong Kong Academy for the Performing Arts, with support since 1990 from the Hong Kong Council for the Performing Arts under its 'Green Sprouts Plan'. The Carlsberg Wanchai Theatre Company is the most active community theatre group in Hong Kong. Under the aggressive management of its artistic and managing director, Ho Wai-lung (1956–), this modest theatre company in the Wanchai district puts on four to six productions a year with partial funding from the Carlsberg beer company.

Among nearly 100 registered community, college and school theatre groups, the Seals Theatre Company, the Zuni Icosahedron, and the American Community Theatre are the most active. The Seals Theatre Company, established in 1979, produced four to five Chinese and translated works yearly until the retirement of its artistic director Vicki Oi in 1990. The Zuni Icosahedron's daring and controversial productions have featured nudity and homosexual themes. Under artistic director Danny Yung (1943–), the troupe has attracted considerable attention in other Asian countries due to its touring activities. The American Community Theatre is the most active English-language amateur theatre company. It stages eight productions a year including musicals, with casts of resident expatriates and occasional professional English and American guest actors.

Young audiences show increasing interest in traditional Cantonese Opera and new troupes have formed to accommodate budding young talent. With few professional troupes in residence, the Urban Council promotes amateur productions of Cantonese opera by providing funds and venues for performance. In 1980 a Cantonese-opera training school was formed by the Pak Wo Association, an umbrella organization for traditional theatre in Hong Kong. Graduates of this school later formed the Sun Moon Star Operatic Troupe (Yat Yuet Sing). Today, Hong Kong's most celebrated Cantonese-opera companies are the Chung Sun Sing Troupe, formed in 1965 by LAM KAR-SING, and the Cry of the Young Phoenix Troupe (Chor Fung Ming). The latter is an offshoot of the Cry of the Immortal Phoenix Troupe (Sin Fung Ming), which, under the leadership of Yum Kim-fai (?–1990) and Pak Suet-sin, had been extremely popular in the 1950s and

Artists

Chung King-fai (1937–)
Noted stage director and theatre educator, and Dean of the School of Drama at the Hong Kong Academy for the Performing Arts. After receiving an MFA degree at Yale Drama School in 1962, he returned to teach and direct. He has staged several West End and Broadway hits in Cantonese, such as *Equus*, *Noises Off*, and *West Side Story*. He has contributed much to the development of Hong Kong drama.

Lam Kar-sing (1933–)
Cantonese-opera actor who specializes in 'young civil and militant male' roles. Founded the Chung Sun Sing Cantonese Opera Troupe in 1965, whose production style maintains strict adherence to the highest professional standards. He and his younger colleagues have been responsible for raising the artistic level of Cantonese opera in Hong Kong to that of the most respected regional Chinese theatres.

60s. Chor Fung Ming was established in 1973 by seven disciples of Yum and Pak, among whom Lung Kim-sang and Mui Suet-see are star actors. The Company is noted for ensemble acting, emphasis on creating new scripts and adaptation of modern theatre technology in its productions. It gives over 100 local productions annually and has toured Southeast Asia, Canada and the United States.

Hong Kong's first school for vocational training of actors, directors, designers, technicians and playwrights was established in 1985 when the Hong Kong Academy for Performing Arts was officially opened. The Academy has Schools of Music, Dance, Drama, and Technical Services. The 1200-seat Lyric Theatre in the Academy complex is one of the best performance venues in Hong Kong. Since Hong Kong is at the crossroad between East and West, the Academy designs its curricula to take advantage of the performing traditions of both Asian and Western countries. The School of Drama, headed by CHUNG KING-FAI, includes the study of the traditional theatre of China, with courses in T'ai Chi, Beijing-opera acting and acrobatic training, and traditional Chinese dance and music, as well as Western theatre.

Another impressive addition to the contemporary Hong Kong theatre scene is the Hong Kong Cultural Centre opened in 1989. Its Auditoria Building houses a 2100-seat Concert Hall, a 1750-seat Grand Theatre, and a 350- to 500-seat experimental Studio Theatre. In the 1980s and early 90s the Urban Council constructed some ten district theatres to accommodate cultural events in various areas of the territory and more are planned. It is estimated that by the year 2000 there will be a five-fold increase of theatre-seating capacity in Hong Kong, promising a considerable growth of theatre activities. (See also China and Taiwan.)

Genres

Yueju

Yueju, also known as 'Cantonese opera', is a regional Chinese theatre form in the Guangdong and Guangxi provinces of mainland China and adjoining areas such as Hong Kong and Macau. Immigrants from these areas also brought the form to overseas Chinatowns in such widely separated areas as Singapore, Djakarta, San Francisco, Honolulu and New York. The term yueju is not to be confused with 'Shanghai opera' (Shaoxing opera) which has the same pronunciation and romanized spelling (see China, YUEJU). Yueju was formed in the early Ching dynasty (1644–1911), much affected by the Beijing opera (see China, JINGXI), southern kunqu opera (see China), and Bangzi opera whose troupes performed in the Guangdong and Guangxi areas. The most unique element in Cantonese opera is its music. In its Hong Kong form especially, the orchestra combines Chinese instruments with those of the West, such as violin, saxophone, and double bass. Its staging technique, affected by the Western drama and opera, utilizes realistic scenery, lighting and sound effects. In the 1940s and early 50s Cantonese-opera performances became racy and vulgar, apparently as a result of commercialization. After the establishment of the People's Republic in 1949, its policies did much to raise the artistic qualities of Cantonese-opera productions on the mainland, including abolishing some earlier vulgar elements. This reform later affected Hong Kong actors and troupes, who in turn introduced further improvements and innovations in the 1970s and 80s. Although purists may look upon its music and the female singing style with a certain disdain, the form has regained much of its former reputation. Noted actors in Cantonese opera who have contributed to the Hong Kong yueju scene include: Lee Man-mau (?–1861), Ma Si-tsang (1900–64), Sit Kwok-sin (1904–1956), Law Bun-chiu (1912–) and Hung Sin-nui (1927–).

Bibliography

F. Bowers, *Theatre in the East*, New York, 1956; J. R. Brandon, *Brandon's Guide to Theatre in Asia*, Honolulu, 1976; A. Leigh, 'A Report on Drama in Hong Kong' (unpublished document of Hong Kong Government), Hong Kong, 1983; Li Wan-wa, 'Man-tan Xianggang huaju fazhan' (Random talks on the development of spoken drama in Hong Kong), *Hong Kong Literature Monthly*, 3 (March 1985); A. C. Scott, *Literature and the Arts in Twentieth Century China*, New York, 1963; Selected Documents of Council on Performing Arts, Hong Kong Government, 1984 to 1990; B. Yung, *Cantonese Opera: Performance As a Creative Process*, Cambridge, 1989.

INDIA

India is among the world's most populous nations, with nearly 850 million people inhabiting a vast and contrasting land bordered on the north and east by the Himalayan mountain range, on the west by the Great Thar Desert and with the southern half of the country a peninsula surrounded by the Arabian Sea on one side and the Bay of Bengal on the other. Because of its strategic location, Indian civilization has been shaped over time by a multitude of social, political and religious forces which, in turn, have had a direct bearing on the shape of its theatre.

The Indus Valley Civilization dating from 2300 BC was the first great culture to inhabit areas of the north, along the Indus River basin. But the advanced city-states that were formed there came to an abrupt and inexplicable halt by 1750 BC, and eventually India was populated by Indo-Aryans who migrated from Persia. Over the centuries, the Aryans developed a body of rituals and religious customs which came to be known as Hinduism. The Sanskrit language was the medium of communication among the priests and kings who dominated the social life. Myths developed which reinforced their ideas and the resulting society prospered and grew to take its place among the world's great ancient civilizations. Sanskrit drama and theatre came into being and flourished during this relatively peaceful period between the 1st and 10th centuries AD, reinforcing the beliefs of the civilization.

India also served as the cradle of other great religions – Buddhism, Jainism, Sikhism and, though it did not originate there, Zoroastrianism. Even the Christian faith took root and flourished in parts of India.

Among the social and political influences that have had a major bearing on the development of Indian theatre was the introduction of Islam to the Indian subcontinent. After an initial period of conquest around the 10th and 11th centuries, the Middle Eastern people who introduced Islam integrated with the Indo-Aryans and produced powerful empires centred in Delhi, such as that of the Emperor Akbar. Owing to their religious convictions, the followers of Islam discouraged, or forbade entirely, the performance of theatre. Under the threat of mass conversion to Islam, the decline of Buddhism as a popular religion and the loss of social and political power, a new movement of Hinduism was born known as Vaisnavism. As a result of renewed faith in the values and ideas which were essentially indigenous to India, Vaisnavism nurtured the growth of theatre in village settings throughout the subcontinent. Theatre grew to service the needs of millions of people in a multitude of regional languages (by some counts today, there are 16 major regional languages in India). The period of development and growth of rural theatre forms began about the 15th century and continued through to the 19th century.

The British came to India in the 17th century, although they did not dominate the country until 150 years later. They established a presence at strategic locations on the subcontinent. Through their effort modern urban society was born. The colonial period extended from the mid 19th to the mid 20th century bringing with it the centralization of power, industrialization, the development of mass systems of transportation and communication, as well as staggering growth in the population. During the colonial period modern theatre developed. It continues to develop in all the major regional languages as a reflection of the ideas and concerns of urban Indian audiences.

In order to understand Indian theatre, it is necessary to investigate each stage of its growth separately, beginning with the Sanskrit theatre, continuing through the rural theatre forms and concluding with modern theatre.

Fragments of the earliest known Sanskrit plays have been traced to the 1st century AD. The sophistication of the form of the fragments suggests that a living theatre tradition must have existed in India at a somewhat earlier date. The earliest traces of civilization in India date from between 2300 and 1750 BC and yet the enormous wealth of archaeological evidence provides no hint of the existence of a living theatre tradition. Dance and music seem to have been enjoyed by the people of those times, perhaps as part of religious celebrations, but theatre is not in evidence. A search of the *Vedas* – sacred hymns, among the world's earliest literary outpourings, dating from approximately 1500 to 1000 BC – yields no trace of theatre, even though a few of the hymns are composed in a short, elementary dialogue. Some of the ritual practices of the Vedic age have the potential of developing into drama but do not seem to have sparked a theatre tradition.

The period between 1000 and 100 BC saw the rise of the great Hindu epic literature, particularly the *Mahabharata*, the longest and arguably the most comprehensive document of ancient Indian life, the *Ramayana*, a somewhat shorter but no less important epic work, which, like the *Mahabharata*, still provides rural and urban dramatists with source material, and the *Puranas*, a major collection of stories dealing with the life and exploits of Krishna, incarnation of the god Vishnu, all of whose incarnations have provided inspiration for dramatic compositions. There are references to a class of performers (*nata*) who may have been actors, which are to be found in major epic stories.

The earliest reference to events which may have been the seeds of Sanskrit drama is in 140 BC by Patanjali in his *Mahabhasya*. The work itself is a text of grammar. In order to make a point, Patanjali indicates that action may be determined in several ways; through; (1) pantomime; (2) recitation; (3) song; (4) dance. Reference is made to individuals who recite and sing (*nata*). Given the existence of dramatic rituals, of ample epic stories which were later interpreted in dramatic form and of traditions of song, dance and recitation firmly established in Indian tradition, it is feasible that Sanskrit drama came into being about this point in time.

Sanskrit theatre has left no physical evidence of its early history. Only in the plays and dramaturgical texts which survive in palm leaf manuscript, and in descriptions from other sources may one glean the outlines of the Sanskrit theatre.

The most important single source for establishing the character of the Sanskrit theatre tradition in ancient India is the vast compendium *A Treatise on Theatre* (*Natyasastra*) attributed to BHARATA MUNI and variously dated between 200 BC and AD 200. *Natya* means 'drama' or 'theatre'. *Sastra* is a generic term referring to any authoritative text.

The mythological origin of theatre is related in the *Natyasastra*. Theatre is said to have been the inspiration of Brahma, the god of creation, and Bharata figures prominently in its origin. In chapter one, Bharata tells a charming story of how theatre came into being.

When the world was given over to sensual pleasure, Indra, king of the gods (one of India's earliest major deities), approached Brahma and asked that he create a form of diversion that could be seen as well as heard and that would be accessible to the four occupational groups (*varna*) – priests, warriors, tradesmen and peasants. Out of his state of meditation, Brahma created drama (*natya*), which he referred to as a fifth *Veda* or sacred text.

Brahma requested that Indra compose plays and have the gods enact them. Not considering it appropriate for gods to act, Indra asked that the priests (*brahmana*) be recruited to take on this task. Bharata and his sons were summoned by Brahma and persuaded to serve as the first actors, which they willingly agreed to do. And Brahma, knowing what he had in mind when he created theatre, taught them the art himself.

To fulfil additional personnel needs, Brahma created heavenly nymphs to act and dance, and musicians were recruited to play and sing to accompany the show. The occasion of the first performance was established to depict and coincide with the defeat of the demons by the gods, celebrating Indra's victorious leadership.

All seemed well until malevolent spirits disturbed the dramatic action. Eventually Brahma summoned Visvakarma, his architect, to devise a space which would be sanctified and prevent spirits from bringing harm to the actors and the action to a complete halt. The architect did as he was bid and produced a facility all the parts of which were consecrated with rituals, from the very ground-breaking to the inauguration ceremony.

The show resumed in the newly sanctified theatre structure but the evil spirits continued to plague the actors. At last Brahma summoned the demons and in a mood of reconciliation explained the purpose of drama and the objective for which it was intended. In short, he indicated that no class of individuals is excluded from seeing it, including the demons, and that it is meant to educate and entertain, and thus no subject may be excluded from consideration, even the defeat of the demons in battle. As a final step to silence the objections of the malevolent spirits, Brahma proclaimed that those who correctly observe the ritual sacrifices connected with performance will be protected from evil and will enjoy success in their undertakings.

Bharata's simple story reveals many important facts about Sanskrit theatre: (1) it is composed of sacred material; (2) a specialist should witness it; (3) it should be performed by members of the priestly caste, the top rank in the hierarchy of the caste system; (4) its execution requires special knowledge and skill; (5) training is a hereditary process coming from father to son and descending directly from God; (6) special skills are necessary to execute theatre, such as dance, music, recitation and ritual knowledge; (7) it should be performed on consecrated ground; (8) its purpose is to entertain as well as to educate.

It is difficult to measure the influence of the *Natyasastra* in its historical context and virtually impossible to compare the multitude of dicta in it with actual stage practices. Perhaps a measure of its importance to scholarly concerns today is that it sheds light, sometimes the only light available, on many subjects of importance to a comprehensive understanding of the theatre in ancient India. Perhaps we cannot hope for more.

The work consists of thirty-six chapters and is the most complete book of ancient dramaturgy in the world. The *Natyasastra* covers acting, theatre architecture, costuming, makeup, properties, dance, music, play construction, as well as the organization of theatre companies, audiences, dramatic competitions, the community of actors and ritual practices, to name only a few of the more important subjects of the book. Coupled with the extant texts of plays, it is possible to develop a picture, incomplete though it may be, of the classical Indian theatre.

At the heart of the theatre companies was the stage manager (*sutradhara*) who may have also been a leading actor. It was his job to direct the players; perhaps he also served as their teacher. Like Bharata in the mythological story of the origin of theatre, he literally held the strings of the performance within his grasp (*sutradhara*, literally means 'holder of the threads or strings', that is, a puppeteer, an architect or a manipulator). He also seems to have been assisted in his duties, perhaps by an apprentice who may have been one of his sons.

The actors studied under the guidance of a drama teacher (*natyacharya*), probably the stage manager, who was usually an older and respected individual, perhaps, like Bharata, the father of the actors. Under his guidance, it was their job to keep physically and vocally fit for performance by undergoing rigorous periods of training. Also, through observation, they gained much insight from their elders in performance practices.

Men and women both seem to have been permitted to act together or in separate troupes of their own sex. They either played characters their own age or they played those of a contrasting age range. Younger actors might play the roles of older people and older actors might portray the young. Actresses were regarded as better suited to enact certain sentiments, not considered appropriate for men to perform. Given the plays, it may be assumed that the actors and actresses needed to be highly skilled in speech and singing, as well as adept at bodily movement, both realistic and abstract. The ability to dance may also have been required.

The Sanskrit plays that survive confirm the use of stock character types. Thus actors may have specialized in a particular role category, such as hero (*nayaka*), heroine (*nayika*), clown (*vidusaka*) and so forth.

The Indian system of acting is laid out in considerable detail in the *Natyasastra*. Many chapters are devoted to its discussion, more than for any other subject covered by the book. Two styles of acting appear to have been common – the realistic (*lokadharmi*) and the conventional (*natyadharmi*), the latter of which receives almost exclusive attention in the text.

Acting (*abhinaya*; literally, 'to carry towards') is defined as having four elements – bodily movement (*angika*), voice (*vacika*), spectacle (*aharya*) and sentiment or emotion (*sattvika*). Of these, bodily movement receives lavish attention in four chapters of the *Natyasastra*.

The body is divided into major and minor parts which are discussed in relation to the way they convey emotions to the spectators. A wide variety of hand gestures are described, indicating that a sophisticated language of communication had to be studied and perfected in order to act in the conventional style. Specific glances, movements of the eyebrows, cheeks, lips, chin and neck are all discussed according to their ability to communicate meaning. Broad categories of movement involving the whole body are also described, such as poses (*cari*) and gaits (*gati*) thought suitable in various situations depending on the age, sex, rank and temperament of a character. These discussions apply, in varying degree to the actor and the dancer.

Another five chapters of the *Natyasastra* are devoted to voice, focusing on grammar, language and metres. Forms of address appropriate for characters of various ranks are discussed and regional dialects, thought appropriate to various characters according to their rank and station in life, are mentioned.

Costumes, ornaments and makeup of the actor are discussed as a vital part of character and of acting. Stage properties, too, are seen as an extension of acting and receive treatment in several chapters. Elaborate decorations (*alamkara*) of the body are described in detail – garlands, ornaments and costumes. From the top of the head to the tip of the toe, hardly any part of the human anatomy was not decorated according to the caste, station in life and occupation of the character. Real ornaments were considered inappropriate for stage use since their weight might tire the actor. Instead, ornaments were crafted of light wood and painted to resemble the actual object. It

is not clear if the costumes were reproductions of historically accurate apparel, if they were the actual dress of the times or whether they were fanciful in shape, size and colour. A curtain (*yavanika*), held by two attendants, was used to mark entrances of characters and became a theatrical device for first introducing the character to the public.

The well-rounded actor of Sanskrit plays was expected to go beyond external representation of character through correct execution of movement, speech and ornamentation. The *Natyasastra* states that there is something invisible (*sattva*) about performance, an intangible quality that transcends externals and reaches the hearts and minds of the spectators. This process has to do with conveying sentiments and emotions (*sattvika*) of the play through the content of the work. It is this intangible something, difficult to describe which completes the Sanskrit actor's circle of obligations.

Although acting is obviously a very important part of theatre, the social status of the actors does not seem to have been particularly high in ancient India. Bharata may have been a Brahmin priest, but Sanskrit actors were classed with bandits and prostitutes according to most ancient authorities. In the final chapter of the *Natyasastra*, Bharata and his sons were cursed by respected sages who took offence at the caricatures of themselves by the actors. On the verge of suicide, the outcast actors were patronized by kings in order to preserve the art from extinction; thus began the historic practice of royal patronage which seems to have survived through ancient times.

Dancers and musicians were fundamental for performances and may have been commissioned to participate in a particular performance or as regular members of ancient companies of players. Among the musicians were male and female vocalists, flautists, who performed on bamboo instruments, players of stringed instruments, like the *vina*, a classical south Indian instrument, drummers and cymbal players. Ankle bells worn by dancers helped to accentuate the rhythmic patterns of the music and further contributed to the sophistication of the sound.

When reading a Sanskrit play it is difficult to determine how dance and music might have been integrated into the fabric of performance. Indeed, at first glance, the plays appear to be dialogue dramas. The stage directions do not indicate where music is to be inserted nor do they reveal when a dance should occur or whether a particular poetic passage is to be danced or sung. The *Natyasastra* does mention that songs (*dhruva*) were to be composed in the Prakrit language and inserted for specific purposes. Apparently these songs were composed for introducing characters, to mark a character's exit, to establish the middle or end of an act, to reinforce a dramatic mood, to establish the change of dramatic moods and to fill the gap when a temporary halt occurred in the action, for instance, when a costume had to be adjusted and the actor was forced to leave the stage.

None of the *dhruva* have survived the passage of time and it appears that the music in which they were composed may have differed considerably from that which we now know as Indian classical music, owing to the influence of Middle Eastern music after the Muslim invasions beginning in the 10th century AD.

Sanskrit theatre was performed to celebrate important religious occasions, in connection with temple festivals. The *Natyasastra* calls dramatic performance a visual sacrifice (*yajna*) to the gods and thus clearly identifies it as a sacred event. And yet we also know that performances were organized to celebrate secular events: a coronation, marriage, birth of a child, the return of a traveller or the defeat of an enemy.

The audience for theatrical events was known as 'those who see' (*preksaka*), clearly implying that seeing a performance was as important as hearing it. Owing to the sophistication demanded of the actors, it is not surprising that the *Natyasastra* identifies spectators in terms of certain ideal characteristics. Those of good character and high birth, who were quiet and learned – partial, advanced in age, alert, honest, virtuous, knowledgeable in drama, acting, music, dance and the arts and crafts which figure in their execution, were considered to have the attributes of an ideal spectator. Perhaps because few measured up to that ideal, God is the ultimate witness to the dramatic event, possessing all the attributes demanded.

Performance competitions, in which critics judged the merits of the acting and awarded prizes to those who excelled, are known during the classical period. Ultimately, those whose occupation was depicted were thought the best judge of the actors. Kings were thought fit to judge actors who portrayed kings, courtesans might judge those who played courtesans and so forth.

The *Natyasastra* laid down rules for the composition of plays and for rituals connected with their presentation. Published editions of the plays normally include a short benedictory verse (*nandi*) and a prologue (*prastavana*) along with the text of the work, if the original text contains a benediction and a prologue; however, the *Natyasastra* lists 18 separate preliminaries (*purvaranga*) among the steps that may have taken place prior to the first lines of a text, including the benediction and prologue. These preliminaries provide a gradual bridging between the world of the audience and that of the play. It begins with musical performances followed by dances and ritual observances. Eventually, events like those of the prologue occur in which the audience is addressed directly by the characters and their conversation leads to the introduction of the first character of the play. This special method of introduction to a play accomplishes the goal of warming the performers and the audience to the events at hand, sanctifying the performance area, blessing the proceedings, introducing the story in a novel way and focusing attention on the dramatic action.

Sanskrit playwrights had ten types of drama in which they could choose to compose their work. The best-known and most significant was the *nataka* which was required to have a well-known story concerning a hero who might be a king or a royal sage. The theme of the *nataka* should exploit the sentiments of love and heroism. This type of drama was restricted to between five and seven acts. *Sakuntala and the Ring of Recognition* (*Abhijnanasakuntala*), *The Vision of Vasavadatta* (*Svapnavasavadatta*), and *The Latter History of Rama* (*Uttara-ramacarita*) are three of the better-known examples of this dramatic type.

The *prakarana* was the second major type. Of the two examples of this form which survive,

The Little Clay Cart (Mrcchakatika) is the better known. According to the Natyasastra, it was to have an invented story; a Brahmin, merchant or minister was to serve as the hero; a courtesan was to serve as the heroine; and love was to be the dominant sentiment. It was restricted to between five and ten acts.

The other types of plays listed in the Natyasastra were less complex forms, often in one or two acts, with small casts – one form was a monologue – and lacking some of the possible dramatic or theatrical elements of the longer, major play forms. Examples are best seen in the works of BHASA.

The smallest possible unit of a play was an act (anka) in which the hero's basic dramatic situation might be portrayed. Acts were to be made up of a series of incidents surrounding the main characters; the concerns of minor figures were not permitted to dominate an act. Curses, marriages, battles, loss of a kingdom or death were strictly prohibited from being depicted on the stage. Events such as these might be reported, but they could not be shown.

The plot (vastu) was considered the body of the play. Each stage in its development was carefully identified and thought to follow a prescribed pattern. Normally, the seed (bija) of the plot concerned the desire of the hero to achieve a specific end. The plot moved the dramatic action toward that goal with a reversal of fortune as an inevitable stumbling block to its achievement. Finally, the goal which was reached was to relate to one of the three ends of Hindu life – duty (dharma), pleasure (kama) or wealth (artha).

Sanskrit drama served as a model of ideal human behaviour. The idealization of the characters, their values and actions, all point to this lofty ultimate aim. Sanskrit drama is not a drama of protest or of reaction but a theatre of elevated ideals. Guided by the Natyasastra's rules, the writers co-operated with and lived within their society rather than breaking down barriers or exhibiting individualistic points of view.

Among the unique contributions of Sanskrit drama to world literature is its aesthetic theory. The theory of sentiment (rasa) relates to the audience's perception of the theatre event, as well as the contribution of theatre artists to the process. According to the Natyasastra, which first articulated the theory of rasa, human experiences are divided into eight basic sentiments – the erotic (srngara), the comic (hasya), pathos (karuna), rage (raudra), heroism (vira), terror (bhayanaka), odiousness (bibhatsa) and the marvellous (adbhuta). These sentiments are aroused in the audience by corresponding emotions or feelings (bhava) represented by the actors. These emotions are achieved with the aid of 32 transitory feelings (vyabhicaribhava) and eight states of emotion or feeling (sattvika).

Every play has a dominant emotion (sthayibhava) which produces a corresponding sentiment (rasa) in the audience. And yet the play of the other bhava and resulting rasa are permissible in a work, as long as balance is maintained and one sentiment dominates the others.

The theory of rasa is much like the experience of savouring a good meal, excellently cooked and served, with contrasting complementary tastes abounding. The playwright provides the basic menu which the performers translate into an appropriate presentation. Given the refinement of the system, it is little wonder that spectators were expected to be cultivated and well-educated in the arts, as well as in other aspects of life.

The place of performance of these refined works of art is still something of an enigma. No sketches remain, no drawings, floor plans, paintings or models, no ruins to contemplate. The Natyasastra is our only guide for a description of the physical facilities of the Sanskrit theatre building. And it speaks of the structures it describes as though they were ideal models rather than actual edifices.

Because the medium-sized rectangular building (vikrstamadhya) is spoken of in great detail, it may have been the favoured model. Bharata regards it as the most suitable space to see and hear a performance. The structure is comparatively small, perhaps holding between 200 and 500 people, certainly no more than 500. Although ideal for achieving intimacy between spectators and players, it seems to have been an exclusive space in contrast with the theatre structures of Ancient Greece and Rome, or those of Elizabethan England.

The Natyasastra sets out specific steps in the selection and preparation of a site for a theatre structure. Rituals accompanied its construction and sanctification, following the plan described for the first theatre structure created by Visva-karma, the heavenly architect. A roof with high windows protected it from the elements and the walls and pillars were decorated with paintings.

Half of the 48 x 96 ft structure was assigned to the spectators. It may be that they sat on risers. Different castes were assigned different seating locations according to their rank. The stage and dressing room made up the other half of the building. The stage space was 48 x 24 ft and fur-ther subdivided in half. A space 48 x 12 ft was raised above the floor of the building by perhaps a foot. The 48 x 12 ft space near the dressing room was elevated still further. Two doors separated the dressing room from the acting area. The space between the doors was reserved for the musicians and one of the doors may have been used for entrances and the other assigned for exits. Curtains could have covered the doors.

Little is known about the dressing room and about the acting area. It appears from the plays that the acting area was regarded as a neutral space endowed with symbolic meaning depend-ing on the dramatic action. By walking around (parikramana) the actors symbolically changed the locale of the action. The stage was also thought to be divided into separate zones (kaksya), although just how this was achieved is not clear from the text. There is no evidence that furniture was used to identify place. Perhaps a stool was the only item of furniture needed to symbolize various objects, such as thrones, benches and so on.

The Natyasastra also describes square and trian-gular theatre structures and indicates that there were small, medium and large varieties of all these shapes.

Although the Natyasastra categorizes play-wrights (natyakara) among the members of theatre companies, historical evidence suggests that they were more likely to have been members of the courts of kings, if not kings themselves. Literally hundreds of plays were written from the 1st to the 10th century AD, the high point of the Sanskrit dramatic outpouring. Of these, several dozen have survived. The earliest are those of Asvaghosa, whose fragmentary works of the 1st century AD came to the attention of scholars in the early part of our own century. His plays concern Buddhist teachings and follow the rules pertaining to dramatic composition laid down in the Natyasastra.

The author for whom we have the greatest abundance of works is Bhasa whose 13 surviving plays cover a wide range of subject matter and at least one of which, The Vision of Vasavadatta, is among the best and most important works of Sanskrit dramatic literature.

Among the major dramatic works of classical India, the most monumental and perhaps one of the most popular is The Little Clay Cart attributed to SUDRAKA. No other works have been traced to Sudraka and yet it is hard to believe that a writer could have produced only one brilliant work and remained silent the rest of his life.

The Little Clay Cart is similar to Bhasa's unfin-ished work Charudatta (Charudattam). Scholars speculate whether Sudraka and Bhasa were one and the same individual, or whether Sudraka bor-rowed Bhasa's play and added his own poetic style to it, as well as embroidering the political plot into the fabric of the story.

The Little Clay Cart is a superb example of prakarana. It involves Charudatta, a hapless Brahmin merchant who is generous to a fault, brave and virtuous and who is in love with Vasantasena, a rich, beautiful and faithful courte-san. Their deep affection for each other is nearly spoiled by Samstanaka, a jealous ne'er-do-well brother-in-law of a corrupt king who is the very antithesis of Charudatta. He attempts to murder Vasantasena and blame the crime on Charudatta only to find his plot is spoiled by fate. Despite its serious moments, the play basically centres on love and humour and historically has been one of the few popularly staged pieces of the classical Indian repertory.

Arguably India's greatest playwright is KALIDASA. His acknowledged masterpiece is Sakuntala and the Ring of Recognition, which, like The Little Clay Cart, has been produced frequently in modern times. The play is a delicate explo-ration of human love. The source of the story may be found in the Mahabharata. Kalidasa took liber-ties with the epic sources to suit his own particu-lar needs. The plot surrounds King Dusyanta, his infatuation, love, marriage, separation and

Bahorupee's version of *The Little Clay Cart*, directed by Kumar Roy in Calcutta in 1979.

reunion with Sakuntala, daughter of a heavenly nymph and a sage. When the play opens, Sakuntala is a young girl on the verge of womanhood. Her unspoiled beauty attracts Dusyanta, who is sporting in a forest nearby Sakuntala's hermitage home. The first three acts explore the delicate relationship between the dashing king and the modest young maiden. After agreeing to a marriage by mutual consent, Sakuntala prepares to follow her husband to the city to take up residence in his palace as his chief queen. Her departure from the sacred grove provides ample food for some of the most beautiful lyrics in all of Sanskrit literature. They also parallel the anguish that parents experience when their children leave home for good.

Due to a seemingly minor offence to a saintly guest, on her arrival at court Sakuntala is punished when the king forgets her. Stricken with anguish, she is whisked away by a heavenly nymph and, up to the final act, the story revolves around the torments of the king, whose memory is restored too late and who learns that Sakuntala has disappeared. Ultimately fate intervenes and the king finds Sakuntala in the hermitage of the mother and father of the gods. She has given birth to a handsome son, his only child, who bears the marks of royalty. Dusyanta identifies the child, finds Sakuntala and experiences a tearful but happy reunion.

Among the major playwrights of a later period of Sanskrit drama, Bhavabhuti stands out above the others. He appears to have lived around AD 700 and was a member of the court of a north Indian king. His *The Latter History of Rama* is among the best plays of Sanskrit drama. The work adapts incidents from the epic *Ramayana* and develops unique and creative twists to the plot. Like other later writers, Bhavabhuti succumbs to the temptation to embellish his writing with lengthy poetic expressions.

Although there are other distinguished playwrights worth mentioning, none of them achieved the reputation of Bhasa, Sudraka, Kalidasa and Bhavabhuti. For all practical purposes, Sanskrit plays which deserve critical attention were not written after the 10th century AD.

The 10th century marks the end of the Sanskrit

theatre as an active force in Indian art. Internal and external forces were at work several centuries prior to that time which brought about its demise. The successive invasions of Mohammed of Gazzni weakened the kingdoms of north India and eventually the temples and kingdoms could no longer patronize theatre troupes. Also the exclusivity of Sanskrit theatre must have weakened its ability to survive. The language of the courts and temples was Sanskrit, but various regional languages and literary traditions were on the verge of emerging in the rural areas. Then too, the rules laid down by the *Natyasastra* exerted a stranglehold on the creative imagination of some later writers. Few were able to make use of them without stifling their creativity. The flexibility that existed in the earlier period disappeared later, and the possibility of new ideas was suppressed.

In the great Mogul empires of the 15th century where Islam became the state religion, theatre no longer thrived because the religion did not condone it. Only at the southern tip of the subcontinent did a form of Sanskrit theatre manage to survive, KUTIYATTAM of Kerala. Little is known about other theatres of this period. For example, it is not known if the actors, once securely patronized at the court of Hindu kings, took to the road, abandoned Sanskrit and performed plays in vernacular languages of the rural areas, catering to the less sophisticated tastes of village spectators. To have done so would have been inconsistent and uncharacteristic but possible, given the will to survive. There is evidence of the existence of jugglers, acrobats, story-tellers and singers who are mentioned in various texts of the period. Certainly entertainment did not totally disappear.

Beginning around the 15th century, theatre emerged again in India through a dazzling array of village theatre forms, each with its own unique manner of presentation and, more importantly, in the vernacular language of a particular region to meet the needs of the people of that region. Sanskrit theatre had exhibited a national character because of the widespread use of Sanskrit at the court and in the temple: rural theatre forms did not travel beyond the boundaries of the communities in which they were originally created.

The village troupes which sprang into being might be either amateur or professional. Many were itinerant groups that worked a particular area, sometimes operating within one community or religious group. From the 15th to the 19th century, forms of theatre developed in virtually every pocket of the subcontinent. Some of the earlier forms have disappeared today, but a large number of them still survive and continue to serve as a testament to the richness and variety of the creative minds of the people who invented them and invested them with a unique life.

A major catalyst for the re-emergence of theatre was Vaisnavism, a religious movement which centres on devotion (*bhakti*) of man for god in the person of Krishna, the incarnation of Vishnu. Unlike orthodox Hindus, followers of Vaisnavism believe that man may approach god directly, rather than with the aid of rituals. The simple act of repeating god's name is regarded as an act of faith. Thus, theatre became an excellent vehicle for communicating the faith by depicting the acts of god. Those who witnessed it, as well as those who performed it, were engaging in a religious act. Many theatre forms arose at different times and in different places to address the needs of Vaisnavism: ANKIYA NAT, BANDI NATA, BHAGAVATA MELA, BHAMAKALAPAM, DASHAVATARA, DHANU JATRA, GOLLAKALAPAM, KRISHNATTAM, KUCHIPUDI, NONDI NATAKAM, PRAHLADA NATAKA and RAMLILA and RASLILA.

Most rural theatre forms in India begin with preliminaries and conclude with rituals. Some of these forms arose as an expression of religious zeal and have since made the transition to more secular concerns. Dozens of other regional theatre forms were originally secular in inspiration and are today played in commercial environs by professional troupes. Among these are: BHARATLILA, BHAVAI, BIDESIA, BURRAKATHA, CHAITA GHODA GATA, DANDANATA, DASKATHIA, GHUDIKI NABARANGA NATA, JATRA, KARIYALA, KATHAKALI, KHYAL, KURAVANJI, MAACH, NAQAL, NAUTANKI, PALA, RASDHARI, SVANGA, TAMASHA, THERUKOOTHU, VEEDHI NATAKAM and YAKSHAGANA.

Most of India's rural theatre forms were created by Hindus primarily for Hindus and their content is derived from Hindu mythology. However, BHAGAT of Agra, and the BHAND JASHNA of Kashmir were created for Muslim consumption and CAVITTU NATAKAM of Kerala focuses on Christian concerns.

All of the above have their own unique form. In execution, organization, costume, makeup, staging and acting style, they differ one from the other; yet there are some broad similarities that may be noted here. The south Indian forms lay stress on dance; indeed, some of them qualify as dance dramas, such as kathakali and krishnattam of Kerala. The north Indian forms emphasize song, among them khyal of Rajasthan, maach of Madhya Pradesh, nautanki of Uttar Pradesh and svanga of the Punjab. Those that lay stress on dialogue are jatra of Bengal, tamasha of Maharashtra and bhavai of Gujarat. The last two mentioned forms are among the few which emphasize comedy and satire.

An amazing array of puppet-theatre forms are also part of the heritage of Indian village life. Shadow, glove, doll and string puppets have a place in various regions of the country. The shadow forms include GOMBEYATTA, PAVAIKUTHU, RAVANA CHHAYA and TOLLU BOMMALU. The glove forms include GOPALILA, PAVAI KATHAKALI and PAVAI KOOTHU. The doll forms are BOMMALATTAM and PUTUL NAUTCH. The string forms are KATH-PUTLI and SAKHI KUNDHEI.

The proliferation of forms of the performing arts does not end here. Dramatic content may be found in the various solo forms of Indian classical dance – bharata natyam of south India, north Indian kathak, odissi from the east and mohiniyattam from Kerala – and in folk forms, such as gambhira of Bengal, seraikella chhau of Bihar, mayurbhanj chhau of Orissa and purulia chhau of Bengal. Also, dramatic content is richly woven in the ritual ceremonies of some areas, particularly those of Kerala state with its mudiyettu and teyyam. Storytelling too is part of the dramatic heritage of India. The acting in cakyar koothu and nangyar koothu of Kerala, the dance, acting and singing of solo performers of tullal, also of Kerala, and the songs and simple dances of the Khavads of Rajasthan, provide hints of the enormously rich variety of India's rural areas.

Modern theatre

The seeds of the modern Indian theatre were sown in the late 18th century with the consolidation of British power in three distinct areas of the subcontinent – Bengal, Maharashtra and Tamil Nadu. More particularly, the British developed fortifications and centralized authority in villages which were later developed into the thriving metropolises of these three areas, Calcutta, Bombay and Madras, respectively. There they introduced their own brand of theatre, based on London models. In those days the playhouses tripled as performance spaces, meeting houses and storage rooms. Initially theatre was meant to provide entertainment for British soldiers and citizens who were serving out their days in an alien land and climate.

Before long it became evident that elaborate machinery was needed to govern a country much of which was already under British control. India, at that time, was a nation of a multitude of princely states most of which were weak and governed by ineffectual leadership in Delhi. To achieve their ends, the British introduced the English system of higher education as a means of developing a class of Indians educated in British ideas, tastes, morals and values. The theatre became an extension of that aim – a tool for conveying the British way of life.

At the same time, educated Indians were not content to merely watch the performance of British works, in the mid 19th century, rich young Bengalis in Calcutta established private theatres in their homes, which had space large enough for temporary acting areas and auditoria. There they produced plays for the consumption of their friends and family. Eventually they began to write plays following British models which wove in Indian music and songs. The work of RABINDRANATH TAGORE, the Nobel-Prize-winning poet, was the product of this initial effort. He showed great empathy for the lives of poor villagers and his plays take such ordinary people as his subjects. Among his dramatic achievements were Red Oleanders (Raktakurabi) and The King of the Dark Chamber (Raja).

These experiments stimulated the establishment of commercial public theatres during the last quarter of the 19th century, managed by Indian artists and designed to appeal to Indian urban taste. Thus, the modern Indian theatre was born.

The pattern of development of modern theatre

Tripti Mitra and Sombhu Mitra, well-known actors of the Calcutta stage, in Rabindranath Tagore's *Visarjan*, produced by Bohurupee.

differs from region to region, but it ultimately led to the same thing – construction of theatres with proscenium-arch stages, lighting with equipment suited to the needs of the space, audience control through sale of tickets, a sophisticated system of theatre management, an acting style suited to the demands of an enclosed building, separation of the audience from the actors by a raised stage and a front curtain, scenery designed to establish the place and time of the dramatic action, costumes, ornaments and makeup geared to the particular lighting effects, organization of the text into units which provided intermissions, and content which addressed issues pertinent to audience concerns. And, perhaps more importantly, the works were composed in the local regional languages. In Calcutta, Bengali was the language of the new and thriving theatre, in Madras it was Tamil and in Bombay, which was more cosmopolitan than the other cities, plays were composed in Marathi, Gujurati, Hindusthani, Urdu and sometimes in a blend of all these languages, plus English.

Dissatisfaction with British rule led some early patriots to produce works critical of the unfair and harsh treatment of Indian labourers. An itinerant band of Calcutta actors produced *The Mirror of the Indigo Planters* (*Nildapana*) in Lucknow in 1875, which criticized white planters for their cruel treatment of Indian peasants. The attempt led British audiences to send the actors packing. Sensitive to the potential of theatre to foment resentment and protest, the government passed the Dramatic Performances Act of 1879 which began a practice of censorship that persisted until recently. Nevertheless, many Indians resorted to masking their protests under the guise of history and mythology. This practice continued, more or less unabated, until independence was achieved in 1947.

The period of the late 19th and early 20th centuries saw the proliferation of theatre buildings, touring companies and an entrepreneurial spirit. Theatre was a popular art in urban areas and in small towns influenced by city commerce and trade, although not all companies were successful.

Sweeping changes in taste occurred in the early 20th century. The enormous popularity of cinema with the middle classes and its easy access led to the closing of live theatres virtually everywhere in the country. Artists abandoned the stage in large numbers to seek more lucrative careers in films. India quickly developed into one of the world's largest producers and consumers of films. Great studios thrived in Bombay, primarily creating films in Hindi, the language which constituted the largest potential market. Tamil-language films followed a close second. Today there are film studios in almost every major city and films are made in every major language of the country. While theatre retains some of its vigour, particularly in Calcutta and Bombay, the number of theatre troupes has declined from a peak in the early part of the century.

Commercial theatre companies performing modern drama exist in large cities today. The largest number of companies are in Calcutta, in the heart of the Bengali-speaking section of the city. The Star Theatre is among the oldest and best known, working out of a building constructed in 1888, renowned for famous theatre personalities that once performed there. Commercial companies also stage plays in the Circarena, Rangmahal, Biswaroopa, Minerva, Rangana and Bijon theatre buildings. In Kerala, the Kerala People's Arts Company (KPAC) and Kalidasa Kalakendra, both communist organizations, operate itinerant groups. The National Theatre of Madras still clings to 19th-century staging techniques, producing slick shows at various theatres and halls in the city, the state and even abroad. Trivandrum's Kalanilaya Vistavision Dramascope Company follows along the path of the National with melodramatic 19th-century fare still popular with a segment of Kerala's population.

The heart of the modern theatre in India today consists of amateur companies. Among the better known are Bohorupee, Little Theatre Group and Nandikar in Calcutta, and Goa Hindu Association's Theatre wing, Abhishek, Indian National Theatre, Theatre Unit and Theatre Group in Bombay. Many of the players who work with these organizations are theatre professionals who eke out a living performing a wide variety of jobs in films, television and advertising, as well as working on the stage. The groups retain their amateur status in order to benefit from tax concessions and because they cannot make enough money at the box office to support the players on a consistent basis.

Calcutta is said to have some three thousand registered amateur groups; Bombay may have as many

Goa Hindu Association in a production of *Raigadala Jevha Jug Yete*, Bombay, 1962.

as five hundred; Madras boasts of at least fifty and Delhi several dozen.

Characteristically, each amateur organization has a director, or core of directors, at its head to choose plays, organize productions and provide momentum for its activities. Without a director these groups would collapse for lack of continuity and leadership. Distinguished directors with national reputations in the amateur theatre are Sombhu Mitra, UTPAL DUTT and Rudraprasad Sen Gupta of Calcutta; Kamalkar Sarang, Mansukh Joshi, Satyadev Dubey, Alyque Padamsee, Pearl Padamsee, Vijaya Mehta of Bombay; EBRAHIM ALKAZI, HABIB TANVIR, Bansi Kaul and M. K. Raina of New Delhi; Manohar and Cho of Madras; and Kavalam Narayan Pannikar of Kerala.

Productions are normally organized on a show-by-show basis. Subscription seasons are virtually unknown. If a show is successful, it is repeated as many times as audiences will come to see it in sufficient numbers to warrant a showing. Often shows are kept in a group's repertory for years.

The bane of amateur theatre is the fact that virtually all the groups must rent theatre facilities which are owned by co-operatives, governments and private individuals. Only one theatre group, Theatre Centre of Calcutta, owns its own building, a tiny space seating less than a hundred people. This means that groups in all the cities vie with each other for theatre space. In Bombay, the situation has led amateur theatre producers to consolidate their efforts and to agree to a booking schedule that gives the busiest and most popular groups access to prime booking dates in the better houses.

Among the most popular amateur theatre houses are the Academy of Fine Arts in Calcutta; the Tata Theatre of the National Centre for the Performing Arts, Shivaji Mandir, Ravindra Natya Mandir, Gadkari Nangayatan, Baidas, Bhirla, Tejpal, Prithvi and Patkar in Bombay; and Kamani Auditorium, Gandhi Memorial Theatre, Sri Ram Centre and Sapru House in New Delhi.

Production expenses are relatively high for amateur theatre. Few of the groups have access to space to build scenery and props. Costume storage is virtually unheard of. Lighting equipment, such as it is, must be rented for each performance. Production costs in Bombay and Calcutta range from two or three thousand dollars for a single-set show to ten thousand dollars for a historical play

Manohar, actor-producer of Madras's National Theatre productions, performing the role of the gluttonous epic character Kumbakarna.

or musical. In cities with a lower cost of living, such as Madras, Bangalore, Ahmedabad and Hyderabad, production costs are somewhat lower.

One of the greatest expenses is advertising. Newspaper advertisements are virtually prohibitive. Each one may run into hundreds of rupees for a small space on a single day. Negotiations for concessions are almost always going on between editors and heads of amateur groups. Word of mouth is considered the best, and certainly the cheapest, means of advertising a production.

If a performance fails at the box office, it may mean the demise of an amateur theatre organization. In recent years, organizers have realized that once a production has met with some degree of success in a large and prominent urban theatre, then it can profitably be marketed to organizations in smaller towns and cities. These so-called 'call' bookings have become a lucrative source of income for many groups and may make the difference between financial success and failure. Yet, they are hard on organizers and performers, many of whom hold down jobs or have other commitments. By its very nature, amateur theatre in India is itinerant.

Plays that provide grist for the commercial and amateur theatre mill vary greatly from group to group, depending on the demands imposed by the organization. In the 19th century, plays were a blend of music, song and dialogue. During the 20th century music and song were dropped in favour of dialogue, as in modern Western drama. Today the trend, especially in major cities, is towards the incorporation of music and song into performance either as a primary or a secondary ingredient. The playwrights who create this work are as varied as the works themselves. Hack writers whose names do not appear on any marquee or in any programme are often engaged to develop an idea for the commercial theatres of Calcutta and Madras, much as hack writers do for films and television in the West. Socially committed playwrights like Thopil Basi are often commissioned by Communist groups in Kerala. They frequently serve as playwright-director negotiating script changes directly with the actors. Utpal Dutt is also known for his contributions to the socially committed theatre of Calcutta. Dutt usually works as a playwright, director and actor. BADAL SIRCAR, Girish Karnad, Vijay Tendulkar, G. Sankara Pillai and K. Narayan Pannikar join Utpal Dutt among a small band of playwrights who have achieved national prominence and whose works have been produced beyond the confines of their own language and area of the country. These artists are concerned with social and political issues and their work is primarily serious in tone.

Examples of playwrights who deliver safer, more predictable works designed to appeal to the taste of the vast majority of urban audiences in their respective languages are N. N. Pillai of Kerala, Jaywant Dalve of Bombay and Cho of Madras. These writers focus on family life and the plight of the individual in a modern mechanized country. Comedy and melodrama are freely mixed in their work leaving audiences satisfied at the conclusion of the show rather than disturbed or moved to take radical action.

Experimental work with limited public appeal has been presented in various areas of the country. Badal Sircar launched experimentation in Calcutta with his Satabdi group by producing work in

Andanun Adakodanum by the Kerala playwright G. Sankara Pillai, with the Calicut University Repertory Company.

'found' spaces rather than in rented theatre halls, forgoing expensive lighting equipment, scenery and elaborate costuming. The work is presented every Friday evening on a regular basis with little or no advance advertising. A mere pittance is charged for admission. The Living Theatre of Khardah, a theatre group in a suburb outside Calcutta, attempts the same thing – a theatre of ideas, accessible to the public but free of commercial constraints. Experimental work has also been attempted in Bombay by Avishkar in a rented school hall and at the moderately expensive Prithvi Theatre in north Bombay. Work that is expected to attract limited audiences is also found in New Delhi and Madras. And in Kerala the work of Kavalam Narayan Pannikar has achieved critical acclaim for its integration of folk and classical theatre traditions.

For several decades the National School of Drama of New Delhi has been a leader in educational theatre by training young actors, directors and designers in modern theatre techniques. Under the guidance of Ebrahim Alkazi, it gained a national and international reputation during the 1960s and 70s. Theatre is taught at university level at the M. S. University of Baroda in Gujurat state, Rabindra Bharati University in Calcutta, Calicut University in Trichur, Kerala, and Chandigar University in the Punjab.

Short training programmes, workshops and retreats are among the various methods used by teachers and leaders of amateur theatre organizations to promote theatre among the young. Regional and state competitions are also conducted to encourage interest in theatre. State and national governments help in a limited way to support the study of traditional and modern Indian theatre through grants to teachers, students and organizations. They also award annual prizes to distinguished individuals for their accomplishments. The government has helped to focus national attention on theatre.

Genres

Ankiya nat

Ankiya nat is a religious theatre form in Assam, a beautiful state in remote northeastern India. *Ankiya nat* was created by Sankaradeva

(c. 1449–1568), who was an ardent devotee of Lord Vishnu, an earthly manifestation of Krishna worshipped by many Assamese Hindus. *Ankiya* means 'act' and *nat* means 'drama'. Thus, *ankiya nat* means a one-act drama composed in a particular form.

Sankaradeva created *ankiya nat* and wrote many plays as a means of maintaining and spreading the tenets of Vaisnavism among his people. His plays became very popular and he established the practice that all leaders of religious orders should write at least one play about Krishna's life during their lifetime.

Performance of *ankiya nat* usually takes place within the confines of a prayer hall (*nam-ghar*), a roofed structure open at the side, located in the sacred confines of a monastery. The acting area is a narrow central corridor marked off by ropes running down the length of the building. Usually audiences sit on the ground or stand at the back facing each other while the players make their way up and down the narrow acting corridor. At times, scenes are played behind one side of the audience, literally enfolding spectators in the dramatic action.

At one end of the prayer hall is a shrine (*manikut*) where the sacred text (*Bhagavata Purana*) is kept, symbolizing the presence of the words, the teachings, of Krishna (Vishnu). Entrances are usually made at the end opposite the shrine and, to begin the performances, the players progress down the passageway in a slow ritual dance toward the text. The large orchestra of musicians provides a hypnotic musical background during the overture and throughout a show.

Usually companies consist of about 15 amateur actors, either made up of monks who regard it as their sacred duty to portray the stories of their god, or village artists who take particular pride in playing the roles of the gods and goddesses of the plays. Men normally play all the parts in the monastery productions, but women may participate in performances in communities where taboos do not forbid it. The boys who take the role of Krishna and his brother Balarama are thought to be temporarily possessed by the spirit of god and are approached with great reverence, particularly by female spectators.

Shimmering white costumes are worn by the musicians, and leading characters wear colourful costumes and crowns to symbolize their stations in life. Perhaps the most striking characters are giant effigies made of bamboo covered with papier-mâché and painted to represent demons and animals. Some of these figures, which are at least 15 ft high, must be manipulated by several actors. Masks of birds, snakes, monkeys and bears are worn when actors portray such fanciful characters.

Typically, performances are organized to coincide with religious festivals, such as the birth of Krishna, the memorial-day celebration of Sankaradeva or some local preceptor, or on a full-moon night. The holiday season coincides with harvest and planting (mid January to mid April). A performance event usually begins around 9 p.m. and continues until sunrise.

Performance begins with an elaborate ritual of drumming. Songs and dances commence at an archway of lights (*agni-gad*) constructed on the acting area, opposite the sacred shrine. Special songs are sung in praise of Krishna and distribution of sacred food (*prasada*) to the musicians follows. At last the stage manager (*sutradhara*) makes a spectacular entrance from behind a curtain at the archway. He is accompanied by fireworks and dancing. In a stately dance before the shrine, he offers his humble respects to Krishna. Then he recites a verse from the play to be enacted and concludes with a song. A red curtain is held up and Krishna makes his entrance, dancing majestically towards the shrine. Only now does the actual drama begin. Throughout the action which follows, the stage manager stands near the actors referring to the text of the play in order to make certain that they perform all the dialogue correctly. He inserts the necessary directions to the musicians and interprets the action of the play for the audience when necessary. In this respect, the stage manager reminds one of the medieval directors depicted in the famous painting of the martyrdom of Saint Apollonia.

Like other forms of traditional theatre, scenes of conflict between the forces of good and evil highlight an evening of *ankiya nat*. Brief songs and dances close the performance in the early hours of the morning.

The strength of *ankiya nat* lies in its close links

to the religious beliefs of the Assamese people, particularly devotees (*bhaktas*) of Krishna. It has sustained itself for centuries because it is prominent among the religiously minded Hindus of the state. It seems to be relatively unchanged over time, even though Assam has undergone many dramatic changes in its economic and social organization in recent times.

Bandi nata

A regional theatre form in central and western Orissa, which takes its name from Bandi, the nickname of the sister of Chandrasena, Radha's husband in the mythological tales surrounding the life of Krishna. The stories concern Bandi's self-sacrifice for her husband Krishna so that he may sport with Radha. The form is acted by members of the untouchable community. The actors mix with the spectators and only join in the action when their turn comes. They are accompanied by the *dhol* drum. Performance lasts about three hours. Dances, songs, actions and humour are freely mixed to keep the spectators entertained.

Bhagat

A Muslim regional theatre form confined to Agra, the site of the Taj Mahal and an important historic city in north India. Headed by a leader (*khalifa*), a group performs for the benefit of individuals in their area of the city. Competition between groups of players can occur.

Bhagavata mela

A folk dance drama in Melattur, a village in Tamil Nadu state in south India. The term *bhagavata* refers to the *Bhagavata Puranas*, collections of Indian epic stories about Lord Vishnu's incarnations. Those who perform these stories are known as *bhagavatar* or *bhagavatulu*. *Mela* refers to a troupe of dancers or singers.

The origin of *bhagavata mela* is traced to the state of Andhra Pradesh where it appears to have been inspired by KUCHIPUDI dance drama around 1502. After the fall of the Hindu Vijayanagar Empire, which included Andhra Pradesh, in 1565, cultural activities came to a virtual standstill. About 500 Brahmin families who performed *kuchipudi* in the Telugu language were left homeless. They travelled south to Tanjore, a Tamil-speaking region, and appealed to King Achyutappa Nayak (1561–1614) for support. The ruler granted them cultivable land and six villages near the city of Tanjore. Today, Melattur, one of the six villages, retains *bhagavata mela* as an annual performance. The other villages also present truncated versions of *bhagavata mela* during the annual festival season.

In Melattur, during the last few weeks of April or early May, two troupes of devotees present an annual performance before the Varadraja Perumala Temple and at the village tank in celebration of Narasimha Jayanti, a festival honouring Vishnu's terrifying man-lion incarnation which destroyed a demon king. Venkatarama Sastri (1759–1847) sparked new life in the form by creating appealing musical compositions to suit about a dozen dance dramas which he also wrote. The object of Sastri's compositions was to spread among the people of this region the devotional movement of Hinduism (*bhakti*) which began in the Middle Ages and continues unabated up to the present day.

The traditional site for the so-called 'temple performance' is on a narrow raised proscenium stage erected in the street between rows of houses of Brahmin families opposite the Varadraja Perumala Temple. A long protective roof of thatch is stretched from the top of the proscenium about 100 ft down the street. Before performances begin around 9.30 or 10.00 p.m., the temple deity is carried in lavish procession through the streets of the town. Then he is installed on a special roofed structure opposite the stage, so that performances take place in the divine presence.

Performance begins with the entrance of the clown (*konangi*) who dances and jests with the spectators. Then musicians enter and sing invocations praising Vishnu and songs appropriate to introduce the particular play to be enacted. Next, the chief teachers of the art are honoured with sandal paste and flowers. This is followed by the appearance of a small boy wearing the mask of Ganapati, the elephant-headed god of good fortune. It is said that the child is chosen because his parents have made a vow to present their son on the stage in this role. After brief dances and songs asking Ganapati's blessings, the drama begins.

All the actors who participate are men, the younger and more attractive of whom play female roles. Elaborate entrances of each character are made behind a curtain held by two attendants. The dance entrances incorporate stylized gesture and intricate patterns of movement characteristic of Indian classical dance. An entrance song (*patra pravesha daru*) introduces each character.

The scenes that follow depict episodes of the drama through dialogue, song and dance. Actors combine stylized and complicated patterns of gesture-language with naturalistic movement and gesture to convey the meaning of the text. The climax of performance occurs in the early hours of the morning when a dramatic crisis is reached.

One particular drama is noteworthy for its dramatic impact and ritual significance – that of *The Story of Prahlada* (*Prahlada Charitram*).

This story demonstrates the faith of Prahlada, a youthful prince who worships Lord Vishnu. Forsaking his father's love for that of his god, Prahlada's faith is tested in various ways. With each successive test his wicked father becomes more and more furious. Eventually Prahlada's father is tricked and loses his life when Lord Vishnu, in the form of a man-lion (Hiranyakashipu), rips open the tyrant king's guts and kills him. (See also PRAHLADA NATAKA.)

According to tradition, the actor who portrays the role of the man-lion fasts and prays before wearing a special mask depicting the god. The mask is said to possess special powers endowed by the deity and the actor goes into a trance to become the violent man-lion. To protect actors playing the other roles, this actor is restrained by attendants. After the ritual killing all the actors climb down from the stage and walk to the temple where they circumambulate the deity. Songs appropriate to the early hours of the morning are sung by the chief musician. Offerings of rice are then received at households along the street, and the ritual ends with a visit to another temple on the outskirts of the village where the actor playing the man-lion takes off his mask. Immediately he falls into another trance and lies motionless on the ground until revived by water sprinkled over him to restore him to consciousness and symbolically return him to his normal state. To conclude the ceremony, benedictory verses are chanted and the exhausted actors return to their homes.

Owing to family conflicts, two parties of performers now work in this tiny village. They share the performance space considered sacred for the festival and each presents a dramatic work as part of the celebrations.

The music of *bhagavata mela*, following the Karnataka style of classical music, has garnered much praise from music critics. Classical musical instruments are used in performance – the *mridangam* drum, traverse bamboo flute, a violin played in the Indian manner and bell-brass cymbals. The voice of the singer is a particularly important instrument completing the musical ensemble.

The dance techniques are a mixture of those inherited from *kuchipudi* and those adapted from the classical *bharata natyam* of Tamil Nadu.

Bhamakalapam

A regional devotional dance drama of Andhra Pradesh state. The word is composed of two parts: *bhama*, an abbreviation of the name of Lord Krishna's beautiful and jealous wife Satyabhama, and *kalapam*, meaning 'dialogue' or 'argument'. *Bhamakalapam* is both a play and a theatre form. The play was written in the 17th century by Siddhendra Yogi for use as a devotional ritual by KUCHIPUDI performers. Several versions of the story have been created since that time, but none is better known or more popular than his. Although *bhamakalapam* is called *vithi natakam* by some scholars, in form and content it is markedly different from VEEDHI NATAKAM, the well-known street drama of south India.

Bhamakalapam is enacted by all-male troupes (*mela*) which function throughout Andhra Pradesh. Until recently it was patronized by local landowners (*zamindar*) and other wealthy patrons. Owing to the general deterioration of folk arts and traditions in modern India, the form is in serious danger of disappearing altogether.

Unlike the dance dramas KATHAKALI, YAKSHA-GANA or THERUKOOTHU, which emphasize masculine dance movements (*tandava*), *bhamakalapam* provides a superb example of graceful feminine dance movements (*lasya*).

Today there is less scope for *bhamakalapam* than *kuchipudi* because it has gained little recognition among dance critics and scholars and, as tastes have changed, the support of wealthy patrons has disappeared.

Bhand jashna

The primary popular theatre form among Muslims of rural Kashmir state at the extreme northern tip of India. *Bhand* means clown and *jashna* means festival. The form emphasizes farce and satire. Lively plays (*pather*) are improvised primarily in the Kashmiri language, with words and phrases from Urdu, Hindi, Punjabi and Persian freely added to suit the particular political and social situation. Actors mercilessly ridicule corrupt officials, money-lenders and the dowry system, while making fun of everyone from the simplest peasant to the most powerful political leader. Many of the plays have semihistorical settings and concern popular folk heroes to avoid the accusation of slander, but their contemporary relevance is nonetheless clear.

A performance may take place during the day or in the evening. To the accompaniment of music, actors make their entrances through the audience to the playing area, which may be any open space in the village. Musicians stand and accompany the actors who work the crowd seated around the playing area.

The performance begins with a ritual invocation (*poozapath*) honouring Allah. This is followed by a farcical imitation of the solemnities performed by the clowns (*maskhara*). Costumes are a mix of contemporary local and semihistorical dress. Colourful headdresses and cloth pieces add flair.

Bharatlila

Also known as *dvara nata*. A folk theatre of Orissa that dramatizes episodes from the epic *Mahabharata*, particularly those concerning Arjuna and his wife Subhadra. The character of Dvara interprets the events to the audience. Three actors plays the main characters, exchanging remarks and adding considerable humour to the events. Performance takes three to four hours.

Bhavai

Raucous, bawdy, obscene, satiric, poignant – all these terms describe *bhavai*, a rural theatre over a broad area of north Gujarat and Saurashtra, Madhya Pradesh state and Rajasthan state in western India. Once extremely popular, the number of troupes has declined today. Local legend has it that *bhavai*'s origin may be attributed to Asaita Thakar, an outcast Brahmin who lived during the mid 14th century in what is now Gujarat state.

The story goes that Asaita Thakar was born a Brahmin and served as the family priest of Patel Hema, headman of Unza, a small village in north Gujarat. One day Hema's daughter Ganga was abducted by a Muslim captain who had an eye for a pretty face. Asaita felt obliged to save the girl and so he sought audience with the captain on the pretext of entertaining him with songs. After winning the captain's praise, Asaita begged that Ganga be released saying that she was his only daughter. The shrewd captain suspected that Asaita was lying, but he agreed to release Ganga if Asaita dined with her in his presence. The wily captain knew that Brahmins were strictly forbidden to dine with lower caste Hindus, indeed it was an unpardonable act. To the captain's amazement Asaita readily agreed and did as he was bade, thus gaining Ganga's freedom. When Asaita returned to Unza with Ganga safely in tow he was promptly excommunicated by his Brahmin brethren. In ancient India excommunication meant that Asaita could no longer practice his hereditary profession and consequently could not earn a living. A lesser man would surely have been ruined by this sudden reversal of fortune, but Asaita accepted his fate and turned to singing and dancing for a living, which has historically been considered an appropriate profession for many of India's outcastes. With the help of his sons and other outcaste Brahmins he formed Gujarat's first company of strolling players (*bhavaiya*, literally, 'those who arouse sentiment' in the spectators through their performance). This community still preserves the hereditary right to perform *bhavai* in Gujarat.

In gratitude for the safe return of his daughter, Patel Hema bestowed a small plot of land and financial support on Asaita, thereby initiating a pattern of village patronage of *bhavaiya* which persists today.

Bhavai is traditionally performed in connection with religious festivals in praise of mother goddesses, such as Ambaji and Bahucharaji, the latter regarded as the patroness of *bhavai* actors. *Navaratri*, the nine-night festival in September–October honouring the goddess, is particularly auspicious. A performance is normally arranged in the sacred confines of a temple courtyard or a street in front of the temple. The performance space (*paudh*) is sanctified by the stage manager who draws a large circle of oil on the ground and lights a torch symbolizing the presence of the goddess. Songs in praise of the goddess are also sung prior to other ritual overtures and the actors and audience alike sometimes shout 'Long life to the Goddess!' during the show.

Despite the highly charged religious atmosphere of the place and occasion, the contents of most performances centre on the vices and virtues of members of various communities in village society. The Brahmin, the tailor, the potter, the scavenger, the money-lender are all satirized. Some performances deal with Hindu mythology; others provide vignettes of famous historical personages of the area.

Humour is the dominant sentiment (*rasa*), although a variety of other emotions may be evoked. The predominance of humour makes *bhavai* unique in the catalogue of regional forms of traditional Indian theatre.

The language of performance is a generous mix of Gujarati, Hindi-Urdu and Marwadi, indicating the historical connection of many castes and communities throughout this wide geographic region. Songs in verse, set to a wide variety of metres, and prose dialogue characterize the structure of the stories.

Bhavai is linked to the past through performance rather than through written stories. Texts were collected and published in Gujarat for the first time in the 19th century. The stories are known as *vesa* (literally 'costume') and they bear the names of the chief characters around which they are composed. For example, *Ganapati-no-Vesa* is the ritual introduction and dance of the elephant-headed god Ganapati; *Juthana-no-Vesa* tells the story of the trials of a Muslim crown prince,

Juthana; *Zhanda Zulan-no-Vesa* concerns the love affair between a Muslim policeman and a wife of a rich Hindu merchant; *Brahmana-no-Vesa* depicts the mad antics of a priest, and so the catalogue goes on and on. There are said to have been 360 *vesa*, one for every day of the year, but far fewer survive in the repertory today.

Commonly used musical instruments are *bhungal*, *pakhawaja*, *tabla* drums, small cymbals (*jhanjha*), harmonium and the classical north Indian stringed instrument, *sarangi*. *Bhungal* are unique to *bhavai*. They are 4-ft-long copper pipes which are blown to provide a forceful cadence during dance sequences and to announce the entrance of important characters. Normally, two *bhungal* are used, a male and a female instrument. On occasion, other instruments are introduced for special effects.

Performance begins around 10 p.m. after villagers have taken their evening meals. Music accompanies the action and initially serves to attract the spectators to the performance area. Hindustani, or north-Indian-style, music predominates but popular local tunes and rhythms are integrated throughout. When a sufficient number of spectators have been drawn to the playing area and important guests have been seated, prayers to Ambaji commence. These are followed by songs describing the love affair of a famous couple from Marwad. The songs serve as a cue to the stage manager (*nayaka*) to enter the arena and begin the rituals.

Asaita Thakar must have considered this phase of the preliminaries important because he formalized the pattern of the preliminaries in a separate *vesa*. On cue from the musicians, an actor dressed to represent Ganapati, the elephant-headed god of beginnings and successes, enters holding a brass plate before his face. As he dances, the musicians sing his praises. Like all of the dances of *bhavai*, the style is a simplified version of *kathak*, the classical dance of north India, combined with *garba*, a folk dance of the region. After Ganapati makes his exit, another actor enters impersonating the goddess Kali. The stage manager asks her name and business but gets nothing other than monosyllables as a reply. Kali dances in a frenzy to loud songs of praise. At the end of the dance the musicians implore her to remove all impediments that might hinder their performance, which she symbolically does by forming a circle over their heads and cracking her knuckles on her temples.

To conclude the preliminaries, an actor dressed as a Brahmin priest comes from the dressing room through the crowds of spectators which circle the arena. He provides the first bit of humour of the evening. When questioned by the stage manager as to his name and business he gives a ridiculous reply, using all kinds of obscenities to the delight of the spectators. His costume caricatures a Brahmin priest. Sometimes an actor portrays the role wearing small clay pots on his stomach and on his hips which are concealed under the folds of his costume. His grotesque appearance provokes roars of laughter. When he dances his movements are the very antithesis of grace. After his antics have been completed the Ganapati preliminaries are concluded by a song. At this point the regular story begins.

Although rural interest in *bhavai* has waned over the last several decades, urban theatre people have been attracted to it for a variety of reasons. First, in the wake of a national desire to preserve valuable and endangered folk traditions, urbanites have sought to support *bhavai* performances and prominent educational institutions have recruited some of the best actors to be part-time teachers at college level. In this way *bhavai*'s folk traditions are being preserved and passed down to future generations in this rapidly industrializing society. Second, the form of *bhavai*, its attention to comedy, satire and political details, accompanied by music with stylized movements and dance, has been imitated by urban theatre groups.

Actors in modern drama troupes have taken *bhavai* and rendered their own versions of the form to the delight of city audiences. More faithful imitators have attempted to replicate *bhavai*'s rural flavour. *Mena Gujari* and *Jasma Odan*, produced by Deena Gandhi and Shanta Gandhi respectively, two well-known theatre directors, have run successfully in Ahmedabad, Bombay and Delhi in recent years. With all the expressed interest, no major movement has occurred which has led the way toward a genuine revival of *bhavai*, and so the original actors and their community continue to struggle to survive.

The National School of Drama Repertory Company of New Delhi in *Jasma Odan*.

which the actors, who are all male, stamp their feet vigorously on the stage. In posture and walk, the actors exaggerate masculine movement patterns to the extreme. Battle scenes loosely incorporate martial art techniques of the region (*kalarippayatt*) which have been adapted to suit the demands of the plays, especially in conflicts with swords and shields. The style of movement contrasts markedly with that of Hindu theatre forms popular in the same region – KATHAKALI, KRISHNATTAM and KUTIYATTAM. Some hand gestures and facial expressions seem to have been borrowed from classically derived forms but the traces are faint.

The master of the performance is the teacher (*asan*) who stage-manages and trains the players in martial arts, acrobatics, singing and dancing, not to mention the memorization of the parts. Most plays are written in Tamil, which is not the language of the players, who speak Malayalam. The teacher sets up a schedule of work at his household, and after ritual initiation into the art, provides regular lessons in the specific roles that are to be learned. General training is not given. Those who play kings come from special families of Christians. Each of the actors is assigned to a character of an appropriate play according to his family connections.

The *cavittu natakam* stage is unique. Located in open ground in a village or town near a church or cathedral, it may be 30 ft wide and 100 ft long. Flanking each end are tall wooden platforms that must be scaled from the stage by ladders. The kings hold court on the high platforms while the action scenes and battles take place centre stage. A door up right serves for all entrances and one up left serves for exits. A small opening up centre provides a clear view of the stage for the chorus and musicians who work backstage. A large bell-metal lamp fed by coconut oil and cloth wicks is located down centre, although it is used more for ritual purposes than for illumination. The main illumination is provided by electric lights such as floods, scoops and fluorescent tubes.

Costumes are local versions of historical Western dress, sumptuous in appearance and very colourful. Makeup is realistic, except for false beards, moustaches and wigs. Villainous characters often wear sunglasses and tennis shoes, which are thought to be appropriate for individuals of an evil nature. The clown character (*katiyakkaran*) keeps spectators amused with various antics, especially when he parodies the songs and dances of the other characters. He even makes cutting remarks about the teacher, who stands on stage throughout performance guiding the progress of the action. The clown interprets the action in Malayalam so that spectators are able to follow the meaning of the Tamil songs and they can appreciate his satiric comments.

Chief among the musical instruments are the barrel-shaped drum played by two sticks (*centa*) and the large bell-metal cymbals (*elattalam*). The teacher controls the tempo of performance with small hand cymbals and he may cue scene changes and entrances with a whistle. A wide variety of other musical instruments may also be used – harmonium, clarinet, *mridangam* drum and *tamboora*, a stringed instrument made from a gourd, among others. Even snare and trap drums make an appearance adding to the general chaos of sound that typifies the *cavittu natakam* performance.

Cavittu natakam is best known in the Cochin and Quilon districts of central Kerala where Latin Christians make their home. The season lasts from December to March coinciding with major church festivals. A group of performers can count on perhaps a dozen shows a season; therefore, they all have other occupations and even the teachers resort to outside income to survive.

Chaita ghoda gata

A folk performance enacted by fishermen of Orissa state in northeastern India on full-moon nights in the spring. Three actors play all roles and two musicians accompany them with drums and cymbals. One of the actors represents a horse-dancer. One is the singer-commentator (*rauta*) who delivers discourses on mythological themes. And one is his wife (*rautami*), chorus, co-singer and dancer. Improvised dialogue and humorous episodes punctuate the evening event.

Dandanata

Thought to be the oldest form of drama in the state of Orissa, northeast India. The evening performance begins in an open arena with dances, music and dramatic episodes. Mythological and religious figures, including gods such as Shiva and Krishna, are introduced through song and dance. Loosely connected episodes link characters that appear during the evening. Moral lessons and religious messages are reinforced by the exalted nature of the characters.

Dashavatara

A popular form of rural theatre in Konkan and Goa on India's west coast. Literally, 'ten' (*dash*) 'incarnations' (*avatara*) of Lord Vishnu, two of whom, Rama and Krisha, are widely worshipped in India.

Dashavatara is thought to have been introduced to the area by a Brahmin 400 years ago. Some claim that it is derived from KUCHIPUDI; others maintain that it owes its origin to YAKSHAGANA. The actors who preserve *dashavatara* worship a small image of a diety which is said to have been brought from Kerala. Most of the actors come from the lower strata of society, although a few Brahmins also perform. The all-male troupes are itinerant, moving from village to village half the year, carrying simple baskets and trunks and sleeping out in the open most of the time. Their earnings are generally meagre.

Performances usually begin around 11 p.m. with songs in praise of Ganapati, the elephant-headed god, sung by the stage manager (*sutra-dhara*). A Brahmin enters and comic dialogue ensues. Two men dance dressed as women. An elementary dance is then performed by an actor who impersonates Saraswati, goddess of learning. After the dance, two women enter symbolizing rivers. With them is Madhavi, a comic Brahmin. Next the frightening figure of Shankhasura bursts on the playing area dressed from head to foot in black and sporting a red cloth representing a tongue. Shankhasura is thought to be capable of exposing the scandals and private lives of the villagers. He carries on a lively improvisational conversation with the stage manager. Then an actor playing the god Brahma, the creator, enters and a story about the theft of the sacred *Veda* is related, in which Shankhasura and the stage manager participate. The events in the elaborate overture described above continue for approximately two hours.

Finally the drama (*akhyana*) begins, lasting until sunrise. The drama includes well-known episodes from epic literature and introduces mythological and historical characters with whom village audiences are familiar. The decision as to which episodes should be performed is negotiated between the village patron and the stage manager, sometimes less than an hour before the show.

A small boy dressed in the costume of a woman moves among the spectators during the performance soliciting contributions from the villagers. The job is said to help cure the boy of stage fright and his costume gives him access to the women, who usually huddle together apart from the village men.

A harmonium and drum (*mridangam*) assist the actors with their songs and set a lively tempo for the simple dances. Tunes from popular film music are also liberally used as accompaniment to song lyrics.

The stage area is simple – an open space in a temple hall or a temporary raised platform set up in the village, surrounded on three sides and roofed by thatch and leaves. A rough wooden bench from the local town-council hall or school serves as the only piece of furniture. Special properties, such as swords, spears and clubs, are introduced by the actors when the need arises. A company's belongings include an elaborately carved ten-headed wooden mask depicting Ravana, the demon king of Lanka, and one representing Ganapati's elephant head. Costumes and ornaments are rather elaborate, considering the simple means the actors have of transporting them. Various cloth pieces, saris, jewellery and headdresses are worn to symbolize nobles, gods and goddesses; red and white makeup distinguishes the characters from their village patrons.

Very little has been written about this form and scholars have only recently begun to reveal the extent and nature of its impact on village life in this area of India.

Daskathia

A two-person storytelling theatre unique to Orissa in northeast India. Several hundred pairs of performers are active, primarily in the Ganjam district. The main singer, *gayaka*, is accompanied by a *palia*, who chants the name of Rama, the epic hero and incarnation of Lord Vishnu, in rhythmic refrains. A mythological story of about three hours' duration is related in which artists play many roles and accompany themselves with cymbals and wooden clappers or castanets. Social commentary and humorous anecdotes enliven the action. The artists wear regal attire. Ankle bells add percussive effects to their rhythmic storytelling.

Dhanu jatra

An open-air passion play depicting events in Krishna's life, staged at Baragarh in Sambalpur district, Orissa. Villages, towns and countryside are incorporated into the dramatic action and symbolically become places in the mythological story. Processions, enactment of scenes using elephants and large-scale replicas of palaces and characters require the spectators to participate in the action.

Ghudiki nabaranga nata

A folk theatre of Orissa state. Also known as *dhukuki nabaranga nata*. *Ghudiki* is the local name of a drum played during performance. Eight to ten actors sing, dance and act in the midst of spectators. The *ghudiki* player acts as the director, jesting with the other players, commenting on the dramatic action and dancing simple steps to add variety to the show. Various improvisational skits characterize the three-to-four-hour performance.

Gollakalapam

Golla means a 'female cowherd' (or *gopi*) and *kalapam* is a 'dialogue' or an 'argument'. Also known as *vithi bhagavata*, 'religious street stories'. *Gollakalapam* is both the name of a play and also a theatre form. It was created in Andhra Pradesh, in the late 19th century by Bhagavatulu Ramayya who developed the form out of *KUCHIPUDI* dance drama. Unlike *kuchipudi*, which is now the exclusive province of Brahmin men and boys, *gollakalapam* is performed by both women and men and has its own teachers knowledgeable in Sanskrit and the *Natyasastra*.

A typical performance proceeds as follows. A Brahmin acting as stage manager (*sutradhara*) performs the preliminaries and makes announcements. Then the main dancer (*golla*) enters and dances behind a curtain held by two attendants. Eventually the curtain is pulled aside and the dancer performs stylized dance patterns (*jati*) which are essentially the same as *daru* used in other dance-drama forms of the area. The dance includes intricate footwork and visual interpretation of songs through elaborate gestures. Following this, the Brahmin returns in the role of the clown (*vidushaka*) and converses with the dancer. They talk of the futility of religious rites, the superiority of the soul over the mind, the ideal family and so forth. The object of their conversation is to satirize the foibles of society and its conventions. A secondary female usually accompanies the chief dancer and performs less elaborate dances throughout the performance.

Songs are set to classical Karnatic melodies (*raga*) and the hand drum (*mridangam*) produces lively rhythmic accompaniment. Verbal recitations of the rhythmic patterns repeated in the dance (*jati*) make for very exciting moments and enrich the variety of an evening's performance.

Originally, *gollakalapam* was an all-night event which continued over three consecutive evenings. At its inception, it was a popular part of temple festivals and rich families invited parties to their homes to celebrate marriages or other happy family occasions. Today the form is rarely performed, owing to the absence of sympathetic patrons. It is somewhat less complicated to perform than *kuchipudi*, its parent form, and there are fewer restrictions regarding the time, place and process of performance.

Gombeyatta

Shadow-puppet theatre of Karnataka, a state in the southwestern part of the subcontinent. Puppets are made of goatskin and the largest puppets are 30–40 in tall. When constructing puppets of Ganapati, the elephant-headed god, and the epic hero-gods Krishna and Rama, the puppeteer performs ritual sacrifices and takes care in preparing and cutting the hides.

Performance requires at least 50 puppets from a set of more than a hundred figures. Puppet size generally indicates social rank and puppets fall into the following categories: divinities, demons, humans, monkey generals, clowns, animals of various kinds and natural objects, such as plants and trees. For some stories, a group of characters are clustered together to form a single puppet. As in other forms of shadow theatre, several puppets may be needed to represent the various moods of a single character.

A company of shadow players consists of the puppeteer, several male members of his family, his wife, who plays the harmonium, sings and speaks the female roles and a *tabla* drummer who also speaks the voices of some male characters. Three or four manipulators are needed to produce a shadow-puppet show and the number of instrumentalists may vary, depending on the wealth of the company. The construction of the stage, its size, shape and location, follow the pattern of TOLLU BOMMALU.

It is thought that about 300 families of shadow puppeteers make their living in Karnataka state. The Karnataka Chitrakala Parishath of Bangalore has pioneered collection and preservation of puppets and supports artists in maintaining their art.

Shadow performances in Karnataka are closely connected to religious holidays. Companies affiliated with particular temples must perform on demand, since temple authorities support them financially during the year. The main seasons for religious festivals are February–April and September–October. Plays are adapted from stories in the *Ramayana* and *Mahabharata* epics.

Gopalila

A simple form of itinerant glove-puppet theatre of Orissa state. *Gopa* refers to the cowherd boys in the life of Lord Krishna and *lila* means 'play'. Also called *kundhei nata*. Puppets are made of wood and paper and their bodies are padded with cloth, the lower half being covered with a long skirt.

Puppeteers usually travel in pairs from village to village carrying their basket of puppets and a small box-like stage, large enough to mask the performer while he manipulates the puppets above his head. The second member of the party sits nearby, playing the drum (*pakhavaj*), singing and narrating incidents from the life of Lord Krishna. Religious occasions, especially those related to Krishna, provide puppeteers with the opportunity to entertain local villagers and to earn a living. Few performers are active today.

Jatra

The most popular regional theatre form in the rural areas of Bengal and among Bengali-speaking people of neighbouring Bihar, Orissa, Assam and Tripura. It also holds sway over village audiences in Bangladesh (formerly East Bengal, and later East Pakistan), where Bengali is spoken. Versions of the form have been created in the Oriyan language as well and will be discussed later.

Jatra means 'procession'. The form may have come into existence in the 16th century as a part of the Vaishnava devotional movement, introduced by Chaitanya, which swept the population into its fold through songs, dances and plays designed to propagate the faith. The earliest extant *jatra* scripts (*pala*) date from the late 18th century. Prior to that plays were preserved as a part of the oral tradition of the region.

Up to the early 19th century, *jatra* plays focused on religious themes and were instructive and moralistic in tone. Companies of actors were owned and managed by the chief singer or actor. In the 19th century, amateurs, mostly the sons of the bourgeois of Calcutta, developed their own *jatra* groups and chose secular themes for their subject matter rather than traditional religious fare. This led the older companies to adapt the secular stories as well. With the advent of the modern theatre movement in the mid 19th century, *jatra* borrowed the scenic displays of the proscenium-arch stage and imitated the Western style of acting and writing that was beginning to be popular among the middle and upper class of Calcutta. From the late 19th to the mid 20th century, *jatra* maintained its rural audiences, but urban audiences viewed its music, tone and style as old-fashioned and corrupt. It did not return to favour in urban areas until 1947, when the Communist Party employed it to win sympathetic support for its cause.

Jatra companies are generally professional and itinerant, booking throughout the Bengali-speaking regions of India. Today some 20 major troupes operate from their central headquarters in Calcutta. There, an agent books shows over the telephone confirming engagements in the tea estates of Assam, in the steel towns and coal-mining centres of the northeast or anywhere along the way that a group can afford to pay for the services of a *jatra* company. Troupes are dispatched to a locale for a flat fee, including food and shelter. Actors are hired by the company manager for the season, written contracts protect the interests of both parties and wages are paid according to a scale. Star performers' wages are handsome by Indian standards. Comedians and vocalists are paid somewhat less.

In the early history of *jatra*, actor-managers ran companies and exercised artistic control. Today, the owner-manager is normally not an artist but an entrepreneur who seeks a profit on his business and who has little motive other than to please the public no matter what the artistic consequences.

Generally, actors come from the lower strata of society, joining companies at an early age because they fall in love with the romance of fame, fortune and travel. Boys aged 11 and 12 who join *jatra* companies are rigorously trained to sing, dance and act in *jatra* style. Frailer youths eventually train to play the female characters and those with powerful voices and strong bodies act the heroes and villains. Actors with a natural sense of humour become the comedians.

The *jatra* season begins in earnest in September, at the end of the monsoon, and extends to May or early June when the heavy rains return. A lucrative time for *jatra* in Bengali villages coincides with the major religious festivals, *Durga Puja* in late September and early October, *Kali Puja* three weeks later, and *Ratha Jatra* and *Manasa Puja* later in the year. The marriage of a daughter, the birth of a son or the winning of a lawsuit serve as an occasion of rejoicing and reason for a family, wealthy village merchant or headman to sponsor a *jatra* performance.

Jatra is highly melodramatic in character, with a liberal dose of songs and dramatic scenes. Actors are adept at vocal projection and can play before thousands of patrons out of doors without the aid of microphones. Among the more interesting of the old *jatra* characters is the Conscience (*bibek*) who is an allegorical figure who moves in and out of the action, commenting on its meaning and foretelling the consequences of evil deeds. The character of Fate (*niyati*), like that of the Conscience, comments on the action and warns characters of potential dangers. Traditionally this character is played by an actress.

The acting area (*asar*) is usually on ground level, covered with cloth mats (*durries*) or carpets and bounded by short bamboo poles linked together by string. Or a low, square wooden platform is used. The platform is connected to the dressing room by a rampway marked by bamboo posts or a wooden construction in the shape of a ramp. The ramp serves as an extension of the acting area and is used for dramatic effects, similar to those of the *hanamichi* in KABUKI theatres in Japan.

The audience enfolds the whole acting area creating a sense of intimacy in the playing, even when thousands of spectators gather on the ground, sit on chairs, stand on the verandas of nearby houses, or hang from the boughs of trees to watch. Women usually sit separately from the men.

Scenes flow rapidly one into the other, punctuated by songs which mark act intervals. The acting area is regarded as a neutral space, even when performing on a proscenium stage, to which meaning is assigned depending on the play's action. Scenery is not necessary and, indeed, would intrude. Experiments with scenery were undertaken in the 19th century in imitation of Western theatre practices; ultimately they failed.

Jatra music is provided by a drum (*pakhwaj*), harmonium, violin, clarinet or flute and bell-metal cymbals. Musicians normally sit at one side of the acting area so that they have a full view of the stage, the ramp and the dressing room. Normally a prompter sits with them, following the action in the script.

The performance begins with a musical concert which continues for an hour or two before the dramatic action starts. The concert is divided into two parts. In part one, evening melodies (*raga*) are played. Part two emphasizes fast-pace rhythms and virtuoso drumming. The concert attracts spectators to the playing area and entertains those who have already gathered. Mood music is inserted throughout a performance to accentuate a bit of dramatic business, to heighten the melodramatic sentiments of a scene or to underscore a character's emotional state.

The performance space is lit by a variety of means, ranging from simple oil torches in remote villages, to petromax pressure lamps, electric bulbs and even fluorescent lights in areas where there is access to better equipment. No attempt is made to vary the intensity of illumination or to control colour.

A chair is the only furniture found on stage. Like the stage itself, it is regarded as a neutral object until it is endowed with meaning. It may serve as a throne, a bed, the steps of a temple, the shrine itself, whatever is demanded by the action.

In the early 1960s, *jatra* underwent something of a revival among the middle classes of Calcutta. Before that time, it had been regarded as 'folksy' and not worth the attention of serious theatre patrons. In 1961, a *jatra* festival was held in the palace courtyard of the Shabhabazar Rajas in north Calcutta. It was a great success and has been repeated yearly with renewed acclaim.

Periodicals and newspapers devote space to *jatra*. *Jatra* scripts may be found in paperback editions in stalls and shops along the streets of Calcutta. And in 1968 Phanibhusan Bidyabinod became the first *jatra* artist honoured by the Sangeet Natak Akademi in New Delhi for his services to the art.

The Communist Party made use of *jatra*, as of other popular forms of rural theatre elsewhere in India, to propagate its political messages. In the 1930s and 40s, plays were written in *jatra* style and artists were recruited to the Communist cause. Since that time, artists have taken a neutral political position so they may please the widest possible audience. In their headquarters it is not uncommon to find pictures of Communist Party leaders at home and abroad alongside those of popular Western politicians and Indian and Western religious leaders and prophets. In recent years the form has served as the model for various contemporary stage directors, actors and playwrights who have experimented with the application of contemporary social issues through the adaptation of the form.

The *jatra* of Bengal was introduced to the neighbouring state of Orissa in the 19th century. Local Orissi troupes soon took up the form and became popular in rural areas. *Jatra* of Orissa is similar to the Bengali version in most respects. However,

the parties of actors prefer to use the words opera and *natya* to describe their work rather than the term *jatra*.

In the Orissi form, the entrance and exit passageway, literally the 'flower way' (*puspa patha*), connects the low temporary wooden stage to the dressing room (*vesha ghara*). Plays are written in the Oriyan language following the structure and style of Bengali *jatra*. During the independence movement from the early 20th century up to 1947, Orissa *jatra* companies launched veiled attacks on their British rulers. Like Bengali *jatra*, Oriyan works emphasize virtuous upright characters pitted against villains and blackguards. Comic scenes add variety and spice to an all-night performance and sustain the interest of the audience.

Kariyala

Also spelled *kariala*. A rural theatre form of Hindu villages in Himachal Pradesh state in northern India.

The performance space or arena (*akhara*) is located between hillocks, permitting spectators to see the action easily. Musicians sit at one side of the playing area and the actors make a slow procession through the spectators from the dressing room to the playing area. As is typical in many rural settings, the men sit together on mats (*durries*) on one side and women huddle on the other. Children crowd close to the playing area to get a good view of the action and are carried home or join their parents in the early hours of the morning, when the all-night performance is over. Costumes are usually contemporary local dress to which brightly coloured headdresses and cloth pieces are added. Like BHAND JASHNA, *kariyala* can be performed during the day as well as at night.

Performances begin when a clown and a female character dance and pantomime as the chorus sings songs of praise to the deities. Plays are loosely structured, simple stories built around character types and their acts (*swang*). Satire and the reinforcement of well-known moral lessons characterize *kariyala*. Stories about moneylenders, village policemen, shepherds, religious medicants (*sadhu*) and old men who marry young wives are popular fare.

Kathakali

A major dance drama of Kerala state, south India. It has gained a considerable international reputation in recent years for its vigorous masculine style of physical movement, bold superhuman characterizations and vivid emotionalism. Dance, music and acting blend in dramatizations of stories adapted from the *Ramayana* and *Mahabharata* epics and the *Purana*.

Kathakali emerged in the 17th century, borrowing heavily from various theatre and dance forms of a region rich in cultural traditions. Ritual elements and emphasis on elaborate facial and eye expressions and hand gestures were perhaps adapted from earlier KUTIYATTAM. Its devotional character, style of dance, movement and music may have been borrowed from KRISHNATTAM. *Kathakali*'s direct predecessor was *ramanattam*, a form of theatre in which plays were composed from events adapted from the *Ramayana*. It is a popular belief that *ramanattam* was created because the Maharaja of Kottayam was jealous of the popularity of *krishnattam* and developed his own form of theatre as a form of self-aggrandizement.

When it became apparent that the fledgeling form of theatre needed a broader base for stories than the *Ramayana* provided, enthusiastic playwrights and patrons came forward to create dramas which included a wide range of popular epic material. *Ramanattam* then became known as *kathakali*, which literally means 'story play'. *Kathakali*'s patrons included rulers and rich landowners. The actors were Nairs, a caste trained in martial-art techniques which were long used in Kerala to develop soldiers to engage in ritual battle. Today actors hail from many different castes and communities, although prominent *kathakali* actors are Nairs.

Actor training is a long and arduous process, often taking from six to ten years to complete. As in many of the world's great art forms, it takes a lifetime to achieve greatness. Training usually begins between the ages of 10 and 14. Traditionally the sons of actors were trained in the art by their fathers, near relatives or trusted teachers.

Today the selection of potential candidates is a difficult task because so much time and energy is invested in the student once he is selected to participate in a programme, that the teachers must have a keen eye for spotting potential talent in the very young. Once selected, the student undergoes extensive body training to develop flexibility and the stamina needed to endure long hours of performance. Stress is placed on eye and facial exercises, and on mastery of an elaborate code of about 600 hand gestures.

The training day begins before dawn and extends until just before midnight. During a typical day, dance sequences suited to specific plays are taught. The rhythm and tempo of the action must be drilled into the physical being. And choreographic sections, including gestures, facial expressions and foot work, are committed to memory. Play texts (*attakatha*) are also learned by heart.

Actors do not speak, so the ideas of a play are conveyed through the lyrics of the song, sung by two singers, and by the actor's hand gestures, facial expressions, and body movements. Therefore precision and size of visual expression are crucial. The lead singer (*ponnani*) holds a heavy brass gong, striking it with a curved stick made of banana root. The second singer plays large bell-brass cymbals. The singers interweave their voices throughout the performance moving systematically through individual verses and dialogue portions of the text in a style of singing known as *sopana*. Three chief drums accompany the dramatic action. The large horizontal drum (*maddalam*) is carried across the waist of the drummer. It provides flexibility of pace and intonation. The vertical drum (*centa*) is used for battle scenes and scenes which require special sound effects and high drama. The small hourglass drum (*itekka*) has a delicate sound and is especially effective when female characters take stage. A harmonium keeps the singers on pitch and the conch shell (*sanka*) is used when gods or important ritual events are at hand. A close bond must be established between the musicians and the actors in order to create a unified dramatic effect.

Performance begins around nine or ten at night following an elaborate percussion overture and preliminaries danced by young apprentices. These take about two to three hours to complete. Any spot is considered appropriate for a *kathakali* performance – temple compound, family home, large hall or proscenium-arch stage. Although a performance seems designed to be played on a rectangular space, 20 to 30 ft square and demarcated by four poles, audiences prefer to gather at the front, near the brass lamp, opposite the musicians. No matter how audiences organize themselves, actors still play to the front.

The atmosphere at *kathakali* is charged with excitement, with children and women relegated to the front and to one side of the house and men arranged on the other.

Troupes of actors, musicians and backstage technicians and costumers, who are commissioned to perform, are able to choose a play at short notice from a limited repertory. The exact play may not be decided until a few hours before the performance begins, just in time for the actors to get into appropriate costumes and makeup.

A programme may include several favourite scenes from various *kathakali* plays or a single play performed from beginning to end. In village performances, shows conclude around 6 a.m. A band of enthusiastic devotees, awake to the very end, trudges wearily home with the sound of drums still ringing in their ears.

Kathputli

The string puppet theatre of Rajasthan in northern India. *Katha* means 'story' and *putli* means 'puppet'.

The puppets are doll figures, up to 2 ft tall, manipulated by a puppeteer who stands above and works the puppets by strings connected to the head, waist and hands. Usually puppets do not have legs and feet and the lower part of their bodies is covered by a long skirt.

Puppeteers carve the heads and trunk of the body from mango wood, patterning the figures after traditional designs, such as those seen in traditional Rajput paintings. The figures are dressed in colourful turbans and crowns to identify their social status and they sport painted beards and moustaches. Women too have a special iconography. Puppet arms are stuffed with cloth to give them a human appearance. Properties, such as swords and shields, may be stitched to the hands. Popular animal figures include camels, horses and snakes.

Today puppet figures are sold in government emporia throughout the country, and special puppets and dolls are mass-produced to satisfy the tourist trade. These puppets are not used in the puppet theatre.

Puppeteers come from the Bhatt community and are known as *nat bhatt*, 'those who perform plays'. They lead nomadic lives travelling from village to village. Troupes of puppeteers consist of the main puppeteer (*sutradhar*, literally 'string puller'), an assistant, usually one of his brothers or sons, a narrator-singer (*bhagavat*) and musicians, including drummer, cymbal player and harmonium player. The puppeteer's wife also may sing during a performance. An unusual instrument which accompanies Rajasthani puppets is a shrill, reed-like bamboo vibrator. It attracts attention to the puppets' vigorous movements and helps to sustain spectators' interest.

Plays centre on the heroic deeds of Amar Singh Rathor, a Rajput warrior king, Prithvi Raj Chauhan of Ajmer and Delhi and King Vikramaditya of Ujjain. The events from the lives of these famous kings provide ample material for the puppeteers to demonstrate their expert skill with the puppets, such as juggling, tumbling, horseback riding, swordsmanship and dancing. Through clever manoeuvres of the strings puppeteers endow the figures with life.

A stage may be arranged anywhere there is room to stand two wooden cots (*charpoy*) on end and stretch cloth masking to create a proscenium arch, known to puppeteers as the 'Taj Mahal'. A dark curtain about 3 ft high is stretched just behind the proscenium to mask the puppeteers. Electric lights, torches or coconut-oil lamps illuminate the acting area.

Today, although *kathputli* is among the best-known of India's puppet forms, it has deteriorated to little more than a sideshow entertainment. Hardly more than an hour is taken to demonstrate the various tricks of the little figures. Unfortunately, the dramatic urge has been replaced by sheer entertainment to satisfy the cravings of the spectators.

Khyal

A popular village theatre form in Uttar Pradesh

and Rajasthan states in northwest India. Also known as *khyala*. Some evidence suggests that *khyal* existed as early as the 18th century and that the city of Agra was its home.

Various styles of *khyal* exist and are named after a city, for example *Jaipuri khyal*, a community, for example *Gadhaspa khyal*, an acting style, for example *abhinaya khyal*, or the author of the work, for example *Alibaksh khyal*. Subtle differences in the music and language of performance, as well as staging techniques, distinguish the various styles.

Khyal stages are unusually elaborate. A main stage 3 to 4 ft high is built as well as an adjacent acting area, either a lower-level stage (*laghu* or 'little stage') or an area demarcated by white sheets spread on the ground. At the four corners of the main stage platform, trunks of banana trees are placed in the ground and decorative flags are strung between the pillars to provide a festive appearance. Behind the main platform stage a balcony-like structure 12 to 20 ft tall is erected on poles or supported by the roof of a nearby house. The balcony is wide enough to hold a few actors and is curtained at the sides and back. The high platform stage is connected to the main stage by a wooden ladder. Thus, *khyal* performances use three distinct acting areas to achieve a dramatic effect. Petromax lanterns, strategically placed at the corners of the main stage and at the front of the balcony, give off a harsh undirected white light which illuminates both acting areas and audience (originally oil lamps cast a flickering yellow light over the acting area). Today electric and fluorescent lights are fast replacing the petromax lamps as sources of illumination. The audience sits on three sides.

Prior to the building of the stage, there is a ceremony in which a pole is installed at the performance site, perhaps an ancient reminder of ritual practices found in the Sanskrit drama.

A performance begins with prayers to Ganapati, the elephant-headed god, and includes invocations to other gods and goddesses. This is followed by comic antics by clowns. The main play which follows is mythological, semi-historical or fanciful.

An accent on melodrama and evocation of moods of romance, valour and pathos are typical.

Like other rural theatre forms, music accompanies performance, played on *nagara* or *dholak* drums, bell-metal cymbals and harmonium. The human voice provides a strong melodic line and drums set various tempos for the action.

Male actors play all roles. The costumes of wealthy companies are elaborate and derived from long-vanished historical periods and styles. The action is carefully controlled by the director-producer (*ustad*) who sits in a chair on the main stage where he carefully follows the sequence of events in his prompt script.

Krishnattam

A religious dance drama performed at the famous Guruvayur Temple in the pilgrimage town of the same name in the coastal region of Kerala state, south India. The form was conceived by a Zamorin king, Raja Manaveda, in the mid 17th century as a means of glorifying the name of Krishna, one of Lord Vishnu's most beloved incarnations. *Attam* is 'story' in local Malayalam language, hence *krishnattam*, 'dramas of Krishna'.

A legend says that Manaveda, a devout follower of Krishna, prayed that he might see the god, who had been seen by a seer at Guruvayur Temple. To his amazement Krishna appeared before him as a small boy playing in the temple courtyard. When Manaveda reached out to touch the boy the vision vanished and a peacock feather in Krishna's hair was left behind. Thereafter generations of actors who portrayed Krishna wore this feather in their crown until it was destroyed by fire several decades ago.

The legend continues that, inspired by his miraculous vision, Manaveda wrote *Krishnagita*, recounting incidents from the life of Krishna. Based on the *Bhagavata Purana*, it serves as the basis for the eight plays comprising the entire dramatic repertory of the form.

Given the fact that Kerala possesses a long history of notable forms of theatre, such as KUTIYATTAM and KATHAKALI, it is not surprising that *krishnattam* shares many features with them, while retaining its own individual characteristics. As in *kutiyattam* and *kathakali*, dancer-actors interpret a text in performance through a highly sophisticated code of gesture language. Nonetheless, preliminary studies reveal that the meaning of many of the shared gestures and their execution is different from that of all the other Kerala performing arts. The dance movements closely resemble those of *kathakali* but they have their own definite character which stresses a lyrical, feminine quality of group movement rather than the masculine vigour of *kathakali* or the more abstract angularity of *kutiyattam*.

Makeup patterns for mythological characters – humans, demons and animals – reveal striking similarities to those of *kathakali* while, at the same time, they display their own flair. To a sophisticated theatregoer, the makeup, costumes and ornaments, which, at a casual glance, seem the same as those of *kathakali*, have shapes and patterns which could only belong to *krishnattam*.

The actors of the one troupe which performs *krishnattam* are all male devotees of the god. Many were offered in grateful service to god and the temple when they were small boys, in exchange for a boon that was granted to their parents. Others came freely to devote their lives to Krishna's service. The high level of devotion of the participants is echoed by the religious fervour of pilgrims who watch the performances.

Traditionally pilgrims, who come from all over India to worship at the temple, pay temple authorities to have a *krishnattam* performed as a part of their ritual sacrifice. The devotee may choose to have any of the eight stories enacted. Favourite stories are associated with requests for particular boons. The play which includes Krishna's marriage is auspicious for a devotee celebrating a marriage; the story which depicts Krishna's miraculous birth ensures the birth of a male child to barren parents; and the story which shows the destruction of the wicked King Kamsa will ward off the evil eye. If all eight plays are performed in sequence, they must be followed by the re-enactment of the first night's play showing the birth of Krishna (it is inauspicious to end a sequence with Krishna's death).

Performances are generally held in the courtyard of the temple, northeast of the main shrine; however, a special proscenium-arch stage has been constructed outside the temple compound so that non-Hindus who have a desire to see *krishnattam* may do so. In recent years, *krishnattam* has been played in towns and cities elsewhere in India and in Europe and the United States. Any open space about 15 ft square with room around it for spectators may serve as an appropriate place for performance. Scenery is not used and a simple stool symbolizes a throne, mountain or bench. A 4-ft-high bell-metal oil lamp provides a flickering glow to the performance. In the proscenium house, two scoop lamps situated on the floor to the right and left of the oil lamp illuminate the space. This lighting deadens and flattens out costumes and ornaments which were designed to be seen under lamp light.

A performance takes place between 9 p.m. and 3 a.m. It may only be presented after the temple rituals are concluded and before the doors of the *sanctum sanctorum* have been opened for the morning prayers. The reason for the strict time frame is explained in a charming story. Many years ago, when the doors of the temple shrine were inadvertently left open, the effigy of Krishna was so moved by the music that it came to life and danced with the actors causing considerable dismay to the temple priests. Care is now taken not to allow the same incident to happen again.

Texts of the plays are sung by two chief singers in the *sopana* style of singing popular in Kerala. The actor-dancers do not speak. Basic rhythmic patterns are played on two *maddalam* drums struck at both ends and suspended around the waist of the drummers, an hourglass drum (*idakka*) played at the drummer's side, and bell-metal cymbals. A harmonium provides the pitch around which the singers weave their intricate melodies. A conch shell is played during auspicious dramatic actions.

In recent years, owing to the continual flood of pilgrims that come to the temple to perform austerities, *krishnattam* is performed nearly every night of the year. The performers are now unionized and the company divided into two groups that alternate in performing and thus no one is exploited. Experts complain that the death of the older generation of artists has led to a serious decline in the quality of *krishnattam*. The performance of the same material over and over again has led to a lethargy among artists whose work has become routinized. No new work may be added to the repertory and only on rare occasions is the full cycle of plays performed.

Kuchipudi

Kuchipudi is the name of a village in the Krishna River delta of Andhra Pradesh, south India. It has given its name to the religious dance drama performed by male Brahmins of that village, as well as to solo concert dances performed by men or women in this style.

The village of Kuchipudi was granted in perpetuity to Hindu actor-devotees by Abdul Husan Qutab Shah, the Muslim Nawab of Golconda, sometime between 1672 and 1687. As early as 1505–9, the Brahmin artists had performed before King Vira Narasimha Raya of the Vijayanagar Empire. Some authorities claim *kuchipudi* began even before this because it is similar to *bharata natyam*, the oldest surviving form of Indian classical dance. In the 17th century Siddhendra Yogi, called the father of *kuchipudi*, composed important dance dramas for players and required all male Brahmins of Kuchipudi village to take an oath to perform the role of Satyabhama, Krishna's jealous wife, in his drama *Bhamakalapam*, at least once during their lifetime. The practice continues today and the Brahmin men and boys of Kuchipudi village who practise the art are the direct descendants of ancestors who received Siddhendra Yogi's instruction three centuries ago.

Kuchipudi is the best-known 'classical' form of dance drama in the Telugu language. Like BHAGA-VATA MELA, its plays deal with the incarnations of the god Vishnu. The following dance dramas are part of the *kuchipudi* repertory: *Prahlad Charitram, Usha Parinayam, Sashirekha Parinayam, Mohini Rukmangada, Harishchandra Nataka, Gayopakhyanam, Rama Natakam* and *Rukmini Kalyanam*. The dramas *Bhamakalapam* and *Gollakalapam* have become so popular that they are now regarded as separate performance forms (see BHAMAKALAPAM, GOLLAKALAPAM).

Kuchipudi performance style is similar to *bhagavata mela* but is executed with more sophistication and more attention to the classical hand gestures (*hasta*) described in the *Natyasastra*. *Kuchipudi* performers exhibit considerable feats of physical skill, executing intricate foot work and using difficult hand gestures while dancing on the sharp edge of a metal plate with a round-bottomed water pot balanced on their heads.

Kuchipudi performers tour constantly. Usually the troupe improvises an acting area in an open space before a temple, such as the Ramalingeshwara Temple of Kuchipudi village. Four poles are firmly planted at the corners of the playing area and a thatched roof is stretched overhead. The spectators sit around the area and witness performances through the night. A curtain is used for entrances of characters and illumination is provided by torches fed by castor oil and held by village washermen. Resin powder is thrown on the torches to produce spectacular flashes of light which accentuate the entrances of important characters.

The performance begins with a prayer to the goddess Amba. Following this, a young boy enters carrying the flagstaff (*jarjara*) of Indra. Then the lamp and incense are carried on and a dancer performs sacrifices. Another dancer, carrying a pitcher of sacred water, sprinkles and sanctifies the acting area. The stage manager (*sutradhara*) enters carrying a crooked stick and announces the title of the play. He joins the musicians and then he accompanies them by playing cymbals during the performance. These sacrifices and preliminaries are in direct imitation of practices described in the *Natyasastra* that are some two millennia old.

Stage attendants hold a curtain behind which a dancer enters wearing a mask of Ganapati, the elephant-headed god of good fortune. The curtain is removed and a dance follows. The curtain is brought forward once again and the chief character performs an elaborate dance entrance using the curtain to tease the audience. Eventually he tosses it aside and is fully exposed to the waiting spectators. Special dances (*patra pravesha daru*) follow, some emphasizing abstract form and style, and some requiring elaborate gesture-language coordinated with the precise meaning of the songs. Songs and dances form part of major scenes in the play being performed, adding variety and emphasing dramatic moments. Humorous and witty remarks are also interspersed in Telugu, which is the regional language.

Music in classical Karnatic style is played on instruments, such as the *mridangam* drum, the violin played in the south Indian manner, transverse bamboo flute, *tutti*, brass cymbals and harmonium.

Rich costumes and ornaments are characteristic. Occasionally, artists attempt to incorporate wing-and-drop settings, but traditionally performance takes place without scenery and properties allowing for total focus on the performers and permitting the free play of the spectator's imagination. Should a particular performer excel, he is rewarded with necklaces of fresh flowers. Enthusiastic spectators will stop the dramatic action to honour a favourite artist.

On the concert stage, dances adapted from the dance-drama repertory are now performed as solo items. Master-teachers have also choreographed new items using themes from a variety of sources while retaining the fundamental characteristics of the form.

Owing to its popular reputation as a branch of classical Indian dance, few members of urban audiences are aware that *kuchipudi* is still practised as a full-scale dramatic performance in the villages of Andhra Pradesh. Nor are they aware of *kuchipudi*'s close association with the religious convictions of rural performers and the ritual significance of the dance drama in village life.

Kuravanji

Literally, the 'dances' (*anji*) of the Kurava people, a nomadic clan of hunters who inhabit the hilly regions of Andhra Pradesh, whose women are said to be excellent fortune tellers. Also called *kuram* and *kuluva natakam*.

Kuravanji originated in the 17th century, perhaps as an offshoot of dance and song entertainments presented at holy shrines in Andhra Pradesh by bands of actors during festival seasons.

Performances in Tamil Nadu state begin with a procession in praise of Sri Vighneswara, the elephant-headed god. Then the clown (*kattiakaran*, also a character in THERUKOOTHU) announces the gist of the story to be enacted. During the proceedings, the heroine appears with her maids and, after being announced, she dances to depict her yearnings and sufferings. Her companions, usually spritely maidens, tease her as she tries to persuade them to convey her love messages. She implores the clouds, the wind,

birds and the moon to act as intermediaries, but to no avail. The lover she is pining for never makes an appearance in any of the plays. Then a gypsy woman (*kuratthi*) appears and boasts of her expertise. At the request of the young heroine she reads her palm. The heroine denies that she is in love but eventually admits that she is. The gypsy is richly rewarded for her efforts. Then a hunter (*kurava*) enters the scene in search of his wife, the gypsy. She accuses him of infidelity but he convinces her of his innocence. The play comes to a happy conclusion.

The form has been used for modern stories as well. Maharaja Serfoji II (1798–1833) taught students world geography through *kuravanji*: the gypsy's song and dance presented the scientific material in an entertaining way. S. D. S. Yogi, a distinguished contemporary poet of Tamil Nadu state, recently composed a *kuravanji* entitled *Bhavani*, centring on the gifts of the river Bhavani after the construction of a dam.

Kutiyattam

Perhaps India's oldest continuously performed theatre form and one of the few surviving art forms of the ancient world. *Kutiyattam* is unique to the state of Kerala, a lush tropical region located on the southwestern coast of the Indian subcontinent. As early as the 10th century, *kutiyattam* seems to have been 'reformed' by King Kulashekara Varman. A high stage of development, at this early point in its history, suggests an origin linking it with the traditions of ancient Sanskrit theatre.

Kutiyattam preserves a tradition of performing plays in Sanskrit, the classical language. Plays by well-known playwrights of ancient drama – BHASA, Harsha and Mahendra Vikrama Pallava – are popular in the *kutiyattam* repertory. In addition to using Sanskrit, actors use the Prakrit language and an old form of Malayalam, the regional language of Kerala, to convey the contents of the plays, much as ancient actors are thought to have used various regional dialects in their performances.

The artists who have preserved this unique theatre form with such dedication over ten centuries are members of the Cakyar caste, a sub-branch of temple servants. Traditionally, it has been their duty to perform *kutiyattam* as a ritual sacrifice to the chief deity in selected temples and to entertain the spectators who assemble there to pay their homage. Musicians who play the *mizhavu*, a large pot-shaped drum peculiar to *kutiyattam*, are traditionally of the Nambiyar communities, while women of the same social group, the Nangyar, act female roles, as well as play the small bell-metal cymbals which sustain the basic tempo of production. Today members of other castes may study *kutiyattam* and appear on stage. Members of other castes may not act in temple performances, however, because that would violate agreements made between temple authorities and the hereditary caste artists.

Kutiyattam has developed the only permanent traditional theatre structures (*kuttampalam*) in India. About nine theatres have been built in various temples in Kerala since the 16th century, the largest and most impressive in Vatukumnathan Temple in Trichur. The interior of this impressive structure is about 72 x 55 ft and, like all existing structures, it is rectangular in shape. According to traditional practice, the theatre building is a separate structure located in the walled compound of the temple and situated in front and to the right of the main shrine. From the solid base of the building, pillars support a high central roof. The stage of the Vatakumnathan Temple is a large, square, raised, stone platform, the front edge of which divides the whole structure in half. Clusters of three pillars extend upward from each of the four corners of the stage to support an interior roof reminiscent of those used for *Nō* stages in Japan. A back wall separates the dressing room from the stage. A narrow door in the wall upstage left is used for entrances and a door upstage right is reserved for exits. Downstage, between the doors, the large pot-shaped drums are suspended in heavy wooden stands. The surface of the stage, in all but a few of the theatres, is convex which allows easy drainage of the stage after washing. Intricate wooden carvings of decorative floral motifs, deities and mythological characters are all but unseen to the spectators who watch the performance under the flickering but weak light of a large bell-metal lamp placed downstage centre.

A typical *kutiyattam* performance extends over a period of several days. During the first few days, the characters in the play are introduced to the audience and historical incidents about them are explored in considerable detail. On the final day of the performance the entire action of the play is performed in chronological order from beginning to end, just as it was written. Performance begins around 9 p.m., after the final rituals have been performed before the deity in the *sanctum sanctorum* of the temple. Segments of the performance finish between midnight and 3 a.m., just before the morning rituals are performed in the *sanctum*. On the last day the performance lasts until 5 or 6 a.m.

Elaborately dressed actors with fantastical makeup and headdresses perform the various roles of mythological characters, gods and demons. They use an elaborate code of gesture-language, chanted speech and exaggerated facial and eye expressions. Much of the action is accompanied by the *mizhavu* drums, small bell-metal cymbals, a small hourglass shaped drum (*idakka*), a wind instrument resembling an oboe (*kuzhal*) and a conch shell (*sankha*).

Ritual actions occur before and during performances, reflecting the sacred character of performance and the great respect for religion shown by the actors. Ancient manuals of instruction are consulted by the actors in order to ensure that correct procedures are followed.

Kutiyattam is performed once a year at Vatukumnathan Temple and nearby Irinjala-gauda Temple. Other temple performances are rare owing to the decline in interest and the fluctuating fortunes of the large temple complexes. Measures have been taken by the state and national government and private institutions and individuals to support *kutiyattam* through performances in theatres outside the temple compounds, in various towns and cities in Kerala and elsewhere in India, as well as tours to Western countries, where non-Hindus may see performances of this ancient art form.

Instruction in the art is provided in Kerala at three schools – the famous Kerala Kalamandalam in Cheruthuruthy village, a school run by Madhavan Cakyar at Irinjalagauda and that run by Margi in the capital city of Trivandrum. Although much effort has been made to bring local, national and international attention to *kutiyattam*, its importance to the history of theatre has still not been fully realized in India or outside the country.

Maach

A form of sung folk theatre popular in villages of central India. *Maach* is thought to have originated in Rajasthan about 300 years ago; today it is found principally in villages of Madhya Pradesh state. *Maach* was introduced to the Malwa area of Rajasthan by Sri Gopalji Guru who is reputed to have composed several *maach* plays and who served as the first of a long line of rural playwrights.

Originally *maach* was associated with the holiday festivals surrounding Holi, a spring celebration. Today it may be performed on any festival occasion, usually on a raised stage approximately 15 x 12 ft built at the end of an open space in a village. A curtain at the back serves as scenery and a $1\frac{1}{2}$-ft-wide border stretches across the front of the stage, masking the feet of the actor-dancers.

Maach is a sung drama into which some dialogue may be introduced and folk dances added for spice and variety. Performance is accompanied by *sarangi*, the classical north Indian stringed instrument, *dhol* drum, and harmonium.

Traditionally men have played all roles, although today some women distinguish themselves in the female parts. Well-known performers earn their reputations because of their excellent singing voices.

Performance usually begins around 10.30 or 11 p.m. and continues until dawn. It begins with a sung *bhisti raag* which, like similar ritual overtures in other Indian theatre forms, is meant to sanctify the proceedings and call villagers to the playing area. Next a set of preliminary dances and songs (*bhisti-farrasan samvad*) provide an overture to the drama.

Among the important characters is the *bidhab* or *shermarkhan*, a comical adviser or consultant to the chief character, frequently a king. The clown enlivens the performance. He knits together the various threads of the complicated plot and he converts songs into dialogue, thus interpreting their meaning to the spectators. Historical, social and religious plays satisfy the taste of village audiences for romantic sentiment charged with strong morals.

Naqal

A rural theatre form of Uttar Pradesh, Punjab and Kashmir states in north India. Also called *naqqal* and *nakkal*. It may have originated among lower-class Muslims during the Mughal era. The number of troupes has greatly declined in recent years.

Naqal plays stress farce and clowns mercilessly satirize the audience and provide fast-paced entertainment through their witty words and actions. Men play all roles. A troupe performs for weddings and other household celebrations in towns and villages. Any open space in a house, yard or street will suffice for the players who work in and among the crowd, confronting the spectators at close range.

Nautanki

Until recently one of the most beloved and popular forms of theatre in the heavily populated central Indo-Gangetic plain of north India, primarily Uttar Pradesh, Punjab, Rajasthan, Hariyana and Bihar states. A musical play which bears the name *The Story of Princess Nautanki* (*Shehzadi Nautanki*) may provide the origin of the name. It was popular in the 19th century and evidence solidly suggests that it was closely related to SVANGA and BHAGAT.

Nautanki's popularity is due in part to the strong singing voices of its actors, who train to reach audiences sometimes numbering in the thousands, and to catchy rhythms produced on kettle drums (*nakkara*). It is said that spectators make up their minds to attend a *nautanki* performance based on the reputation of the singers and the drummers. A typical company consists of 10 to 12 actors. Actors are generally Hindus of various lower castes; musicians are Muslims.

Nautanki may take place virtually anywhere, in an open space of a village, in a farmer's field, in the courtyard of a patron, in an enclosed proscenium theatre or under a tent (*shamyana*). A raised stage 3 to 4 ft high is erected. Actors may commandeer the balcony or veranda of a nearby house or a tree in the village if needed. In early times the site was demarcated by a special post of wood inserted with great ceremony by the company head several days before the stage was erected. Performance is hired to celebrate a special occasion – a wedding, birth of a male child, festival occasion or fair.

The usually serious and highly moralistic dramas stress melodrama and romantic love. They draw on mythology, history, semihistory, popular folklore and original sources. They are either epic or narrative in form. The stage manager (*ranga*) links diverse elements of the plot together. Following preliminary rituals, he informs spectators that they are going to see a particular story and the dramatic action commences.

Music is provided by small and large drums (*nakkara*). A *dholak* drum, bell-metal cymbals and harmonium may be added. *Nautanki* music is a blend of classical, folk and film music. Under the influence of film songs, musical style has changed enormously in recent years. The wooden *sarangi*, the classical north Indian stringed instrument, for example, is now often replaced by wind instruments, such as the clarinet. The dominant element of singing is broken by dialogue, simple dances incorporating film and folk elements, and improvised comic skits.

With the introduction of women performers after the 1930s, the predominantly male audiences demanded actions and dances which are somewhat provocative. In traditional companies young boys always play the female roles. Whatever the sex of the players, enthusiastic patrons make donations of money to the singers during the performance. The women take the welcome gift and stick it in their blouses and repeat the song or dance to please the adoring follower. In other companies the stage manager takes the money and names the donor loudly to the public indicating how much he gave to the player. Today, *nautanki* players find it difficult to survive in a society in which films dominate the public imagination and where television is on the verge of becoming readily accessible to millions of rural patrons. Troupe leaders usually hold odd jobs and assemble available players when commissioned to give a performance.

Two styles of *nautanki* dominate today. The style of the city of Hathras is regarded as the older and was popularized by Indarman and his pupil Natharam in the 19th century. They established a training centre (*akhara*) for disciples. The leaders of the group (*khalifa*) established strict discipline and as master-teachers exercised enormous control over the form. Natharam printed and distributed *nautanki* scripts to the voracious reading public of peasants and lower-caste townspeople, gaining for the style a wide popular following. Artists of the Hathras style sing in a high pitch and ornament their songs with elaborate flourishes. Performers work on simple raised platform stages with little or no scenic decorations, inviting the audience to use its imagination.

The second style, of the city of Kanpur, was created by Sri Krishna Pahalvan after 1913. His goal was to crack the tight *akhara* system which admitted no one other than those who adhered to the dictates of its teachers. He replaced the opening prayers with a chorus in simple metre sung by the entire cast, which proved popular with audiences. He accepted performers who demonstrated promise and inspiration in singing, regardless of length of training. Kanpur style singing is in a lower pitch and the dramatic story line is emphasized over vocal ornamentation. Typically the style incorporates great scenic detail. Wings and drops are used to set locale. 'The garden' and 'the court' are typical stock set pieces. This has forced audiences into a frontal juxtaposition to the acting area, virtually abandoning the three-sided or arena performance spaces with their neutral acting area typical of the Hathras style.

Nondi natakam

Literally, a 'play' (*natakam*) by 'one who limps' (*nondi*), that is, a one-legged person. Also called *ottraikkaal natakam*, *nondi natakam* was created in Tamil Nadu state in the late 17th or early 18th century and is performed in the region of Madurai city.

The play is narrated by an actor with one leg tied up to impersonate a one-legged thief. The thief sings about his escapades with a courtesan. She takes all his earnings and persuades him to replenish his funds by stealing. His obsession with debauchery is insatiable. Finally he travels to a distant town ruled by a local chieftain. He impresses the ruler as a man of means but at night he attempts to steal one of the royal horses. Caught in the act, the thief is brought to the ruler who orders the amputation of one of his hands and legs, a common punishment for thieves in mediaeval India. The cruel sentence is carried out. After a time, a saintly person finds the poor thief and takes pity on him by relieving his pain with soothing balm. He also offers spiritual counsel. The thief accepts his advice and goes to the temple to express his devotion. God appears and restores his hand and leg leaving no trace of mutilation. Obviously the play centres on the theme of forgiveness and devotion, but rustic, humorous vulgarities are sprinkled liberally throughout.

Pala

A dramatic form of Orissa state in eastern India that honours Satyapir, a deity worshipped by Hindus and Muslims. It is performed by groups of players who sit (baithaki) or stand (thhia). The chief player (gayaka) holds a yak's tail fly whisk and plays small bell-metal cymbals. The other players (palia) form a chorus. Preliminary rituals are said to closely resemble those described in the Natyasastra. Thhia pala has a high literary level. Humour is provided by one of the party. After each song the chief player explains the meaning of the text. Any open space may be used for a performance. Two groups of pala players may compete for prizes.

Pavai kathakali

A glove-puppet play of Kerala state, in which wooden dolls imitate various characters in the repertory of KATHAKALI dance drama. The figures are 1–1½ ft tall. Their faces are painted and bodies costumed in the distinctive patterns and colours of kathakali. A puppet is operated by a manipulator who sticks his middle finger into the head of the figure while thumb and little finger move its hands. At least four puppeteers are needed in performance, standing behind a curtain stretched between poles. They hold the glove puppets above their heads to perform.

Stories are drawn from the Mahabharata and follow the kathakali pattern of organization. Musical accompaniment is by bell-metal cymbals and cenda drum. The artists come from the village of Kavadi Parambu in Palghat district and are relatively secretive about their art form which they generally show only on religious occasions.

Pavai koothu

A glove-puppet theatre performed in Thiruchendoor city in Tamil Nadu. It may have originated in the 16th century. The language of performance is Tamil.

Plays centre on Vali, a female attendant of Shiva, and her love for Subramanya, one of Shiva's sons. Hence the name of the form: pavai, 'woman', and koothu, a 'play'. On Shiva's advice Vali was born to a deer in the forest. A hunter found her and he and his wife reared her. Seeing the beautiful maiden one day in the forest, Narada, divine troublemaker, hastened to tell Lord Subramanya. Infatuated by Narada's description, Subramanya disguised himself as an old bangle-seller and came to the hunter's cottage in the forest. Through a ruse, he took Vali far from her home and then revealed himself in his heavenly form. They embraced and received the blessings of Ganesha, who appeared to them in the form of an elephant, an auspicious sign.

Puppets are about a foot tall. Heads and arms are made of papier mâché. Costumes are constructed of cloth and garlanded with coconut fibre or paper. Performance is given by a single manipulator who sits cross-legged behind a wooden box which masks him from view. (This can be compared to WAYANG in Indonesia and Malaysia.) He is accompanied by an idakka drummer and a singer who keeps time with bell-metal cymbals. Popular tunes are sung, liberally borrowing from folk melodies of the region.

Pavaikuthu

Pava means 'figure of a shadow' and kuthu means 'play'; the shadow-puppet theatre of Kerala state, south India. Also called tholpavaikuthu.

Plays are based on a Tamil version of the Ramayana called Kambar Ramayana, named after Kambar, its author, and written for a Chola king in the 9th century. It has unique characteristics which distinguish it from other forms of shadow-puppet theatre in south India, including the fact that the people of the region in which the performance takes place speak Malayalam not Tamil, the language of the drama. *Pavaikuthu* is usually performed near the *sanctum sanctorum* of a Kali temple as a ritual form of entertainment for the goddess. Processions and general celebrations are part of every programme.

The short, stout silhouettes, as small as 4 in and as large as 3 ft tall, are made of thick, opaque antelope-doe skin, thought to be holy. The silhouettes projected on the screen appear as almost solid black, for only minimal perforations in the leather delineate costume and ornament, and unlike other shadow puppets in India, they are not translucent. The puppets are held tightly against the screen by a thorn pin or spike. The shadows are articulated by movable heads, arms and hands. Puppets of less important characters have no movable parts. The puppets (*ola pava*) are similar to Javanese WAYANG.

Performance is held in a specifically constructed enclosure (*kuthumadom*) which is about 42 ft long, 9 ft deep and 4 ft above ground level. These special stage houses are placed at an elevated end of a broad stretch of temple compound. The shadows face south, or in the direction the temple deity faces. The long narrow opening in the *kuthumadom* is completely draped to create a screen about 18 ft long and 5 ft high, the upper portion of which is white and the lower portion black.

Below the white screen a long strip of bamboo is stretched horizontally in which grooves are cut, and coconut halves or small earthen vessels are placed in the holes to serve as lamps to cast shadows on the screen. Manipulators squat below the white portion of the screen masked by the black curtain and operate the puppets from behind the lamps.

A performance usually begins when drums are played and a wick from the *sanctum sanctorum* of the Kali temple is brought in procession to the *kuthumadom* to light the wicks of the oil lamps. This ritual is called *kotti kayattam* which means 'installing the puppets to the sound of the drums'. Next a special ritual sacrifice is offered to Ganapati, the elephant-headed god of success and beginnings. After the installation ceremony, all but two of the puppets are removed from the screen.

Gangayati Patter and Muther Patter, the remaining characters, praise the master-teachers of *pavaikuthu*, past and present, invoke the blessing of specific gods and, if patronized by a family, bless the household. Then they provide a summary of the previous night's story which serves as a prologue to the events about to take place. The episodes of the local version of the *Ramayana* are enacted in sequence.

The conclusion to the story is the grand coronation of Rama. On this night a procession takes place, beginning from the innermost part of the temple to the *kuthumadom*, to pay homage to Rama whose spirit is worshipped in the puppet. The performance ends when the sacrifice to Ganapati is again performed, the clown puppet (*kirita pava*) performs a ritual, and finally Rama appears wearing his crown.

Prahlada nataka

Literally, the 'play' (*nataka*) of Prahlada. Some 40 village companies in the district of Ganjam in Orissa state in eastern India preserve a style of performing this play demonstrating the faith of the child-prince Prahlada, who worships the name of Vishnu despite the evil machinations of his wicked father-king. The play is thought to have been adapted from a classical text popularized by Raja Ramakrishna Deva Chotterai, a local ruler of the mid 19th century. A special mask endowed with great power is worn by the actor who plays Narasimha, the man-lion incarnation of Lord Vishnu, who ultimately destroys the wicked king.

Troupes enact the play on special festival occasions on a bleacher-like platform placed in an open field. The performing style includes dialogue and song, accompanied by the music of *mridangam* drums, harmonium, wind instrument (*mukha veena*), cymbals and conch shells. At the climax of the dramatic action, the actor dons the mask of the man-lion, becoming possessed. He must be forcibly restrained by attendants from inflicting harm on the person of the actor playing the king. Symbolically, when the king is killed by Vishnu, order is restored to the universe.

Putul nautch

Literally, 'dancing dolls'; a rod-puppet theatre in Bengal state in eastern India. In the past puppets

2 to 3 ft in height were constructed of plaster on a bamboo frame covered by banana leaves to give shape to the different parts of the body. Nowadays dolls are carved from wood, hollowed to reduce weight and to allow rods and strings to pass through the body.

Manipulators work the dolls from below. To their waistband they tie a cup in which they support a long rod which goes through the centre of the puppet to its head. Through a system of strings connected to various parts of the figure, they manipulate and dance the puppets giving life to the figures.

Today performances are presented in connection with fairs and festivals, though not as frequently as in the past. Some plays centre on events from the *Mahabharata*. Other plays draw on local folk tales, such as that of Manasa, the snake-goddess sister of Sesha, the serpent-king, and stories concerning Radha and Krishna.

Ramlila

Celebration of Lord Rama, hero of the epic *Ramayana*, through depiction of dramatic episodes from his life is an all-India phenomenon. At no time is it more prevalent than September–November and nowhere is it celebrated with greater verve than in north India. Activities leading up to the destruction of evil, symbolized in effigies built for the Dassahra Festival, provide the opportunity for the Hindu community to express its renewed faith in the restoration of world order. Following soon after Dassahra is Diwali, the Festival of Lights, which welcomes Rama home from his self-imposed exile from Ayodhya, his kingdom and his home. Millions of tiny oil lamps that decorate the exteriors of countless village homes throughout the north symbolically light Rama's path. This great public outpouring of faith over a three-month period is accompanied by public performances of the devotional theatre form, *ramlila*. Although performances in different localities share the same subject matter, they differ considerably in the manner of their execution and length.

Lila means 'play' or 'sport'; *ramlila* is the 'play of Rama'. The generic term applies to a variety of different theatre events performed on festival occasions that centre around Rama's life. Historical

Lakshmana, Rama and Sita are seated on the shoulders of priests, ready to be carried to the performance area in Ramnagar, North India. Because *ramlila* is a sacred event, it is not thought proper that the incarnation of these gods should walk to the performance area.

evidence places the beginning of *ramlila* in the 17th century when a version of the story was staged, based on the poet Tulsidas' famous Hindi version of the *Ramayana*, entitled *Ramcharitmanas*.

Some centres for large-scale *ramlila* spectacles are the cities of Ramnager, Allahabad, Mathura and Delhi. In Ramnagar alone, over a million pilgrims arrive annually for the vast processions and performances organized by the Maharaja Udit Narain Singh (commonly known as the Maharaja of Benares). The Ramnagar festival is supported by a grant of public money which helps the upkeep of the temples in the great pilgrimage city of Varanasi, across the river from the Maharaja's palace.

The usual procedure for establishing small-scale versions of the *ramlila* begins with the formation of committees, often democratically elected, by constituents of an area of a town or city. Although members of the *ksatriya* caste are thought to dominate the committees in many areas, in Mathura and Allahabad members of the merchant community control the organization. Obviously, besides expressing his religious devotion through public service on a *ramlila* committee, a merchant might reap profits from the festival occasions, especially since people purchase new clothing and prepare special sweets and foods, as well as increasing their charitable contributions, at this time of year. The bulk of the money to support festival activities is raised by small subscriptions collected from thousands of eager patrons.

Ramlila is performed by amateurs drawn from the community. In some areas actors have come from the same Brahmin families for centuries. It is customary for the roles of the five chief characters – Rama, his three brothers, Lakshmana, Bharata and Satrugna, and his wife, Sita – to be played by Brahmin boys who have not yet reached the age of puberty. Normally the youths are required to live in the house of the head of the *ramlila* committee prior to the opening of the performance because they are thought to take on the aspects of the gods they represent, to become *svarups*, embodiments of divinities.

The person who trains the boys and who heads the entire *ramlila* performance is called the *liladhari*. He inherits the right to instruct the amateur players in proper stage deportment, to lead the singing and to make sure that correct procedures are followed in the preparation of scenery, costumes, makeup and music.

The stage space varies depending on the city where a performance is held and the community that prepares the festivities. In Ramnager, which literally means 'Rama's city', 30 days are assigned to the *ramlila*, each day's events occuring in their own particular locations in the city and surrounding area. The Maharaja often travels from one event to another in his horsedrawn carriage or rides atop his elephant to better see the activities. During the great battle scenes between the monkey soldiers of Rama and the demon soldiers of Ravana, the symbolic representation of evil, hundreds of youths take part. The spectacle ends in the burning of the effigies of Ravana and his demon brothers. The effigies are four to five storeys tall. At the conclusion of the evening they are shot with burning arrows and they burst into flames and explode with fireworks falling in a heap at the feet of the actor playing Rama, as the crowd fervently chants 'Victory to Rama'.

In village performances, an earthen platform 3 to 4 ft off the ground topped by a colourful canopy will serve as the stage on which all the dramatic events are enacted. Processions of floats (*chauki*), separate chariots designed for Ravana and Rama, and processions of elephants and camels represent various events in the story. Microphones and loudspeakers carry the songs, music and dialogue in some performances. In others the actors must project their voices valiantly in open spaces, but are rarely heard by the thousands of participants who jam the area just to be a part of the ritual occasion.

People from many walks of life participate in the *ramlila* – Hindus, Muslims, Christians, Sikhs, and Parsis; rich and poor; maharajas and beggars – whoever comes to witness the events may participate. Those who consider the events sacred often reverently touch the feet of Rama and Sita when the boy *svarup* draw near.

Costumes differ considerably among the various groups. Because hundreds of actors typically participate in the major performances, costume houses in the area specialize in *ramlila* costumes which they rent out for the duration of the season. The makeup of the five central characters is usually a pinkish-white base over which stencil designs in the shapes of flowers and stars are drawn. Sequins and mica are added to provide a glittering, colourful and unrealistic appearance. The moment the actor playing Rama wears his crown, he is thought to be invested with the spirit of the god-man he portrays.

The actor who plays Ravana wears a mask depicting the ten heads that mark the demon king. His brothers usually have various distorted and deformed features, as do his demon hordes, many of whom smear black makeup on their faces to symbolize their evil nature.

The music of *ramlila* follows the folk-music tradition of the area with the addition of religious tunes as well as classical pieces. Bell-metal cymbals, drums and harmonium are the chief musical instruments. Chanting of the whole of the *Ramcharitmanas* is a part of the ritual activities in many areas and priests capable of excellent recitation regard this as a ritual obligation, no matter what the hour of the day or night.

In Andhra Pradesh state a popular form of presenting the *Ramayana* is *chiratala ramayanam*. The actors, mostly amateurs from different communities, wear makeup and costumes appropriate to the characters they portray and gather in an open place for the celebration. They stand in a circle and dance, keeping time with *kartal*, a pair of wooden pieces with small metal disks held in the hand and struck against each other. *Kartal* are associated with devotional music (*bhajans*). The musicians sit in the centre of the circle and accompany the performers with *tabla* drums and harmonium. When a passage of music is used for dance, the clown, who keeps a whistle in his mouth, blows it in time to the rapidly accelerated music. He governs the performance and moves the action forward.

Rasdhari

About 160 years ago, the RASLILA of Mathura was introduced to Rajasthan when artists from Braj performed at the Shrinathji Temple at Nathdvara, a principal centre of pilgrimage for the followers of Krishna. Initially the form appealed to the Vairagis community which developed its own version of the form in the late 19th century, principally in the Phulera area of the state and primarily in Rojdi village. From the beginning the companies that formed were professional. Before long, they developed performances around Vaishnava shrines throughout the state, such as those of Kishangarh, Jaipur, Bharatpur, Kota, Nathdvara and Kankroli. The original organizers of *raslila* performances in Rajasthan were known as *rasdhari* and hence the word came to indicate the theatre form, with its own unique Rajasthani characteristics.

Two types of *rasdhari* companies evolved. In some companies the plays remained devotional and adults were cast in the leading roles of Krishna and Radha, rather than boys as in *raslila*. Other companies were less religiously oriented and adapted stories from a wide variety of mythological and historical sources.

Today itinerant troupes of actors and musicians perform in any open meeting area in the village. Spectators generally ring the performers in a close-packed crowd. It is not uncommon for spectators to lean out of the doors or windows of surrounding houses, to settle into a comfortable fork of a nearby tree or to rest on any raised space where they may get a better view. Musicians sit among the spectators and entrances and exits are negotiated by the actors through the crowd.

No stage scenery is needed to relate the stories. Vivid word pictures in speech and song help spectators visualize the action. If a simple prop is needed, it is easily obtained from a nearby household.

Songs and musical accompaniment are borrowed from other styles of music and theatre popular in the region and do not have their own unique character. Improvisation is freely used in dialogue and song as the actors test the audience's interest in possible themes and dramatic action. Dance too is improvised. Fast-paced, energetic acting creates a strong positive rapport between artists and spectators which makes the form very popular.

Costumes are the local dress of the spectators and the manner and behaviour of mythological characters imitate those of local inhabitants. The simplicity of the form allows considerable latitude in interpreting and altering the classical stories and reinforcing moral behaviour.

Raslila

The generic term throughout India for various dances and dance dramas dedicated to Krishna, seventh incarnation of the god Vishnu. *Ras* refers to Lord Krishna's joyous, melodious, circular dance with the wives of Brahmin cowherds of Vrindavan, a holy city in north India, described in mythological sources. *Lila* means 'play' and implies the god's playful tryst with man and earthly beings. Because they are devoted to Krishna, KRISHNATTAM of Kerala and ANKIYA NAT of Assam are also *raslila*. *Ras* dances in Gujarat and other states are not included here because they do not have a significant dramatic structure.

The *raslila* performed in Vrindavan is perhaps the best-known in India. Vrindavan is in the Braj region along the Jumna River, a 90-mile-square area south of Delhi. The present form probably came into being in the 16th century on the crest of the devotional (*bhakti*) movement dedicated to

Vishnu-Krishna which swept this part of north India.

Krishna is said to have been born in the city of Mathura, a few miles from Vrindavan where he spent his childhood and youth. Thus, the whole area is considered holy ground and enactment of raslila is an extension of the religious fervour of the inhabitants and the hundreds of thousands of pilgrims who flock to the area every year to join in the holy-day celebrations and to walk the very ground which Krishna is reputed to have trod. To witness raslila is tantamount to experiencing darshan (revelation of god).

Performance centres on aspects of Krishna's earthly life and the miraculous experiences of lovers and devotees in association with him. The first part of a performance begins with a tableau: Krishna is seated enthroned, with Radha, his beloved chief consort (sakhi), on his left, and less important consorts arranged on lower steps of a platform to his right and left. The chief singer and other musicians reverently touch the feet of the divine couple, at that moment regarded as incarnations of god requiring respect. Ritual prayers are sung in praise of them and other deities. A tray with a lighted lamp is waved in a circular motion in front of them (arati), the same ritual which is performed in the temple before idols. Then Krishna and Radha perform a series of dances (nitya ras), joined in some by Krishna's consorts. Songs accompanying the dances move through different rhythmic patterns, slowly raising the level of religious fervour of the spectator-devotees. When particular sections are well executed the spectators shower verbal praise on the gods, not on the artists. Sometimes fervent devotees are moved by an action or moment in the performance and stand and sway to the infectious rhythms or make their way to the playing area and reverently bow down and touch their heads to the ground in front of the actors. When the latter have returned to their throne decorated with sumptuous fabrics, other songs and a short discourse by Krishna may follow.

After a short interval, the second part of the nitya ras begins in which songs predominate and dance plays a secondary role. Group singing involves the spectators in the emotional fervour which climaxes in a duet sung by Krishna and Radha, particularly relished by the crowd. Then Krishna, Radha and the sakhi perform a final group dance which culminates in a tableau. At this point devotees surge forward to touch the feet of the divine couple. After they have prostrated themselves before the god-actors, they leave gifts of money, the musicians singing popular hymns all the while. Curtains close on the tableau and a short interval follows.

The final part of the evening's performance is a short play (lila) based on an episode in Krishna's life. The plays are composed primarily of dialogue and song, with relatively little dance. The particular audience, season or holiday will often dictate which lila out of the nearly 150 that have been composed is appropriate for performance. Plays concern episodes connected with Krishna's birth, his mischievous childhood, his sport with the young milkmaids of Vrindavan and his adult life. At the conclusion of the lila, devotees shout 'Victory to Krishna of Vrindavan!' and the performance and rituals end.

Performance lasts about two and a half hours. Unlike many forms of rural theatre, raslila must be completed before midnight. Since it is regarded as a religious ritual, shoes must be removed outside the performance area, spectators must sit on the ground and may not presume to sit or stand above the heads of the actors who play Radha and Krishna, and smoking or talking are strictly forbidden.

The proper place for a raslila performance is in a temple, a private garden, a bungalow or holy resting place for travellers. It is not considered appropriate to perform such a sacred event in the street.

A raslila performance area is a circle (mandal), echoing the circle dance of the nitya ras. A throne is placed at one side with several platform steps leading down to the ground. A curtain strung on wire masks the platform from spectators sitting opposite. A rectangular area (about 15 x 20 ft) is marked out on the playing area in front of the throne. To one side of the playing area and facing the throne, the musicians (samaji) arrange themselves. The musical party consists of two singers, each with a harmonium, a tabla drummer and a cymbal player. The musicians act as a chorus and the chief singer (rasdhari) takes the lead and controls the progress of the performance.

A *raslila* party consists of 10–18 males. Only boys who have not yet reached the age of puberty may play the divine couple and consorts and Radha and Krishna are carefully chosen from among sons of traditional Brahmin families of Braj. When the young actors wear the crowns of Krishna and Radha they are thought to be the gods and are treated with great deference. They are carried on the back of the troupe leader to the playing area so that their feet do not touch the ground. Adults who have distinguished themselves for their playing skill take the roles of adults in the *lila*.

The young boys study with a teacher (*swami*) who serves as the leader of the troupe. The texts of the songs and the various *lila* are taught verbally to those who are not literate. The chief singer (*samaji*) acts as the prompter. He may correct the actors or jump in to aid them to speak a line properly or support them when they fall out of character or forget a particular section of dance. In performance, actors often seem to drop out of character, staring at the audience indiscriminately. No standard of excellence exists, even though the companies are professional. The religious fervour of the experience seems to outweigh aesthetic considerations.

The high season for *raslila* performance in Vrindavan is the monsoon season and the holy days connected with Krishna's birth and special events in his life.

Ravana chhaya

Literally, 'shadow' (*chhaya*) play of 'Ravana', the demon king of Lanka, Prince Rama's foe in the *Ramayana* epic. A form of shadow-puppet theatre in Orissa state in eastern India. The puppet of Ravana is interesting and large in size. Some scholars see the influence of the Jain religion and Buddhism in naming this genre after the reputed villain of *Ramayana*. In the Jain version of the *Ramayana*, Ravana assumes considerable dignity. Or it may be that players were hesitant to speak of Rama as a shadow, for he is the incarnation of Vishnu, a popular and important figure of worship and respect.

The one story in its repertory concerns the life of Rama and his struggles with Ravana as described in the *Vichitra Ramayana*. This Oriyan-language version of the Sanskrit epic was written by Viswanath Khuntia sometime between 1692 and 1720. Episodes have been drawn from this work to make up seven plays.

The simple shadow puppets are 6–8 in tall. About seven hundred puppets are required to perform the seven plays in the repertory. A character requires more than one puppet to depict its various moods. Besides the characters of the epic, there are stock characters of village barber and his grandson, and numerous properties and scenic items which lend interest to the story.

Puppets are made of deerskin mounted between strips of bamboo. Unlike other shadow figures in India, they have no movable parts. After they are created, life is breathed into them through a simple ritual sacrifice. When they can no longer be used due to excessive wear, they are symbolically cremated and reverently disposed of in a nearby river.

Performance is a simple affair and may be arranged at any convenient location where two poles can be fixed in the ground six or seven feet apart. An oil lamp casts the puppets' shadows on a white curtain about four feet wide that is stretched between the poles. Straw mats threaded together provide masking for the puppeteer who squats behind the screen.

Performance begins when a coconut is broken and a sacrifice (*puja*) invokes the blessings of the elephant-headed god Ganapati and Rama. The leader of the troupe steps to the side of the acting area in view of the audience and offers a prayer to Rama. Then he introduces the story in a prose narrative. The puppets of the village barber and his grandson enter on the screen and the play begins.

The narrator speaks the parts of all characters, joined only by two singers. A blend of Oriyan folk and classical melodies set to lively rhythmic patterns accompanies dialogue and songs.

Although the action is limited by the static construction of the puppets, the religious atmosphere of the event and the magical transformation of the screen coupled with poetic language and music heighten the effect of the evening performance.

Sakhi Kundhei

Literally, 'doll dance'; a form of string-puppet performance found in Orissa state in eastern India. Also known as *sakhi nata*, *kundhei nata* and *gopa lila* (*GOPA LILA* is also the name of a glove-puppet theatre in Orissa). Puppet heads and hands are made of light wood and paper. Their costumes follow those of *JATRA* actors of the region, especially in the well-known character roles. Some puppets are made with moveable legs, others have a skirt, like their Rajasthani counterparts, covering the legless torso. Animal puppets include tigers, elephants, goats and horses. Stories centre on events in the life of Lord Krishna.

The stage, like that of *KATHPUTLI* of Rajasthan, may be decorated with colourful cloth pieces of the region, depending on the wealth of the players. Itinerant families of four or five performers work fairs and festivals, collecting what they can in donations from villagers.

Musicians sing folk tunes and adaptations of film songs to narrate the story. A cymbal player, *pakhavaj* drummer and harmonium player provide the basic rhythm for the narrator-singer.

Svanga

A rural theatre form in Haryana, Uttar Pradesh and Punjab states in north India. Also known as *swang*, *sang* and sometimes *sangeet*. *Svanga* is thought to have originated in the late 18th century. In urban as well as rural areas, Hindu festivals and family celebrations, especially marriages and the birth of a son, provide the occasion for *svanga* performance. Plays concern conflicts between rivals found in popular ballads and semi-historical tales. Stories of love, honour and duty abound.

Performance takes place in an open space of the village or on the veranda of a patron's house. Actors, all male, wear costumes which are simple village garments, exaggerated headdresses and brightly coloured cloth pieces. False hair and beards 'theatricalize' a performance to satisfy village tastes.

An evening's entertainment begins with songs in praise of Hindu deities, especially Ganapati, the elephant-headed god of good fortune. A strong plot line emerges in which characters express their feelings in vernacular dialogue and punctuate their emotions with songs which have a strong poetic line.

Svanga can also mean an act of a *KARIYALA* play.

Tamasha

A major form of rural theatre in the state of Maharashtra, in west-central India. Approximately 10,000 artists in some 450 *tamasha* troupes serve a population of about 62 million people. In sheer numbers alone, this makes *tamasha* among the more popular forms of theatre in India. Also, few of India's many forms of rural theatre stress humour as extensively. *Tamasha* satirizes and pokes fun at contemporary society, often at the expense of politicians and businessmen, priests and prophets, clothing its barbs in the guise of historical or mythological stories.

Evidence suggests that *tamasha* developed in the 16th century as a bawdy entertainment both for the Mogul armies that occupied the Deccan plain and among insurgent Maratha forces determined to free their people from their oppressors. The term itself is a Persian word meaning 'fun', 'play' and 'entertainment', and was probably introduced to the area by Urdu-speaking soldiers of the Mogul armies. The form that we call *tamasha* today is probably the amalgam of many different influences which may be traced back over many centuries. Some scholars have suggested that *tamasha* developed out of the decaying remnants of two short forms of classical Sanskrit entertainment – the *prahasana* and the *bhana*. Just how this transpired is not certain. Other scholars suppose that diverse pieces of musical, dance and dramatic entertainment coalesced to form *tamasha* sometime in the 16th century. There were certainly plenty of forms of entertainment available from which artists might draw inspiration – classical *kathak* dance of north India, with its infectious rhythms and sensuous appeal; Muslim *kavali* and *ghazal* songs designed to assault the ear with rich melodies and exotic rhythm; *DASHAVATARA* musical plays and *bharud* dramatic poetry recitals; *lalit* religious plays and *gondhal* religious songs; *kirtan*, a one-man musical sermon; and *kal sutri* puppet shows among them.

The diverse elements found in *tamasha* performance indicate eclectic borrowing as suggested above. All *tamasha* performances open with a *gan*, a devotional song in praise of the deities, lustily sung by the chief male singer and musicians. This is followed by the *gaulan*, a dramatic segment in which Krishna and his clown attendant wittily converse with milkmaids on their journey to market. Songs and dances punctuate the raucous humour. Following this is the *vag*, a short dialogue play drawn from historical or mythological sources and laced with satirical incidents and broad slapstick humour. After the *vag* was introduced to *tamasha* in the 19th century, it quickly became the soul of the art form.

The performance practice above typifies *dholki-baari* folk drama troupes, who present one of two varieties of *tamasha* performance. *Dholki-baari* troupes get their name from the popular drum used in *tamasha*, the *dholki*. A troupe consists of a leading male actor, half a dozen male actor-singers, one or more female dancer-singers and several instrumentalists.

Sangeet-baari, or song troupes, represent an older style that emphasizes song and dance. They do not use the *vag* as part of their entertainment. *Sangeet-baari* troupes are relatively small in size, consisting of half a dozen dancers and singers and several instrumentalists. The clown character (*songadya*), whose improvised humour is so integral to the success of *tamasha* performance, is common to both varieties.

Tamasha's popularity is partially due to love songs (*lavani*) which are interpreted through singing and dancing. *Lavani* entered the form during Maharashtra's Peshwa period (1707–1818). Until the end of the 19th century, they were sung by male singers dressed as women. Today *lavani* are sung by professional dancing girls whose physical charms, as much as their vocal abilities, help to sell a song. Enthusiastic patrons pleased with particularly brilliant singing, or perhaps taken with the beauty of the singer, are encouraged to go to the performance area and offer a token of their esteem to the singer in the form of a rupee note. These special requests (*daulat-jadda*) are often honoured by the singer who repeats the song to the enchanted enthusiast. Poetic dialogues coupled with mime (*chakkad*) are also honoured in this way. The songs themselves have provided the inspiration for many popular Hindi and Marathi film songs, while film songs popular

with rural audiences are taken into *tamasha*.

In addition to the *dholki* drum, *tamasha* musicians play the *tuntuni*, a single-string drone instrument; the *manjeera* cymbals; the *daf*, a large tambourine-like instrument with a single leather surface; the *halgi*, a small version of the *daf*; the *kade*, a metal triangle; the *lejim*, an instrument resembling buttons strung like beads on a wooden rod, producing jangling sounds; and the harmonium. Many strings of *ghungrus*, or ankle bells, worn by the dancers accentuate the rhythm of the music.

Tamasha dance is an amalgam of *kathak* classical dance technique and indigenous folk dance, broadly described as 'filmic' by some local critics.

Historically, *tamasha* has been linked with two untouchable communities of Maharashtra – the Kolhati and the Mahar. Training has largely been kept within the confines of family units long associated with the art. With the introduction of female dancers in the late 19th century however, the general public assumed that the artists were little more than prostitutes; consequently they have continued to be the subject of censure by puritanical and conservative forces in Maharashtrian society.

During the 18th century, poet-singers (*shahir*) were chiefly responsible for raising the artistic level of the narratives and love songs. As company leaders they gained an enviable reputation with the rulers of the day and helped to lift the reputation of the *tamasha* artists. This tradition of *shahir* leadership brought the idea of freedom from British rule to the heartland of India during the independence movement in 1947. In the 1930s and 40s, some popular *shahir* became associated with Communist causes. In response to the recent diminishing of *shahir* influence, an association of *shahir* was formed in 1969 to revitalize *tamasha*.

Tamasha is performed almost anywhere that there is a suitable open space. Throughout most of the year performances are presented out of doors; during the heavy monsoon rains indoor performances are given in urban, proscenium-arch theatres in Bombay, Pune, Nagpur, Nasik, Aurangabad and smaller cities. Troupes that perform in these theatres are regarded as 'raw' *tamasha* and are welcome at venues in working-class districts.

Artists

Alkazi, Ebrahim

Director, educator. Arguably the most influential Indian theatre artist of the 20th century, Alkazi started his theatre career after basic college education in Bombay in the 1940s. He studied in London at RADA and the Royal Academy of Art. In 1951 he returned to Bombay where he and friends and relatives founded Theatre Group, an English-language theatre organization. Shortly thereafter he founded Theatre Unit where he successfully produced plays in Hindi. His reputation for organization and his workshops in theatre education earned him the post of Director of the National School of Drama in New Delhi in the early 1960s, which he brought to national and international prominence. Alkazi was responsible for forging a respected team of teachers who established the standard for theatre education for the contemporary generation of theatre artists, many of whom are now leaders in film, television and theatre. After resigning from the National School of Drama in the late 1970s he returned to his earlier love – collecting and selling modern art for Indian and foreign dealers . In 1991 he made a brief return to the New Delhi stage with several new productions, among them *The House of Bernarda Alba* and *Othello*.

Bharata Muni

Bharata Muni is the reputed author of *A Treatise on Theatre (Natyasastra)* in which is formulated the ideas which have shaped centuries of dramatic literature and patterns of performance practice throughout much of South Asia. The work has served actors, dancers, playwrights and musicians over the centuries and is the earliest complete text of Indian dramaturgy and among the most important works of its kind in the world. Bharata is not only the author's name, but also the name of the first tribe of India and has come to mean 'actor' as an occupational group. 'Muni' is scholar or seer. Although many stories about the author speak of him as a Brahmin and the father of a hundred sons, the man remains a mystery.

Bhasa

Major playwright of ancient Sanskrit drama. Bhasa probably worked between the 4th and 5th centuries AD in the city of Ujjain in north central India. He composed plays based on dramatic incidents from the *Ramayana*, the *Mahabharata*, and the *Purana*, as well as semihistorical tales. He also created original stories. Bhasa's works follow many of the dramatic rules of the *Natyasastra*; when he violates them at times it is with outstanding results. Bhasa seems to have been a man of the theatre, as well as a capable poet. His works are as fresh today as they must have been when he first wrote them. Many modern Indian directors have been drawn to Bhasa's plays and have given them new, and often lively, modern interpretations.

The texts of 13 plays attributed to Bhasa were discovered in 1912. The most important and one of the most elegant in Sanskrit literature is *The Vision of Vasavadatta (Svapnavasavadatta)* a play fusing the pain of love in separation with a political intrigue. Among Bhasa's short plays are *The Broken Thighs (Urubhangam)* and *Karna's Task (Karna-bharam)*, dramatizations of episodes in the great battle which concludes the *Mahabharata*.

Dutt, Utpal (1929–93)

Director. Perhaps India's best-known exponent of theatre for political and social purposes. He began his career in the 1940s with the Shakespeareana International Theater Company. Later he produced many of Shakespeare's plays in English for the Little Theatre Group of Calcutta. Attracted to political causes, he joined the Indian People's Theatre Association in 1950 but remained for less than a year, needing more independence and flexibility. As director, playwright, stage and film actor, Dutt has been acknowledged for his dynamic personality, energy and determination. Among his memorable productions are *Coal (Angar)*, *Invincible Vietnam (Ajeya Vietnam)*, *Arrow (Teer)*, and *Barracade*. For a time he wrote performance pieces for JATRA, the popular folk-theatre form of Bengal.

Kalidasa

Most revered playwright of the classical Sanskrit theatre. Kalidasa may have been court poet for King Chandragupta II of Ujjain in north central India during the mid 5th century AD. He is known to have written the plays *Malavika and Agnimitra* (*Malavikagnimitra*) and *Urvasi Won by Valour* (*Vikramorvasiya*) and the dramatic poem *The Cloud Messenger* (*Meghaduta*). His most important work is the play *Sakuntala and the Ring of Recognition* (*Abhijnanasakuntala*) which has served as the ideal example of the *nataka* type of classical Sanskrit drama. Kalidasa adheres to the classical rules without sacrificing his own artistic integrity and his works are recognized as representing some of the finest examples of Sanskrit poetry.

Karanth, B. V. (1928–)

One of South India's most important contemporary directors, B. V. Karanth began his career producing experimental works in Bangalore where he attended college. He attended the National School of Drama and eventually became its director. Apart from many controversial stage productions he has also directed experimental films. He has headed Bhopal's Bharat Bhavan theatre school where he forged numerous successful musical productions. Currently he heads the Karnataka Repertory in Mysore.

Mitra, Tripti

Actress. Considered one of the great women performers of 20th-century India. Born in West Bengal, she made her reputation performing in the Calcutta amateur theatre. She was attracted to the theatre as a college student during the mid 1940s because of its political and social potential during this time of great social unrest and famine. Appearing in the Indian People's Theatre Association's original production of *New Harvest* (*Nabanna*) in 1944, she later gained fame for her sensitive portrayals of Tagore's heroines in *Red Oleanders* (*Raktakarabi*) and *King of the Dark Chamber* (*Raja*), as well as Nora in Ibsen's *A Doll's House*. Most recently she has appeared in one-woman shows, designed by herself, which have successfully toured India, Europe, Russia and the United States.

Sircar, Badal (1925–)

Playwright and director. Born in Calcutta, he studied to be a civil engineer and town planner. He began his theatre career in 1953 as a director and actor. In 1956 his first original script was produced in Calcutta. In 1957 he went to London for further education in his original profession. National recognition came with *And Indrajit* (*Evam Indrajit*), composed while he was abroad. Between 1966 and 1967 he worked in Nigeria as a town planner. Shortly after returning to India in 1967 he formed his theatre group Satabdi and shortly thereafter toured the USSR, Poland and Czechoslovakia where he saw productions by Lyubimov and Grotowski. Tiring of structured plays, he returned to India and restructured his group in 1969, beginning a period of experimentation requiring little of the scenery and lighting elements characteristic of urban theatre in Calcutta. Among his notable recent productions are *Spartacus*, *Bhoma* and *Procession*. Today he teaches workshops in creative process throughout India and has inspired several generations of contemporary artists with his ideas.

Sudraka

Playwright of ancient Sanskrit theatre who lived around the 5th century AD. He apparently produced a single work, *The Little Clay Cart* (*Mrcchakatika*), a complex and dynamic play about the love of a Brahmin and a courtesan and the overthrow of a despotic ruler. The preface to the play describes the author in considerable detail, indicating that he was a king, mathematician, knowledgeable in love and skilled in the training of elephants. According to the verse, he was a hundred years old when he committed suicide. Obviously it is impossible that a writer could discuss his own death in the preface of one of his plays; hence numerous questions about the authenticity of the preface and the author of the work. Whatever the circumstances, Sudraka certainly produced a master-piece.

Tagore, Rabindranath (1861–1940)

Winner of the 1913 Nobel Prize for Literature, author of India's national anthem, painter and poet, this towering figure is perhaps India's best-known modern playwright. Tagore was born into a large family of wealthy and artistic Bengalis in 1861. He founded a unique school, Santiniketan, in 1901 in rural Bengal aimed at melding the best of Indian and Western culture, and in 1935 Visva-Bharati University dedicated to the arts. He travelled and lectured widely in Europe, America, China, Japan, Malaysia and Indonesia. Although his many plays are not frequently produced outside Bengal today, they are an important contribution to the world's dramatic literature. They include, *Chitra* (*Chitrangada*, 1892), *The King of the Dark Chamber* (*Raja*, 1910), *The Post Office* (*Dakghar*, 1913), and *Red Oleanders* (*Raktakarabi*, 1924).

Tanvir, Habib

Contemporary North Indian director. He began his theatre career in 1948 after his basic education in rural Madhya Pradesh. Between 1945 and 1953 he was a radio producer and writer, film actor and song writer in Bombay. Like other prominent contemporary performers in the late 1940s he became an active member of the India People's Theatre Association. In 1954 he moved to Delhi where he founded the Hindustani Theatre. In the late 50s, after studying at RADA and the British Drama League in London, he spent nearly a year at the Berliner Ensemble. His notable productions include *Agra Market* (*Agra Bazaar*, 1954), *The Little Clay Cart* (1958), and *Thief Charandas* (*Charandas Chor*, 1975). Between 1972 and 1978 he served as a Member of Parliament from Madhya Pradesh. Recent works include film and television appearances, as well as experimental productions which he has directed with rural artists from his home state.

Loknatya, or 'people's theatre', companies play a more refined style of *tamasha*, cleansed of obscene remarks and actions typical of rural companies. They play in expensive urban playhouses for patrons who can afford the relatively high-price admission and who want wholesome family entertainment.

Like other forms of rural theatre, *tamasha* serves as a source of inspiration to modern urban directors and actors. Prominent productions developed in imitation of *tamasha* technique in recent years include Vijaya Mehta's Marathi versions of *The Caucasian Chalk Circle*, *The Little Clay Cart* and *Hayavadana*, written by Girish Karnad; Jabbar Patel's *Ghashiram Kotwal*, written by Vijay Tendulkar; and *Teen Paishacha Tamasha*, also directed by Jabbar Patel and adapted from Brecht's *Threepenny Opera* by P. L. Deshpande.

Therukoothu

Theru means 'street', *koothu* 'play'. As the name suggests, *therukoothu* has a rustic origin. It is usually performed by members of the Koothadi community and is most frequently seen in the north and south Arcot and Chingleput districts of Tamil Nadu state. Its players and audiences come from the lower strata of urban and rural society. Some scholars suggest it was inspired by YAKSHAGANA of Karnataka state, others by KATHAKALI of Kerala state. One thing seems clear, *therukoothu* is not like any other form of traditional theatre in south India.

A troupe performs in an open space in a village. Four tall posts of bamboo or wood are fixed in the ground bounding the acting area. A large banner proclaiming the company name hangs above the musicians who assemble in the space upstage centre. Colourful banners are strung overhead between the remaining posts. The makeup of central characters is bright blue and red accentuated with white and black lines. Heavily waxed moustaches accentuate the virility of the heroic characters of the epics and *Puranas*. Colourful wooden ornaments decorate their chests and arms and impressive crowns adorn their heads. Special short grass skirts are worn under the outer cloth skirts. In some respects the makeup and ornaments resemble those of the *yakshagana* of

Andhra Pradesh and south Kanara in Karnataka state, and the skirts resemble *kathakali* skirts of Kerala actors.

As part of large-scale ritualistic events in a village, the actors parade through its streets along with the temple deities. Following an all-night performance, they participate in the symbolic destruction of evil under the watchful eye of temple effigies and thousands of enthusiastic villagers. The ceremony concludes when they walk across beds of hot coals to prove their faith in god.

Plays centre on stories drawn from epic literature and concern events in the lives of famous epic characters. Among popular fun-loving figures is the *kattiakaran*, a clown figure who combines the functions of the fool with those of the stage manager.

Traditional *therukoothu* music is a blend of classical and folk music. Melodies are first sung by the actors and then repeated by musicians singing in chorus. About half of a performance is made up of songs and the other half is improvised prose dialogue spoken in Tamil. *Therukoothu* songs characteristically require a high shrill pitch demanding sustained vocal power.

The musicians' space is called the *pin pattu*, or 'back song'. When an actor is not in character, he joins the musicians and sings from the *pin pattu*. The harmonium provides the basic pitch. A reed instrument (*kurukuzhal*) provides melodic background. Small hand drums played on both ends and bell-metal cymbals complete the musical ensemble.

Dance steps are simple and violent, involving circular movements with quick turning leaps. There is no symbolic code of hand gestures. Dance provides an element of fast-paced spectacle demonstrating the emotional state of the character, or forms part of a battle scene.

Few companies remain today. Highly praised is the Raghava Thambiran Company named after its founder. Other companies playing in and around the slums of Madras city have abandoned traditional costumes and use film music to attract people to their performances.

Tollu bommalu

Also *tholu bommalatta*. One of the best-known forms of puppetry in India and one example of the wonderfully varied forms of shadow-puppet theatre in Asia. It is found in several regions of Andhra Pradesh state in south India. *Tolu* means a 'doll' and *bommalu* means 'leather'. According to the oral tradition, the form originated in 200 BC when it was patronized by the rulers of the Satavahana dynasty. In the 16th century during the reign of King Kona Reddy, a ruler of the Vijayanagar Empire, a Telugu manuscript entitled *Ramayana Ranganathana* was composed specifically for the shadow theatre. Besides providing a dramatic text of the famous epic story, the manuscript includes instructions for the construction and decoration of shadow puppets. Families of puppeteers even today jealously guard copies of the manuscripts from outside study.

Puppets are cut from various types of hide and processed in a special manner. Most puppets, including humans and saints, are made of goatskin. Demons are carved of buffalo hide, and gods and heroes of deerskin. Puppets are large, translucent and multicoloured. Their sizes depend upon the area of the state in which they are produced. For example, puppet figures from Madnapalli district are generally around 4 ft tall and those from Kakinada as tall as 5 ft.

The leather puppet is wedged into a split bamboo strip and tied along the length of the strip from the head to the crotch to provide support. Different emotional states of a character are depicted by separate puppets. Some puppets incorporate a scenic environment around the figure. For example, Rama's wife, Sita, is depicted beneath an Ashoka tree in King Ravana's garden.

Many puppets have movable hands and legs and some movable heads and necks. The hands are moved by sticks and the legs allowed to dangle from the trunk of the puppet. The skirt of a dancing girl is hinged at her waist and, through a clever device contrived with strings and knots, she may even turn her head and torso from side to side.

Refined characters have a delicate physiognomy, whereas demons have exaggerated and gross features revealing their excessiveness and crudity. Some puppets are delicately carved with traceries of fine perforations. Puppets are dyed black, red and green; for females and sages the dominant colour is yellow.

The colourful shadows are cast on a wide, white screen made of a sturdy cotton *sari* or cloth pieces stretched between two poles temporarily fixed in the ground about 6 to 12 ft apart. The total height of the screen depends on the size of the puppets used, ranging from 5 to 7 ft. The stage behind the screen is raised about half a foot above the ground and encased by thatch matting to provide privacy for the performers and their families during the long hours of the performance.

About 11 in above the bottom of the screen a rope is stretched on which the puppets may be rested when they are on stage. Puppets are pinned in place on the screen with acacia-thorn pins. Traditionally the flickering mellow glow of oil lamps and torches produced the shadows on the screen. Nowadays companies use petromax lamps which give off a harsh blue-white glow that changes the true colour of the images. The chief manipulator stands pressing the large puppets firmly against the screen. With his free hand he manipulates the arms of the puppet. When big puppets are used for fight sequences, two people manipulate each puppet. Puppets are passed from hand to hand when they are moved across the wide screen. A manipulator wears a set of bells on one of his ankles which accentuates his dance steps. A loose elevated board on the floor of the performance booth provides additional sound effects when struck with his foot.

A typical troupe of between 6 and 10 people is composed of manipulators, singers, dancers and instrumentalists. Women speak the female parts and the stage manager manipulates the shadows during dance numbers.

While songs have a written text, dialogue sections are improvised and extend as long as the puppeteers can hold the audience's interest. Musicians play a *mridangam* drum, bell-metal cymbals, and sometimes harmonium and *mukavina*, an oboe-like wind instrument. A metal barrel is struck with long thin sticks, like a drum, and a piece of leather slapped by the hand provides special sound effects. Folk and classical melodies are integrated. Even film music has crept in because of its popularity.

During performance puppeteers chant and speak dialogue to each other rather than through the puppets. The puppets seem to act only as symbols of the characters portrayed to which the manipulators add their own highly effective emotional reactions.

Special effects delight the audience. For example, when a character is shot with an arrow during a battle, a whizzing noise is produced by a small whistle as a leather arrow on a rod is whisked across the screen. When it strikes the victim, severing his head, the puppet head is detached quickly by a string and made to roll across the screen. Drummers accentuate the action with loud thuds.

Popular characters are the clowns – Katikayata, the drunken lecher and womanizer, and Bangavaka, his fat, scandal-mongering wife. They provide comic interludes within the familiar stories of the *Ramayana*, the *Mahabharata* and the *Puranas*. A company has six to a dozen plays in its repertory, each of which takes four to eight hours to perform.

Lord Shiva is regarded as the god of puppeteers. During Shiva's birthday in May, some companies perform special nine-night programmes in his honour outside temples of the region. This tends to be one of their most lucrative engagements. The playing season extends between the monsoons which strike Andhra Pradesh twice a year.

Performance begins when the puppet of Ganapati, the elephant-headed god, is placed on the screen and songs of praise are sung in his honour. Then Saraswathi, goddess of learning, appears and is praised. A comic interlude takes place between the husband and wife. Jokes are made about local spectators. Then the stage manager introduces the subject of the play. Nearly two hours are devoted to preliminaries and introduction of characters. Finally, the drama based on an epic story is enacted. About sunrise performances end with songs of thanksgiving.

Veedhi natakam

Veedhi (or *vithi*) means 'street', *natakam*, 'drama', hence a street theatre. At one time *veedhi natakam* was the most popular form of traditional theatre in Andhra Pradesh state in south India. Artists moved freely among the people of the countryside where they found patronage. A rural form of theatre, its roots are uncertain. Scholars believe it was in vogue at the height of the Vijayanagar

Empire during the 16th century. It may have been the dramatic counterpart of YAKSHAGANA and KUCHIPUDI may have adapted its dramatic form from *veedhi natakam*.

Stories performed in *veedhi natakam* are drawn from the epics and the *Puranas*. Troupes of players perform throughout the state from November to May, playing in the open air, usually in squares or before village temples. Today popular film music may replace traditional folk melodies. The actors sing all the songs and a chorus of musicians repeats lines and phrases for emphasis. A harmonium provides the basic melodic line and *tabla* drums keep the basic tempo. Performances are given in the open air in any space large enough to accommodate a crowd. Rugs or mats demarcate the playing area which is shaped like an arena. Musicians sit on stage in full view of the spectators.

Yakshagana

Yakshagana is a generic term identifying a variety of theatre forms of south India, the best-known of which is found in the south Kanara region of Karnataka state. *Yaksha* are the demigods associated with Kubera, god of wealth, and *gana* is a song. Thus, *yakshagana* means 'songs of the demigods'. Historical evidence suggests that the *yakshagana* of south Kanara originated in the 16th century or earlier. The earliest written playscript for Kanara *yakshagana* dates from the first half of the 16th century when Kandukuru Rudrakavi wrote the play *Sugrivavijaya*, the story of the monkey king who overthrew his powerful brother, based on incidents from the *Ramayana*.

Yakshagana is popular with rural audiences. Companies are itinerant organizations managed by temple authorities. The manager of the troupe contacts the players (a minimum of 15 people are required to produce a performance) and the musicians (a minimum of five are needed). Touring begins from the home temple and engagements are organized during the festival season which lasts approximately six months between November and May. The manager makes all the formal arrangements with a patron, including place of performance, cooking arrangements and living accommodation which is either in a local temple or the home of a Brahmin. During the

initial contact, a ritual exchange takes place between patron and manager, usually on the morning of performance, and the full payment for the show is provided the morning after, just prior to the departure of the actors for their next engagement. The manager usually hires a staff of at least ten helpers to assist in the cooking, to prepare the accommodation and to transport costume and prop boxes.

Yakshagana is a lively, fast-paced form in which songs, dances and improvised dialogue mix according to a prescribed structure. At the heart of *yakshagana* are the poetic songs (*prasanga*) sung by the chief musician (*bhagavata*), who thus controls the pace of the performance. The most popular of these songs have been transcribed and published, even those from hundreds of years ago. With their particular melody (*raga*) and metre intact, they constitute a major part of the historical record of regional Indian dramatic literature. Today published editions of *prasanga* are to be found in paperback editions in bookstalls along the roadside in rural areas of Karnataka.

Improvised dialogue (*matu*) by the actor-dancers expands on the content of the songs. Until recently, this portion was not written down because it changed from night to night and from actor to actor. Most *prasanga* are based on stories from the great Hindu epics, the *Mahabharata* and *Ramayana*, and from the *Purana* and concern serious events from the lives of well-known epic figures. Humour is inserted in the performance by the clowns (*hasyagar*) through comic antics and witty remarks.

The acting area (*rangasthala*), a space near the house of the patron, may be a paddy field cleared of stubble, or the open ground in front of a temple compound. Tall bamboo posts demarcate the four corners of a rectangle 15 x 20 ft. Mango leaves, flowers, coconuts, plantains and coloured paper provide a festive, simple decoration. At the centre of one of the narrow ends of the acting area a wooden table is placed on which the chief musician sings and plays the *maddale* drum. Behind this is a collapsible four-wheeled cart, the only functional piece of furniture and scenery used during performance. Standing between the musicians is a man who plays the *shruti*, a simplified version of the harmonium which keeps the underlying pitch necessary to guide the singer's melodies. On the right side of the playing area, sitting on a chair facing the acting area, is the *chende* drummer. The area between the pillar and the table up left is used for entrances. Some distance away on the left side of the acting area, actors gather in an improvised dressing room made of thatch walls. A space between the *chende* player and the table is reserved for exits.

The audience sits on three sides of the rectangle, the women and children separate from the men. Oil lamps are placed stage right and left facing the acting area but electric lights and petromax lanterns have become popular today to help the spectators to see the action better. A simple curtain with the troupe's name embroidered on it is used for dance entrances of major characters or groups of dancing characters.

Admission is usually free to the public. Petty merchants display their wares, such as sweets, tea and snacks, outside the audience area and conduct a brisk business among the spectators through the long hours of the night. Performances begin with rituals about 9.30 p.m. and continue uninterrupted until sunrise when they are concluded by ritual prayers.

Some troupes give performances in a tent in order to control attendance. Tickets are sold and folding chairs are provided for a fee. A raised proscenium stage is used for these performances and the style of dance and acting has assumed unique features which distinguish it from that of the open-air troupes. These performances are known as tent drama (*tent atta*).

During the monsoons which hit the area from June to September, *yakshagana* is presented in the homes of patrons or in enclosed halls. The actors sit on the ground to sing the *prasanga* and perform truncated improvised dialogue with musical accompaniment. These performances are known as *tala maddale*.

Costumes and makeup for the *yakshagana* of south Kanara are unique. Big heart-shaped headdresses are worn by the warriors, crowns of wood covered with tinsel paper are worn by kings and large impressive headdresses are worn by demons whose spiky makeup distorts the actor's facial features beyond recognition.

In the same region another style of *yakshagana* is practised, called *yakshagana tekutittu* ('the southern style of *yakshagana*'). Its vigorous dances and music are reminiscent of KATHAKALI dance drama of neighbouring Kerala state.

The term *yakshagana* is also applied to performances in Andhra Pradesh and Tamil Nadu states. Some say that the term *isai* used in *Silappadikaram*, a famous Tamil epic poem of the 8th to 10th centuries, refers to a prototype of *yakshagana* which came from Kerala and imitates *kathakali*. Others say that the *yakshagana* of Andhra Pradesh originated in the 14th century and that it began as a dance interpretation of one character who took many roles.

Later it added a second character, a female counterpart. In this phase, the male was called *yaksha* and the female was known as *yakshi*. In the course of time, a clown was introduced to provide humour and finally a fortune teller came into the picture. At this stage, it is said that *yakshagana* served as a model for KUCHIPUDI which 'upgraded' the form by bringing in classical Karnataka music and elaborate acted dances that follow the dictates of the *Natyasastra*. In any case, *yakshagana* performed in Andhra Pradesh is different from that of Karnataka and less sophisticated visually.

Bibliography

GENERAL: S. Awasthi, *Drama: The Gift of Gods: Culture, Performance and Communication in India*, Tokyo, 1983; C. Choondal, *Christian Theatre in India*, Trichur, 1984, and *Classical and Folk Dances of India*, Bombay, 1963; B. Gargi, *Theatre in India*, New York, 1962; M. Khokar, *Traditions of Indian Classical Dance*, Delhi, 1979; K. Kunjunni Raja, *Kutiyattam: An Introduction*, New Delhi, 1964; K. D. Kurtkoti (ed.), *The Tradition of Kannada Theatre*, Bangalore, 1986; G. Panchal, *Kuttampalam and Kutiyattam*, New Delhi, 1984; A. Rangacharya, *The Indian Theatre*, New Delhi, 1971; F. P. Richmond, D. L. Swann, and P. B. Zarrilli (eds.), *Indian Theatre: Traditions of Performance*, Honolulu, 1990; M. L. Varadapande, *Religion and Theatre*, New Delhi, 1983; K. Vatsyayan, *Classical Indian Dance in Literature and the Arts*, New Delhi, 1968, *Indian Classical Dance*, New Delhi, 1974, and *Traditional Indian Theatre: Multiple Streams*, New Delhi, 1980.

CLASSICAL SANSKRIT THEATRE: R. Van M. Baumer and J. R. Brandon (eds.), *Sanskrit Drama in Performance*, Honolulu, 1981; Bharata Muni, *Natyasastra*, ed. and tr., M. Ghosh, Calcutta, 1961; G. K. Bhat, *The Vidusaka*, Ahmedabad, 1959; C. M. Byrski, *Concept of Ancient Indian Theatre*, New Delhi, 1974; A. B. Keith, *The Sanskrit Drama in its Origin, Development, Theory and Practice*, London, 1964; E. W. Marasinghe, *The Sanskrit Theatre and Stagecraft*, Delhi, 1989; B. S. Miller (ed.), *Theatre of Memory, the Plays of Kalidasa*, New York, 1984; S. P. Pandya, *A Study of the Technique of Abhinaya in Relation to Sanskrit Drama*, Bombay, 1990; I. Shekhar, *Sanskrit Drama: Its Origin and Decline*, Leiden, 1960; H. W. Wells, *The Classical Drama of India*, New York, 1963, and *Six Sanskrit Plays*, Bombay, 1964.

REGIONAL AND FOLK THEATRE: M. Ashton and B. Christie, *Yakshagana*, New Delhi, 1977; S. R. Desai, *Bhavai*, Ahmedabad, 1972; R. A. Frasca, *The Theater of the Mahabharata*, Honolulu, 1990; B. Gargi, *Folk Theatre of India*, Seattle, Wash., 1966; J. S. Hawley, *At Play with Krishna*, Princeton, N. J., 1981; N. Hein, *The Miracle Plays of Mathura*, New Haven, Conn., 1972; C. R. Jones and B. T. Jones, *Kathakali: An Introduction to the Dance-Drama of Kerala*, San Francisco, 1970; K. S. Karanth, *Yakshagana*, Mysore, 1974; D. R. Kinsley, *The Divine Player: A Study of Krsna Lila*, Delhi, 1979; J. C. Mathur, *Drama in Rural India*, Bombay, 1964; M. Neog, *Sankaradeva and His Times*, Gauhati, 1965; G. Panchal, *Bhavai and its Typical Aharya*, Ahmedabad, 1983; R. Schechner, *Performance Circumstances from the Avant Garde to Ramlila*, Calcutta, 1983; M. L. Varadapande, *Krishna Theatre in India*, New Delhi, 1982; P. B. Zarrilli, *The Kathakali Complex: Actor, Performance, Structure*, New Delhi, 1984.

MODERN THEATRE: R. Bharucha, *Rehearsals of Revolution*, Honolulu, 1983; C. Choondal, *Contemporary Indian Theatre: Interviews with Playwrights and Directors*, New Delhi, 1989; S. D. Desai, *Happenings: Theatre in Gujarat in the Eighties*, Gandhinagar, 1990; U. Dutt, *Towards a Revolutionary Theatre*, Calcutta, 1982; C. H. Kullman and W. C. Young (eds.), 'India', in *Theatre Companies of the World*, vol. 1, Westport, Conn., 1986; S. K. Mukherjee, *The Story of the Calcutta Theatres, 1753–1980*, Calcutta, 1982; B. Narayana, *Hindi Drama and Stage*, Delhi, 1981; M. Aslam Qureshi, *Wajid Ali Shah's Theatrical Genius*, Lahore, 1987.

INDONESIA

This performance-rich Southeast Asian nation has a population of about 180 million located on over 3000 islands which extend from Sumatra to Irian Jaya (West New Guinea). Although most of the some 300 ethnic groups which speak over 250 languages have distinctive performance traditions, research in Western languages is just beginning to clarify their nature. The better-documented theatres of Java, Bali, and Sunda (West Java) are fusions of drama, dance and music. Information on the arts of these areas has often been passed on by oral tradition, and taken with archaeological and performance evidence, reconstruction of the probable evolution is possible.

To understand the major theatres of Indonesia, it is important to comprehend four concepts: WAYANG, type, gamelan, and structured improvisation.

Wayang is the puppet tradition of the islands. The most venerable types of wayang are the recitation of stories from painted scrolls (wayang beber) and wayang kulit purwa (leather puppetry telling Ramayana and Mahabharata stories). Wayang uses a dalang ('storyteller', 'puppeteer') to direct the story. This individual manipulates the puppets or, in human theatre modelled on the puppet tradition, forges the narrative link between characters' dialogue and episodes. Wayang is generally performed to a gong-chime orchestra, called a gamelan. Over its long history, its repertory changes from Hindu epics to indigenous legends (babad) to Muslim-influenced stories about King Amir Hamzah. And its medium changes from leather puppets (kulit) to round wooden puppets (golek) to masked dancers (TOPENG) to unmasked dancers (orang). Throughout, general rules of narration, music, structure and characterization identify the forms as variants of wayang.

Second is the concept of type. Actors strive to present the essence of a character type rather than a realistic portrait. Five characters types – refined noble, proud refined aristocrat, strong male warrior, ogre king, and clown – appear in both puppetry and what is considered the oldest form of dance-acting, topeng masked dance. Later genres developed from these forms and, despite refinements, these five basic character types still form the substructure of theatre throughout Indonesia. The range from alus ('refined') to kasar, gagah ('rough', 'strong') characters underlies everything. Stylized gestures for mimetic action – walking, adjusting costume, gesturing – and pure dance movements are set for each type. Since all classical dance portrays one of these basic character types, all dance is dramatic. The refined hero, be he Rama from the Ramayana, Panji the prince of East Java, Amir Hamzah the uncle of Mohammed, or Arjuna from the Mahabharata, will be identical in terms of movement, vocal usage, and demeanour. Only the costume, the dialogue and story line will betray the individual identity.

Thirdly, music is a necessary component of all traditional performance. A tune, a tempo, a particular percussive pattern will alert a blind audience member that a character like Rama is on stage and making a specific gesture. In former times particular scales were probably linked with certain story materials: the five-tone slendro scale is widely found with the Hindu-derived tales, and the seven-tone pelog scale is more consistently used for local legends and Muslim tales (Amir Hamzah). In current Central Javanese practice, however, larger ensembles that can play either tuning have developed, blurring the earlier division. Most theatre forms are accompanied by some variant of gamelan, an orchestra in which instruments are a set tuned to each other rather than any absolute pitch. Hanging and horizontal gongs on racks generally sound on specific beats of the cyclical musical patterns. Smaller metallophones and xylophones play melodic patterns in interconnected parts. Drums provide the rhythmic lead – signalling starts, stops, and changes of tune – and may make sound effects or accent the moves of the dance. Singers, flute or a bowed lute (*rebab*) provide an elaborate melody within the structural frame the other instruments supply. The *dalang* cues the musicians with a wood mallet and/or metal plates. Specific tunes are associated with set scenes, character types or dramatic action (that is, battle). The *dalang* sings mood songs which have similar dramatic specificity. The *gamelan*'s singer, if present, will try to choose lyrics that reinforce the atmosphere of the scene. Voices of character types may be pegged to specific notes of the scale and defined by set vocal patterns.

Finally, one must consider the role of structured improvisation: traditional performances have no written text, nor are the songs to be played during a show preplanned by the troupe. The genre's set dramatic structure in conjunction with the scenario and rules of type allow performers to generate the text and song sequence in performance. A traditional epic episode or even a newly devised story can be presented by a good troupe at a moment's notice. Of the many theatre genres currently performed, only the recently developed Western-influenced genres like SANDI-WARA and modern drama use a written script. Performances traditionally take place outdoors or in the pavilion of an aristocrat's house, and food stalls and other entertainments sprout just outside the performing area. Children wake up for clowning and battles, others turn their attention to the stage for love scenes or philosophical discussions. Audience members come and go, eat, gamble, sleep or visit neighbours throughout the night. The drama is only a part of a larger event in which audience and performers improvise within their set constraints.

These organizing principles provide a basis for considering theatre history. Four major categories of performance exist: (1) proto-theatrical practices; (2) traditional court or folk performance; (3) popular urban drama of the last 100 years; and (4) modern spoken drama. By considering each of these strata as representing stages of development, a sense of the history of theatre may be deduced, though the interplay of strata is more complex than this evolutionary model implies.

Proto-theatrical practices

Throughout the archipelago features that characterize performance in most Malay cultures can be seen, notably: (1) epic recitation; (2) poetic dialogue games; and (3) use of performance for spirit communication. Singing of verse epics is found in many Indonesian cultures, and this custom seems to have continued with new content and metres as new cultural influences became accepted. For example, among the Sundanese of West Java, a *pantun* storyteller composes, in performance, his tale based on indigenous legends. Accompanying himself on a zither (*kecapi*), he sings octosyllabic, metred lines in nightlong presentations. Similar entertainments may have been a base from which puppet theatre developed after the advent of Hindu culture about the first century AD.

Javanese written epics of the 9th–14th centuries were probably presented in oral performance by

A Dayak dancer emulates the movement of the hornbill bird, Kalimantan.

reciters who are mentioned in early court records. These epics, based on Indian sources and written in Sanskrit-derived metres and language and known as *kakawin*, are still sung in Bali and may form the literary base for *wayang*. Tales include the *Ramayana*, which chronicles Sita's rescue by her god-incarnate husband, Rama, when she is kidnapped by the demonic Rawana. Other *kakawin* are based on the *Mahabharata*, telling of the exploits of five heroes, the Pandawa brothers, who fight their hundred Kurawa cousins in the *bharata yudha*, a great war that leaves the heroes heartbroken in their hour of victory. Middle-Javanese-language *kidung* were stories written in indigenous verse forms, dealing with the story of the heroic Panji and other indigenous tales. Although these texts, by virtue of being written, are more set than traditional theatre genres of today, they correspond to the story materials of most theatre. Such texts, presumably growing from and intended for oral performance, may have had interplay with theatrical enactment from an early period. Indeed, a few mood songs of the shadow-theatre repertoire correspond to passages from such texts.

Sintren, a trance dance of the Cirebon area of West Java. The entranced dancer is said to be possessed by a goddess who is called into her body by the *dukun*, here holding an incense burner in his hand.

Poetry games using indigenous verse forms are a root of some folk-theatre forms. The Sundanese four-line riddle poetry, *sisinderan*, is an example. These verses could be improvised courting games in which a male singer vied with a female, or sung in other contexts. A number of Sundanese folk-theatre forms, such as GODANG, dog-dog, calung (each of which uses a different kind of musical instrument to accompany singing), expand on such games by adding humorous improvised skits about village life.

Also significant are performances that communicate with spirits. Trance performance is common throughout the islands, since such dances allow spirits to enter the world in a controlled mode. In Balinese SANGHYANG *dedari*, a trance performance done in times of epidemic or difficulty, two small girls are put into trance by the chant of a male chorus and allowed to speak for the spirits. In West Java *sintren* or *lais*, the trance dance of a child medium, is probably a related form. In Central Java entranced dancers may rock a doll figure, *nini towong*, to make rain. In other islands of Indonesia, too, masks and puppets are used in rites for the dead, and a preference for puppet and mask in this culture may relate to such forms. (See also Malaysia, ULEK; Burma, NAT PWE.)

In Sunda, entranced dancers doing martial arts dance (*pencak silat*) may be entered by the spirit of a tiger (*pamacan*) or monkey (*pamonyet*). Horse trance dances are found in Bali (*sanghang jaran*), Java (KUDA KEPANG, *jatilan*) and Sunda (*kuda lumping*) as well as in Malaysia. Dancers entered by horse spirits are able to eat glass or walk on hot coals. An important animal figure associated with trance performance is the lion-like being, BARONG, perhaps derived from a Buddhist protective figure and related to the Chinese lion. In Bali the image has become linked to a magico-religious dance drama in which the protective *barong* pits its power against the malevolent witch, Rangda ('widow'). She prompts entranced dancers to turn their weapons against themselves; however, their trance prevents wounds.

In most trance performances a *dukun* (ritual specialist in dealing with spirits and curing) or a priest will be the significant figure who, by mantras and incense, calls the appropriate spirit into the performer. Often an assistant makes sure the trancers remain within acceptable bounds and adds comic quips to the possession rite at the same time. These two roles have some features in common with respectively a *dalang* who controls and narrates for a performance but does not 'act' himself, and a clown character who is part of every genre.

Content is also significant for placating the spirit world. *Wayang*'s exorcistic story, *The Origin of Kala (Murawakala)*, is a case in point. In Java, Sunda and Bali certain individuals are believed to be threatened by the demon Kala, whose name means 'time'. The potential victim lives in danger of misfortune until a *dalang* plays the story of how the first *wayang* exorcism (*ruwatan*) calmed Kala's wrath. Another story, *Mikukuhan*, about King Mikukuhan was used in Java and Sunda to prevent diseases threatening rice crops, while *Watugunung*, named after its hero who married his own mother, was used in East Java to make rain. The Balinese *Calonarang*, named after the witch-widow of the title, tells how a king of East Java foiled her machinations. It may be presented in Bali as a shadow play or in conjunction with *rangda-barong* dance drama.

Performances are traditionally part of rites-of-passage ceremonies for the group or individual, and this tradition seems to have persisted through times of spirit worship, of Hinduism and of Islam. In areas like Cirebon, wooden-rod-puppet shows telling local chronicles (*wayang golek cepak*) take place annually at the cemetery to honour the dead. Indeed some scholars believe pre-Hindu performances told of ancestral exploits as a means of gaining the forbears' aid in promoting fertility. In Bali much performance takes place in the context of temple festivals when Hindu and local spirits are thought to be visiting earth. Throughout Muslim Java and Sunda weddings, circumcisions, a ceremony for an unborn or newly born child or a ritual cleansing of the village from bad spirits are important occasions for a performance that often lasts all night, since that is when spirits are nigh. Performances include food offerings for the spirits, and open with mantras and music meant for spirit propitiation. Although today most performances are primarily intended for the amusement of the audience who attend for free (the family celebrating the rite of passage pays the troupe), such evidence hints that old relationships of dancer and spirit medium, and of *dalang* and shaman, give the performer an aura of power.

Traditional court and folk performance

The elaboration of early performance practices into strong theatrical traditions seems largely to have come after Hindu–Buddhist religion was adopted by the ruling elite. In the kingdom of Sriwijaya (7th–13th centuries), centred in Sumatra but having influence in Java and the Malay peninsula, the ruler used ceremony as a mode of dramatizing his magico-religious power. In Java various dynasties perpetuated syncretic animistic-Hindu–Buddhist practices. By the 9th century Javanese inscriptions indicate that female dancers, clowns, mask performers and shadow players were resident in courts and temples. Indian influence may have been stronger in this early period: dancers in temple reliefs assume strong stances similar to current Indian dance and unlike contemporary Javanese style. The sign-mime gestures of India (*mudra* or *hasta*) are not, however, apparent. Local aesthetics must soon have remoulded any strong outside stimuli: by the 13th century temple reliefs in East Java show scenes in which the costume, space usage and character typology bear a striking resemblance to current Balinese *wayang*.

In the 9th–15th centuries distinctive Javanese versions of the *Ramayana* and *Mahabharata* were developed. These epics probably reached Indonesia from Bengal and eastern India, but soon events of the epics were believed to have occurred at specific sites in Java and the heroes were considered ancestors of the Javanese. Masked dance, female dance and shadow theatre became integral parts of ritual to enhance the aura of the king in magico-religious, as well as aesthetic dimensions. The importance of performance to such systems has led anthropologist Geertz to characterize such cultures as 'theatre states': court performance and ceremony became the way rulers acted out their power and, thereby, were empowered. The concept that *gamelan*, dances, puppets, masks and performers focused spiritual power and hence were necessary regalia for kings seems to have crystallized in this era. Tantric Hindu–Buddhist thought seems to have promoted such thinking. Kings in Cambodia, Thailand and Malaysia eventually adopted similar strategies for articulating their glory, influenced, in part, by Sriwijayan and Javanese models.

Scholars currently debate the impact of Indian and Chinese culture in developing the arts. For example, female dance, shadow puppetry and mask theatre are all found in India. Though these are the oldest performance modes in Indonesia, each of these arts manifests itself in quite a different way than in Indian models. It seems likely that Indonesians largely borrowed forms which reinforced indigenous performance tendencies, upgrading them with Indian stories and the aura of a higher culture. The fact that theatre only developed strongly in areas of Indonesia where Hindu culture was firmly implanted implies that the impact of India was, indeed, important. Trade with China was a significant feature in developing the economic base of the major kingdoms in Indonesia, and it is possible that puppetry techniques and typology of character were influenced by Chinese practice. Martial-arts dance and wooden-rod-puppet techniques, for example, are often associated with Chinese communities. Though less scholarship has focused on the connection between performance in Indonesia and Oceania, common threads might usefully be pursued. The importance of female dancers and child performers is a common link.

Muslim conversions began in the 13th century, and gradually all Java accepted Islam. The aristocrats of the last Hindu–Buddhist court, Majapahit, retreated to the neighbouring island of Bali around 1520. Balinese performance has developed greatly since these culture bringers slipped across those two miles of ocean, yet it seems likely that the aesthetic of Bali today may give some insight into Hindu Javanese arts. The Balinese hold that their theatre is the legacy of Majapahit, citing two forms in particular, GAMBUH dance drama and *wayang parwa*.

Bali

Gambuh is said to have been developed in Majapahit Java and have changed little since the 16th century. The plays, presented in the inner temple courtyard during temple festivals, last all day or all night, and tell stories drawn from Javanese legends, notably the *Panji* cycle. The heroic characters speak Kawi (old Javanese), which the audience cannot understand, while the clowns use colloquial Balinese, and the narrator mixes Kawi and Balinese. This linguistic difference

Cak, or 'Monkey Dance', in Bali.

between epic characters and clowns is a significant part of traditional Balinese performance. Other Balinese dramatic forms, including *LEGONG*, *topeng*, *wayang wong*, *ARJA* and *baris melamphan*, are said to derive from this ur-genre, which is preserved at Batuan, Gianyar and a few other places.

The other form considered as a direct legacy of Majapahit is *wayang parwa*, the hide-shadow-puppet theatre of Bali telling *Mahabharata* tales. The figures, the music ensemble and performance technique are more vigorous than current Javanese style, perhaps indicating an older practice. Less stylized puppet images, a simpler orchestra composed of four metallophones called *gender*, a smaller screen, a shorter performance duration and a more elaborate opening ritual are some of the characteristics differentiating it from Javanese practice. This vibrant puppet tradition is the most popular theatre form in Bali and performances are required for many life-cycle ceremonies.

The Balinese *legong* dancer, with darting eyes, high elbow placement, and dynamic changes of position, offers a more energized vision of the female than Muslim Java cultivates. The vibrancy may hint at an aesthetic more aligned with the Hindu–Buddhist heritage of Majapahit. In *legong* the most abstract of dramas is hidden in the movements of three prepubescent girls. The form as currently practised developed around 1800 when prince I Dewa Agung Made Karna, after dreaming he saw heavenly maidens dancing in a style similar to the sacred trance, *sanghang dedari*, ordered girls to be trained accordingly. As other rulers elaborated on this first attempt, *legong* was established. In times past, *legong* dancers often became wives of the ruler when they reached puberty.

Topeng is the mask dance of Bali: the stories are taken from Javanese and local legends. Major characters wear full masks, while clowns, who translate, wear half-masks. Some masks are said to be magically charged, and the oldest masks in the island are said to have been brought back from East Java in the Majapahit era by an aristocrat of the Jelantik clan. His descendants eventually used these masks and added new ones that tied at the back rather than being held by the teeth as in Java. The oldest Balinese *topeng* is the solo *topeng pajegan*, performed in the sacred inner courtyard of the temple. Four introductory mask dances begin the performance, then the dancer acts out a story alter-

nating noble and clown masks. Finally, he puts on the mask of an old man, Sidha Karya ('Accomplishing the Task'), and enacts a dance ritual to bring a desired blessing. Ritually potent *topeng* dancers today include: I Made Jimat, I Made Sidja, Anak Agung Cebang and I Ketut Kantor. I NYOMAN KAKUL's death in the early 1980s was a major loss.

In the last hundred years two new *topeng* forms have become popular as entertainment. *Topeng panca* ('five'-person *topeng*) uses a larger group to present the traditional repertoire with more interaction and clown scenes. The Sidha Karya mask ritual is not presented in this version nor in the eclectic *topeng prembon* ('combination' *topeng*) created around 1940. The latter melds the *topeng* repertoire and clowning with females dancing and singing in *arja* (dance opera) style.

Gambuh, *wayang parwa*, and, to a lesser extent, *legong* and *topeng* may hint at Majapahit theatre practice and aesthetics. More recent Balinese genres continue to draw on these older forms. *Wayang wong* was created in the late 1700s when the ruler of Klungkung asked performers to use ancient masks in his collection. In the resulting form masked humans tell tales derived from the *Ramayana*. A parallel form is *Wayang (orang) parwa* in which unmasked dancers and masked clowns enact *Mahabharata* stories. Sukawati was a centre for this genre, but the currently active group is in Bonkasa, Badung. Both these forms use a *dalang* and follow shadow-theatre performance practices. Masked *JAUK* originated in the 18th century as dance dramas of *Ramayana* and *Mahabharata* stories.

More modern genres, created as secular entertainments, include: *JANGGER*, *arja*, *KECAK*, *baris melamphan* and *SENDRATARI*. *Jangger*, a group dance for young men and women, was considered daringly modern between 1920 and 1950, and it continues to be popular today. *Arja* is a romantic dance opera that began in the 1900s and features female performers. It is perhaps the most popular genre on the island today. *Kecak* is a modern creation devised for tourist audiences. The expatriot painter Walter Spies commissioned the first performance in Bedulu village for a German film *Island of Demons* in the 1930s. Thereafter it became a popular tourist genre. In its standard form, a 150-strong male chorus makes interlocking 'cak-cak' calls, playing a chorus of monkeys, as the stirring background for a danced episode of the kidnapping of Sita from the *Ramayana*. The abstract warrior dance drama *baris melamphan* uses *Ramayana* and *Mahabharata* stories. The all-male cast speaks in ancient Kawi language. The dancers are not distinguished from each other by costume or characterization, but by action and the talk of the translator-clowns.

SENDRATARI (literally, art-drama-dance) is a form of pantomimic dance drama developed at the High School of Traditional Music (KOKAR, now SMKI) in 1962. This genre was created simultaneously in Java and Sunda in government art schools. The narrative of the traditional *dalang* and dialogue were cut to eliminate the language barrier that kept members of other ethnic groups from understanding regional performance. In Bali *sendratari's* appeal was heightened by the use of the most popular *gamelan* style of the last 25 years, *kebyar*, 'lightning' style, which has brilliant tone and quick transitions. The expert performance of the young dance students who often come from the best families of traditional dance, the proscenium stage, theatre lighting and costumes adapted from traditional dance apparel, all make the form popular. *Sendratari* as choreographed by I Wayan Beratha, I WAYAN DIBIA, and I MADE BANDEM show much continuity with the past, but the imposition of a set choreography and the absence of the Kawi language and of a *dalang* show movement from the older theatre pattern.

Currently the Balinese maintain a vibrant theatrical life. Performers and cultural conservators, aware of potential contradictions between religious aims and modern commercial strains have attempted to provide guidelines for usage of the different genres so that commercial and religious values need not clash. In the late 1970s the categories of sacred (*wali*), ceremonial (*bebali*) and entertainment (*bali-balihan*) were established, and different genres divided into these categories in an attempt to prevent commercial cannibalization of the *wali* genres. On any day dozens of tourist performances can be seen around the island and the glut of tourists has created a surplus of capital in many villages which is reinvested in performances for temple festivals, cremations and the annual Bali Arts Festival. At this point these attempts to distinguish tourist from religious performance appear successful.

Java

With the energized Balinese drama as a perspective, the transitions made in 15th- to 17th-century Java toward a more subdued, inwardly focused and stylized theatre style become clear. A generation of Muslim teacher-rulers rose in cities along the north coast. Rather than abandoning the arts, these leaders promoted them. Johns has suggested that Sufi mystical orders introduced Islam, and this would explain the performative orientation of Islam in Java. Further research is required to test the hypothesis: for example, a close comparison of *wayang kulit purwa* with the dervish-related Kargoz shadow-puppet theatre of the Arab world, supposedly created in 1366 by a Sufi mystic, Mehmend Kushteri, might establish firmer links.

Documentation from earlier periods proves that shadow, mask and dance performance actually developed in the Hindu-Buddhist period. Still traditional Javanese artists invariably trace the origin of their theatre practice to the *Wali Sangga*, the 'Nine Saints' who converted the island to Islam. Wali Sunan Kalijaga is credited with devising *wayang kulit purwa*, performing it in mosques and requiring the Muslim confession of faith as the price of viewing.

Though not necessarily historical facts, these statements reveal inner truth – the local tradition was redefined, and new features characterized Muslim–Javanese as opposed to Hindu–Balinese arts. A greater stylization of puppet and mask was introduced, supposedly to circumvent the Islamic prohibition on representing the human form. A more inward-turning focus and flowing dance style were adopted, especially for refined character types. The Kawi language was abandoned for Javanese, though traces of the older tongue haunt mood songs and narration. The *Mahabharata* cycle, on which 95 per cent of current stories are based, was revised to suit a Muslim ethos: Indian religious figures were devalued and the polygamy of the five Pandawa and their wife, Drupadi, edited out. New content was introduced, including the Amir Hamzah stories glorifying that Muslim hero and tales of the nine *wali* themselves were soon developed. Pan-Islamic forms like Sufi DIKIR group chanting and the Muslim trance dance *dabus*, in which performers stab and cut themselves with impunity, also began in this era.

Many changes were made in Java's *wayang* tradi-

Islamic figures in *wayang golek cepak*, the rod-puppet theatre of the north coast of Java.

tion, leading toward the well-known *wayang kulit purwa* of today. On an expansive screen a *dalang* presents the monodrama, manipulating about 50 leathers-shadow-puppet figures through a complex plot lasting from 8.30 p.m. till morning. The puppetmaster controls the entire performance, cuing the *gamelan* which also accompanies the female singer. His story will ordinarily be based on Javanese-invented tales concerning the Hindu heros of the *Ramayana* and *Mahabharata* and will follow a strict performance structure: opening court scene, battle episode, hermitage and clown scene (*gara-gara*), second battle against ogre characters called the 'flower battle' (*perang kembang*), and closing battle. Individual scenes required for a story are added as necessary. The performance is divided into three parts, marked by change in musical pitch. The set character types of hero, strong warrior, clown and ogre, and known epic materials form the base for each improvised performance.

The meanings of these plays are multiple. For example, the three parts of the night correspond to youth, adolescence and adulthood. The child's precarious first steps become firm in the testing of youth, the 'flower battle'. There we overcome 'ogres' of greed and sensuality if we are to succeed in life. Another mode of looking at plays is to understand that the classes of characters correspond to different categories of Javanese society: the heroes are the Javanese elite; the clowns are the common people; the ogres, the demonic and non-Javanese powers or peoples. The myths of the Pandawas fighting their own cousins remind Javanese of the colonial experience. The Dutch used royal-family rivalries, splitting the royal house in 1755 into Surakarta and Yogyakarta and later subdividing these to form four competing royal houses. The inter-family quarrels helped make the rulers weak, and have given these stories deep resonance. Other scholars see old tribal patterns, spirit communication, royal propaganda or philosophical tolerance as important features of the form.

Other forms of Javanese *wayang* tend today to follow the structural-musical model of the *wayang kulit purwa*. The now infrequently played *wayang beber*, which tells various cycles using picture scrolls, may actually be older than the *wayang kulit purwa*. The oral tradition holds that this was the genre used to tell the exorcistic Kala tale until the early 1600s. Since *dalang* still fear changing this magically powerful story, earlier practices of it might have been maintained longer. Another genre that follows the *wayang kulit purwa* style is *wayang gedog* which uses *pelog gamelan* and leather puppets to tell *Panji* and other Javanese tales. It was supposedly created in 1553 by the wali, Sunan Giri. *Wayang golek cepak*, which has wooden doll-like rod puppets and tells Javanese chronicles and Amir Hamzah tales, was credited to Sunan Kudus' innovation in 1584. This form continues to thrive along the north coast, where Aliwijaya of Cirebon claims to be the 27th generation of his family to present the art. In East Java *wayang klitik* adopts flat wooden puppets to tell Javanese tales. One feature that distinguishes some of these genres from *wayang kulit purwa* is that there is no concept of 'branch' stories, and therefore *dalang*, in general, need to be better versed in all the particulars of the epic than the young *purwa dalang*, who may invent many of their tales. Another distinction is that puppet headdresses and costumes vary from *purwa* style and are reminiscent of Javanese court dress of the 17th century.

Some newer shadow forms are found only in the palaces or government offices, since they validate and glorify particular rulers: *wayang madya* uses leather puppets to tell tales of historical Central Javanese kings, while *wayang suluh* was created in 1947 and tells of figures like Sukarno who forged the new Republic of Indonesia. There are many other *wayang* forms, but none rival *wayang kulit purwa*, which remains a favoured entertainment for weddings and circumcisions. Cassettes of performances by superstars like NARTO SABDHO or Anom Suroto are found in every record shop. At institutions like Habiranda, a puppetry school founded by the Bureau of Performing Arts of the Yogyakarta palace in 1950, one can find many students studying formally what *dalang* of past generations learned by apprenticing themselves for a number of years.

The mask dance of the north coast, *topeng babakan*, is also attributed to Sunan Kalijaga. Over eight hours a solo dancer (who is also a *dalang*) presents a sequence of four or five masks. Today most *dalang* specialize only in dance; in times past performers, who might be male or female, often performed shadow plays as well. *Topeng* performances would be given during the day and *wayang kulit purwa* would be presented in the evening. The white-faced refined Panji, conceptually an innocent infant, yet spiritually perfected, opens the presentation. Then comes Pamindo ('two'), often a blue mask – a refined but proud and flighty adolescent; the third figure is a strong, mature male, Temenggung ('minister'), whose mask has a reddish cast; and the final figure is Klana a red-faced figure with bulging eyes and fangs, furiously grasping for life, even in the moment of death. A fifth mask, Rumiang, may sometimes be added. A second dancer plays the clown, and his half-masks let him engage in verbal as well as physical humour. The abstract story is less significant than the types which represent the different aspects of the personality that lie behind and within each person. The symbolism of the masks is complex: they are correlated with the four directions, the elements and emotions, and may be derived from rice-harvest ritual. Today SUJANA ARDJA of Salangit, Cirebon, is a major performer of this genre.

The second major mask theatre of Java is said to have evolved from this solo tradition. Multiple masked dancers enact stories in *wayang topeng* as a *dalang* delivers all the dialogue or just the narration, mood songs and cues. This form persists in rural areas especially along the north coast and on the island of Madura, while the courts and commercial theatre have largely abandoned it for unmasked dance drama.

The final legacy of this early Muslim period is the female dance of Java. Even more abstract than *legong*, it remains a potent symbol of past court glory. In BEDAYA nine refined female dancers move through intricate floor patterns via slow, stylized gesture. Somewhere within the piece a highly stylized struggle may be enacted, representing both an actual combat in the story and the extinction of worldly desire in the soul of the true aesthetic. The interplay of eroticism and enlightenment colours the form. Some practices of tantrism may have affected the genre, and the choreography creates a mandala-like floor pattern that works on a magico-religious level to simulate enlightenment in the ideal spectator – the ruler. The dancers would often become the wives or ladies-in-waiting of the ruler, and he might take them into battle to unleash the spiritual forces they represented against his enemy.

The oldest *bedaya* choreography still performed dates from the 16th century, but the genre is believed to be related to older Hindu–Buddhist forms. The *Bedaya Ketawang* is the inheritance of the Surakarta court of Central Java. It is said that Sultan Agung of Mataram (1616–45) was meditating on the shores of the southern ocean when the goddess of the seas tried to seduce him with this dance. Thereafter, it has been ritually performed once a year on the anniversary of the coronation day of his kingly descendants, perpetuating the spiritual compact between goddess and ruler. The goddess herself is believed sometimes to appear among the dancers.

Bedaya Semang, the similar ritual performance of the Yogyakarta court, lapsed around 1920. *Bedaya Madiun* presents the suppression of a rebellion by the Mataram monarch, and *Bedaya Arjuna Wiwaha* re-enacts the ritual union of the *Mahabharata* hero, Arjuna, with a heavenly nymph. In recent years *bedaya* has become a popular choreographic genre for new dances. *Srimpi*, a related form for four female dancers, dates from the 17th century. Performers were traditionally daughters of rulers who, again, presented a stylized battle. *Srimpi*

Renggawati, for five female dancers, shows the battle between two princesses in love with Amir Hamzah.

Solo female court dances do not have the same aura of the sacred as these group dances. It seems likely that they rise from the popular RONGGENG (female singer-dancer) tradition which is found in many manifestations throughout Indonesia. *Tayuban* is a dance party in which a female dancer opens the performance by dancing classical character types but which ends up with the lady (or, in some instances, a female impersonator) doing partner dances with various male spectators. *Ronggeng* has always had an aura of prostitution attached, but the role has a significance that Western society does not accord the courtesan. Some scholars attribute these forms to archaic links between female dancers and rice fertility rituals, which are still found in some villages and require the presence of such a performer.

Beksan lawung ('lance dances') are 17th-century male court dances depicting military prowess performed at both the Surakarta and Yogyakarta courts. Perhaps because of the military expertise of its founder, Hamengku Buwana I, the Yogyakarta sultanate is especially noted for these dances, which recreate the pageantry and battles of the court. The Surakarta court, with its legacy of *bedaya*, is felt to excel in female-style dance.

Unmasked dance drama, *wayang orang* in Indonesian or *wayang wong* in Javanese, is also a speciality of Yogyakarta since it was supposedly created there after the split in the royal line. The first court dance drama, *Gondowerdoyo* (*Scent of the Heart*), was presented under the personal direction of Hamengku Buwana I in the 18th century. Then, as today, the performance used *wayang kulit purwa* and *wayang topeng* as models. The function of the *dalang* and the dramatic structure came from puppet theatre. Dancers took the puppet roles, and the flat plane of the blocking and the flowing quality of movement probably derived from the shadow play aesthetic. Female impersonators were the theatrical norm for *wayang wong* in Yogyakarta until the 1920s. Dance, in this era, was considered a necessary study for royalty, since it refined the spirit. Hence, princes were often fine dancers and apt to play major roles in these dance dramas. Performers were cast according to body type and personality, and would play the same role type for

life. Though the conceptualization of role types was expanded from four to twelve in the court, the increased types can be considered a refinement, rather than a rejection of, the old four-character system.

The resources of the court promoted precision and elegance inconceivable in village performance. Performances ran three to four days with hundreds of dancers rehearsing up to a year in preparation. Twelve such epics were staged in the Yogyakarta court in the 1920s–30s, with the repertoire primarily drawn from *Mahabharata* material. The distinctive older headdress of the masked dancer, constructed of matted hair, was abandoned in favour of headpieces like those of *wayang kulit purwa* figures. Exquisitely dyed batik fabrics with set designs designated for specific characters wrapped the bejewelled dancers. Dance scarves, tossed and held as part of the dance technique, were prescribed for each role. The 'green-room' area where dancers waited to make their entrance to the dance area of the palace was called by the same name as the puppet chest of *wayang*. Still, behind the splendour of these costly court extravaganzas the *dalang* role of the ruler was already in decline.

In the first quarter of this century two major alterations in court support of theatre occurred. Firstly, Krida Beksa Wikrama was founded in Yogyakarta by Prince Surjodiningrat and Prince Tedjokusumo in 1918 to train dancers for performances outside the palace. Secondly, palace performers began producing *wayang orang* for a ticket-buying public in Sriwidari, a park in Surakarta opened in 1899. Originally commercial, travelling *wayang orang* companies played there, but by 1920 palace dancers took over the venue. The box office went into the palace treasury, and performers got a set salary. This early democratization and commercialization of palace arts accelerated after 1949, when, with independence, court resources diminished. Sriwidari itself came under city administration at that time.

Current commercial *wayang orang* troupes perform on a proscenium stage equipped with wing-and-drop scenery. Women often play refined male roles, a practice first introduced in the 1930s in Surakarta. Troupes have in recent years shortened performances to three hours and introduced new repertoire – Javanese legends, in addition to *purwa* tales – to attract audiences. Actors find these new materials difficult and must undertake unaccustomed rehearsals: *purwa* materials are easily improvised from the scenario, since actors generally play the same set character from performance to performance. Though the 1980s have brought declining audiences, major troupes like Ngesti Pandawa in Semarang and Surakarta's Sriwidari continue.

Other court dramas have largely disappeared. Surakarta's *langendriya* is rarely seen. This dance drama contained sung dialogue presented by a female troupe. It tells the story of Damar Wulan, a 14th-century Majapahit ruler. The form was created in 1876 by Raden Temenggung Purwadiningrat and Prince Mankubumi. Also rare, *langen mandra wanara* was created by Danureja VII in the same era to present the *Ramayana* story. Related forms told stories of King Amir Hamzah (*langen asmara*) and Prince Panji (*langen pranasmara*).

As in Bali, a textless *sendratari* has grown popular in Java since the 1960s for both tourist and local audiences. Major tourist performances can be seen in the dry season at Prambanan and Pandaan temple complexes, where *Ramayana* and East Javanese tales, respectively, are presented. Noted *sendratari* choreographers, including Wisnu Wardhana, BAGONG KUSSUDIARDJO, Sudharso Pringgobroto, SARDONO S. KUSUMO, and Sudarsono, create works for urban Javanese and overseas tours. They sometimes incorporate techniques from Sundanese, Balinese, or even Western experimental dance in innovative productions. Story materials, music, and costume may also diverge from traditional sources. Still, the strong continuity with the classical tradition is apparent in most performances, which can also be seen at government academies of dance in Yogyakarta and Surakarta.

Sunda

Since the 18th century the Sundanese, a distinct ethnic group living in western Java, have developed a rich artistic tradition. As in Bali, genres show their relation to Javanese models while the aesthetic, movement style, music and language are Sunda's own. Sundanese performance strikes the viewer as occupying the middle ground between the almost frenetic dynamism of Bali and the mesmerizing, flowing aesthetic of Java. The drummer accents the dancers' steps with drum patterns appropriate for the movement, rather like the drum-dance syllables of Indian performance. This makes the movement and sound system seem more transparent than Java's. In conjunction with the lively musical style, the constant calls and quips that musicians are free to add to the performance, it also makes Sunda's arts seem earthy and spontaneous. This aesthetic probably results from the fact that palaces have had little part in forming the Sundanese arts – these are village arts.

Storytelling, harvest rituals, and poetry traditions involving skits were part of Sunda's indigenous culture. In the early 19th century Javanese officials assigned to govern parts of this area began importing *dalang* from the Cirebon area where north-coast Javanese had their own distinctive variants of Javanese arts. About the same time itinerant troupes from the north coast availed themselves of the road the Dutch colonial administration had opened into the Sundanese highlands. *Topeng* dancers and *ronggeng* singers might be found as part of market-day entertainments. As these artists settled in Sunda and intermarried with Sundanese, a new hybrid of *wayang*, *ronggeng* and *topeng* performances developed. Meanwhile, *wayang golek purwa*, a rod-puppet theatre, was created about 150 years ago in the city of Sumedang when performers of Javanese *wayang kulit purwa* began to tell their Hindu-based *purwa* stories in the Sundanese language using wooden rod puppets. Until that time only leather puppets had been used to tell the *purwa* story, but the local preference for the comparative realism of the three-dimensional figures (used to tell Javanese and Muslim stories along the north coast) prompted the local regent to commission a set of wooden puppets with the distinctive *purwa* headdresses. From this start *wayang golek purwa* became a lively village entertainment. The most popular genre in Sunda, it is performed at life-cycle ceremonies and broadcast on radio and television. The story structure roughly follows the Javanese model, but much more freedom is allowed to the puppeteer in shaping his story, especially when the clown and ogre characters appear. At present some performers also do Sundanese chronicle tales and Amir Hamzah stories using the same set of *purwa* style puppets. These tales are the speciality of Bogor-city *dalang* who find Islamic fundamentalist audiences favour such material.

Today the SUNARYA family of the Bandung area is probably the most popular *dalang* family: five major performers from two generations of the family are active. The eldest *dalang* in such a family can make holy water, used to cure and bring luck, or perform spiritually dangerous exorcisms. However, since major *dalang* are culture idols and command high fees, many boys who do not come from families of *dalang* aspire to the role, creating a current pool of about 2000 who have trained via the apprentice system. The female singer (*pasinden*), who was incorporated into the form around 1900, is given more prominence than her Javanese counterpart, and the audience requests songs during interludes in the story. The first *pasinden* was, reportedly, a *ronggeng* dancer-singer who married a *dalang*. The popularity of these dynamic women rivals that of the *dalang* themselves.

Sundanese folk theatres like *topeng banyet* and *ronggeng gunung* are linked to the *ronggeng* tradition. They often open with solo character dances by a female, short sketches on village life, and culminate with performers dancing *ketuk tilu* partner dances with male audience members. Songs by the performers may come between sketches. Featured roles are the female actress-singer-dancer and clown. In recent years this *ronggeng* style has been reinterpreted for urban audiences in a performance called *jaipongan*. Begun in the late 1970s by Gugum Gumbira, *dalang* Nadang Barmaya and actress-singer Tatih Saleh, this dance-song-comedy genre became a pan-Indonesian craze.

Topeng mask dances came to Sunda from the north-coast area. The aggressive Klana character with his red face and demon energy has long been the favoured dance. Currently many Sundanese study with masters from the north coast and are reintroducing many mask dances into the highlands.

Wayang orang developed in Sunda, as in Java, by substituting people for puppets, and corresponds in most particulars to the *wayang golek purwa*. The dance of the performers has the grounded, three-dimensional feel of the wooden rod puppet that the dancer tries to emulate. *Sendratari* has emerged in the last 25 years, with ENOCH ATMADIBARATA, Abay Subarja, IRAWATI DURBAN ARJO and Endo Suwanda as important choreographers. Though *purwa* stories are sometimes presented, Sundanese legends and history prevail. Tales of Pajajaran, the

Sundanese kingdom that retreated to the spirit plane rather than accept the domination of the Javanese, may be presented with haunting Sundanese songs derived from the old *pantun* (storytelling) tradition. Where Javanese and Balinese may look for new materials from other areas, Sundanese tend to look to their own past.

Popular urban drama

In the last hundred years popular drama forms which emphasize dialogue over dance, performed in permanent theatres for a ticket-buying audience, have arisen in the cities. Many of these forms developed in the early part of this century in response to touring BANGSAWAN troupes from Malaysia. The Malaysian troupes presented a model of a commercial theatre where entertainment was the prime aim and presenting new plot materials was standard practice. Actors played set character types and generated the script from a scenario. A *dalang* was not needed, and the archaisms of language, rituals for spirits and formulaic phrases that characterize *wayang* were dropped. Plots could be set in modern times. Plot and language were emphasised and movement and the whole performance tended toward greater realism. The prominence given clown characters and tendency of plots to turn on problems of lovers and their parents make the forms reminiscent of *commedia dell'arte*. Usually performances would be given in structures boasting a proscenium stage, painted scenery and a darkened auditorium. Though some forms, like KETOPRAK, show considerable continuity with *wayang*'s epic world, others, like LUDRUK, look more to the present.

Ketoprak is a Central-Javanese form created in the early 20th century based on musical rhythms elaborated from rice-pounding music. The music became a craze in court and villages around Surakarta, and dialogue-oriented, improvised dramas based on Javanese chronicle tales became associated with it in the 1920s. By 1927 *gamelan* replaced the original musical instruments. Current troupes like Ketoprak Mataram and Sapta Mandala in Yogyakarta perform nightly, and the backstage visitor will see actors checking the posted scenario before going on stage. Plot structure and character types correspond in many ways to *wayang orang* minus its dance and archaic language.

Ludruk is the urban popular theatre of Surabaya in East Java. It developed from folk entertainments into a drama-oriented genre under the influence of *bangsawan*. Performances begin with a dance, followed by a clown sequence and singing by the female impersonator. Then comes the story, usually a domestic melodrama with comic interludes, though some traditional stories are still presented. Though the female impersonator dances in a style rudely recalling the traditional female court dancer, the core of the show is the realistic spoken drama that probes problems of the modern urban audience.

Sandiwara, Sunda's response to *bangsawan*, has two major forms. The first is comparable to *ketoprak* and combines indigenous *gamelan*, Sundanese history tales, and *wayang*-like dramatic structure. The second variant is now more common and focuses on domestic melodramas climaxing in martial-arts scenes. A village girl may be kidnapped by a bandit, but rescued by her sweetheart, or the attempts of parents to marry a daughter for money will be foiled by her true love and the good offices of her clownish servant.

Other examples of similar 20th-century improvised forms aimed at popular audiences are found in Sumatra (*randai* of the Minangkabau), around Jakarta (the circle dance *lenong*), in Cirebon (*tarling*, accompanied by flute and guitar), and in Kalimantan (*mamanda*). Many troupes, however, have folded in recent years under the competition from rock bands, film and television. Sri Mulat, a company which has branches in Jakarta and East Java, is an exception, and its fine comedians perform often on television.

The traditional theatre comments on this world through the multifaceted clown, while music, dance, types and formulaic patterns communicate its deep message. It asks the audience to look at epic and archetypical worlds beyond and within, assuming the performance, crafted by forebears, will make viewers see a reality that the daily world obscures. Modern spoken drama, the youngest genre of theatre in Indonesia, on the other hand, demands that the audience look at the real world around them and take action on pressing social problems confronting the modernizing nation. Spoken drama is presented in contemporary Indonesian language, rather than the regional languages that characterize traditional dramatic forms. In hopes of reaching a wide audience with their message, playwrights and directors of modern theatre have increasingly in the last two decades moved toward television drama and film. For this reason, the history and development of modern theatre have had a profound influence on these two mass media and, conversely, some playwrights and directors work on the stage in a filmic manner. ARIFIN C. NOER'S work appears in film, television and on the stage. PUTU WIJAYA's ironic sense of humour translates well into filmic scripts. Director Teguh Karya whose company excels in Stanislavski-based realist theatre, has generated strong films like *Mother* (*Ibunda*). Within the limits of often strict government censorship, modern drama, film and television speak tellingly of the faultlines and foibles in current Indonesian society. Producers who dictate what gets funded exert even stronger control, based on what they believe will draw audiences. These media play for a living, consumer audience.

Modern Spoken Drama

The 1926 verse drama written by Rustam Effendi, *Bebasari*, opened the curtain on modern Indonesian theatre. Rustam's allegorical tale recalls the famous episode about the kidnapping of Sita in the Hindu epic, the *Ramayana*. Princess Bebasari (Indonesia) is abducted by Rawana (Holland) but she is subsequently rescued by Bujangga (Indonesian Youth). Performance of the play was obstructed by the Dutch colonial government and when Rustam published the play himself, it was proscribed.

Young literary dramatists such as Rustam and Mohammed Yamin, and those who belonged to the influential 1930s literary group, New Literati (Pujangga Baru), were pioneer writers in the newly proclaimed (1928) national language, Bahasa Indonèsia. Collectively, they saw themselves as a beacon leading the nation towards the formation of a new culture. Their Western education had instilled in them progressive ideals, yet they were pulled towards fables of 'legendary and historical warriors' (*dongeng ksyatria*), gleaned from Indonesia's aristocratic classical literature. A leading figure of New Literati, Sanusi Pane, wove stories about imperious figures of the past in plays such as *Kertadjaja* (1932) and *Twilight of Majapahit* (*Sandhyakala Ning Majapahit*, 1933). But unlike

Rustam's traditional hero, Sanusi's champions are flawed men, and vaguely tragic, surrendering either to fate or passion. Sanusi's ideal modern man, a synthesis of East and West, was raised in his only play with a contemporary setting (India), *New Man (Manusia Baru*, 1940). The most thoughtful play of the era was never performed.

Performance, however, was a main objective of the theatre company, Maya, formed by Usmar Ismail in 1944 at the close of the Japanese occupation. A literary intellectual and playwright cut in the same mould as the New Literati writers, Usmar was also a director and theatre professional. But this short tradition of professional modern theatre disappeared when Usmar turned to films in the 1950s, and was not revived again until the contemporary period.

In the 1950s, following Indonesia's independence in 1949, a proliferation of one-act plays pointed to two realities: firstly the modest capacities of the playwrights; and secondly, the primary aim of writing plays was publication, preferably in literary magazines. Regarded as the father of Indonesian realistic drama, Utuy Tatang Sontani gained prominence because of his fecundity, deftness in creating verisimilitude, and his vision of the times. He wrote numerous one-act plays – one of the best-known, both in Indonesia and Malaysia, is *Awal and Mira (Awal dan Mira*, 1952) – and a few full-length dramas, that often alluded to that singular modern condition, alienation.

The inchoate in Indonesian realism was infused with a formal sensibility by the Indonesian National Academy of Theatre (Akademi Teater Nasional Indonesia, ATNI), instituted in 1955. The first modern theatre academy in Southeast Asia, ATNI taught Stanislavskian performance methods. Between 1955 and 1963, ATNI principally staged Western dramas, including Molière, Gogol, Chekhov and Sartre. ATNI's choices reflected and reinforced theatre people's lack of confidence in indigenous modern plays. Nevertheless, ATNI raised the status of theatre in the national consciousness, and acted as a catalyst of increased theatre activity in major Indonesian towns and cities.

In the meantime, a doctrinaire 'socialist realism' in the arts was beginning to be preached in the late 1950s, following the ascendancy of the Indonesian Communist Party during President Sukarno's 'Guided Democracy' government. The aggressive promotion of the Marxist-Leninist line in the arts compelled neutrals and anti-communists to protect themselves against communist onslaughts, some surreptitiously supported by the army, the other major player in the Byzantine power game plaguing the late Sukarno era. The consequences were an intense politicization of and sectarianism in the arts, including modern theatre. Sukarno was discredited and the communists swept away in a holocaust of mass killings and arrests which followed an abortive coup against the generals on 30 September 1965. Soon after Suharto's New Order military government emerged in 1966, theatre too began to reveal a new visage.

In the growing mythology of contemporary Indonesian theatre, two persons are credited with its origins: W. S. RENDRA and Arifin C. Noer. The watershed event was Rendra's staging of *Bip-Bop* in 1968. Nothing could have been more defiant of the literary, realistic theatre than this improvised and starkly non-verbal theatre exercise. Its principal resources – an ensemble of performers and a leader – collectively assembled a succession of non-linear images made up of movement and sound (natural and human and, occasionally, song). The overall impact of the piece was poetic, suggestive of a conflict between the mass and the individual – a theme that reverberated with political connotations in 1960s Indonesian society. Generously featured in the national press and on television, Rendra, also a considerable poet, soon rose in national perception to be a modern cultural hero. In subsequent years his communitarian-based company, Bengkel Teater Jogjakarta, staged Rendra's original plays, and various 'confrontations' with Western classics. Rendra, for example, transplanted the ambience of the Javanese folk theatre clowns into Beckett's *Waiting for Godot* (*Menanti Godot*, 1969). Sophocles' *Oedipus Rex* (1969) was mediated with a Balinese style of theatre, complete with Balinese masks and costumes.

Rendra's theatre became increasingly and explicitly political in the mid 1970s, as shown by the performances of *The Struggle of the Naga Tribe* (*Kisah Perjuangan Suku Naga*, 1974) and *District Secretary* (*Sekda*, 1977). Framed within Javanese *wayang kulit* shadow-theatre performance, the former warned that foreign exploitation, abetted by high-placed indigenous corruption, was jeopardizing the natural and harmonious order. From May to October 1978, Rendra was detained by the Indonesian authorities, and subsequently prohibited from public performance for seven years. In 1986 he returned to the stage with *Honourable Reso* (*Panembahan Reso*), a seven-hour event just two hours short of the traditional all-night *wayang kulit* performance. Staged in Jakarta's Senayan Stadium, the performance emphasized that Rendra, a charismatic actor with a unique Indonesian epic manner, is the only Asian avant-garde theatre personality who can command a mass audience cutting across age and class barriers.

Folk and popular theatre have also been Arifin Noer's resources in his explorations of a genuinely Indonesian theatre. His use of traditional sources is, however, informal, born of instinct and cunning, rather than of an *a priori* schema. He began his task with *Clouds* (*Mega-Mega*, 1964), and reached a momentary epiphany with *Moths* (*Kapai-Kapai*, 1970), which has become the best-known of all modern Southeast Asian plays. *Moths'* written text is as austere as a poem, but in its Jakarta premiere it was a multidimensional performance, profuse with non-linear events, crystallized by folk songs, children's games, irreverent popular-theatre comedy, topical commercial jingles and stylized movement. By so doing, Arifin wrested freedom from the thrall of the literary text. The relentless images revolved around the worker, Abu, whose plight was raised to spiritual and metaphysical heights by the performance strategy. (All of Arifin's contemporary plays focus on the spiritual vitiation of the underdog.) Mercurial juxtapositions of events and images were the means that opened up entry points to a reflexivity: juxtapositions between illusion and reality, sense and nonsense, tragedy and comedy, horror and farce. In *Moths*, Arifin was the quintessential middleman, negotiating an autonomous status between Western and Asian theatre. The actor and playwright-director, Ikranagara, calls this stance, 'post-modern'.

Throughout the 1970s, Arifin and his theatre group, Teater Kecil, forged ahead with a widely emulated style of play and performance. In 1985, after six years spent almost exclusively in film, Arifin staged *Interrogation or In the Shadow of God* (*Interogasi Atau Dalam Bayangan Tuhan*). His sense of play, provoking contrasts in tone and sensibility, was still intact. But he showed a renewed faith in story and verbal theatre. He explained that words, after all, are the last refuge of human contact in a world gone excessively rational and materialistic.

Once Putu Wijaya formed his theatre group, Teater Mandiri, in 1974, it was possible to talk of a 'Yogyakarta School of Contemporary Theatre'. (At separate times in the 1960s, both Arifin and Putu worked in Rendra's Yogyakarta theatre company.) Prominent also as an innovative and prolific novelist, Putu brought a posture of severe detachment to Indonesian contemporary theatre. Conventional characters were entirely absent on Putu's stage: his people appeared as dislocated beings in *Ouch* (*Aduh*, 1974) and *Insane* (*Edan*, 1973), dependent on the content of their dialogue to acquire 'character'. His evocation of the 'tragedy of language' made a mockery of human communication in plays titled *Dag-Dig-Dug* (1972) and *So and So* (*Anu*, 1974). Most of his plays present assemblies of contentious people caught in a state of shock or 'terror' over the power that mysterious individuals and happenings have on their lives, as in *Shit* (*Tai*, 1983). The sense of the mass on stage, initiated by Rendra, is amplified into a mortifying experience of paranoia. In contrast to his arid written texts, his performances, executed by a singularly stable and athletic ensemble, were as sensual, irrepressibly playful and grotesque as the Balinese folk theatre he imbibed as a high-born Balinese child. His last performance, *Front* (1985), however, also hinted at Putu's return to a narrative theatre.

In contrast, Teguh Karya, theatre director, filmmaker and master of formal realism, has expanded his vocabulary of non-realistic gestures in recent performances staged by his group, Teater Popular. *Randai* Sumatran folk theatre was the informing style of his revival of Lorca's *Blood Wedding* (*Pernikahan Darah*, 1987). The Indonesian perception of Teguh as a prime mover of contemporary theatre is paradigmatic of the culture's plural and remarkably tolerant aesthetics. An ATNI product, Teguh, since his repertory days in the Bali Room of Hotel Indonesia (1968–72), gained fame and following mainly for his formalistic and finely-wrought performances of Western dramas.

Direct contact with a 'concrete' audience is the root cause accounting for the ubiquitous 'rough and rude' (*kurang ajar*) humour characterizing much of contemporary Indonesian theatre. A specific audience, mostly young and numerically and geographically confined, was created in the 1970s, particularly in Jakarta's Ismail Marzuki Park (Taman Ismail Marzuki, TIM). TIM has been called 'the most successfully conceived arts centre in Asia'. Although financially supported by the Jakarta municipality, it is run by the artists themselves represented by their peers sitting on the Jakarta Arts Council (Dewan Kesenian Jakarta, DKD). Since 1968, TIM has housed a stable, diverse, innovative repertory of folk and popular theatre performances. TIM is also the mecca of regional contemporary theatres, notably those led by Wisran Hadi (Padang, Sumatra), and Suyatna Anirun (Bandung, Java). Conceived as a sanctuary of artistic freedom, TIM, however, has not been entirely immune from political interference. In the 1980s, TIM began to show signs of a creeping bureaucratization. Actually, TIM never fully recovered its glory days since the banning of Rendra and the prolonged absence of Arifin and Teguh due to film work.

In the 1990s the delicate equipoise between politics and the arts nurtured at TIM is threatened by the rise of liberal political parties. They represent a swelling middle class caused by the spread of education and economic stability under the New Order. Progressive cultural thinkers call for a socially 'contextual' literature and art. While TIM's leading lights, Arifin and Putu, have not demurred from contending with the social problems of poverty and oppression, their stance, shaped by the trauma of excessive politicization of the arts in the 1960s, is 'sly' and allusive while being responsible.

Teater Koma in Jakarta and Teater Gandrik in Yogyakarta exemplify the new shapes of theatre that emerged in the 1980s. Founded in 1977 by Nano Riantiarno, the former already has amassed new audiences from Jakarta's upper and middle classes. Teater Koma's 'operas', notably *The Cockroach Opera* (*Opera Kecoa*, 1985), reflect an accessible blend of Western rock and indigenous folk and popular performance applied to contemporary themes of poverty, slums, homosexuality and transvestism and to characters who live in the subterranean world of the dispossessed. Riantiarno's latest play, *Succession* (*Suksesi*, 1990), deals candidly with Indonesia's most controversial political issue – the succession to Suharto. Under the guise of folk *ketoprak* figures, he introduces extravagantly corrupt characters reminiscent of the president's

family. The play was banned by the authorities in the midst of a hugely successful run in the Gedung Kesenian, Jakarta's newly renovated 'colonial' theatre.

Dwelling at the crossroads of town and country, Teater Gandrik leads a growing movement, centred in Java, that strives to inject contemporary theatre with the rural values of community through the malleable comic folk form of *dagalan mataram*. From its first performances in 1987, its style has been 'coarse', some of which seems to be erased in its most recent production, *Tree Spirit* (*Demit*, 1990). Gandrik's productions unveil the personal and political greed that lurks under the cover of commercial and intellectual pretence.

Genres

Arja

A sung dance drama based on *Panji* and other romantic stories created in the 1900s, widely performed in Bali today. Originally an all-male form, by the 1920s women had taken over the major roles, since their voices seemed appropriate for the *tembang* singing style, while men performed only the clown roles. Singers rose to star status, especially after radio broadcasts began in 1958. The noted troupe from the Radio Republic Indonesia station performs throughout the island. Audio cassettes of *arja* plays based on Hindu, Javanese, Balinese and even Chinese sources are sold in shops.

Barong

The term in its narrow usage means a large body mask found in Bali or Java which may be of a variety of creatures (elephant, boar, tiger, cow, lion, and so on). Its most spectacular theatrical manifestation is the ritual *barong kekek* a mythical creature who is lord of the forest (*banaspati raja*) and may be associated with the protective power of the afterbirth. In Bali this creature is pitted in an exorcistic performance against the mask of *rangda*, a witch-widow, who may be identified as Calonarang, a famed sorceress of the mediaeval period. Men and women may stab themselves with knives (*kris*) while in trance produced by the spell of the witch until they are released by the beneficent power of the *barong*, hence the common name 'kris dance' for performance. The *barong* is perhaps the most popular tourist presentation on Bali and can be seen daily in several villages.

Bedaya

Court dances performed by the ladies–consorts (*bedaya*) of traditional Javanese rulers. Many of these choreographies came to have ritual significance since spiritual power was felt to infuse the dance and dancer. The *bedaya* of a small court might be done by a pair of dancers or a small group. Dances at large courts, such as Surakarta (Solo) and Yogyakarta in Central Java, were chore-

Bedaya dancers performing in the central Javanese court of Yogyakarta.

ographed for up to nine dancers and were created to commemorate important events in the history of the court. The dance would then be passed down as a royal heirloom (*pusaka*) from generation to generation. Descendants might fight over the disposition of a choreography, especially when royal houses split upon the death of a monarch. The most powerful descendant could prove his priority by carrying away the most important choreography. The *Bedaya Ketawang* of the royal court of Surakarta, supposedly taught by Lara Kidul, the goddess of the South Seas, to Sultan Agung in the 17th century is the most noted choreography danced today. Many modern *bedaya* have been introduced in this generation and SASMINTA MARDAWA of Yogyakarta is a noted choreographer who has used this genre. The form compares with Thai LAKON FAI NAI, Cambodian LAKON KABACH BORAN, Balinese LEGONG, Burmese *yein* and Malay MAK YONG.

Dikir

A Sufi-influenced religious song-chant of the Malay world in which a group moves and sings in unison. It often forms a framework from which local theatres arise in Muslim areas, and is well developed among the Gayo of Sumatra.

Gambuh

Dance drama of Bali, now rare, a legacy of the 16th century when Javanese brought the form to the island. It is the ancestor of many genres that developed later. Noble characters speak in archaic Javanese (Kawi) while clowns translate the material into modern Balinese. Episodes from the story of Prince Panji are danced. The orchestra is composed of four long flutes (*gambuh suling*), bowed string *rebab*, drums, cymbals, bells, gongs and a *gumanek* (struck idiophone used in some of the oldest Javanese dances). The structure of each story is predictable: a maid dances, ladies-in-waiting and the princess enter, they speak. In the next scene, two portly ministers and four retainers dance and the refined hero, Panji, and his clown servant enter. In the third scene the antagonist, a strong but greedy king, and his ministers appear. The conflict ensues. In decline since court support waned in 1906, the form continues to be presented in some villages for temple festivals.

Artists

Atmadibarata, Enoch (1928–)

Noted Sundanese choreographer-researcher who has been significant in maintaining traditional arts. Born in Bandung to an aristocratic family he studied with masters of the last generation including Pak Wirakusumah, who set movements for aristocratic dance. He choreographed major dance dramas on Sundanese subjects in the late 1960s and took over the government Project to Develop Sundanese Arts in the 1970s and 80s.

Bandem, I Made

Major choreographer and scholar of Balinese performance. He is noted for his influence on reviving older forms and incorporating study of them into the curriculum of the Academy of Arts (ASTI, now STSI–Advanced School of Indonesian Arts) in Denpasar where he is director. His work on GAMBUH and wayang wong have had significant impact on those arts. He frequently tours to the United States and Europe.

Dibia, I Wayan

Balinese choreographer and dancer of JAUK. In both capacities Dibia is a noted exponent of the present generation. As a faculty member at the Academy of Dance (ASTI) in Denpasar he was instrumental in choreographing major dance dramas in KECAK style on new themes like the confrontation of the Monkey king-siblings Subali and Sugriwa.

Durban, Irawati (?1942–)

Major Sundanese choreographer of this generation. She began studying with dancemaster Tjetje Somantri in the 1950s and became, with Indrawati Lukman, a major exponent and extender of his work. She directed the Academy of Dance (ASTI) in Bandung in the early 1980s and began to introduce stronger, more martial dances for women. She frequently tours to Asia, Europe and the United States.

Kakul, I Nyoman (1905–1985)

Dancer and teacher. Born in Batuan, Bali he performed TOPENG in the Balinese style from age thirteen to his death. He was one of the first to teach women strong martial dances like baris in the 1950s. He toured the world from the 1950s to the 1970s and had many students in Bali and the West.

Kussudiardjo, Bagong (1928–)

Noted Javanese choreographer and visual artist. Born in Yogyakarta, he studied dance there under G.P.H Tedjokusumo. He explored the dance of Sunda, Sumatra and Bali. After studying modern dance in the United States and Europe in the 1950s, he established his own studio. His choreography has been part of cultural missions abroad. In his choreography, based on classical Javanese dance, he borrows freely from the movement of the other parts of Indonesia and the West.

Kusumo, Sardono S. (1946–)

Major Jakarta-based contemporary choreographer. He trained in the Surakarta (Solo) court and at the Martha Graham Studio in 1968. His innovative work is frequently seen at the Jakarta Arts Center (TIM) and abroad. In 1974 he collaborated with Balinese master artist Pasek Tempo and villagers from Teges, Bali to create The Story from Dirah which told of the 12th century widow who sends pestilence on the Kingdom of Kediri when her daughter's hand is rejected by the ruler. In Plastic Forest he collaborated with dancers from Kalimantan, exploring the destruction of the rain forest.

Mardawa, Sasminta

Major contemporary choreographer of Yogyakarta and head of the Mardawa Budaya troupe and school of Yogyanese dance. His versions of Arjuna's Meditation (Arjuna Wiwaha) were highlights of the 1978 Jakarta Festival.

Noer, Arifin C. (1941–)

Playwright and director, recipient of the Arts Award (Anugerah Seni) of the Indonesian government. Born in Cirebon, he began writing plays as a student in Surakarta (Solo). In the 1960s he worked with RENDRA and with Teater Muslim in Yogyakarta. He founded his Little Theatre (Teater Ketjil) in Jakarta in 1968, where he has directed *Caligula* and *Macbeth* and his own plays. His works evince poetic gifts and a sense of the sacred which mesh with social concerns. *Moths (Kapai-Kapai)* has been translated and performed in the West. His company performed *The Bottomless Well (Sumur Tanpa Dasar*, 197(1) in English while touring the United States in 1992. He writes and directs regularly for films and television.

Rendra, W.S. (1935–)

A charismatic actor, director and poet who revolutionized contemporary theatre in the 1960s. He grew up in Surakarta (Solo) and in 1967 founded the Workshop Theatre (Bengkel Teater) upon his return from study in the United States. In 1969 he introduced a series of movement–sound studies he called *minikata* ('minimal words'). Attacking exploitive economic development, government corruption and limitations on democratic expression in works like *Struggle of the Naga Tribe, Mastadon and Eagle*, he also comments on the failings of modern Indonesia in *Honorable Reso*. Despite constant censorship and periods of government arrest, he continues to influence the direction of all modern drama in Indonesia.

Riantiarno, Nano (1949–)

Actor, director and writer. Born in Cirebon and educated in Jakarta, he worked with Teguh Karya's Popular Theatre until 1977. In 1977 he established Koma Theatre which has created more than 13 drama productions and produced over 17 television dramas. Major scripts include *Paper House, Sam Pek Eng Tay* (a Chinese romance named after its hero), and *Time Bomb. Cockroach Opera* recounts the life of a poor Jakarta transsexual who lives in the shadow of the grand monuments of the economically surging city.

Sabdho, Narto (1925–85)

An innovative *dalang* of WAYANG kulit of Central Java. He began as a musician working as a drummer for travelling theatre groups, joined the *wayang orang* troupe Ngesti Pandawa in 1945, and became widely known as a *dalang* in 1955. His innovations include highlighting the female clown-servant and modernizing musical accompaniment.

Sidja, I Made

Major Balinese *dalang* of WAYANG parwa. He is one of the top performers of the present generation noted for balancing religious philosophy, humour and performance technique in his work. He directs Sanggar Seni Paripurna (Paripurna Arts Group) and created in 1976 a new form of *wayang* using the opera-singing style, *wayang arja*.

Somantri, Tjetje (?1900–63)

Choreographer of Bandung, West Java. He transformed Indonesian female dance in the 1940s. After studying Javanese dance, mask dance and other genres he created a style of refined female dance, mixing Javanese and Sundanese elements, that became an important part of every cultural exchange programme until the time of his death.

Sudirja, Nugraha (?1930–)

A major choreographer and teacher of Sundanese dance from 1950. He takes Sundanese traditional forms like the mask dance and gives them a new dynamic energy. He is especially noted for his portrayals of greedy king, Klana, and a prime minister, Temengung.

Suid, Gusmiati

Major Jakarta-based director and choreographer from Padang, Sumatra. She is noted for use of martial-arts movement and has created works based on *randai* theatre and other genres from the Minangkabau area of Sumatra.

Sujana [Ardja] (?1935–)

Master mask dancer of TOPENG babakan of Cirebon. He is noted for the clarity of his movement and precision of his characterization. He heads the Panji Asmara group in the village of Slangit.

Sunarya, Asep Sunandar (?1953–)
Top Sundanese puppetmaster of this generation. His innovations have influenced most performers of the rod-puppet genre WAYANG *golek purwa*. His slow-motion fight scenes, ogres that vomit blood and musical innovations are widely emulated. He appears regularly on television and cassettes of his performances are extremely popular.

Wijaya, Putu (1944–)
Director and playwright. Born in Bali and educated in Java, he worked with Rendra's Workshop Theatre in the late 1960s and Arifin Noer's Little Theatre in the early 1970s before studying in Japan and the United States. He has taught in the drama department of the Jakarta Arts Institute and at American universities, and he chaired the theatre committee of the Jakarta Arts Council. He directs his own avant-garde work, which includes plays like *Roar* and *Geez*, and produces many film scripts. The surrealistic humour of his work is striking.

Godang
A Sundanese theatre of West Java inspired by rice-pounding music. Two groups, males and females, alternate in singing verse riddles (*sisinderan*) most often about love matters, and playing out skits. The form probably grew from rice-harvest-festival celebrations. Analogous to Cambodian *ayay*, Lao *mawlum* and Vietnamese *trông quân*.

Jangger
Literally 'humming'; a Balinese group dance done by young males and females. Developed after the turn of the century, the form incorporated the SANGHYANG vocal style (also found in KECAK). The chant accompanied traditional or modern stories and, between scenes, the large chorus did group dances which included acrobatic formations. Actors could wear Western dress mixed with traditional costuming and wing-and-drop sets were used. This once popular theatre form is now seldom performed.

Jauk
Balinese masked dance drama originating in the 18th century that tells *Ramayana* and *Mahabharata* stories. A *jauk* is a demon character identified by strong dance style, long fingernails, fanged mask and large wig. A prominent contemporary practitioner is I WAYAN DIBIA.

Kecak
Sometimes called 'monkey chant', the Balinese term means the interlocking vocal singing of a large male chorus which imitates the 'cak-cak' sound of monkeys, as well as dance dramas that incorporate this chant. In its theatre form developed around 1930, the vocal element from SANGHYANG trance performance was combined with a pantomime version of the *Ramayana* story and narration by a *dalang* of the WAYANG tradition. The chant had already been borrowed for JANGGER, a popular theatre form. These performances in the dim light of the oil lamp made an impact on tourist audiences; soon many villages were in the *kecak* business. Today several generations of Balinese have grown up doing the form, and younger choreographers are now creating *kecak* with different stories and using new choreographies for Balinese viewers.

Ketoprak
A popular Javanese-language theatre of Central Java which rose around the turn of the century using rice-block-pounding music as its inspiration. *Gamelan* music was later incorporated. Dialogue is improvised according to a scenario by actors who specialize in specific role types. The repertoire includes traditional Muslim stories, Hindu-based stories and popular, melodramatic tales. Wing-and-drop scenery is standard, as is the practice of charging for entrance to the large pavilion with woven bamboo walls where performances take place.

Kuda kepang
Literally, 'horse of woven bamboo'; a Javanese

dance in which performers are said to be entered by a horse spirit. Skits, clowning or story episodes may intersperse entertainment feats such as fire-walking, self-stabbing, and eating lightbulbs.

Legong
Balinese female dance genre accompanied by *gamelan pelegongan*. Developed after 1800 as an abstract dance drama of prepubescent girls who were selected by the palace and trained in the movement style derived from the SANGHYANG *dedari* (child trance dance). An episode from the Panji story, where a greedy king encounters his doom, is a popular theme. Modern choreographies employing *dalang* ('puppetmaster') and WAYANG-style narration may enact fuller stories with older dancers emulating the children's puppet-like movement style.

Ludruk
Popular Javanese-language theatre of the Surabaya area which features a transvestite singer, clowning and *gamelan* accompaniment. Interludes, singing and plays telling modern and traditional stories are presented by the troupe. As an exorcistic form in which the clown had the main ritual role, its roots may go back to the 13th century. As a modern entertainment it goes back to the 1920s when a performer named Besut was active.

Ronggeng
Improvised dance-theatre forms, in which a female singer-dancer-actress (*ronggeng*) works in conjunction with a clown, are found throughout Java and Malaysia. *Gamelan* accompaniment is common and masks are used in some cases. In a village context dancers were associated with rice-harvest ceremonies or rain-making. Singer-actresses tend to perform melodramatic and romantic song or theatre material. Performers dance with audience members after the presentation, and prostitution with Tantric connections is frequent. *Ronggeng gunung*, *topeng banyet*, *topeng bekasi*, *ketuk tilu* and *gandrung banyuwangi* are all variants of this genre.

Ruwatan
Literally 'to make well'; an exorcistic theatrical performance on Java. The most common drama, *The Origin of Kala* (*Murawakala*), protects potential victims from bad luck caused by this man-eating demon. The story is related to the *Sapuleger* (*sapu*, 'sweep', *leger*, 'naked') story in Bali and the *berjamu* (*jamu*, 'medicine') rite of Malaysia and south Thailand. Most often *ruwatan* is done as a WAYANG puppet performance, but sometimes it is presented through other storytelling genres.

Sandiwara
1 Popular Sundanese-language theatre of West Java which thrived 1920–70 using *gamelan* and Sundanese dance-acting style to tell traditional and modern tales. Stories include local histories, popular ghost stories, romances and tales drawn from WAYANG theatre. Dialogue is improvised from a scenario with actors portraying codified character types: refined male or female, strong male, villain and clown. Wing-and-drop scenery and electric lighting are incorporated and presentations are staged in permanent theatres where the public buys tickets to enter. A few groups are still operative though popularity has declined.
2 Early modern spoken drama in Java and Sunda based on Western scripted models which developed in the 1920s–60s and had a major impact on the aesthetics of film and television. Troupes formed in major cities under a director and played on a proscenium stage using Western scenic conventions. Scripts were relatively realistic portrayals of modern life or historical stories.

Sanghyang
The trance performance of the Balinese. Impersonation of animals, such as horses (*sanghyang jaran*) and monkeys (*sanghyang monyet*), are variants. In *sanghayng dedari* ('divine nymph'), young girls become possessed by heavenly goddesses and express the divinities' wishes. The form is used for healing and protecting the community as well as for entertainment. Later entertainment forms like KECAK and LEGONG are related to these dances.

Sendratari
Wordless dance dramas in Java, Bali and Sunda popularized after the foundation of government dance academies in major cities in the 1960s.

Faculty and students of the academies vied to present brilliant, large-scale, somewhat modernized versions of traditional *Ramayana* and *Panji* dance plays to the pan-Southeast Asian world at new international festivals sponsored by ASEAN nations. The lack of a common language between countries resulted in the abandonment of text. Choreographers after graduating from the academies have continued to work in this genre, especially when preparing a work for international, inter-island or modern urban performances.

Topeng

Masked dances of Java and Bali. *Topeng* literally means 'press': the wood masks are held in place by biting a piece of leather tacked to the mask's mouth. Current genres of *topeng* usually trace their heritage back to the north coast of Java. In both Bali and Java the solo mask dance in which a single individual dances all the masks is considered older than multiple-person mask theatre. On the north coast of Java, solo mask dancers of the Cirebon area dance a sequence of four or five characters, from refined to emotionally uncontrolled, to *gamelan* accompaniment for rites-of-passage ceremonies in villages in a form called *topeng babakan*. Single dances representing these characters out of the context of the cycle are popular dance interludes in both Java and Sunda. The dance of the greedy king, Klana, is particularly popular. The masks may be used in a form of *WAYANG* called *wayang* (*orang* or *wong*) *topeng* in which a *dalang* narrates the story and delivers the dialogue while the dancers pantomime the action. This form corresponds to Thai *KHON* and Cambodian *LAKON KHOL*. In Bali, *topeng pajegan* by a solo performer is considered the older and more sacred genre, but *topeng panca* ('five'-person *topeng*) includes more clowning, and *topeng prembon* incorporates actresses from popular *ARJA*. Historical chronicles provide most stories in Bali, while in Java tales of Prince Panji or from the *Mahabharata* are the most frequent themes.

Wayang

Wayang, 'shadow' or 'puppet,' is a term broadly encompassing numerous forms of traditional theatre in Java, Sunda and Bali that grow from

Javanese *wayang kulit* shadow-play scene showing Kresna in audience with members of his court.

the art of the puppetmaster or *dalang*. This performer narrates a story, generally accompanied by a percussive orchestra, called a *gamelan* on Java, improvising in performance according to the constraints of the genre. The *dalang* provides narration and, in puppet forms, dialogue and manipulation, and cues the musicians. His performance activates the archaic literary language, Kawi, and his mood songs and mantra can be powerful in a ritual sense, hence a *dalang's* art is often practised at rites-of-passage events. Performers of sufficient spiritual practice may also carry out *RUWATAN* or other exorcistic rites via performance. Performers in different areas use different media (flat hide puppets, round wooden puppets, painted scrolls, human actors) and different story cycles (*Mahabharata, Panji, Amir Hamzah*). The name of the genre changes as medium and story cycle change, hence there are hundreds of kinds of *wayang*. Within a language or culture area one genre tends to predominate and its rules of performance tend to be applied to the less popular forms in that area. Major genres are *wayang parwa* in Bali, *wayang kulit purwa* in Java and *wayang golek purwa* in Sunda. The first term in each name indicates that the genre is in the style of the puppetmaster's art, *wayang*. The last terms indicate that the story cycle is Hindu-derived (*parwa, purwa*). The middle term, when included, usually indicates the medium: *kulit* are hide puppets popular on Bali and in Java, and *golek* are round wooden puppets most popular in Sunda.

In Balinese *wayang parwa* the *dalang* manipulates hide figures 1–2 ft in height against a screen about 6 ft wide by 4 ft high. The Kawi language of the heroic characters distances them, while the ever-present clowns provide colloquial equivalents for their noble visions. The *dalang* opens the play chanting incantations and dancing the 'tree of life' (*kayon*) puppet in the creation of the world. Swinging the oil lamp he lets the shadows of the puppets quiver: he represents God breathing life into man and woman. Then he raps for the second 'tree' dance and the ensemble of four *gender*, metallophones, strikes up again. The dance represents the new imbalance in the universe, now that human desire has been born. At this point the story of the evening begins. Performance lasts from about 9 p.m. to 1 a.m. and usually takes place in the context of a temple festival, cremation or similar ceremony.

Wayang parwa is currently practised by 300 *dalang* on Bali, mostly men born to *dalang* families. Beginning in 1974, a few women have been trained, primarily under I Nyoman Sumandhi, a teacher the High School of Traditional Music (SMKI, formerly KOKAR) in Denpasar. Performers of sufficient spiritual power can make holy water used for curing and exorcism, play ritual stories like those of *Sudamala* (literally, 'averting evil') and *Calonarang* (named after a witch who threatens humans), and comprehend the mantras of the *dalang*'s handbook, *The Book of the Wayang* (*Darma Pawayangan*). Related Balinese shadow genres tell *Ramayana* and *Panji* tales. *Dalang* Rajeg, *dalang* Wija, and *dalang* Sidja are noted exponents at present.

In Central Java the *dalang* cues his *gamelan* players who play the appropriate tunes on the martial-sounding *slendro*- or more melancholy *pelog*-scale instruments in the *patet*, key or mode, appropriate to that part of the story. The pitch of the three *patet* matched to the three successive sections of each performance is progressively higher, underlining the rising tension of the plot. The glamorous female singer was not a feature of the early period, but an innovation of the last hundred years.

The Hindu epic material is normally presented, but most performances do not dramatize events of the Indian versions, but 'branch' episodes that show the epic character in moments not defined by those 'trunk' stories. Typically, Arjuna of the *Mahabharata* or some other refined knight, with the counsel of his clown-servants, struggles with ogres to restore balance to the order they threaten. The *dalang* develops his performance according to a set dramatic structure from the story outline acquired in one of four ways: (1) his teacher told it to him in a few paragraphs; (2) he saw it performed; (3) he read it in a *dalang* manual; (4) he devised it himself. The plot will usually contain the following standard scenes.

As in Bali, an opening mantra-like narration and a 'tree'-puppet dance begin the performance. The action begins in a palace with a court audience scene: a problem is discussed and an army is sent to deal with it. A second and perhaps a third audience scene follow the same pattern. The armies despatched by the rulers then meet in the first of the evening's three major battles.

The *patet* changes, now the scene is a mountain where clown-servants of a refined prince wait as he undertakes a meditation causing cosmic imbalance. In this *gara-gara* (world in disorder) scene, which comes about midnight, clowns comment freely on current politics and events, in contrast to the other characters who live in epic time and cannot refer to the present. Semar, the chief clown, farts and frets – but the audience knows that this fat old hermaphrodite's insights veil deep truth, since Semar is a high god sojourning in the world. After a hermitage scene, the hero goes down from the mountain where he encounters four ogres in the 'flower battle' (*perang kembang*) – the manipulation highlight of the show. The first blood of the evening is Cakil, a boastful ogre who serves a giant king. He dies in every *wayang*, proving the hero is spiritually prepared for future challenges.

With the hour advancing toward 2 a.m., the less structured scenes of the third *patet*, required by the plot of the particular story (*lakon*), come. The performance climaxes in the 'great' battle in which the hero defeats all opponents. The final audience scene is concluded by planting the 'tree' puppet in the banana-log puppet-stand as dawn approaches. Scenes may be omitted and others, not noted here, added, but most performances are improvised within this frame. Dalangs Anom Suroto and NARTO SABDHO are major Javanese performers of this generation.

Wayang golek purwa is the rod-puppet theatre of Sunda in which the *dalang* performs amazingly realistic dances and gestures with the dolls of *Mahabharata* and *Ramayana* characters. A night-long performance serves the same ritual and entertainment functions as shadow puppetry in Bali and Java. A puppet screen, of course, is not used and figures are merely placed in the banana-log stage. The 11 artists (puppeteer, singer, 9 musicians) sit on a 15 ft x 15 ft wooden stage, constructed for the occasion to face the porch of the host's house. The *slendro*-tuned *gamelan* ensemble is much smaller than that of Central Java. The exuberant music and the dancing are distinct from Java's repertoire and technique. Plot interpretations reflect a peasant's perspective on the court ethos, and clowns receive great prominence. The structure of the performance is looser than in Java (for example, there is no 'flower battle' with its set ogres). It is possible that the simpler pattern reflects a form from which the more complex Javanese shadow theatre evolved within the court context. Among the top performers of this genre are the *dalang* ASEP SUNANDAR SUNARYA and Dede Amung Sutarya.

Less significant, but still vital *wayang* forms in Java include: *wayang topeng purwa*, whose human dancers wear masks (*topeng*) while enacting *purwa* plays; and *wayang orang purwa*, where unmasked human (*orang*) dancers relate the same Hindu tales. In contrast, *wayang klitik, wayang golek cepak* and *wayang gedog* all tell stories about the East Javanese prince, Panji, the King of Arabia, Amir Hamzah or other Javanese chronicle tales (*babad*). The first uses flat wooden puppets (*klitik*); the second, three-dimensional wooden figures (*golek*);

and the last, leather figures. *Wayang beber* (scroll performance) is rarely found, but this narration of scenes painted on scrolls is said to be the oldest genre from which all the others have descended. *Wayang cepak* tells Amir Hamzah or Panji stories along the north coast.

Bibliography

P. Abdurachman, *Cerbon*, Jakarta, 1982; I M. Bandem and F. deBoer *Kaja and Kelod*, Kuala Lumpur, 1981; J. R. Brandon (ed.), *On Thrones of Gold: Three Javanese Shadow Plays*, Cambridge, Mass., 1970, and *Theatre in Southeast Asia*, Cambridge, Mass., 1967; J. Emigh, 'Playing with the Past: Visitation and Illusion in the Masked Theatre of Bali', *The Drama Review*, 23, 2, 1979; K. Foley, 'Of Dalang and *Dukun* – Spirits and Men: Curing Performance in the *Wayang* of West Java', *Asian Theatre Journal*, 1, 1, 1984, and 'The Sundanese *Wayang Golek*: The Rod Puppet Theatre of West Java', PhD. diss., Univ. of Hawaii, 1979; C. Geertz, *Negara*, Princeton, N.J. 1980; C. Holt, *Art in Indonesia*, Ithaca, N.Y. 1967; A. H. Johns, 'Islam in Southeast Asia: Reflections and a New Direction', *Indonesia*, 19, 1975; G. Kam, 'Wayang Wong in the Court of Yogyakarta', *Asian Theatre Journal*, 4, 1, Spring 1987; C. H. Kullman and W. C. Young (eds.), 'Indonesia', in *Theatre Companies of the World*, vol. 1, Westport, Conn., 1986; A. C. Noer, *Moths*, tr. Harry Aveling, Kuala Lumpur, 1974; R. Long, *Javanese Shadow Theatre: Movement and Characterization in Ngayoyakarta Wayang Kulit*, Ann Arbor, Mich., 1982; Mangkunegoro VII, *On the Wayang Kulit (Purwa) and its Symbolic and Mystical Elements*, Ithaca, N.Y. 1957; G. Mohamad, *Modern Drama of Indonesia*, New York, 1991; J. Peacock, *Rites of Modernization: Symbolic and Social Aspects of Indonesian Proletarian Drama*, Chicago, Ill., 1968; T. Pigeaud, *Javaanse Volksvertoningen*, Batavia, 1938; W. S. Rendra, *Struggle of the Naga People*, tr. M. Lane, New York, 1979; Soedarsono, *Wayang Wong*, Yogyakarta, 1984; B. de Zoete and W. Spies, *Dance and Drama in Bali*, Kuala Lumpur, 1973.

JAPAN

Ancient and traditional

Theatre permeates Japanese culture. Today, in spite of a surfeit of television and film, live theatre continues to draw huge audiences in major cities – Tokyo, Osaka and Kyoto – and in villages through folk festivals. There are arguably more theatre buildings in Tokyo than any other city in the world; 40 high-tech theatres and performance spaces were constructed in the 1980s alone. Perhaps because Japanese proscribe strong emotional display in daily life, they value sophisticated expression of emotion in the theatre. For whatever reasons, theatre-going is a normal facet of life for millions of modern Japanese.

Japanese share with most Asians the attitude that theatre is an open-ended form, with room for dialogue, song, music, dance and expressive elocution. The mode of expression may be first-person enactment, third-person narrative voice, a chorus substituting for the actor or a combination of modes. Masks and puppets are important expressive media. With few exceptions, traditional theatrical performance is exceptionally dynamic and based almost equally on textual and performance elements. The traditional word for theatre in Japanese is *geinō*, 'artistic skill', a linguistic indication that theatre arose primarily from the body and the voice of the performer. The Japanese conception of theatre as a complete performing art thus stands in marked contrast to Western critical analysis in which, historically, precedence has been given to drama (Aristotle's plot, character, thought) while performance (Aristotle's spectacle, song, diction) has been felt to be unworthy of philosophic concern. With the exception of European opera and American musical comedy, the main line of Western performance development has been toward specialized arts: concert music, ballet, spoken drama. The naturalism of Zola and Stanislavski, which took life, not art, as both subject matter and medium, was a movement consistent with the Western emphasis on dramatic content and its corollary, disdain for performance as an expressive art. Western visionaries such as Artaud, Meyerhold, Eisenstein and Brecht responded to the wholeness of Asian, and Japanese theatre, a wholeness that embraced all possible expressive means. Even today Japanese rarely treat play scripts as literature (*bungaku*). Text and performance together make up a single art which is understood to be quite distinct from written literature.

Significant theatre genres include Shintō-based celebratory dances and sketches (*kagura*), Buddhist dances and sketches (*gigaku*), semidramatic dances of the imperial court (*BUGAKU*), serious masked dance dramas of the samurai class (*NŌ*) and their companion comic plays (*KYŌGEN*), flamboyant commercial urban theatre (*KABUKI*), commercial puppet theatre (*BUNRAKU*), and, in this century, modern spoken drama inspired by Western models (*SHINPA* and *SHINGEKI*). Each genre reflects the historical period in which it was first created and the interests and the tastes of the social class which patronized it. Theatre's 2000-year history in Japan has not been 'cannibalistic', as has been the Western experience: succeeding genres did not devour existing genres, but rather coexisted in different societal niches. Performing traditions mentioned above (with the exception of *gigaku*) continue unbroken down to the present day. To see traditional theatre in Japan today is akin to entering a theatrical time capsule that transports the spectator to every period from the present to the ancient past.

Early religious performance: kagura

Written history began in Japan in the 6th century, so we can only speculate about the origins of Japanese theatre. At excavations of Yayoi period settlements (350 BC to AD 250), clay miniatures of flutes, stringed instruments (*koto*), drums and masks have been found. Clay *haniwa* figures of the same era represent men and women singing, dancing and playing musical instruments. A great variety of folk dances and skits (*kagura*) celebrate Shintō festivals of the new year, rice planting and harvest in thousands of villages, leaving no doubt that performing arts trace their ancestry back to ancient times. The earliest written records of theatre are found in the *Records of Ancient Matters* (*Kojiki*, 712) and *Chronicles of Japan* (*Nihon shoki*, 720). They describe the origin of performance in Japan in a proto-shamanic myth. The Sun Goddess, Amaterasu, angered, has withdrawn from the community of deities into a rock cave, thus plunging the islands of Japan into darkness. Another goddess, Ame-no-Uzume, tries to lure her from the cave by showing her breasts, lowering her skirt, and dancing with a joyful beat of her feet. Hearing the laughter of the assembled gods and goddesses, Amaterasu leaves the cave to see what is causing their merriment and thus light is restored to the world. This is not only a mythological description of the 'first *kagura* performance'. It tells us theatre came into existence as a joyful welcome to a deity to enter a community, thus assuring the continuing life and prosperity of that community. This continues to be the function of *kagura* performances and Shintō festivals (*matsuri*).

Kagura came to be written with the Chinese characters meaning god-entertainment, but its original meaning was a deity's residence. *Kagura* performances occur at the site where the deity resides. The centrality of *kagura* to Shintō worship is clear from the fixed three-part structure of Japanese festivals: summoning the deity, entertaining the deity, and bidding the deity farewell. *Kagura* is that performance which entertains a deity during the mid section of a Shintō festival and it may take many forms. In the lion dance (*shishi kagura*), the deity is present in the large lion mask and it brings protection to those who invite it onto their premises. In folk *kagura* (*sato kagura*) a villager wears the mask of a deity and enters the village compound. Possession, role playing, and the enactment of a story, the fundamentals of drama and theatre, exist in prototypical form in village *kagura*. Female shamanic dance (*miko kagura*) by shrine priestesses uses music and dance to induce trance and to evoke a deity who speaks prophetically through the mouth of the priestess-dancer. *Mikagura*, court *kagura*, are performed by court musicians and dancers (courtiers in the past)

as part of major Shintō rites sponsored by the imperial court to assure the prosperity of the land and the continuity of imperial rule.

A number of significant characteristics of Japanese theatre are first found in *kagura*. The journey of the deity along a sacred path, from the spiritual to the mundane world where the performance occurred, was marked out as a passageway of the gods. Open passageways to the stage – the bridgeway in *nō* and the flower path in *kabuki* – have their origins in this deeply ingrained conception of god–man relationships. In subsequent theatre forms, scenes of travel, journeys and impressive entrances became normal, indeed essential, parts of dramatic structure. *Kagura*'s square, raised wooden stage, permanent or temporary, is Japan's earliest theatre structure. In the form that influenced the development of *nō* and early *kabuki* theatres, it was covered with a roof and was a freestanding dance pavilion (*kagura den*), usually located at the entrance to the inner shrine compound. *Kagura*'s celebratory and joyous humour continues in *kyōgen* and in *kabuki*. Social or psychological humour that takes the form of satire or farce in Western theatre is not a part of traditional theatre. Nor is there a clown or buffoon role, as there is in Indian, Southeast Asian, Chinese and Western theatre. The buffoon is a social outcast and the butt of humour, often cruel, that is based on ineptitude and failure, characteristics that do not fit the communal, egalitarian, felicitous nature of *kagura*. The easy acceptance of theatrical performance as part of both community and religious ritual carries forward into Japanese attitudes toward theatre today. We do not know whether the masking found in some *kagura* derives from ancient indigenous sources or is a later adoption influenced by Chinese or Korean theatre.

Early popular theatre: dengaku, sangaku, sarugaku

Other early, popular entertainments are variously described, in personal diaries and official records of the 10th–12th centuries, as field entertainment (*dengaku*), miscellaneous entertainment (*sangaku*) and monkey music (*sarugaku*). It is difficult to know what kind of performances the terms refer to because sacred and secular, urban and country arts are mentioned first under one term and then under another. In part they referred to itinerant artists – acrobats, tight-rope walkers, jugglers, and magicians – who worked the streets of Nara and Kyoto. *Sangaku*, a term borrowed from China, suggests arts introduced from China (and Korea). Until the 15th century, *dengaku* dramas were as popular as *nō* plays. Sacred *dengaku* rice-planting songs and dances have celebrated spring festivals as far back as records go; they are still performed as imperial rituals today. Professional *sarugaku* troupes gave variety shows in this early period. They set up in shrine or temple compounds at festival times or performed by invitation at the homes of court nobles. In the 14th century, *sarugaku* actors developed the serious dramas that came to be called *nō*.

Chinese and Korean influence: gigaku, bugaku

Between the 7th and 10th centuries, Chinese and Korean culture, including theatre, was widely admired and imitated in Japan. Chinese ideographs were adopted for writing and Chinese poetic forms and styles were learned at court. In 612, a Korean performer Mimaji (Mimashi in Japanese) introduced a Chinese-origin Buddhist dance play at the Japanese imperial court. Scattered masks, musical instruments and costumes of this form may have been brought from China as early as 550. This court-supported form, known as *kiak* in Korea, became *gigaku*, 'elegant entertainment', in Japan. The Japanese regent, Prince Shōtoku (r. 593–621), ordered Mimaji to establish a school of music and dance at the court and he assigned boys to be his pupils. Other Korean musicians and dancers followed Mimaji to Japan.

Gigaku propagated Buddhism, a religion new to Japan which Shōtoku avidly proselytized during his reign. A 13th-century account describes a *gigaku* performance: first, ritual Buddhist music (*netori*) is played on flute, drums, gong and cymbals; then chanting monks masked as Buddha figures pass in procession (*gyōdō*) followed by a second procession of ten actors wearing masks of a Chinese woman, a king, Baromon (an Indian Brahman), Karora (Garuda, the King of Birds in Indian myth), lion tamer, wrestler and others. Finally, the masked figures mount a temporary outdoor stage and perform comic skits cautioning against Buddhist sins. By the 12th century, *gigaku* had lost imperial support and performances gradually ceased – an unusual case in Japan of a signifi-

cant theatre form dying out. Some 250 *gigaku* masks are preserved in temple collections; the oldest date from the 7th century, the time when *gigaku* was first introduced, and may be of Chinese make. They are beautifully carved and painted, and are rare works of art.

A rival form of dance entertainment, *bugaku*, was introduced to the court from China via Korea in the 8th century. In 701 an Imperial Music Bureau was established at the court for instruction in *bugaku* and its music (*kangen*). (The composite dance-music art is called *gagaku*, 'musical entertainment'.) From the beginning, *bugaku* was an eclectic art. The Bureau had divisions for Chinese music and dance (*tōgaku*) and for Korean (*komagaku*) and apportioned its 255 performers to various specialities within the two divisions. In 736 performers were assigned to learn and perform new dances introduced from southern India and from Vietnam. The Emperor Ninmyō (r. 833–49) was so devoted to *bugaku* he journeyed to the Tang court of China to study the original music and dance. He also composed many new dances. From the 13th to the 16th centuries *bugaku* entered a period of serious decline. An impoverished imperial court could not afford to support hundreds of performers after it lost political power to the rising samurai class. Many pieces in the repertory were lost and the early dramatic vitality of the genre was largely forgotten. The oldest dance pieces, such as 'Bunomai', a martial dance, suggest the present style of performing is considerably less dynamic than in the past. The dance 'Genjōraku' presents an intensely dramatic situation: a hero of Indian myth fights a poisonous snake, is victorious and returns triumphant to his castle. A number of the *bugaku* dances were borrowed and then absorbed into provincial performance genres, such as Buddhist longevity dances (*ennen*), because of their dramatic qualities. Today, however, *bugaku* is danced to instrumental music only and there is virtually no role-playing or dramatic interaction. Unison or mirror-image dancing in geometric patterns by two or four dancers is typical. Thus the earlier storytelling elements, song lyrics (and possibly dialogue) have not survived. *Bukagu*'s serene, stately qualities reflect the art's patronage by the imperial court and later by large shrines and temples closely associated with the throne, an association that is maintained at the present time.

Theatre of the samurai: nō, kyōgen

In Japan's medieval period (1185–1600), samurai generals wrested power from the imperial court and assuming for themselves the title of Shōgun, or General, ruled from lavish courts first in Kamakura and then in Kyoto. The chief theatre forms patronized by the samurai class were *sarugaku*, also called at that time *sarugaku nō*, and then later simply NŌ ('skill'), and its companion comic form KYŌGEN. In the middle of the 14th century, dozens of professional *sarugaku nō* troupes were attached to important shrines and temples. Four large troupes were based in Nara, the ancient capital city, where they performed for festival occasions and in public (*kanjin nō*). The head of one of these troupes, Kan'ami Kiyotsugu (1333–84), is credited with transforming *sarugaku* into *nō*. A skilled actor and troupe head, he conceived of combining a popular narrative song of the time (*kuse*) with rhythmic dance (*mai*) and used the resulting narrative sung-dance (*kuse mai*) as the climactic scene of a performance. He structured his plays as virtual monodramas (in contrast to multirole plays of competing *dengaku nō* troupes), in which the crucial event in the life of the chief character (the *shite*, or Doer, role), often the grieving spirit of a dead person, was remembered and re-enacted in a *kuse mai* scene. Kan'ami's son, ZEAMI MOTOKIYO, was an actor of singular genius whose superb acting focused even more attention on the Doer role. Kan'ami stressed convincing physical and vocal characterization (*monomane*) through observation of real people, hence he is considered the father of acting, as distinct from dancing and singing, in Japanese theatre.

Kan'ami's troupe, competing with other *sarugaku nō* and with *dengaku nō* troupes, had the good fortune to act before the Shōgun Ashikaga Yoshimitsu in 1374. The 14-year-old Shōgun was attracted by the playing of Zeami, who was 11 at the time, and invited him to be his companion in the palace. During the ensuing 50 years, Zeami performed at court and received shogunal patronage. Zen Buddhism was the official religion of the Ashikaga court, and under Zeami's guidance Zen artistic principles of restraint, austerity and economy of expression were incorporated into *nō* performance and plays. The unadorned stage, the deliberate pace of performance, masks for major characters and the significant gesture reflect Zen

ideals. Zeami's advice to the actor to 'move seven if the heart feels ten' is a succinct expression of Zen precepts. Suggestive beauty (*yūgen*) was the quality most sought by Zeami in performance. Zeami became troupe leader when his father died and in his later years wrote important treatises on *nō* acting. He was succeeded by his eldest son Kanze Motomasa (?1394–1432), author of the play *The Sumida River* (*Sumidagawa*), and, following his early death, by his scholarly son-in-law KOMPARU ZENCHIKU. The last of the great actor-playwrights was Kanze Nobumitsu (1435–1516). He composed highly dramatic plays – *Benkei in the Boat* (*Funa Benkei*), *The Ataka Barrier* (*Ataka*), *The Maple Viewing* (*Momijigari*) – that used large casts and pitted Doer (*shite*) against Sideman (*waki*) in a dramatic conflict (originally he was a *waki* actor).

Shogunal patronage drastically declined during the civil wars of the 16th century. When Kyoto was burned, troupes fled to the provinces. To support themselves, actors instructed provincial samurai lords, priests and wealthy commoners in singing and dance. Texts for chanting (*utaibon*) were first printed and sold to the public in 1512. Hundreds of *nō* plays became available in print, as well as descriptions of staging, costumes, masks and music. *Nō* spread among the lower classes giving rise to amateur performances. Many surviving provincial *nō* styles trace their origins to this time. *Nō* troupes returned to the centre of political power when the country was unified at the end of the 16th century. The ruler Toyotomi Hideyoshi (1537–98) studied *nō*, ordered *nō* plays to be written about his battlefield victories, and played himself in them. The first Tokugawa Shōgun, Ieyasu (1543–1616), patronized the Kanze troupe even before he assumed rule in 1603. His successors ruled from the new capital of Edo (Tokyo), where they designated *nō* a 'ceremonial art' (*shikigaku*) to be performed on formal occasions through the long Tokugawa era (1600–1868). The third Tokugawa Shōgun, Iemitsu (1604–51), codified every aspect of *nō* and forbade deviation. *Nō* actors were given samurai rank and only the sons of actors were allowed to become performers. The troupe head (*iemoto*) was given absolute authority, and was held responsible for the actions of all members of the troupe. The freshness of performance (*hana*) that Zeami had prized was smothered by tradition and regulation. Popular audiences were forbidden to see or study *nō*. Actors devoted themselves to ever greater refinement and subtlety in their acting until, by the close of the 19th century, a play took two or three times as long to perform as during Zeami's time.

Nō evolved eclectically, its plays based on borrowed stories and its poetic forms mirroring earlier literature. Zeami advised playwrights to dramatize events from history and legend for these would be familiar and easily grasped: Chinese legend, and Japanese mythology and history, especially the 12th-century civil war between the Heike and Genji clans, are the source of most plays. *Nō*'s sonorous singing style grew out of Buddhist chant (*shōmyō*) and early popular songs (*imayō*); its restrained movement style shows the influence of professional female dance (*shirabyōshi*) as well as popular and religious performances (*jushi hashiri, ennen, dengaku, kōwaka*). The refined masks that mark *nō* as a uniquely suggestive art have antecedents in *gigaku* and *bugaku* masks of the court tradition and in village *kagura* masks as well. Masks for women's roles are especially beautiful. Often said to be 'neutral', in fact they express, usually in subtle fashion, a wide range of human emotions – happiness, pride, innocence, melancholy, elegance, grief. Except for the lavish costumes of the Doer role, dress is restrained in keeping with Zen precepts. Few properties are used and these tend to be symbolic – a fan as a drinking cup, a cloth-wrapped frame for a boat, for example.

Kyōgen, 'inspired or "mad" speech', is a performance genre that is both related to and separate from *nō*. *Kyōgen* actors perform in *nō* plays and they enact independent celebratory, often comic, plays that alternate in performance with them. (The term *nōgaku* encompasses the art of *nō* and *kyōgen* together.) *Kyōgen* plays and acting style are at least as old as *nō*. Some accounts trace *kyōgen*'s origins to comic dances – such as Ame-no-Uzume's – from the prehistoric Age of the Gods. The ritual play *Okina*, performed as an auspicious prayer for longevity at the beginning of a *nō–kyōgen* programme, is in both the *nō* and the *kyōgen* repertories and there is some evidence that the latter version is older. The humorous titles of 11th-century *sarugaku* plays (*A Nun Seeks Baby Napkins, Pranks by a City Boy*) show that *kyōgen* plays were a vital part of the *sarugaku* repertory. During Zeami's time specialist performers of *nō*, of *kyōgen*, of drums and of flute were combined into a comprehensive *sarugaku nō* troupe. When *kyōgen* actors of the Ōkura, Sagi, and Izumi families received direct patronage from the Tokugawa rulers toward the end of the 16th century, they became semi-independent of *nō* troupes. As with *nō*, all performers are men and acting is generally a hereditary profession passed down from father to son.

Within a *nō* play, the role of a commoner, servant or labourer is played by a *kyōgen* actor. Rarely is more than one *kyōgen* actor called for in a *nō* play, but in dramatic plays, such as *Benkei in the Boat*, the role is major and essential to the play's plot. The *kyōgen* role is also important in the interlude (*ai* or *ai kyōgen*) between parts one and two of the typical two-part *nō* play. When the Doer retires from the stage to change costume, the *kyōgen* actor recapitulates the story, in a monologue or in dialogue with the Sideman. Published *nō* texts do not contain the interludes, for these sections are the sole prerogative of *kyōgen* performers. Finally, *kyōgen* actors perform all roles in the independent comic plays that make up the separate *kyōgen* repertory. Most plays have two to four characters, a major role (*shite*), a second role (*ado*), and subsidiary roles (*koado*, 'small *ado*'). In all roles the *kyōgen* style of acting, in contrast to *nō* acting, calls for a clear and lively voice and movements that are active and precise. Actors improvised *kyōgen* in performance until at least the 17th century. Scenarios of 165 texts were written in manuscript form in 1578 and a collection of 203 texts of plays as they were performed were transcribed by Ōkura Toraakira, head of the Ōkura acting family, between 1638 and 1642. These were secret texts, shown outside the acting family only under exceptional circumstances. Some 200 *kyōgen* plays were published for the general public in 1660.

A *nō–kyōgen* programme is made up of thematically unrelated plays chosen from the *nō* repertory of 240 plays and the *kyōgen* repertory of 260 plays. Each programme is given a single performance. Plays are chosen to match the season, the occasion and the aesthetic principle of ever-increasing emotional tension and tempo (*jo-ha-kyū*) that regulates performance. The *nō* repertory is divided into five groups based on the nature of the Doer role and the order in which the plays appear on a programme. A typical programme contains, in order, a play with a Shintō deity (*kami*), a male warrior (*asura*), a court lady (*katsura*), a deranged woman (*kyōran*) and a demon (*kichiku*) in the major role. The *kyōgen* plays that follow each *nō* play have as main roles a deity (*kami*), a wealthy land owner (*daimyō*), a small landholder (*shōmyō*), a bridegroom or son-in-law (*muko*), a Buddhist priest or mountain ascetic (*shukke* or *yamabushi*) or a demon (*oni*). A day-long programme in Zeami's time consisted of eight to ten *nō* plays and five or six *kyōgen* plays. Even a complete but shorter programme of five *nō* and four *kyōgen* is too long for modern audiences; shorter programmes, of as few as two or three *nō* and one or two *kyōgen*, fit the busy schedules of contemporary urban audiences. All-*kyōgen* programmes have gained acceptance in recent decades as the social status of *kyōgen* actors has grown.

Popular theatre of the Edo (Tokugawa) period: kabuki, bunraku

Professional, commercial KABUKI and BUNRAKU are products of a restless, assertive, mercantile society that flourished in the great cities of Kyoto, Osaka and Edo (Tokyo) under the xenophobic rule of successive Tokugawa Shōguns (1603–1868). Troupes of the two genres competed for the same audiences. They performed in theatres side by side and over the decades they borrowed each others' successful plays. Alike in certain ways, nonetheless they evolved out of different antecedents and they attempt mutually distinct artistic aims.

Kabuki grew out of popular, urban dances and sketches of contemporary life. In the 16th century, vagabond troupes congregated in Kyoto, then the capital, where they performed secularized forms of religious dances (*ennen*) and folk dances (*yayako odori* and *kaka odori*). Around 1600 one of these dancers, a woman named Okuni and advertised as a priestess of the Grand Shrine in Izumo, made a great success in a new dance called *kabuki*. She performed on a temporary stage set up first in the grounds of Kitano Shrine and later along the dry bed of the Kamo River (hence the disparaging term for *kabuki* actors, 'beggars of the riverbed'). *Kabuki* was unorthodox. It was the rock entertainment of the 17th century. Okuni performed the first Japanese plays of contemporary urban life: numerous painted screens and scrolls show her outrageously garbed as a handsome young warrior, exotic Christian rosary draped on her bosom, con-ducting an assignation with a prostitute. The Portuguese were newly arrived and licensed quarters for prostitution had only recently been established in Kyoto. Okuni's chief imitators were professional prostitutes who performed *kabuki* dances and songs on public stages as a come-on for their evening profession. Paintings of the early 17th century show prostitutes seated sensuously on tiger skins playing the *shamisen*, a lute recently introduced from China via Okinawa, as bevies of girls circle the stage.

The shogunate banned women from public stages in 1629 as part of its general policy of restricting each person to a single occupation; prostitutes could not also be actresses. Early *kabuki* was also performed by troupes of young boys (*wakashū*), doubling as catamites, and they were banned in 1652. After these events *kabuki* began to develop as a serious art. *Kabuki*'s major characteristics became established by the early 18th century: all-day multi-act plays, adult male casts (and therefore the evolution of the art of the *onnagata* or actor of female roles), a yearly season of five or six productions, and unique musical, dance and acting styles appropriate to various styles of play. Standard scene types are identifiable in the 1680s and 90s: the brothel assignation (*keiseigai*), the swaggering parade of a hero (*tanzen roppō*), the flight of lovers (*michiyuki*), the choreographed fight between a hero and a group of opponents (*tachimawari*). Government officials restricted the number and location of *kabuki* theatres and forced actors to live apart from others. Plays about current samurai were forbidden, leading playwrights to disguise contemporary events as history. In spite of government suppression of *kabuki*, samurai lords and their ladies, rich merchants, priests, workers and servants all attended the theatre and the despised art flourished as a major attraction of Japanese urban life.

Uniquely different plays and acting styles developed in *kabuki*'s two centres, Kyoto–Osaka and Edo. SAKATA TŌJŪRŌ performed in Kyoto for relatively cultivated audiences. In 1678 he portrayed Izaemon, the pampered scion of a wealthy merchant in *New Year's Remembrance of the Courtesan Yūgiri* (*Yūgiri nagori no shōgatsu*). In the scene set in Osaka's current licensed quarter, Tōjūrō continued Okuni's original prostitute-buying plays. He developed a 'soft' acting style (*wagoto*) for romantic domestic scenes (*sewamono*).

In contrast, ICHIKAWA DANJŪRŌ I wrote and acted in bravura history plays (*jidaimono*) for an audience of rough samurai and adventurers in the new city of Edo. He created a 'rough' acting style (*aragoto*) and specialized in playing heroes of superhuman strength. The bold red and black makeup (*kumadori*) and exaggerated costumes that mark *aragoto* acting date from Danjūrō's first stage appearance as a boy of 14. Danjūrō's powerful poses (*mie*) and gestures are said to have been suggested by Buddhist guardian statues (the present Danjūrō XII worships at the same temple Danjūrō I did, dedicated to the Guardian Deity Fudō Myōō). Titles of plays in which he and his son Danjūrō II (1689–1758) starred are amply descriptive – *Indestructible* (Fuwa, 1680), *The Thundergod* (Narukami, 1684; trans. 1975), *Immovable* (Fudō, 1697), *Wait a Moment!* (Shibaraku, 1697), *Pulling the Elephant* (Zōhiki, 1701), *Repel!* (Oshimodoshi, 1714), *The Arrow Maker* (Yanone, 1725). Danjūrō II blended rough and soft styles when he created the role of the dandy hero in *Sukeroku: Flower of Edo* (Sukeroku yukari Edo no zakura, 1713; trans. 1975), written by Tsuuchi Jihei II (1679–1760). The wonderfully dramatic confrontations, erotic byplay, impromptu comedy verging on farce and brilliant settings of the licensed quarter justly make this *kabuki*'s most popular play. These and plays added by later generations comprise the Eighteen Favourite Plays (*jūhachiban*) of the Ichikawa family.

Professional puppet theatre, today popularly called *bunraku*, began in the late 16th century from wholly different sources than *kabuki*. Doll figures manipulated by shamans served as scapegoats, carrying away impurities and evil, in religious rites in ancient times and popular puppetry was influenced by travelling troupes of Chinese and Korean performers, as part of *sangaku*. Sophisticated mechanical dolls (*karakuri*) decorated festival floats and attracted audiences to commercial theatres as late as the 19th century. Narrative skills, long admired in Japan, found expression in dozens of religious and secular forms. Today, we can hear raconteurs of comic stories (*rakugo*) and reciters of historical epics (*kōdan*) carrying on their narrative traditions in variety halls. In the 1590s performers of the previously separate arts of puppet manipulation and of narrative storytelling joined forces with musicians who played the plucked three-

stringed lute, the *shamisen*, forming commercial puppet-theatre troupes. One name for this tripartite theatre was *jōruri*, after the musical style used to chant a popular epic, *Twelve Tales of Princess Jōruri* (Jōruri jūni dan). The early 17th-century styles of commercial performance (*sekkyō bushi, ko jōruri*) were built around a narrative, sung, chanted and spoken by a single narrator (*tayū*), accompanied by a single *shamisen* player and illustrated by puppets. This remains the basic style of performance today. At first puppeteers, chanter and *shamisen* musician were concealed, but techniques of performance were of great interest to audiences, and by the early 18th century, when CHIKAMATSU MONZAEMON wrote the first psychologically persuasive 'modern' puppet plays, all performers were visible to the audience.

The first significant commercial puppet theatre was the Takemoto Theatre on the west bank of Dotombori Canal in Osaka. Its leading chanter TAKEMOTO GIDAYŪ specialized in serious, emotional delivery. The Toyotake Theatre (est. 1703) on the canal's east bank was set up by rival chanter Toyotake Wakatayū, whose style was light and flowery, hence a west style (*nishi fū*) and an east style (*higashi fū*) of chanting. The puppets executed simple movements, each manipulated by one puppeteer. Audiences enjoyed the chanting, but early puppet theatre presented no challenge to *kabuki*. Between 1720 and 1740 performers revolutionized *bunraku* art and world puppetry. They adopted characteristics of a first-person theatre, thereby bringing it closer to *kabuki*. Yoshida Bunzaburō (?–1760) invented a three-man manipulation system in 1724. A nearly life-size doll with movable eyes, eyebrows, mouth, hands and fingers moved realistically within elaborately constructed scenery. Puppet-theatre producers and *kabuki* managers perfected the revolving stage (a century before Europe), multiple trap doors and lifts with which to move performers and entire scenes magically into and out of view.

Exciting new plays were written to capitalize on the expressive power of the three-man puppets. At the Takemoto Theatre the playwriting team of Takeda Izumo II (1691–1756), Namiki Senryū (1695–1751), and Miyoshi Shōraku (1696–1775) jointly composed the Three Great Masterpieces of puppet drama: *The House of Sugawara* (Sugawara denju tenarai kagami, 1746), a drama of feudal loyalty; *Yoshitsune and the Thousand Cherry Trees* (*Yoshitsune senbon zakura*, 1747), a war tragedy that pits brother against brother; and *The Treasury of Loyal Retainers* (*Kanadehon chūshingura*, 1748; trans. 1971), Japan's famous revenge play. The convoluted plots of these multi-act history plays are driven by Confucian conflicts between duty (*giri*) and human compassion (*ninjō*). In *The Treasury of Loyal Retainers* the stalwart hero Yuranosuke abandons his wife and debauches himself out of loyalty to his slain lord. The plays contain spectacular puppet effects – a flying fox, a statue coming to life – and horrifying scenes of sacrifice – ritual disembowelment (*seppuku*), verifying the severed head of your child (*kubi jikken*), killing a beloved relative to save one's lord (*migawari*) – draw powerful emotions from the chanters. In *Chronicle of The Battle of Ichinotani* (*Ichinotani futaba gunki*, 1751; trans. 1975), composed by Namiki Sōsuke and others for the Toyotake Theatre, the Genji general Kumagai slays his teenage son in order to save the life of the emperor's son, Atsumori. Then he is forced to show his son's head to his wife. Unable to bear the horror of his act, Kumagai abandons his rank and becomes a mendicant Buddhist monk. Basic to puppet narrative is the pathos of early death, symbolized by the quickly fading cherry blossoms.

Plays were now enacted with remarkable verisimilitude – real water and mud were used in staging the domestic play *The Summer Festival* (*Natsu matsuri*, 1745). Perhaps the *yin-yang* concept of balance through opposites explains why human *kabuki* is stylized while puppet *bunraku* is realistic. If the plays were lacking in dramatic coherence (scenes were parcelled out to the different writers), they provided wonderfully effective theatre. The popularity of the productions – *Chronicle of the Battle of Ichinotani* ran 12 months – was such that within a month or two *kabuki* troupes would mount pirated versions to keep their audiences. In the process of borrowing from each other, *kabuki* and *bunraku* became more alike, sharing a humanistic world view, a common audience and a flamboyant aesthetic.

Kabuki borrowed puppet movement techniques, *gidayū* music and third-person narration. Adaptations of puppet plays came to make up a third of the *kabuki* repertory. Conversely, puppeteers studied *kabuki* productions like *The Vendetta at Iga* (*Igagoe norikake kappa*, 1777) and *Dispute in the*

A folk puppet performance with female and male puppeteers, on Awaji Island.

House of Sendai (*Meiboku Sendai hagi*, 1777), and imitated the actors in later puppet performances. After Chikamatsu Hanji's popular *Moritsune's Battle Camp* (*Moritsune jinya*, 1769) and *Mount Imo and Mount Se* (*Imoseyama onna teikin*, 1771; trans. 1990), *bunraku*'s popularity rapidly declined. The Takemoto and Toyotake theatres closed by 1772 and by the beginning of the 20th century the Bunraku-za in Osaka was the only remaining puppet theatre.

Kabuki attracted fresh audiences with ever-changing performance styles. Playwright Namiki Shōzō I (1730–76) introduced traps, lifts and the revolving stage to enhance *kabuki*'s spectacle. Onnagata stars Segawa Kikunojō I (1693–1749) and Nakamura Tomijūrō I (1719–86) were adored for dancing in new versions of *The Lion Dance* (*Shakkyō*) and *Dōjō Temple* (*Dōjōji*). In 1784, the playwright Takarada Jurai created a new dramatic dance form (*buyō geki*) featuring male roles in *Love's Snowy Barrier* (*Seki no to*) and a new style of music, *tokiwazu*. The form was developed by playwrights Horikoshi Nisōji (1721–?81) and pupil Sakurada Jisuke I (1734–1806), who was also famous for his witty writing style. In Namiki Gōhei III's new dance drama *The Subscription List (Kanjinchō*, 1840; trans. 1966, 1972) all the roles were male. Danjūrō VII (1791–1859) created the leading part of Benkei, now considered the most difficult dance role in the repertory. *The Subscription List* is based on the *nō* play *The Ataka Barrier.* It was the first of a score of *kabuki* dance dramas, serious and comic, based on *nō* and *kyōgen* plays, that borrowed music and acting techniques from these forms.

In spite of the government's Tempo Reforms of 1830–42, which aimed at nothing less than the destruction of *kabuki* by forcing theatres to move to Saruwaka-cho outside of Edo city, *kabuki* flourished. Playwrights TSURUYA NAMBOKU IV, Segawa Jokō III (1806–81), and KAWATAKE MOKUAMI in succession wrote 'raw' domestic plays (*kizewamono*) about thieves and gangsters, reflecting the riots, famines and peasant uprisings of the late feudal period, for actors Onoe Kikugorō V (1844–1903) and Ichikawa Kodanji IV (1812–66). Their scenes of murder (*koroshiba*), eroticism (*nureba*), torture (*semeba*) and extortion (*yusuriba*) illustrate a corrupt and decaying society. Namboku's masterpiece, *The Scarlet Princess of Edo* (*Sakura hime azuma bunsho*, 1817; trans. 1975), weaves together historical and outcast worlds (*sekai*), humour and soaring passages of poetic dialogue, and bloody, arresting visual effects. His imperial princess becomes a prostitute, his gangster becomes an official, and a samurai lord is murdered by a criminal.

The Western room: traditional theatre in the modern world

Western warships forced Japan to open its society to foreign trade and culture in the mid 19th century. The last Tokugawa Shōgun was defeated in a brief civil war by citizen soldiers loyal to the new Emperor Meiji. Cultural, political and economic changes during the Meiji period (1868–1912) profoundly altered the social and economic basis of all existing theatre forms. Paradoxically, Japan's economic miracle since defeat in World War II has increased competition for theatre. Increasingly, traditional genres – *bugaku, nō, kyōgen, kabuki* and *bunraku* – must hold an audience in competition with film, television, rock concerts, travel and other amenities of modern life.

Nō and kyōgen actors suffered greatly when the Meiji emperor abolished feudalism in 1869.

Overnight, *nō* actors lost their samurai status; without work or income, they were forced to sell heirloom masks and costumes to stay alive (hence the fine *nō* collections in Western museums). Within a year, however, actor Umewaka Minoru (1828–1909) began the process of bringing *nō* to the public by charging admission to performances in his home. Later he persuaded the reigning *nō* star Hōshō Kurō to return from retirement on his farm and to join him in performing in public. In Kyoto monthly public performances were started by actors of the Kongō school in 1877. New *nō* theatres were built in Tokyo's Aoyama Palace in 1878 and Shiba Park in 1881, encouraged by statesman Iwakura Tomomi who, returning from a study trip to Europe, realized that *nō* could be Japan's equivalent of Western opera. Former President Ulysses S. Grant, visiting Japan, praised *nō* and urged that it be preserved. Gradually *nō* occupied an elite position in the new society. After a short period of government support, including imperial command performances, public support solidified.

Today the thousand or so professional actors that belong to the five *nō* and two *kyōgen* schools support themselves primarily by teaching many thousands of devoted amateurs, while only a portion of their income derives from performance (theatres seat 400–500 and each programme is performed a single time). Each *nō* school owns one or more theatres and the hereditary master-actor (*iemoto*) of each school exercises total artistic and financial control. On the surface, the repertory and style of performance appear unaffected by the modern world. With rare exceptions, new plays are not performed (Kanze Hideo was banished from *nō* in the 1960s for acting in modern plays).

The livelihood of *kabuki* and *bunraku* performers was not directly threatened by Meiji-period reform because their popular audiences did not immediately change. But through the 20th century both theatres gradually lost their 'popular' audiences and became classical arts favoured by a higher, better-educated social class. In 1872 officials informed *kabuki* playwrights and actors of the emperor's 'command' that they must present only material suitable for family groups or foreign spectators. Throughout its 300-year history, *kabuki* had been 'contemporary theatre' and, like film and television today, everything new in society was eagerly placed on the stage. In the late Meiji period,

Mokuami wrote plays featuring telegraph messages, locomotives and balloon ascents. In 1879, actor-manager Morita Kanya XII (1846–97) hired a British troupe from Hong Kong to act alongside kabuki actors in A Foreign Kabuki set in London. Modern 'cropped-hair plays' (zangirimono), acted by Onoe Kikugorō V (1844–1903), put current life on the kabuki stage. Ichikawa Danjūrō IX played in living-history plays (katsureki geki) that aimed at historical truth. Danjūrō joined the calls of the Society for Theatre Reform, formed in 1886, to modernize and sanitize kabuki in line with Western theatre practice. Leading literary scholars advocated abolishing traditional music, the wooden-clapper sound effects, the hanamichi, stage assistants and the female impersonator, so as to 'modernize' kabuki. These extreme reforms never came to pass, but the raucous nature of kabuki was irretrievably destroyed.

Literary men from outside the theatre replaced staff playwrights as the authors of new kabuki dramas (shin kabuki). Plays such as Tsubouchi Shōyō's A Paulownia Leaf (1904), Okamoto Kidō's The Love Suicides at Mount Toribe (1915), and more recently kabuki scripts by novelist-playwright Mishima Yukio are notable for having achieved de facto the aims of the discredited reform movement. Traditional kabuki dramaturgy is abandoned. Modern authors do not know seven-five dialogue, poetic name-saying speeches or traditional act and scene structure. They rarely incorporate mie poses, shamisen music or stylized battles. New kabuki plays continue to be written and staged at the Kabuki-za in Tokyo, but rarely do audiences like them, rarely are they revived, and rarely do they in any way deserve the name kabuki.

A handful of superb bunraku performers sparked renewed interest in the puppet theatre during the Meiji era, working primarily at two new theatres in Osaka, the Bunraku-za (est. 1872) and its competitor the Hikoroku Theatre (est. 1884). The chanter Takemoto Harudayū V (1808–77) was greatly admired for his powerful and expressive voice. One of the few shamisen players to achieve personal fame, Toyozawa Danpei (1827–98) revolutionized the art of bunraku music. He composed complex scores that closely supported the emotional nuances of scenes rather than merely serving as accompaniment to the chanter. It was said a listener could understand the emotions of a charac-ter just by hearing Danpei play the shamisen. With his wife, he wrote the touching Buddhist miracle play, Miracle at Tsubosaka Temple (Tsubosaka reigenki, 1879), the last important text to enter the traditional repertory. Chanter Takemoto Settsu-Daijō (1836–1917) performed for members of the imperial family and in 1902 was honoured with an imperial title. A decade before this, Settsu-Daijō began the fad of chanting puppet texts without puppets. Amateurs studied chanting under the instruction of professional shamisen teachers; in 1889 perhaps a thousand amateurs were chanting in theatres and recital halls in Osaka. Mass performances by 400–500 chanters were not uncommon. Women chanters (onna jōruri) gained enormous success in commercial variety theatres (yose) in the early decades of the 20th century. Settsu-Daijō attempted to restore 'historical truth' to classical plays, parallel to the efforts of Danjūrō IX in kabuki. He placed the old plays in their proper historical period and called characters by their real names. Lovers of bunraku, however, did not want their plays tampered with and by 1891 Settsu-Daijō had abandoned his reforms. Bunraku's Meiji-period revival did not last when its charismatic performers passed from the scene. The one remaining puppet theatre, the Bunraku-za of Osaka, was purchased in 1909 by the Shōchiku Theatrical Corporation. Performers split into two competing groups following World War II, but in 1963 they rejoined to form the present single troupe under the auspices of the Bunraku Association and with generous financial support from the Ministry of Education. The troupe draws a stable, moderate-sized audience at its home theatre in Osaka and on yearly national tours.

Early in the Meiji period, when the government ceased regulating the number and location of theatres, kabuki-theatre owners moved to elite locations in the centre of Tokyo. In 1872 Kanya XII moved the Morita Theatre, which had opened in old Edo in 1660, into the heart of Tokyo and three years later rebuilt it as the New Tomi Theatre equipped with Western seats and gas lighting where he staged kabuki's first nighttime performances. Foreign dignitaries, including former President Grant, attended this 'modern' theatre. The Kabuki-za, now the premiere kabuki theatre in the country, opened in the fashionable Ginza district in 1889. Kabuki managers were successful in drawing the new upper-middle class, but in doing so they abandoned their traditional supporters, the merchants, artisans and workers.

During World War II audiences for both *kabuki* and *bunraku* declined drastically. Performers were drafted into the army or sent on war-related entertainment tours. Theatres were gutted by bombing. After Japan's surrender in 1945 American-occupation censors banned 'feudal' *kabuki* and *bunraku* plays and it appeared that the survival of both forms was in doubt. The appeal of *kabuki* to a broad segment of the public remained strong, however, and as soon as censorship was lifted audiences again filled the Kabuki-za, the Shinbashi Dance Theatre, and, from 1966, the new National Theatre. The Minami Theatre in Kyoto (remodelled in 1991) and the Naka Theatre in Osaka are located in traditional entertainment districts and retain the flavour of old *kabuki*.

Kabuki family acting traditions have been carried into the second half of the 20th century by a group of charismatic and talented actors: Ichikawa Danjūrō XI (1909–65); Living National Treasure Onoe Shōroku II (1913–89); Matsumoto Koshirō VII (1910–75); Living National Treasure Nakamura Kanzaburō XVII (1909–88); former President of the Kabuki Actors' Association Ichikawa Sadanji III (1898–1964); Morita Kanya XIV (1907–75); and two great *onnagata*, Living National Treasure NAKAMURA UTAEMON VI; and Living National Treasure Onoe Baikō VI (1915–). Today's young

The *Exposé* (*Tekihatsu*), a modern *kyōgen* comedy about a young office worker in Tokyo, performed in the traditional acting style, 1968.

actors BANDŌ TAMASABURŌ, Kataoka Takao I (1944–), Onoe Kikugorō VII (1942–), Ichikawa Danjūrō XII (1946–) and even younger stars are idolized by fans. They have done much to attract a younger audience in the 1970s and 80s.

The imaginative staging by actor-director Ichikawa Ennosuke III (1939–), who insists upon reinterpreting each classic to make it interesting to a modern audience, is unusual. Today *kabuki* is a classical, orthodox theatre in which little change occurs. Spectators are mostly middle-class, block-booking by corporations fills 75 per cent of the house and a first-class ticket costs US $80–100 (£50–60). Once a despised theatre, it calls itself Grand Kabuki on foreign tours. Actors work exceptionally long hours: matinee and evening bills, usually different, begin at 11 in the morning and end at 10 at night. The programme changes monthly, performances are daily for 25 days, and four or five days at the end of the month are spent in intensive rehearsals on the next month's plays. Theatre owners and producers run *kabuki* today and the 500 or so professional actors are rotated among theatres each month as needed. There no longer is a functioning troupe system. Actors often perform in mixed-genre productions today.

Government support of theatre in the modern period has been negligible. *Bugaku* is the chief exception: the main troupe continues as part of the Imperial Household Agency. *Bunraku*, as noted, began receiving government subsidies in 1963. A distinguished artist who is named an Intangible Cultural Asset or Living National Treasure receives a small government annuity. Most significantly, in recent decades the government has built four modern and beautifully equipped theatres containing stages, research facilities and performer-training programmes: the National Theatre for *kabuki* and *bunraku* (1966), the National Variety Theatre (1966), and the National Noh Theatre (1983), all in Tokyo, and the National Bunraku Theatre (1985) in Osaka. Theatre staffs, but not the actors or musicians, are on government salaries.

Traditional performances have been televised regularly throughout Japan since the 1960s (*kabuki* most often), thereby reaching audiences that normally would never have the chance to attend the theatre. *Kabuki, bunraku, nō,* and *kyōgen* troupes are regularly sent out on international tours, so that traditional theatre is no longer isolated.

Transition to modern theatre: shinpa

Shinpa, 'new school', developed as the theatre of the half-Westernized, half-traditional urban middle class that rose to prominence during the Meiji era. It was a transitional theatre whose rationale for existence was the rejection of 'old' values. The first shinpa plays were staged by the failed politician Kawakami Otojirō (1864–1911) who used patriotic events, such as the Russo-Japanese war, as subjects for melodrama. He and his wife, Sada Yakko (1871–1946), a trained geisha, toured the United States and Europe in 1899–1901 where their troupe's emotional performances received astounded acclaim. Sada was compared to Sarah Bernhardt for the 'realism' of her death scenes. Due to Sada, the 1629 law banning women from the public stage was repealed.

Kawakami successfully adapted Western plays such as Othello, Hamlet, and The Count of Monte Cristo to Japanese settings. He introduced Maeterlinck and Sardou, and he produced Japan's first children's drama in 1903 at the Hongō Theatre. Between 1900 and 1915, Kawakami appeared in major theatres in Tokyo and Osaka in competition with rival shinpa troupes in topical plays that had great popular appeal. Titles of plays produced in 1904, the year that the Russo-Japanese war began, suggest their intense nationalist flavour: The Fall of Port Arthur, The Imperial Army That Vanquishes Russia, The Great Russo-Japanese War, Battle Report, and Submarine.

Shinpa producers inaugurated shortened performance hours, they brought actresses back to the stage, and they abolished the theatre teahouses that controlled ticket sales. Seeing that huge country audiences flocked to the cinema (introduced commercially in 1903), they placed live performances in front of film backgrounds in 1910. Most important, they gave new Japanese playwrights an opportunity to see their plays produced. Tsubouchi Shōyō's modern drama The Cuckoo (1904) received its first performance at the hand of shinpa actors. Tsubouchi (1859–1935) was a seminal figure in early modern Japanese theatre – translator of Shakespeare's canon, playwright, acting teacher, director, and founder of the influential Literary Arts Society. Satō Kōroku (1874–1949) wrote five plays in the space of two years (1907–08) for shinpa actors and Mayama Seika (1878–1948) dramatized contemporary novels for

shinpa performance. By the 1920s shingeki had laid claim to Western drama and shinpa declined to routine domestic tragicomedies marked by sentimental nostalgia for a past era. The superlative actress Mizutani Yaeko (1905–79) assured the popularity of the one remaining shinpa troupe through the postwar years, and her daughter, Mizutani Yoshie, continues with that troupe in the 1990s. Often kabuki and shinpa actors give joint performances, indicating the affinity of the two genres.

Modern Japanese theatre: shingeki

The history of modern Japanese theatre, known as SHINGEKI (literally 'new theatre'), has been characterized by a break with traditional theatre forms in the early 20th century and attempts since the World War II to recapture some of the resources lost in that rupture. In essence, the plethora of gods and demons who had populated classical nō and kabuki were exiled from the modern stage in the early period, only to return in force since the war. Five periods may be distinguished in this process: 1887–1928, the establishment of a modern theatre; 1928–45, the politicization of modern theatre; 1945–60, the establishment of an orthodox modernism; 1960–73, the rejection of modernism; and 1973 to the present, diversification.

Exile of the gods, 1887–1945: the classical legacy

In 1887, the government of Meiji Japan formed a blue-ribbon Committee for the Reform of the Theatre (Engeki Kairyō Kai) to clean up kabuki and make it acceptable to a Western audience. The Japanese oligarchy was self-conscious about kabuki because it was a highly erotic and frequently violent form of popular theatre that had provided a relatively harmless release for plebeian libido in the repressive Tokugawa period (1600–1868). The government's goal was to recast kabuki in the mould of 19th-century European realism. A number of attempts were made to achieve this end, including the katsureki, or 'living-history', plays performed by Ichikawa Danjūrō IX (1838–1903) in the 1890s and shinpa (literally 'new wave' drama), originated by Kawakami Otojirō, his wife Sada Yakko, and the actor Ii Yōhō (1871–1932). The experiments of Ichikawa Sadanji II (1880–1940) and OSANAI KAORU in the first decades of the 20th century are also worth noting. Most of these experiments failed, but some, like *shinpa*, survived and continue to be performed.

Nō and *kabuki*, Japan's premier traditional theatre forms, evolved in a pre-modern milieu where little distinction existed between art and religion. While very different from each other, *nō* and *kabuki* are nevertheless both religio-aesthetic forms. *Nō* is a sacred theatre where, typically, a god will appear and catharsis will be achieved through contact with the divine. By contrast, *kabuki* originated as a profane theatre, where catharsis was achieved through exposure to evil. What the Committee for the Reform of the Theatre and other would-be reformers tried to do was deny the religious function of *nō* and *kabuki* and re-establish them as purely aesthetic forms.

Exiled from the classical stage, the gods found little refuge in the emerging modern theatre. Troupes dedicated to producing Western plays and their Japanese equivalents appeared in the first decade of the 20th century. The Literary Arts Society (Bungei Kyōkai) was founded in 1906 by Tsubouchi Shōyō; the Free Theatre (Jiyū Gekijō), named after Antoine's Théâtre Libre, was founded in 1909 by Osanai Kaoru and Ichikawa Sadanji.

While the two troupes differed in their approach to modern theatre, there was little room in either of them for the displaced spirits of the Japanese pantheon. Tsubouchi, one of the Meiji period's outstanding men of letters, was professor of English literature at Waseda University and a translator of Shakespeare. As its name implied, his troupe took an academic and literary approach to the theatre and concentrated on performing Tsubouchi's translations of Shakespeare, including *The Merchant of Venice* (1906), *Hamlet* (1907, 1911) and *Julius Caesar* (1913). In contrast, the Free Theatre concentrated on the works of contemporary European writers, staging Ibsen's *John Gabriel Borkman* in 1909 and Gorky's *Lower Depths* the following year.

The two troupes agreed that a new style of acting would be necessary to successfully perform Western drama (including the training of actresses, who had been banned from the Japanese stage more than 250 years earlier), but they differed on how this goal was to be achieved. The Literary Arts Society hoped to develop a new breed of actor by exposing amateurs to great works of dramatic literature; the Free Theatre sought to re-educate professional actors, like its cofounder Ichikawa Sadanji, to perform European works.

Neither approach was successful. *Kabuki* actors never successfully adapted to the realistic style of acting required by the modern European works staged by the Free Theatre; and the actors Tsubouchi helped to train were unwilling to remain dedicated to his stoic literary philosophy. The Free Theatre continued to perform sporadically until 1919. The Literary Arts Society collapsed in 1913, when the troupe's leading actress, MATSUI SUMAKO, left the troupe with Tsubouchi's erstwhile disciple, Shimamura Hōgetsu (1871–1918), to found their own Art Theatre (Geijutsuza), a more commercially oriented company that capitalized on Matsui's popularity as Japan's first modern actress.

The 1910s and early 20s were an era of much literary but little theatrical activity. Many plays were written but few performed with distinction. Among those writing plays during these years were Kikuchi Kan (1888–1948), Kume Masao (1891–1952), Yamamoto Yūzō (1887–1974), and Tanizaki Junichirō (1886–1965), all of whom are as well or better known as novelists.

It was at the end of this period of literary activity that the Tsukiji Little Theatre (Tsukiji Shōgekijō) was founded. Ordinances had prevented the construction of new theatres in Tokyo, but after the Great Kanto Earthquake destroyed much of the city on 1 September 1923, the municipal administration eased restrictions in the interest of rebuilding the capital. Osanai organized and HIJIKATA YOSHI financed the project. A wealthy young nobleman and theatre devotee who had just left for an intended ten-year tour of Europe, Hijikata hastened home when he heard that a theatre could be built, and he placed the funds earmarked for his sojourn abroad at Osanai's disposal.

The Tsukiji Little Theatre opened on 13 June 1924. It had a seating capacity of just under 500 and was constructed along the most modern lines. The most renowned feature of its stage was a *Kuppelhorizont* that made sophisticated lighting design possible.

Construction of the Tsukiji Little Theatre was greeted with enthusiasm by Japanese playwrights. They had been publishing their works, first in *New Trends in Thought* (Shinshichō), a journal founded in 1907 by Osanai himself, and later in *New Trends in*

Drama (*Engeki shinchō*), and had every reason to believe that the Tsukiji would stage them. They were thunderstruck, therefore, when Osanai announced at Keio University on 20 May 1924 that for a period of two years the Tsukiji would produce only works by Western playwrights.

Osanai's action precipitated a deep split in the *shingeki* movement. After his frustrating experience with the Free Theatre, his travels in Europe and his contact with Stanislavski's Moscow Art Theatre, however, Osanai was determined to create a viable production system for modern plays in Japan, and he was convinced that this required a clean break with traditional methods and sensibilities. Even the remnants of Japaneseness found in the ostensibly 'modern' works of Japanese playwrights could subvert this project, he feared. Only by actually producing European plays in the European manner for an extended period could the goal of a modern theatre for Japan be achieved.

Politicization of modern theatre, 1928–45

By the time of Osanai's untimely death on 25 December 1928, the Tsukiji Little Theatre had established a modern system of theatre production in Japan. It had produced a diverse repertory of representative European works by playwrights including Ibsen, Chekhov, Turgenev, Strindberg, Capek, Pirandello, and Georg Kaiser; and it had trained an entire generation of theatre practitioners. With Osanai's passing, however, the tensions inherent in a troupe so diversely conceived immediately came to a head, and the company collapsed in less than three months.

The Tsukiji Little Theatre split into factions that continued to define the *shingeki* movement into the postwar period. Hijikata Yoshi led the New Tsukiji Troupe (Shin Tsukiji Gekidan), the 'political' faction, which incorporated the activist members of the original company, including such actors as Maruyama Sadao (1901–45) (who died from radiation poisoning he received in the atomic bombing of Hiroshima), Yamamoto Yasue (1905–) (later to become KINOSHITA JUNJI's favourite actress and to create the role of Tsū in his *Twilight Crane*), Susukida Kenji (1898–1972) (a founder of the People's Art Theatre company after the war) and others. Aoyama Sugisaku (1889–1956) represented the Tsukiji Little Theatre Company (Gekidan

The present-day Kabukiza Theatre in the Ginza, Tokyo, built in 1925 and restored in 1949.

Tsukiji Shōgekijō), the 'artistic' faction, which included such notable actors as Higashiyama Chieko (1890–1980) (later of The Actors' Theatre), Tomoda Kyōsuke (1899–1937) and Tamura Akiko (1905–83) (husband and wife, who later joined the Literary Theatre), and Sugimura Haruko (1909–) (also of the Literary Theatre and one of the postwar period's finest actresses). Takizawa Osamu (1906–), one of Japan's most accomplished actors, originally belonged to the Tsukiji Little Theatre Company, but later shifted his allegiance to the politically engaged group.

Playwrights also helped to define the *shingeki* movement in the 1930s. Murayama Tomoyoshi (1901–77) (who was also a talented stage designer and director), Miyoshi Jūrō (1902–58), and KUBO SAKAE were left-wing writers associated with the political mainstream of the movement; Kubota Mantarō (1889–1963), Iwata Toyō (1893–1969), and KISHIDA KUNIO were representative writers for the artistic group. Kubota, Iwata, and Kishida jointly founded The Literary Theatre (Bungakuza) in 1937; and it was the only prewar *shingeki* troupe allowed to perform continuously through the war.

In August 1940, the government ordered the New Tsukiji and the New Co-operative (Shinkyō) troupes, the two remaining left-wing companies, to disband and imprisoned their leaders, including Kubo. Kishida, by contrast, became head of the cultural section of the Imperial Rule Assistance Association in 1940, the year it supplanted all political parties, and after the war he was purged by the Occupation as a collaborator in the war effort.

Modernism becomes orthodoxy, 1945–60: the post-war situation

For a brief period after the war, it seemed that *shingeki* would become the centre, not only of Japanese theatre, but of Japanese culture as a whole. Of all the arts, its ardent devotion to realism had kept it relatively immune to the ultranationalist contagion. It was this same commitment to realism, however, that hobbled modern theatre's attempts to answer the profound questions raised by the war and defeat.

Influential playwrights in the 1950s included Kinoshita Junji (1914–), who represents the politically engaged group, and FUKUDA TSUNEARI, who was a leader of the literary faction. Both of these men were, incidentally, scholars and translators of Shakespeare. Mishima Yukio (1925–1970), whose *Five Modern Nō Plays* (*Kindai nōgaku shū*, 1956; trans. 1957) offers eerily effective one-act adaptations of the *nō* classics, was also an important innovator. Also significant were Hotta Kiyomi (1922–), whose play *The Island* (*Shima*, 1955; trans. 1986) was the first play of national importance to deal with the bombing of Hiroshima; and Tanaka Chikao (1905–95), whose *Head of Mary* (*Maria no kubi*, 1959; trans. 1986) treated the tragedy of Nagasaki from a Roman Catholic point of view.

Institutionally, the postwar scene was dominated by three *shingeki* troupes that reflected the alliances that had existed in the Tsukiji Little Theatre. Mingei (The People's Art Theatre) represented the left wing; the Actors' Theatre (Haiyūza), led by SENDA KOREYA, an actor, director, and translator of Brecht, most closely approximated the catholic, academic approach of Osanai; and the Literary Theatre continued to represent the literary faction.

With the easing of political tensions and the recovery of the postwar economy, the differences between these troupes became more apparent than real, however; and the postwar period was marked by a growing consensus on what modern theatre should be. Modernism, in short, became an orthodoxy. Among the tenets of this orthodoxy were a commitment to proscenium-arch realism, a belief in the primacy of the text and the actor's subservience to it, a commitment to a tragic and humanistic dramaturgy and a conviction that the principal function of theatre is didactic.

When the war ended, modern Japanese theatre faced a severe crisis. Most theatres had been destroyed, and troupes lacked the wherewithal to mount productions. By the 1960s, however, *shingeki* had achieved unprecedented success.

Two factors were responsible for the success of the postwar *shingeki* system. The first was the *gekidan* or company system. In the company system, actors work outside the theatre, especially in films and television, and pay a 'company tax' (*gekidanzei*) of up to 50 per cent of their earnings to support the activities of the troupe. A famous example of the efficacy of this system is the construction of the Actors' Theatre in 1954 with the earnings of actors like Senda Koreya, who performed in 29 films in two years and contributed 65 per cent of his income to the theatre. Actors like Senda, ununionized and unpaid or poorly paid for their stage work, are the altruistic foundation of all modern theatre in Japan. Another example of the success of the company system is the People's Art Theatre company. Founded in 1950 with eleven actors and one director, it had grown by 1970 to 250 members, producing ten plays for 600 performances a year.

The second factor was Rōen. Modelled after the German Volksbühne, Rōen (Workers' Theatre Councils) provided troupes like the Actors' Theatre and the People's Art Theatre with a national audience by selling discounted tickets to members of trade unions. By 1969 the organization was sponsoring as many as a thousand performances each year for its 133,000 members.

In a sense, however, the postwar *shingeki* movement fell victim to its own success. Originality was frequently sacrificed in the interest of fiscal conservatism. Once the most innovative and adventurous form of theatre in Japan, by the 1960s *shingeki* had become a tradition in its own right, ripe for challenge by a new generation of theatre artists.

Return of the Gods, 1960–73: emergence of the post-Shingeki movement

When the United States–Japan Mutual Security Treaty came up for renewal in 1960, the limitations of orthodox *shingeki* became painfully apparent to the emerging younger generation. Massive nationwide demonstrations had been organized to oppose renewal of the treaty, which permits the stationing of American military forces on Japanese soil and places Japan under the United States 'nuclear umbrella', and *shingeki* groups had taken an active part in them. When the demonstrations failed to prevent the renewal of the treaty, however, younger members of the movement began to feel that *shingeki* orthodoxy could no more effectively explain what had happened to them than it had been able to explain the war, and this led to a thoroughgoing re-assessment of theatrical priorities and goals that precipitated a counter-movement in modern Japanese theatre called the ANGURA or post-*shingeki* movement.

The Youth Art Theatre (Seinen Geijutsu Gekijō or Seigei) company provided the transition from orthodox *shingeki* to the post-*shingeki* movement. It had been organized by youthful members of the People's Art Theatre troupe in November 1959. The Youth Art Theatre's leading playwright was FUKUDA YOSHIYUKI, whose early works, including *A Long Row of Tombstones* (*Nagai bohyō no retsu*, 1957), were written under the strong influence of Kubo Sakae and Kinoshita Junji. The experience of the 1960 demonstrations, street theatre in a real sense, changed the perspective of Fukuda and other members of the troupe, however, and the Youth Art Theatre began to develop an independent style that rejected proscenium-arch realism and the other major tenets of *shingeki* orthodoxy.

The Youth Art Theatre became a spawning ground for many of the writers and actors in the post-*shingeki* movement. Among the playwrights who were in some way connected with the troupe were BETSUYAKU MINORU, KARA JŪRŌ, and SATOH MAKOTO.

In 1965, the Youth Art Theatre restaged Betsuyaku's *The Elephant* (*Zō*, 1962; trans. 1986), which eloquently articulated the new generation's frustration with the passivity of the orthodox movement and their desire to create a newly empowering rationale for action. The play deals with survivors of Hiroshima, but it was understood as a protest against a world in which any kind of action was impossible.

There was a widespread feeling after 1960 that if the past was to be successfully explained and a rationale for future action formulated, the dramatic conventions of a half-century would have to be discarded and some means found to make the gods once again appear on stage. In play after play, the writers of the post-*shingeki* movement engineered epiphanies, moments when gods once again came to populate the Japanese stage. This was their means of escaping the debilitating sense of enforced passivity and stasis they had been experiencing.

The mechanism was apotheosis: ordinary men and women were metamorphosed into gods before the audience's eyes. In 1964 the Youth Art Theatre produced Fukuda Yoshiyuki's *Find Hakamadare!* (*Hakamadare wa doko da*, 1964; trans. 1988), one of the first plays to clearly employ the dramaturgy of metamorphosis as an empowering theory of action. Based on a 12th-century legend, the play describes how a band of oppressed peasants take their fate into their own hands and become Hakamadare, their long-awaited saviour, when Hakamadare himself turns out to be a rapacious villain.

Kaison the Priest of Hitachi (*Hitachibō Kaison*, 1965; trans. 1988) by AKIMOTO MATSUYO describes the metamorphosis of a young man in the early 1960s into the immortal Kaison, a warrior from the 12th century who is still reputed to wander through northeast Japan doing penance for sins committed centuries ago. Through his metamorphosis the young man escapes from history into mythic time and is saved from the excruciating burden of guilt he carries from his experience as a child during the war. Kara Jūrō's *The Beggar of Love* (*Ai no kojiki*, 1970; trans. 1988) describes the metamorphosis of oppressed urbanites into their redeemer, an avenging peg-legged sailor named Silver. And Satoh Makoto's *Nezumi Kozō: The Rat* (*Nezumi Kozō Jirokichi*, 1970; trans. 1986) describes the transformation of a rag-tag band of lumpen proletarians into their awaited messiah, a Robin-Hood-like figure from the early 19th century named Nezumi Kozō.

A special feature of the post-*shingeki* dramaturgy of metamorphosis is that 'salvation' in each of these plays is virtually indistinguishable from damnation. Apotheosis into Kaison or Silver or Nezumi Kozō means abandoning historical time and responsibility and being sucked back into the maelstrom of eternal redundancy. This restatement of the existential situation of the Japanese, torn between the cruel reality of history and the ambivalent promise of salvation through assimilation to mythic time, has challenged the tragic–humanistic formula of orthodox *shingeki* and has been the major contribution of post-*shingeki* dramaturgy.

This contribution has been accompanied by innovations in stagecraft that break decisively with orthodox *shingeki* practice. Gone is the hegemony of the proscenium stage: two of the post-*shingeki* movement's major troupes, Kara Jūrō's Situation Theatre (Jōkyō Gekijō) and Satoh Makoto's Black Tent Theatre 68/71 (presently known simply as Kuro Tento or the Black Tent) perform in tents. SUZUKI TADASHI's SCOT (Suzuki Company of Toga), formerly the Waseda Little Theatre (Waseda Shōgekijō), abandoned Tokyo in 1976 for Toga village, a mountain retreat eight hours from the city, where the company lives and works together in a manner similar to Jerzy Grotowski's earlier Laboratory Theatre in Wroclaw, Poland, or Eugenio Barba's Odin Teatret in Holstebro, Denmark. The primacy of the text has been replaced by a renewed emphasis on the creative role of the actor, and Suzuki in particular has made a lasting contribution to actor training by creating a system of exercises suggested by *nō* and *kabuki*.

These three companies continue to perform today. An additional troupe from a slightly different lineage that played a seminal role in the revolt against *shingeki* orthodoxy was TERAYAMA SHŪJI's Tenjō Sajiki (literally, the Upper Gallery). Terayama, who was born in 1935 in Aomori prefecture in northeastern Japan, was deeply influenced by the French avant-garde, particularly Antonin Artaud and Lautreamont; and his first dramatic work, *Blood Sleeps Standing Up* (*Chi wa tatta mama nemutte iru*, 1960), was produced by the Four Seasons (Shiki) company headed by Asari Keita, which gained fame in the 1950s for its productions of the French playwrights Giraudoux and Anouilh. (Shiki is today a multimillion-dollar enterprise specializing in the production of musicals like *Jesus Christ Superstar* and *Cats*.) The multitalented Terayama, who was also a renowned poet, essayist and director, was a true scion of the European avant-garde. His principal aim was to shock the bourgeoisie, and he succeeded in this with happenings, street theatre, multimedia events and themes ranging from incest to transvestitism.

Continuity and discontinuity: 1973 to the present

By 1973 the dialectic of divine exile and return that

Satoh Makoto's *Nezumi Kozō* (*The Rat*).

had governed the evolution of modern Japanese drama for nearly a hundred years had been fulfilled. Orthodox *shingeki* was embattled. In 1971 thirty members of the People's Art Theatre resigned, and eleven members of the Actors' Theatre quit in protest over the troupe's conservative repertory. Mishima Yukio's troupe, the Romantic Theatre (Roman Gekijō), folded in 1972, following the author's suicide two years earlier; and in 1973, writer Abe Kōbō (1924–93) ended his affiliation with the Actors' Theatre to found his own company, the Abe Kōbō Studio.

At the same time, the return of the gods to the Japanese stage reached its apex with the emergence of *BUTŌ* as a full-fledged dance form. The word *butō* is simply a variant of the Japanese word for dance. The style had originated in the 1950s and 60s with the pioneering work of dancer-choreographers Ohno Kazuo (1906–) and Hijikata Tatsumi (1928–86). In 1972 *butō* dovetailed with the post-*shingeki* movement. In that year, Maro Akaji (1943–), formerly a leading actor in Kara Jūrō's Situation Theatre, founded the first *butō* troupe, Dairakudakan (The Great Camel Battleship). Maro had lived and studied with Hijikata, and he effected a marriage of Hijikata's unique choreography with post-*shingeki* dramaturgy and organizational style.

The dancers in *butō* are ghosts and gods. Naked, heads shaven, covered in dead white body makeup, arms raised, eyes rolled back, they are unmistakably apparitions from another world. Hijikata acknowledged this explicitly in a speech delivered in 1985: 'To make gestures of the dead, to die again, to make the dead re-enact once more their deaths in their entirety – these are what I want to experience within me'. The metamorphosis into trans-historical ghosts and gods that is the heart of post-*shingeki* dramaturgy appears in its most overt form in *butō*.

Having successfully challenged orthodox modernism, the consensus that had united various post-*shingeki* troupes in an informal movement began to collapse in the mid 1970s. A number of factors exacerbated this phenomenon. The first was political. The United Red Army Incident of 1972, the murder for 'ideological deviation' of student radicals by members of their own political sect, made theatre artists less sanguine about 'revolutionary' activity and signalled the end of the period of political radicalism that had begun in 1960. Productions like *When We Travel Down the Great River of Callousness (Bokura ga hijō no taiga o kudaru toki*, 1972), written by Shimizu Kunio (1936–) and directed by Ninagawa Yukio (1935–), reflected the impact. The second factor was economic. Following the OPEC oil embargo of 1973, 1974 was the first year since the World War II that the Japanese economy experienced a recession. The concomitant inflation inevitably affected the theatre world.

More important than either of these factors, however, were the long-range changes in society brought about by the rapid economic growth of the 1960s. In particular, prosperity made it possible to construct numerous new theatres after 1973. The scarcity of theatrical space had always been the basic reality of modern Japanese theatre; now the construction of many new theatres accelerated the trend toward dramatic diversification. Similarly, the appearance in 1972 of *Pia*, a biweekly listing of theatre and other performances in the Tokyo area, brought accurate and timely information about the productions of new as well as established troupes to a mass audience. With the advent of easily accessed computerized ticketing in the 1980s, theatre attendance became simpler than ever, precipitating a boom in theatre that continues to this day.

Theatrical diversification began in the 1970s with the emergence of new, younger troupes: The Theatre Group (Engekidan) led by Ryūzanji Shō (1947–), The Gallery Troupe (Tsunbosajiki) led by Yamazaki Tetsu (1946–), and Space Acting (Kūkan Engi) led by Okabe Kōdai (1945–). It was the work of Tsuka Kōhei (1948–), however, that marked a real departure in style. Tsuka was the first playwright born after the war to receive the Kishida Prize for Playwriting, which he received for *The Atami Murder Incident (Atami satsujin jiken)* in 1974. Tsuka's apolitical, insightful human dramas were intensely funny and signalled an end to the underlying intellectuality that had continued to characterize post-*shingeki* productions.

The lure of commercialism was also felt. In 1974 Ninagawa Yukio defected from the avant-garde to direct *Romeo and Juliet* for the commercial Tōhō firm. Known for his highly theatrical effects, Ninagawa has gone on to direct many successful commercial productions. Avant-garde artists also began to work together on an *ad hoc* basis in what has come to be known as the 'producer system', but affiliation with quasi-familial companies remains the rule in Japan and a true system of independent artists and producers is yet to emerge.

Female playwright-directors also began to appear in the mid 1970s. Kishida Rio (1950–) had worked closely with Terayama Shūji beginning in 1974. After his death in 1983, she established her own troupe, The Kishida Office & The Optimists (Kishida Jimusho + Rakutendan), and won the 1984 Kishida Prize for her feminist play *Woven Hell* (*Ito jigoku*). Kisaragi Koharu (1956–) and Watanabe Eriko (1955–) have also been influential. They and their troupes, respectively NOISE and 3OO (Sanjūmaru), have frequently focused on family dynamics and have added a female perspective to contemporary Japanese theatre.

The 1980s have been called the decade of 'metatheatre'. The Dream Wanderers (Yume no Yū-minsha, founded1976) led by Noda Hideki (1955–) and The Third Stage (Daisan Butai, founded 1981) led by Kōkami Shōji (1958–) are representative. A fascination with play and nonsense, a fixation on

A 'soft-style' (*wagoto*) love scene from the *kabuki* play, *Love Letter from the Licensed Quarter* (*Kuruwa bunshō*).

childhood, and maze-like, anti-linear dramatic structure have earned these playwright-directors the title 'postmodern'. More traditional but no less innovative have been troupes like the Shinjuku Ryōzanpaku (literally, the Shinjuku Hideout, founded 1987), a unique ensemble organized by Japanese of Korean extraction who carry on the traditions of the Situation Theatre and the Black Tent, where many of them did their apprenticeship. In a similar vein, Tokyo Group One (Tokyo Ichikumi, founded 1988) has developed a uniquely satisfying combination of post-*shingeki* dramaturgy and the commercial comedy style of the immensely popular actor Fujiyama Kanbi (1929–90).

The 1980s were also a decade of acceptance. Prefectural and local governments began to actively support the theatre. Suzuki Tadashi's theatre at Toga and the Art Tower Mito with its resident theatre company, also directed by Suzuki, are examples of theatres built and supported with public funds. Ota Shōgo (1939–), whose innovative Theatre of Transformation (Tenkei Gekijō) disbanded in 1988, became artistic director of the Shōnandai Cultural Centre Municipal Theatre in Fujisawa City in 1989. And the municipally funded Tokyo Art Theatre (Tōkyō Geijutsu Gekijō) opened in October 1990.

Corporations have also sought to improve their cultural image by building theatres and supporting theatrical activity. The Parco Theatre built in the Shibuya section of Tokyo by the Seibu Department Store chain in May 1973 was one of the first examples of corporate support for theatre. The Spiral Theatre in the Aoyama section of Tokyo was constructed by the Wacoal lingerie company in 1985. More recently, in 1989, the Tōkyū Corporation built the Culture Village (Bunkamura) complex adjacent to its flagship department store, also in Shibuya. The complex contains restaurants, a museum, an opera-concert hall, and the Theatre Cocoon presided over by Kushida Kazumi (1942–) and his Free Theatre troupe ('On Theatre' Jiyū Gekijō).

New theatres have provided expanded opportunities for stage designers. Japanese stage design began with the work of Itō Kisaku (1899–1967), who made his debut at the Tsukiji Little Theatre in 1925 with a modernistic set for *Julius Caesar*. Strongly influenced by Edward Gordon Craig and Adolphe Appia, Itō went on to influence the next

Artists

Akimoto Matsuyo (1911–)

Doyenne of modern playwrights. Influenced by Miyoshi Jūrō (1902–58), Akimoto's *Kaison the Priest of Hitachi* (*Hitachibō kaison*, 1965; trans. 1988) signalled the return of the gods in full force to the Japanese stage in the 1960s. In more recent years, her work with director Ninagawa Yukio and designer ASAKURA SETSU for the commercial Tōhō Company on such works as *The Love Suicides of Chikamatsu* (*Chikamatsu shinjū monogatari*, 1979) has attracted attention.

Asakura Setsu (1922–)

Japan's best-known modern stage designer, a professor at Kuwasawa Institute of Design in Tokyo. Asakura was influenced by Itō Kisaku (1899–1967), who began his career in 1925 with a design for *Julius Caesar* at the Tsukiji Little Theatre. Asakura reached prominence after World War II designing complex sets for a range of commercial, avant-garde, and SHINGEKI productions. She worked with NŌ actor KANZE HISAO and KYŌGEN actor Nomura Mansaku on Seneca's *Medea* (1975). She has designed for directors SUZUKI TADASHI, KARA JŪRŌ and Ninagawa Yukio. For Inoue Hisashi's play *The Great Doctor Yabuhara* (*Yabuhara kengyōgo*, 1974) she used lighting to sculpt and transform a single open space. Typifying her bold and dynamic design sense are the mammoth three- and four-storey sets for Ninagawa's production of Brecht's *Threepenny Opera* (1977), *The Love Suicides of Chikamatsu* (*Chikamatsu shinjū monogatari*, 1979) and Kara Jūrō's *A Tale of Tokyo* (*Shitaya mannenchō monogatari*, 1981).

Bandō Tamasaburō (1950–)

Perhaps the most popular young KABUKI actor of female roles. The adopted son of Morita Kanya XIV (1907–75), he took the name Kinoji for his stage debut in 1957 and his present name in 1964. Tall and willowy with a beautiful face, his somewhat haughty persona draws adoring young fans. He is popular in seductive roles – Lady Taema in *The Thundergod*, Princess Sakura in *The Scarlet Princess of Edo* – and multiple quick-change roles – seven roles in TSURUYA NAMBOKU's *Osome and Hisamatsu*. He has successfully played in films, in Mishima's modern play *Madame de Sade*, and as Lady Macbeth.

Betsuyaku Minoru (1937–)

Playwright. A prolific writer whose minimalist plays, profoundly influenced by the work of Samuel Beckett and Eugene Ionesco, have been a staple of the Japanese theatrical scene for three decades. *The Little Match Girl* (*Matchi-uri no shōjo*, 1966; trans. 1992), one of Betsuyaku's earliest works, treated the deprivation of the immediate postwar period. He subsequently rejected the style as too 'literary' and moved toward more abstract, absurdist works like *The Move* (*Idō*, 1973; trans. 1979).

Chikamatsu Monzaemon (1653–1725)

The most important playwright of KABUKI and BUNRAKU plays in Kyoto–Osaka during his lifetime. Born the second son of a minor provincial samurai and placed in service as a court page in his youth, his background and education are apparent in the literary quality of his texts. His first kabuki play, *Seventh Year Memorial for Yūgiri* (*Yūgiri nananenki*, 1684), was written for SAKATA TŌJŪRŌ and for a decade he was that actor's staff playwright in Kyoto. Abbreviated illustrated scripts (*eiri kyōgen bon*) of 31 of his kabuki plays are preserved, including *The Prostitute and The Whirlpool of Love* (*Keisei Awa no naruto*, 1695), *The Prostitute of Buddha Field* (*Keisei hotoke no hara*, 1699), and *The Prostitute and Prayers to Buddha* (*Keisei mibu dainenbutsu*, 1702). The juxtaposition of religion and eroticism is typical of early kabuki. In these plays Chikamatsu skilfully balanced bravura history scenes with gentle lovers' scenes.

During this period he also wrote puppet plays, such as *The Soga Heir* (*Yotsugi Soga*, 1683) for chanter Uji Kaga no Jō and *Kagekiyo Victorious* (*Shusse Kagekiyo*, 1685) for chanter TAKEMOTO GIDAYŪ. At Gidayū's invitation he moved to Osaka in 1705 and over the next 20 years composed nearly 100 puppet plays for the Takemoto

Theatre. The history play *The Battles of Coxinga* (1715), showing a Japanese hero restoring the Ming dynasty in China, was immensely successful and influential. In a dozen lovers' suicide plays (*shinjūmono*), Chikamatsu carried *kabuki*'s erotic prostitute-buying themes to tragic conclusions, creating a new independent domestic play in *The Love Suicides at Sonezaki* (*Sonezaki shinjū*, 1703), *The Courier to Hell* (*Meido no hikyaku*, 1711), *The Love Suicides at Amijima* (*Shinjū ten no Amijima*, 1721) and others.

Chikamatsu's narrative passages contain sections of great verbal beauty, especially lovers' travel scenes (*michiyuki*). He used verbal techniques of alliteration (*kakekotoba*, 'pivot words') – in which a word contributes one meaning to the phrase preceding and a different meaning to the phrase following – and related words (*engo*), as, for example, mist, rain, dew and wetness convey related images of eroticism. More than any other playwright he created significant dramatic literature for the puppet theatre.

Fukuda Tsuneari (1912–94)

Playwright, critic, director. Fukuda graduated with a degree in English literature from Tokyo University in 1936 and later published a complete translation of Shakespeare's works. He carried on the literary legacy of KISHIDA KUNIO in the postwar period, but, unlike Kishida, idealized Shakespeare and held the Bard up as the model Japanese theatre should emulate. During the 1950s Fukuda was active as a conservative social critic and as a playwright. In 1963 he founded the Contemporary Theatre Association (Gendai Engeki Kyōkai) and its affiliated Cloud (Kumo) troupe, which later became known as Subaru.

A proponent of conservative values in the theatre as in politics, Fukuda's major plays frequently parody Western works and are generally less stimulating than his theories. *Typhoon Kitty* (*Kitii taifū*, 1949), for example, may be read as a parody of Chekhov's *Cherry Orchard*; and *The Man Who Stroked the Dragon* (*Ryū o nadeta otoko*), often cited as Fukuda's best work, is based on Eliot's *The Cocktail Party*.

Fukuda Yoshiyuki (1931–)

Playwright. Influenced by dramatist KINOSHITA JUNJI, Fukuda began his career as an orthodox left-wing playwright but contributed to the creation of the post-*shingeki* movement with plays like *Find Hakamadare!* (*Hakamadare wa doko da*, 1964; trans. 1988), which introduced the dramaturgy of metamorphosis that characterized Japanese playwriting in the 1960s. As a founder of the Youth Art Theatre (Seinen Geijutsu Gekijō or Seigei) he influenced numerous younger playwrights, including BETSUYAKU MINORU, SATOH MAKOTO and KARA JŪRŌ, all of whom worked with the troupe.

Hijikata Yoshi (1898–1959)

Director. Born into the aristocracy, Hijikata soon became disillusioned with the nobility and took a lifelong interest in the theatre. After graduating from Tokyo University, he departed for a planned ten-year European tour in November 1922 but returned to Japan in December 1923 to help found the Tsukiji Little Theatre (Tsukiji Shōgekijō), which he financed almost single-handedly until 1929. As a director, Hijikata was influenced by Meyerhold and other avant-garde directors. In 1933 he left Japan for the Soviet Union. An avowed Marxist, the Japanese government stripped him of his title in 1934. During Stalin's purges Hijikata left the Soviet Union for France, but returned to Japan in 1941 and was immediately imprisoned, spending the duration of the war in jail. After his release Hijikata resumed his theatrical activities, directing and serving as administrator for a number of influential theatrical enterprises.

Ichikawa Danjūrō

Twelve generations in the Ichikawa family of *KABUKI* actors have attained the illustrious name Danjūrō. Because of the importance of this acting family and its long history, Danjūrō is sometimes called the 'emperor' of *kabuki*. A brief description of the genealogy of this one acting name tells us much about *kabuki*'s hereditary acting system in general. Danjūrō, as family head (*soke*), is responsible for preserving

Kabuki actor, Ichikawa Danjūrō as Yūranosuke watches as Lord Enya Hangan (Onoe Baikō) commits suicide by *seppuku*: from *The Forty-Seven Loyal Retainers* (*Kanadehon Chūshingura*), adapted from the puppet play.

the Ichikawa family's famous *aragoto* acting style and passing it on to the next generation. Some early Danjūrōs received the name as children, but, more typically, intermediate names are awarded marking progressive stages in the actor's career: the present Danjūrō XII was called Ichikawa Natsuō at his stage debut when he was 3, Ichikawa Shinnosuke when he was 12, and Ichikawa Ebizō X when he showed mature acting stature by playing the lead in *Sukeroku: Flower of Edo* at 23. He took the Danjūrō name at a three-month ceremony in the summer of 1985. Several Danjūrōs were adopted to continue the family acting line when there was no son.

Danjūrō I (1660–1704).
Son of a country samurai, he was 13 when he played the boy-hero Sakata Kintoki in the play *The Four Guardian Gods* (*Shitennō*,1673) at the Nakamura Theatre in Edo (Tokyo) in bravura style marking the beginning of *aragoto* acting. He wrote heroic roles for himself in a dozen plays under the pen name Mimasuya Hyōgo – an infatuated priest turned thundergod in *Thundergod* (*Narukami*, 1684; trans. 1975), the superhero Kamakura Gongorō in *Wait a Moment!* (1697), the fierce protective god Fudō in *Fudō* (1697; trans. 1975), the powerful priest Benkei in *The Subscription List* (*Kanjinchō*, 1702). He was murdered on stage by a jealous actor when he was 44.

Danjūrō II (1688–1758).
The eldest son of Danjūrō I he became Danjūrō II when he was 17. Over his long lifetime, he originated more than half the plays in the Eighteen Favourite Plays (*Jūhachiban*) collection – *Sukeroku: Flower of Edo* (*Sukeroku yukari no Edo zakura*, 1713; trans. 1975), *The Medicine Seller* (*Uiro uri*, 1718), *The Arrow Maker* (*Yanone*, 1725) and *The Whisker Tweezers* (*Kenuki*, 1742; trans. 1975) among them. He introduced grace and gentleness into *aragoto* acting, especially in the dashing title role of Sukeroku, borrowing from the Kyoto–Osaka soft style of acting (*wagoto*). Having no son, he passed the Danjūrō name to a pupil and acted for the last 23 years of his life as Ichikawa Ebizō II.

Danjūrō III (1721–42).
An adored child actor at 6, he became Danjūrō III when he was 14. He had a beautiful voice and an elegant acting style. He died at the age of 21, after becoming ill while performing in Osaka with his adoptive father.

Danjūrō IV (1711–78).
After Danjūrō III died, no successor was named for 12 years. The elderly Ebizō II (Danjūrō II) adopted 43-year-old Matsumoto Koshirō II, a specialist in villain roles, as his heir. A progressive intelligent actor, Danjūrō IV added a dark tinge to *aragoto* acting in his role of the malicious warrior Kagekiyo, a role he played 16 times in his life.

Danjūrō V (1741–1807).
The son of Danjūrō IV, when he was 29 he changed his name from Matsumoto Koshirō III to Ichikawa Danjūrō V. He was the first actor to announce his new name in a formal name-

no nishikie, 1862; trans. 1976) – for Onoe Kikugorō V. He wrote original 'puppet' scenes, using BUNRAKU-style music. He was the first writer to adapt Western literature to the *kabuki* stage in the 1870s. His impressive skill at composing dance plays, such as *The Ground Spider* (*Tsuchigumo*, 1881) which was witnessed by Emperor Meiji, helped socially elevate *kabuki*. In 120 history, domestic, modern and dance plays, he demonstrated an unrivalled ability to utilize acting technique, music, dance, costuming and staging for dramatic purposes.

Kinoshita Junji (1914–)

Arguably the most influential playwright of the postwar period, 1945 to *c.* 1965. Kinoshita graduated with a master's degree in English literature from Tokyo University in 1941. He specialized in Elizabethan literature and went on to produce an 8-volume translation of Shakespeare's works. An ambivalent Christian, he was deeply influenced by both Hegelian theology and Hegel's theory of history. His work is comparable to that of Arthur Miller in the sense that he re-invented tragedy in a modern idiom. Kinoshita identifies the historical dialectic with tragic dramaturgy, and in works from *Turbulent Times* (*Fūrō*, 1939, rewritten 1947) to *A Japanese Named Otto* (*Otto to yobareru Nihonjin*, 1963) an individual confronts history only to be simultaneously crushed and redeemed by it. Kinoshita has also been fascinated by Japanese folklore, and he has written numerous 'folktale plays', the most famous of which is *Twilight Crane* (*Yūzuru*, 1949; trans. 1956). The tension between his Christianity and his fascination with Japanese shamanism on the one hand and his Hegelian universalism and his sense of Japanese uniqueness on the other informs virtually all of his plays. A good example is *Between God and Man* (*Kami to hito to no aida*, 1970; trans. 1979), a two-part work that approaches the problem of Japanese war crimes through the Tokyo War Crimes Tribunal in the first part and through the eyes of a shaman in the second.

Kishida Kunio (1890–1954)

Playwright. His devotion to drama as a form of literature helped establish an insightful form of psychological realism in Japan. Kishida spent several years in France in the early 1920s and was deeply influenced by Jacques Copeau and the Vieux-Colombier. In 1932 he founded *Playwriting* (*Gekisaku*) magazine as a literary showplace for younger playwrights ignored by the left-wing troupes that dominated the theatre at the time; and in 1937, he was instrumental in founding The Literary Theatre (Bunga-kuza) troupe as an alternative to the politically engaged theatre. The troupe continues to perform today. Kishida's best plays are the one-act sketches he wrote in the 1920s. Examples include *Paper Balloon* (*Kami fūsen*, 1925; trans. 1989) and *Cloudburst* (*Shūu*, 1926; trans. 1989). Multi-act works like *The Two Daughters of Mr Sawa* (*Sawa-shi no futari musume*, 1935; trans. 1989), regarded as Kishida's finest play, generally expand on the themes of his earlier work: family relationships and the inability of people to communicate with one another. In the postwar period, Kishida returned to writing short works like *Adoration* (*Nyonin katsugō*, 1949; trans. 1989).

Komparu Zenchiku (1405–?68)

Second of ZEAMI's successors and head of the Kanze Nō troupe from 1443 until his death. He composed the richly poetic plays *Yang Kuei-fei* (*Yōkihi*), *The Plantain Tree* (*Bashō*), and *Rain and Moon* (*Ugetsu*), which are admired for a profound, delicate and nostalgic sense of *yūgen*. In 23 treatises he developed a metaphysical philosophy of nō aesthetics based on doctrines of Kegon and Zen Buddhism. The actor who achieves unconscious performance enters the 'circle of emptiness', which is the highest level of artistic and religious accomplishment.

Kubo Sakae (1900–58).

Playwright. He succeeded in developing Japanese social realism into a mature dramatic form through skilful characterization. Closely identified with OSANAI KAORU and the Tsukiji Little Theatre, Kubo was a translator of German drama, rendering over the course of his career some 30 plays into Japanese, ranging from Goethe's *Faust* to works by Kaiser, Wedekind and Hauptmann. Kubo's magnum opus is *Land of Volcanic Ash* (*Kazanbaichi*, 1937–8; trans. 1986), a monumental seven-act work that depicts life in a small agricultural community in Hokkaido in the 1930s. Kubo continued to write engaged, positivistic works in the postwar period and influenced major postwar playwrights like KINOSHITA JUNJI and FUKUDA YOSHIYUKI.

Matsui Sumako (1886–1919)

First important *SHINGEKI* actress. Originally a member of TSUBOUCHI SHŌYŌ's Literary Arts Society (Bungei Kyōkai) where she created a sensation as Nora in Ibsen's *A Doll's House*, Matsui went on to help establish The Art Theatre (Geijutsuza) with her lover, Shimamura Hōgetsu, an important literary critic and also a former member of Tsubouchi's group. An important force in the 1910s, The Art Theatre tried to balance commercial success and artistic integrity. In despair over Shimamura's death from influenza in November 1918, Matsui took her own life on 5 January 1919.

Nakamura Utaemon VI (1917–)

Second son of Utaemon V (1866–1940), the most esteemed living *KABUKI* actor of female roles. He is a Living National Treasure and President of the Japanese Actors Association. He took the name Kotarō at 5, Fukusuke VI at 16, Shikan VI at 24, and his present name at the age of 34. He projects a willowy elegance and, overcoming a physical handicap, he excels in dance roles, as in *Sumida River* (*Sumidagawa*) and *Maid of Dōjō Temple* (*Musume Dōjōji*). His mature performances retain youthful delicacy while projecting powerful emotion.

Nomura Manzō VI (1898–1978)

Major 20th-century *KYŌGEN* actor of the Izumi school. A Living National Treasure, noted for his powerful and formal style of acting, he raised the social and artistic status of *kyōgen*, established *kyōgen* programmes separate from *NŌ*,

and brought new audiences to this mediaeval theatre form. His successors are two brilliant sons, Nomura Manzō VII (1930–) and Nomura Mansaku (1931–).

Okuni (fl. 1600–10)

Actress-dancer who founded *KABUKI*. Called Izumo no Okuni, 'Okuni from Izumo', she is reputed to have been a priestess of the Grand Shrine of Izumo. Ticket-buying audiences of commoners were captivated by her popularized version of a Buddhist Prayer Dance (*nenbutsu odori*) and a new dance play, *kabuki odori*. The swaggering dandies she portrayed were known in Kyoto as *kabuki mono* ('far out, outrageous fellows') and Okuni's performance took that name. She was called 'Best in Japan', and she danced for the first Tokugawa Shogun, Ieyasu, in Edo Castle in 1607. Okuni's performances were copied by scores of female performers whose troupes toured throughout Japan, thus assuring the continuation of *kabuki* after her death. There is no evidence that Okuni was a prostitute, but her successors were. The prohibition against their performances, first promulgated in 1629, continued to bar women from Japanese stages until the 20th century.

Osanai Kaoru (1881–1928)

Influential director who helped establish a modern, realistic theatre in Japan. In 1909 Osanai founded The Free Theatre (Jiyū Gekijō) with Ichikawa Sadanji II, a *KABUKI* actor. Unsatisfied with the results of his experiments in training *kabuki* actors to perform the realistic works of Ibsen and Chekhov, Osanai established the Tsukiji Little Theatre (Tsukiji Shōgekijō) in 1924 with the help of HIJIKATA YOSHI, which created a completely new production system for modern theatre in Japan.

Sakata Tōjūrō (1647–1709)

The most popular *KABUKI* actor in Kyoto–Osaka during the period of Genroku culture (1688–*c.* 1730). Little is known of his early life except that he was the son of an actor. In 1678 he created a sensation playing Izaemon, the romantic lover of the prostitute Yûgiri, in *New Year's Remembrance of Yûgiri* (*Yûgiri nagori no shôgatsu*). Yûgiri was an actual prostitute from Osaka who had died the month before and this 'overnight pickles' (*ichiyazuke*) play capitalized on town scandal about this event. Tôjûrô revived the play 18 times in his career, gaining the nickname Sakata Izaemon. In this and similar 'disguised lover' (*yatsushi*) roles in plays about contemporary commoners (*sewamono*) he developed a gentle, humourous 'soft' (*wagoto*) acting style. For 5 years he was actor-manager (*zagashira*) of the Mandayû Theatre in Kyoto, acting in similar plays written by his staff playwright CHIKAMATSU MONZAEMON.

He based his acting on close observation of merchant life. His colleagues, including Chikamatsu, praised his egoless acting, careful attention to the dramatic requirements of the script and 'realistic' approach to directing other actors, insisting that the actor study the actual details of a character's circumstances. His comments on acting were set down by others in *The Actors' Analects* (*Yakusha rongo*, 1776; trans. 1969). The tradition of *wagoto* acting is continued today by Nakamura Ganjirô III (1931–) and a small number of other actors.

Satoh Makoto (1943–)

Playwright and director. The product of a complex intellectual background that included affinities for the ultranationalist right, the revolutionary left, Christianity and existentialism, Satoh received his theatre education at the Actors' Theatre Training School, graduating in 1965. He was a founder of the Black Tent Theatre (Kuro Tento) in 1968. Satoh won the Kishida Prize for Playwriting in 1970 for *Nezumi Kozô: The Rat* (*Nezumi Kozô Jirokichi*, 1969; trans. 1986), and the plays he wrote between 1966 and 1976, from *Ismene* (*Isumene*, 1966; trans. 1992) to *The Murder of Blanqui, Spring in Shanghai* (*Buranki-goroshi Shanhai no haru*, 1976) are among the most challenging and rich of the post-*shingeki* period. In recent years, he has written less and devoted himself increasingly to directing, particularly for the opera.

Senda Koreya (1904–94)

Actor and director. Real name: Itô Kunio. Brother of Itô Michio, dancer in Yeats' productions in London, and stage designer Itô Kisaku. Senda began his acting career at the Tsukiji Little Theatre in 1924 but left the troupe in 1926 to participate more actively in the proletarian theatre movement. He spent the years 1927 to 1931 in Germany, where he remained active in left-wing theatre. In 1932 he produced an adaptation of Brecht's *Threepenny Opera*, and he continued to translate Brecht's work throughout his career. Imprisoned for his leftist affiliations for much of the war, he founded the Actors' Theatre (Haiyûza) in 1944. He was a pillar of the *shingeki* movement; in the 1950s and 60s under Senda's direction the Actors' Theatre pioneered actor training and produced the work of young playwrights like Abe Kôbô (1924–93).

Suzuki Tadashi (1939–)

Director and dramatic theorist. Suzuki originally established his reputation directing experimental works by post-*shingeki* playwrights like BETSUYAKU MINORU, KARA JÛRÔ, and SATOH MAKOTO at the Waseda Little Theatre (Waseda Shôgekijô), which he founded with Betsuyaku and actor Ono Seki. In 1969, however, his fertile collaboration with actress Shiraishi Kayoko began, and he moved away from a text-centred to an actor-centred theatre. He assembled dramatic collages to showcase Shiraishi's talents, *On the Dramatic Passions, I* (*Gekiteki naru mono o megutte, I*, 1969) and *II* (1970), and out of these grew the actor-training method for which he subsequently became famous. In 1976 Suzuki moved his troupe out of Tokyo to the village of Toga in Toyama prefecture and later changed its name to SCOT (Suzuki Company of Toga). Since 1982, he has organized an annual international theatre festival at Toga. As a director, Suzuki's reputation rests on his renditions of Western classics. *The Trojan Women* (1974), *The Bacchae* (1978), and *Clytemnestra* (1983) are representative. Suzuki has taught at the University of Wisconsin–Milwaukee, the University of California–San Diego, and the Julliard School.

He has staged bilingual productions, using Japanese and American actors, including *The Tale of Lear* (1988). In addition to his position as leader of SCOT, Suzuki has been artistic director of the Mitsui Festival since 1988 and artistic director for theatre at the regional Mito Art Tower since 1990.

Takemoto Gidayū (1651–1714)

The puppet chanter who established the powerful musical style, known by his given name, *gidayū* which is used today in BUNRAKU performance. He studied under the older chanter Uji Kaga no Jō. In 1684 he cofounded with theatre manager Takeda Izumo I (?–1747) the important Osaka puppet theatre that takes his family name, the Takemoto Theatre. In the following year he created a 'new' style of chanting that displaced 'old' *jōruri* and all other musical styles in the puppet theatre. Chikamatsu joined the Takemoto Theatre as staff playwright in 1705. This remarkable artistic triumvirate put a human face on a didactic storytelling form and brought contemporary life into their plays. In domestic plays, such as *The Love Suicides at Sonezaki* (1703), Gidayū created reality in the tones of ordinary townsmen. Gidayū published scenes from plays he had chanted, at that time considered the property of the chanter, and a treatise on performance and playwriting that shows familiarity with ZEAMI's writings.

Terayama Shūji (1935–83)

Terayama began his career as a poet but went on to become an innovative and controversial playwright, director and filmmaker. Influenced by Lautreamont, Breton and Fellini, he was a true advocate of European-style avant-garde iconoclasm in Japan. His plays, from *Blood Sleeps Standing Up* (*Chi wa tatta mama nemutte iru*, 1957) through *Heretic's Gate* (*Jashūmon*, 1971), *Knock: Street Theatre* (*Nokku*, 1975; trans. 1992) and *Directions for Servants* (*Nuhikun*, 1978) were meant above all to shock the bourgeoisie. In 1967 he founded the Upper Gallery (Tenjō Sajiki) troupe, which he directed in performances in Europe as well as Japan.

Tsubouchi Shōyō (1859–1935)

One of the fathers of modern Japanese theatre as well as a theoretician of the modern novel in Japan. Tsubouchi was a professor of English literature at Waseda University in Tokyo. A man of diverse talents, he wrote pieces for Japanese dance and staged pageants in addition to translating Shakespeare and founding *Waseda Literature* (*Waseda Bungaku*), an influential literary review. In 1906 he founded one of Japan's first modern theatre troupes, The Literary Arts Society (Bungei Kyōkai). His 40-volume translation of the complete works of Shakespeare was completed in 1928. In 1926 his *En the Ascetic* (*En no Gyōja*), written in 1913, became the first play by a Japanese writer to be staged by the Tsukiji Little Theatre.

Tsuruya Namboku IV (1755–1829)

The dominant playwright of Edo KABUKI in the early 19th century, his nickname was Namboku the Great. His career is typical of traditional playwrights: apprenticed to an actor as a boy, apprenticed to playwright Sakurada Jisuke I at 22, promotion to third assistant playwright and to second assistant playwright, and finally success as staff playwright at the age of 46. He wrote vehicles for the great actors of his time: the *onnagata* Iwai Hanshirō V, Matsumoto Koshirō V and Onoe Kikugorō III.

His 125 plays encompass all genres. In an almost post-modern fashion, he excelled in rewriting (*kakikae*) familiar scenes from old plays and joining them to contemporary material, often with darkly parodic intent. He originated the 'raw' domestic play (*kizewamono*) about criminals and society's outcasts. Against this 'real' dramatic material, Namboku counterposed beautiful, stylized performance techniques: poetic elocution (*shichigochō*), quick costume changes (*hayagawari*), nighttime pantomime (*danmari*), stage tricks (*keren*) and dance scenes. His most often revived work is *The Ghost of Yotsuya* (*Tōkaidō Yotsuya kaidan*, 1825) in which the ghost of Oiwa torments her husband, Iemon, in revenge for having brutally disfigured and murdered her.

Yoshizawa Ayame I (1673–1729)
Genroku-period KABUKI actor. He was instrumental in advancing the art of portraying female characters (*onnagata*) beyond the exhibitionism and eroticism of early cross-dressing. Unmatched in courtesan roles, such as Mitsu in *The Prostitute of Mount Asama* (*Keisei Asama ga take*, 1689), Ayame was praised for 'realistic' characterization, and in his memoirs, *My Advice to Onnagata* (*Ayame gusa*; trans. 1969), he insisted the actor should live totally as a woman offstage in order to bring a sense of reality to his performance of a woman onstage.

Zeami (Seami) Motokiyo (1363–1443)
Actor, troupe leader, playwright, music composer, choreographer and writer of major treatises on performing and composition. Zeami is the foremost figure in the history of Nō. He refined *nō* during 34 years in the Kyoto court under Shogun Yoshimitsu's patronage. He moved beyond playing a role (*monomane*), the strong point of his father Kan'ami Kiyotsugu (1333–84), to striving for a mysterious beauty tinged with sadness (*yūgen*). Representative works among the 20–90 plays attributed to Zeami are: *The Damask Drum* (*Aya no tsuzumi*), The

Old Pine (Oimatsu), Kiyotsune, Visiting Lady Komachi (Kayoi Komachi), and Lady Yuya (Yuya).

He was a practical theatre person, concerned with finding means to attract a varied audience through novelty (*hana*), by doing the unexpected (following the *yin-yang* theory of opposites) and by cultivating a 'beginner's heart' (*shōshin*). Over the last 30 years of his life, he wrote 21 'secret' treatises (*hiden*) for direct descendants in the Kanze family (partial trans. 1984). He advised diligent training through seven stages of one's career (in *The Way of the Flower*), structuring a play through emotional progression guided by *jo-ha-kyū* (in *True Path of the Flower*), acting through a Zen-like state of unconscious mastery (in *Disciplines for Joy*), attaining nine progressive levels of artistic achievement (in *The Nine Levels*), composing plays based on known dramatic subjects (in *On Playwriting*) and how to run a professional troupe (in *Reflections on the Art*). Much of Zeami's advice applies to any theatre. He said there is no single correct way of acting, but only more or less appropriate ways of performing under specific circumstances. Audience approval is the proper criterion of success. His treatises became available to the public in the 20th century.

generation of designers, most prominent among whom are Kanamori Kaoru (1933–80), Takada Ichirō (1929–), and ASAKURA SETSU. Hirano Kōga (1938–), who designed numerous sets for the Black Tent Theatre, and architect Isozaki Arata (1931–), who has designed several theatre spaces for Suzuki Tadashi, have also made original contributions to the conception and use of theatrical space.

Acceptance has also been international. In the 1970s and early 80s, Terayama Shūji made almost annual pilgrimages to perform at theatre festivals in Europe and the United States. Ninagawa Yukio's *Medea*, produced in Rome (1983) and Athens (1984), and *Macbeth*, staged in Amsterdam (1985) and London (1987), established his reputation internationally. Suzuki Tadashi, who has taught and directed in the United States, Europe and Australia, has also established a firm international reputation. In addition, since 1982, Suzuki has

sponsored an annual international theatre festival in Toga, one of a growing number of international festivals being held in Japan.

Mainstream *shingeki* companies have remained active and have achieved a rapprochement with post-*shingeki* troupes. Chijinkai, literally, the Terrestrial Troupe, founded 1982, and the Komatsu Troupe (Komatsu-za, founded 1984) are two new *shingeki* troupes descended from the Literary Theatre. Both remain firmly literary in orientation and feature the work of director Kimura Kōichi (1931–) and writer Inoue Hisashi (1934–).

Genres
Angura
A perversion of English 'underground [theatre]', *angura* refers to the theatrical activity in the 1960s and after, that challenged the hegemony of

Western-style modern drama in Japan. In the 60s this revolt against SHINGEKI sought to recapture the pre-modern Japanese imagination as the source of Japanese theatrical creativity. Also referred to as the *shōgekijō undō* ('little theatre movement'), and the post-*shingeki* movement.

Bugaku

A formal Japanese court dance, dating from the 7th century, that originated in China. A rarefied art, *bugaku* is performed and taught primarily at the Music Department of the Imperial Household Agency and at large temples and shrines in Kyoto, Osaka and Nara. Public performances also are given annually at the National Theatre in Tokyo. *Bugaku* is performed on a square, raised dance floor. Unroofed, its space is demarcated visually by a red-lacquered railing on four sides and by a green silk cloth that covers its surface. The stage is often set outdoors, in a garden or over a pond, to enhance the beauty of performance. Performers, divided into 'left' and 'right' groups and performing different items of the repertory, enter between two enormous drums that stand at the rear of the stage. Masks are worn for some roles. Costumes are court dress of the 7th century: elegant silk robes, black hats, white *tabi* covering the feet. No scenery is used. Musicians playing flute (*ryūteki, komabue* and *hichiriki*), mouth organ (*shō*), gong (*shōko*), drums (*taiko, sannoko* and *kakko*) accompany the dance while seated, often in small pavilions, offstage. There are no singers. The repertory of about 50 dances can be classified into pieces of Chinese or Korean origin; old or new; large, medium or small cast; or, most commonly, into military or civil pieces, a classification well known in China.

Although performance today has lost almost all dramatic function, reminders of *bugaku*'s previous dramatic content can be seen in the grotesque mask worn by the young king Ranryō who wished to frighten his enemy in battle, in Batō where the dancer is supposedly mounted on a white horse, and in some now extinct pieces that were comic parodies of *gigaku* dances. Associated with the imperial court from its beginnings, the decorous, four-square movements and ethereal music of *bugaku* evoke, to a remarkable extent, the refined elegance of the Japanese court of 1000 years ago (the dances from which *bugaku* grew have long since died out in China). *Bugaku* performance was structured into an opening (*jo*), a breaking apart (*ha*), and a fast conclusion (*kyū*). This fundamental aesthetic construct of emotional progression was later adopted in NŌ and other forms of Japanese theatre.

Bunraku

Highly sophisticated, adult, commercial doll-puppet theatre. Since 1652, all professional performers have been male. The name *bunraku* derives from the 19th-century theatre manager, Uemura Bunrakuen (or Bunrakuken), who moved from Awaji Island to Osaka, where he staged puppet plays at shrines and professional theatres. His troupe was the only group of professionals to continue into the Meiji period (1868–1912), hence the association of his name with the current genre. A chanted puppet performance may also be called *jōruri*, after the generic style of narrative music, *ayatsuri* ('manipulation') *jōruri*, or *ningyō shibai* ('puppet play').

In the 1590s *jōruri* narrative chanting and accompanying *shamisen* music was joined to puppet manipulation to form this complex style of puppet theatre. For perhaps a thousand years before this, bards had chanted religious tales and military epics, especially, after the 12th century, *The Tale of the Heike* (*Heike monogatari*). Because of the respected tradition of oral narrative (*katari*), the chanter (*tayū*) took social and artistic precedence over puppeteers and musicians. Until the 20th century, only he was allowed to own property or live outside the confines of the licensed theatre districts. An indication of the status of chanting can be seen in the visit in 1614 of the emperor Go-Yozei to a puppet performance in Kyoto of the Buddhist miracle play, *The Chest-Splitting of Amida Buddha* (*Amida no munewari*). Numerous chanting styles competed in the early 17th century. In Edo (Tokyo), the chanter Satsuma Jōun (1593–1672) joined his highly bombastic chanting style with violent puppet manipulation to create *kimpira jōruri*. It is said that the bravura acting style of KABUKI was in part inspired by performances of the *kimpira* puppeteer Izumi Dayū who decapitated puppets with an iron bar in knockabout battle scenes.

In 1657 the Great Edo Fire destroyed the three professional puppet theatres operating in the capital (as well as four large and eight small *kabuki* theatres). When these puppet troupes fled to Osaka that city became the undisputed centre of puppet theatre. From 1686 audiences thrilled to TAKEMOTO GIDAYŪ's beautiful melodies and powerful interpretations at the Takemoto Theatre. His vocal style displaced all others and today the general term for *bunraku* music and chanting style is *gidayū* (or *takemoto* when played and sung in *kabuki*).

A day's programme traditionally consisted either of a history and domestic play in sequence, or selected scenes. More important than act divisions (*dan*), are the two or three scenes (*ba*) into which they are divided: opening (*kuchi*), middle (*naka*), and conclusion (*kiri*). In performance a different chanter is assigned to each scene: young chanters take early, less important scenes, star chanters take difficult scenes, especially each act conclusion. Occasionally 4 or 5 chanters perform a scene together, each providing the voice of one character as an actor might, an indication of *kabuki* influence.

Influenced by *nō*'s *jo-ha-kyū* structure, most history plays are in five acts and last 8–10 hours in performance. Several subplots intersect, providing opportunity for display of a variety of emotions: love, pathos, the excitement and horror of battle, auspicious celebration. The dramatic high point is the 'final scene of the third act' (*san dan no kiri*), an agonizing scene in which a parent sacrifices a child (*migawari*) or a warrior commits ritual suicide out of feudal loyalty (*seppuku*). Most domestic plays are in three acts. They followed the history play and closed the programme (*kiri kyōgen*). Critics today regard the domestic play more highly than the history form, a reversal of 18th-century opinion. History and domestic plays alike portray an ethical conflict fundamental to feudal society: duty (*giri*) to a lord or master versus human feelings of love and generosity (*ninjō*). In Chikamatsu's *The Battles of Coxinga* (*Kokusenya kassen*) the mother and sister of Coxinga willingly kill themselves to protect the honour of the two male heroes.

A text is composed in alternating sections of prose (*kotoba*), which is usually spoken dialogue, and verse (*fushigoto*), which is usually sung narrative, that call upon various vocal techniques (*ji, naka, kami, suete*, and so on). A chanter must perform at a tremendous pitch of emotional fervour to match the dramatic intensity of the text. Chanter and *shamisen* player sit in audience view on a dais (*yuka*) stage left of the proscenium that revolves to change performers between scenes. The chanter 'reads' from the text (actually memorized) which rests prominently on a lacquered stand before him.

Bunraku is performed on a proscenium stage, somewhat smaller than a *kabuki* stage and without *hanamichi* or revolving stage. It is divided by low railings into two or three zones from front to back. Since a puppet's feet reach to around the knees of the puppeteers, the low front railings provide a ground level on which a puppet character can walk when moving outside. The innermost railing ('first railing', *honte*) is at about hip level, allowing a puppet to be seated on a mat of an inner room. Elaborately painted sets surround the puppets with 'realistic' interior and exterior environments.

Some 50 types of puppet heads match a wide variety of character types; in a long play five heads may be used for one character to show changes in emotion. Heads are carved of paulownia wood, hollowed to hold the mechanisms for moving eyes, eyebrows and mouth, and painted in realistic detail. Fingers may be jointed so the hand can open wide or close in a fist. Puppets of vigorous male characters have the largest number of movable parts. Three puppeteers surround, hold and move a puppet. The chief puppeteer (*omo zukai*) controls a puppet's right arm (with his right hand) and head and body (with his left hand). The second puppeteer (*hidari zukai*, 'left puppeteer') controls the left arm. The third puppeteer (*ashi zukai*, 'foot puppeteer') moves the feet of the male puppet or kimono hem of the legless female puppet. Puppeteers may improvise movements in performance, using a wide repertory of accepted mimetic gestures (*furi*) and stylized movements (*kata*). The former include sewing, smoking, walking or weeping in highly realistic fashion. The latter include displays of technical virtuosity, such as the beautiful one-handed manipulation of a woman looking over her shoulder (*ushiro buri*). Although it is inanimate wood and cloth, the energy infused into a puppet by the manipulators, chanter and musician make it appear lifelike and real, while a *kabuki* character may seem quite unreal. Puppets, puppeteers, chanter and musician all have their own visual presence in *bunraku* and vie for attention. Puppeteers in the West are now borrowing from *bunraku* many of its performing techniques because of their theatrical effectiveness.

Butō

Often referred to as *ankoku butō* or 'dance of darkness', and in Roman transcription *butoh*. *Butō* originated in the 1950s and 60s with the work of Ohno Kazuo and Hijikata Tatsumi. Maro Akaji brought together *butō* choreography and post-*shingeki* dramaturgy when he founded the first *butō* troupe, Dairakudakan (The Great Camel Battleship), in 1972. Other current troupes are Sankai-juku (literally, Mountain-Ocean School, founded 1975), Byakkosha (literally, White Tiger Brigade, founded 1980) located in Kyoto, and Tanaka Min's Dance School (Mai-juku, founded 1981). The essence of the movement is its attempt to recapture the shamanic basis of the Japanese performing arts and rearticulate it as modern art.

Kabuki

The major urban commercial theatre genre from its beginnings *c.* 1600 into the 20th century. *Kabuki*, the noun form of the verb *kabuku*, tilted or off-centre, meant unorthodox, strange, new. The scandalous nature of early performance is clear from the fact that *kabuki* was written with the ideographs song (*ka*), dance (*bu*), and prostitute (*ki*). In response to the tuts of Victorian moralists, in the late 19th century the ideograph meaning 'skill' was substituted for the ideograph meaning 'prostitute'.

Kabuki performers depended on a popular audience, always creating new plays and acting styles to meet the temper of the times. They borrowed from NŌ, KYŌGEN and BUNRAKU. As a consequence, *kabuki* acting encompasses half a dozen substyles, leading the Meiji period scholar Tsubouchi Shō yō to call *kabuki* a multiheaded monster. It is notable that even a wildly successful play was rewritten as a matter of course when revived, which explains the scores of variant texts for an often-performed play like *Wait a Moment!* (*Shibaraku*).

An actor masters forms or patterns (*kata*) of acting perfected over generations in his family. *Kata* are understood to encompass both outer form and inner content, so that varying interpretations are possible within one *kata*. Good actors create new, unique *kata*. The history of the ICHIKAWA DANJŪRŌ acting line illustrates the balance between tradition and creation over twelve generations. Today few actors go much beyond transmitted forms.

Actors in *kabuki* dance and speak. Song is the province of specialist singers who accompany the action from offstage or, in dance scenes, onstage. Actors of female roles (*onnagata*) display their charm and skill through solo dances (*shosagoto* or *keigoto*) that are worked into plays of all types. Actors characteristically freeze in tableau (*mie*) at emotional climaxes, thus intensifying and prolonging moments of dramatic tension. A high level of energy in the actor sustains these silent, motionless moments. Actors command a repertory of vocal techniques, including versions of *nō* speech and *bunraku* chanting. Sukeroku's name-saying speech (*nanori*) requires a machine-gun-like tempo (*ippon chōshi*). Passages of antiphonal dialogue composed in lines of 7 and 5 syllables (*shichigochō*) are delivered in a melodious style (*yakuharai*) based on Buddhist chanting.

Nō and *bunraku* each have a single style of music; *kabuki* has many musical styles to match its many styles of drama and performance. Three basic types of instruments combine in *kabuki*. The *nō* ensemble of drums and flute (*hayashi*) can be seen in paintings of Okuni's performances in Kyoto, *c.* 1600–10. Later these combined with large drums, gongs, bells and other sound-effects instruments, to make up *kabuki*'s percussion ensemble (*narimono*). The plucked lute (*shamisen*) is seen in paintings of *kabuki* performance of the period 1610–20. Today percussion, *shamisen* and singers make up *kabuki*'s basic musical grouping, called *geza* ('lower seat') from its position offstage right. *Geza* musicians perform *nagauta* ('long song') style music and provide sound effects. Their music is ubiquitous throughout a performance: instrumental *shamisen* melodies (*aikata*) set an appropriate mood for a scene; patterns beaten on the large barrel drum (*ōdaiko*) indicate rain, snow, wind, ocean waves or the time of day; *shamisen* and song accompany exits and entrances of characters along the rampway through the audience. More than 500 melodies and rhythms, as well as special gong and bell sounds, are part of the offstage musical repertory. Wooden blocks (*tsuke*) struck on the stage floor provide sound effects for running, walking, striking and other actions, while hard wood clappers (*ki* or *hyōshigi*) provide an aural frame for the opening and closing of the act curtain, for scenery changes, and to alert actors and audience that a scene will soon begin.

In dance plays, the musical ensemble – *nagauta, tokiwazu, tomimoto, kiyomoto* or other style – is seated onstage. The last three musical styles were created in the 18th century specifically for *kabuki* dance plays; they do not use percussion or flute and hence are softer and more romantic than *nagauta* music. *Takemoto* music accompanies borrowed puppet plays (*maruhonmono*) and some

dance plays. The formally dressed musical ensembles contribute to the spectacular stage picture. Several ensembles can be used to provide variety of mood – *nagauta* and *tokiwazu* in *The Zen Substitute* (*Migawari zazen*; trans. 1966, 1972), or *nagauta, takemoto, tokiwazu* in *The Maple Viewing* (*Momijigari*), for example.

The bravura acting style of heroic figures (*aragoto*), developed by the Ichikawa Danjūrō acting family, is expressed through exaggerated costumes and properties, and bold red and black face makeup (*kumadori*). It is familiar through actor portraits in wood-block prints. The comic-erotic acting (*wagoto*) for feckless heroes in domestic plays was developed in Kyoto–Osaka. When an actor acts a 'puppet' role, he may perform in exaggerated puppet style (*ningyō buri*). Styles are mixed within a play or scene. *Kabuki* dance incorporates lively rural and urban dances (*odori*) of the common people, as well as *nō*'s characteristic turning or pivoting technique (*mai*).

A *kabuki* performance is structured to provide changing moods and emotional states over time.

A *kabuki* dance comedy, *Three Misfits* (*Sannin katawa*), adapted from a *kyōgen* play. Singers and *shamisen* musicians perform on the stage.

The productions in the 1st, 3rd, 5th, 7th and 9th lunar months matched the Five Annual Festivals of the lunar calendar; the 11th-month production was the season opening, or *kaomise* ('face showing'). The nature of the play matched the season: love in spring, martial vigour on Boy's Day (5th month), lament for the spirits of the dead in the summer. A day's programme, 10–12 hours in length, began with casual 'practice' plays (*jobiraki* and *futatateme*) before dawn. The main play (*hon kyōgen*), consisting of formal history and legendary acts (*jidai*), domestic acts (*sewa*) and felicitous dance finale (*ōgiri*), ended at dusk.

Detailed information about performance was published in yearly rankings of actors (*hyōban ki*), production chronologies (*nendai ki*) and actors' commentaries (*geidan*). *My Advice to Onnagata* (*Ayame gusa*) by the actor YOSHIZAWA AYAME I, *A Record of Theatrical Matters* (*Kezairoku*) by playwright Namiki Shōzō II (?–1807), *The Playwright's Seasonal Calendar* (*Sakusha nenjū gyōji*) by playwright Mimasuya Nisanji (1784–1856), and *Notes of a Kabuki Playwright* (*Kyōgen sakusha kokoroesho*) by Kawatake Mokuami provide fascinating inside views of *kabuki*'s vibrant place in society.

The Tokugawa government licensed 9 large *kabuki* theatres through most of the Edo period: 3 each in Edo, Kyoto and Osaka. A drum tower over the theatre entrance signified the owner was licensed to use *kabuki*'s unique three-coloured draw curtain, the revolving stage, *hanamichi*, and other *kabuki* symbols. Small, unlicensed *kabuki* houses, numbering up to a dozen in each city, could not. Spectators sat in side balconies, ground-floor boxes and a centre pit, and occasionally on the side of the stage and even behind scenes. Performance was restricted by law to daylight hours; lighting was by candle or indirect sunlight (shutters over the audience could be opened or closed).

In the autumn the theatre owner signed a one-year contract with a troupe actor-manager (*zagashira* or *zamoto*), a leading female impersonator (*tate onnagata* or *tate oyama*), a staff playwright (*tate sakusha*) and a company of 50 to 70 supporting writers, actors, musicians, singers, costumers, wigmakers and technicians. In addition, a staff of 150 barkers, ticket sellers, doormen, ushers, food vendors, cushion vendors and bouncers kept a large theatre running. Theatres were restricted by government decree to a single district of 2 or 3 blocks in each city.

A special theatre structure evolved for playing *kabuki*, an oblong box in which audience and stage are physically part of the same space. A rampway or *hanamichi* carried the stage space through the left portion of the audience nearly to the back of the house. *Hanamichi*, 'flower path', probably meant 'gift path' in the late 17th century, flower being a euphemism for a gift. It allowed an actor to walk through the audience when entering and exiting, or deliver a major speech standing in its midst. A second *hanamichi* ran through the right portion of most *kabuki* houses. In some scenes, two separated characters, one on each *hanamichi*, spoke alternate speeches over the heads of the audience, a technique not dissimilar to cinema montage. By the mid 18th century, theatres were equipped with floor-level revolving stages (often one within another) for moving elaborately painted scenery and actors, traps, hanging wires, pipes for water, and other staging devices. Stage assistants in black (*kōken* or *kurogo*) moved properties and scenery in audience view or lighted a star's face with a candle held out on a flexible pole

Major changes occurred in staging *kabuki* during the 20th century. Cavernous new theatres were constructed, modelled on European opera houses. Auditoriums and stages expanded to three times the size of the traditional theatre – the present Kabuki-za in Tokyo has a 93-ft-wide stage and seats 2600. The actor used to stand out on the traditional small stage; he is now dwarfed by the theatre's dimensions. Acres of painted scenery fill the stage, competing with the actor for attention. Spectators in the overhanging balconies can no longer see actors on much of the *hanamichi*. The transformation of *kabuki* from a despised plebeian entertainment into a classic art of the middle class has been accompanied by the phenomenon of giganticism in theatre architecture and staging.

Kabuki's theatricalism has had a major impact on Western directors in the 20th century: Sergei Eisenstein, Max Reinhardt, Erwin Piscator, Joshua Logan and Harold Prince, among others. *Kabuki* is performed in English at the University of Hawaii and Pomono College, and its performing techniques are increasingly applied to various 'fusion' productions (for example a *Kabuki Macbeth*).

Kyōgen

A traditional theatre genre consisting of a repertory of some 260 short plays, celebratory and usually comic, that are performed by specialist *kyōgen* actors on a *nō* stage normally as part of a joint *nō–kyōgen* programme. *Kyōgen* humour arises in part from poking fun at human foibles – greed, lust, chicanery, cowardice. Characters are not idealized as they are in *nō* but rather their social weaknesses are shown – a priest is ignorant or useless (*Mushrooms*, *The Crow*), a wife domineering (*Fortified Beard*), a servant dishonest (*Poison Sugar*), a demon witless (*Head-pulling*, *Spring Evening*). Humour also arises from punning, onomatopoeia, and physical action. Plays such as *Monkey Quiver* begin seriously – a lord plans to kill a pet monkey to make a quiver from its hide – but conclude in felicitous celebration. Reflecting Shintō beliefs, *kyōgen* plays are fundamentally joyous and affirm the goodness of the natural order.

Language is vernacular prose of the 15th and 16th centuries and easily understood by today's audiences. Actors perform with a high energy level in controlled, clearly articulated vocal and movement patterns which, while stylized, are derived from daily speech and actions. *Kyōgen* is one of the few traditional theatre genres in Asia that is unaccompanied by music. A character may urge a companion 'let's sing a song together' at a play's climax, thus lifting the characters out of their particular, plebeian circumstances and transporting them into a universal state, described by Sakaba as 'rapture'. A handful of plays contain dances accompanied by a *nō*-style musical ensemble (*hayashi*) and a chorus (*ji*). Masks are worn for animals and special characters, but usually the actor performs without mask or makeup. Costume is based on the real clothing people wore in medieval times and is plain in comparison with the gorgeous and expensive silk brocades worn in *nō*. Tarōkaja, the stock servant character, wears a large-checked underkimono, sleeveless vest, bold-patterned bloused trousers and yellow socks. A landowner is identified by trailing trousers and sword.

English-language production of *Pining Wind* (*Matsukaze*) at the University of Hawai'i (1989), directed by Nomura Shirō, follows traditional patterns of movement, song and costuming.

Major acting families are the Nomura and Miyake families within the Izumi school (*ryū*) of *kyōgen* and the Yamamoto, Shigeyama and Zenchiku families within the Ōkura school. Most actors live in Tokyo, Kyoto, and Nagoya, but perform throughout the country.

Nō

A serious and subtle dance drama that evolved in Japan in the 14th century out of earlier songs, dances and sketches. It was originally performed by priest-performers attached to Buddhist temples. In performance, movement, music and words create an ever-shifting web of tension and ambiguity. The combined repertories of the five schools of performing – Kanze, Hōshō, Kongō, Komparu and Kita – consist of *c.* 240 plays.

A play text (*utaibon*, 'song book') contains prose (*kotoba*) and poetry (*utai*) sections. Prose is delivered in a sonorous voice that rises gradually and evenly in pitch, then drops at the end of a phrase. This typically repeating pattern is heard in all plays and varies only slightly by character type. The male actor does not attempt to reproduce the female voice but uses the normal male register when portraying a woman. Verse sections, which make up the bulk of the text, are sung (indicated by the musical term *fushi*, 'melody') by the Doer (*shite*), Sideman (*waki*), or Chorus (*ji*). The singing voice moves flexibly, with many melismas and slides, on and around base notes (three in soft style, *yowagin*, and five in strong style, *tsuyogin*). Verse composed in lines of 12 syllables, each line divided into a first phrase of 7 and a second phrase of 5 syllables, is known as normal rhythm (*hira nori*). This is the metre of the central, narrative song (*kuse*), sung by the Chorus, in which the major character dances a crucial event from his or her past. The vocal pattern of 7–5 syllables is overlaid on an 8-beat rhythm played by hip drum (*ōtsuzumi*), shoulder drum (*kotsuzumi*), and a bamboo flute (*nōkan*). The resulting syncopation produces an inherent musical tension. In contrast, verse in 8-syllable lines (*ō nori*) and 16-syllable lines (*chū nori*), are rhythmically congruent with the musical beat. These rhythms are used to accompany strong dances at the climax of a play, with a stick drum (*taiko*) adding to the rhythmic effect.

Voice, action and music are never precisely congruent, for that would be bare and uninteresting. Tempo continually fluctuates within a play, a scene or a phrase of movement or sound, following the basic Japanese aesthetic principle of *jo-ha-kyū* ('beginning, break, fast'). Each strand of the performance can be perceived separately; the spectator senses a continual advancing and receding of one performance element *vis-à-vis* the others. The well-known finesse of *nō* performance rests on the Buddhist view that the world is in a state of continual flux. This view is exemplified in concrete performance characteristics. Acceptance of change underlies ZEAMI's admonition that the *nō* actor always seek newness or freshness (*hana*, 'flower') in performance. The actor should never do what is expected, but rather, by analysing the performance situation – the audience, the season, the time of day, previous plays on the bill – he should choose a play and an interpretation that will elicit audience interest by being unexpected and therefore novel and interesting.

The 240 or so plays in the current repertory are categorized into one of five play types according to the nature of the *shite* role. Representative plays of each type are – God (*kami*) play: *The Twin Pines* (Takasago), *Chikubu Island* (Chikubu shima), *The Crane and the Tortoise* (Tsurukame); Warrior (*asura*) play: *Atsumori*, *Kiyotsune*, *Sanemori*; Woman (*katsura*) play: *The Well Curb* (Izutsu), *Pining Wind* (Matsukaze), *The Feather Robe* (Hagoromo); Living-person (*genzai*) plays: *The Ataka Barrier* (Ataka), *The Sumida River* (Sumidagawa); and Demon (*kichiku*) plays: *The Earth Spider* (Tsuchigumo), *Benkei in the Boat* (Funa Benkei).

The dramatic development of a play can be analysed into five units according to *jo-ha-kyū* progression (*ha* is divided into *jo-ha-kyū*, as well): Sideman's entrance (*jo*), Doer's entrance (*jo of ha*), Doer and Sideman conversation (*ha of ha*), Doer's main narrative (*kyū of ha*), and conclusion of Doer's narrative (*kyū*). Each of these scenes is made up of smaller modules (*shōdan*, 'small scene'), identifiable by function or form. The typical modules in a play are the opening music and Chorus song (*shidai*), Sideman's speech of self-introduction (*nanori*), travel song (*michiyuki*) and arrival speech (*tsukizerifu*), Doer's arrival song (*issei*), Doer–Sideman conversation, either spoken (*mondō*) or sung (*kakeai*), Doer's opening narrative song (*kuri* and *sashi*) leading into Doer's main narrative dance (*kuse*), interlude by Villager (*ai kyō gen*), Sideman's song waiting for Doer's return (*machi utai*), and Doer's final dance (*mai*) and Chorus song (*kiri*). High-pitched songs (*age uta*), low-pitched songs (*sage uta*), Doer–Chorus songs (*rongi*) and other modules are used where needed.

Around 1600 the stage became standardized as a raised dancing platform about 19 ft square; it was made of polished cyprus wood and covered by a temple-like roof which was supported by pillars at the four corners. The roof protects the outdoor stage from the elements and demarcates the performance area visually, thus helping to focus audience attention on the performing area. A bridgeway (*hashigakari*) 20–40 ft long runs from upstage right diagonally back to the dressing room and serves as an entrance and exit passage.

Role types have conventional locations on the stage. The Sideman sits beside the Sideman pillar, down left, the flautist is beside the flute pillar, up left, and the Doer is either centre stage or near the Doer pillar, up right. Players of the interlude (*kyōgen kata*) sit on the bridgeway, musicians (*hayashi kata*) sit rear centre (*ato za*), stage assistants (*kōken*) wait upstage right, and the Chorus sits in two rows of four or five singers on the left side stage (*waki za*). The Chorus became standard in *nō* after Zeami; its seating area is usually covered by a separate roof.

Today festival performances occur on traditional free-standing outdoor stages maintained by temples and shrines. Nighttime performance by torchlight (*takigi nō*) in late summer became popular in the 1980s, in part for tourist promotion. Contemporary urban *nō* stages are constructed within modern buildings where they can be used daily for training, rehearsal and performance without regard to weather. Major stages include the Kanze, Hōshō, Umewaka, Tessenkai and Kita theatres owned and run by these groups, and the National Noh Theatre, funded by the national government, all in Tokyo, the Kanze and Kongō theatres in Kyoto, and the Yamamoto theatre in Osaka. New plays and fusion productions occasionally occur.

Shingeki

Literally 'new drama', the generic term for modern theatre and drama in Japan. The term is used to distinguish modern theatre from traditional forms like NŌ and KABUKI. At the same time and more narrowly, *shingeki* also refers to one kind of modern theatre: the realistic, Western-based modern drama performed by companies like The People's Art Theatre, The Literary Theatre and The Actors' Theatre. Today in its broadest meaning, *shingeki* refers to the entire gamut of nontraditional theatre performed in Japan.

Shinpa

A genre of modern commercial theatre (see also Korea). The name literally means 'new wave [drama]'. It was one of a number of experiments to 'modernize' KABUKI around the turn of the century. The form was in every respect transitional. It reintroduced actresses to the Japanese stage but retained female impersonators as well. It took up contemporary themes but treated them with a jejune, 'train-whistle realism'. Its style is characterized by a cloying sentimentality. Although it is performed today by one troupe, *shinpa* has had virtually no influence on the evolution of SHINGEKI, the mainstream of Japanese modern theatre. Kawakami Otojirō (1864–1911) and his wife, actress Sada Yakko (1872–1946), are frequently cited as the founders of *shinpa*. They experimented boldly in a variety of areas, including the training of actresses, the use of pyrotechnics to represent scenes of modern warfare, the production of theatre for children and the use of everyday speech to replace stylized *kabuki* diction. They performed in Europe and the USA and attempted to incorporate their experiences abroad into a modern Japanese theatre. When Kawakami died, he was planning a production of Ibsen's *Enemy of the People*, but his work had already been superseded by the nascent *shingeki* movement. It was the work of Ii Yōhō (1871–1932) who had worked with Kawakami in 1891, that prefigured *shinpa* as we know it today. His dramatization of popular novels written for an upper-middle-class female audience and his commercial acumen, bringing *shinpa* under the aegis of the Shōchiku Theatrical company in 1917, are the real source of today's *shinpa* drama.

Bibliography

GENERAL: J. T. Araki, *The Ballad-Drama of Medieval Japan*, Berkeley, Calif. 1964; P. D. Arnott, *The Theatres of Japan*, New York, 1969; F. Bowers, *The Japanese Theatre*, Rutland, Vt., 1974 (1952); E. Ernst (ed.), *Three Japanese Plays from the Traditional Theatre*, Westport, Conn., 1976 (1959); F. T. Immoos, *Japanese Theatre*, London, 1974; Y. Inoura and T. Kawatake, *The Traditional Theater of Japan*, New York, 1981; T. Komiya, *Japanese Music and Drama in the Meiji Era*, Tokyo, 1956; C. H. Kullman and W. C. Young (eds.), 'Japan', in *Theatre Companies of the World*, vol. 1, Westport, Conn., 1986; B. Ortolani, *The Japanese Theatre From Shamanistic Ritual to Contemporary Pluralism*, Leiden, 1990.

BUGAKU: M. Togi, *Gagaku: Court Music and Dance*, Tokyo, 1971; C. Wolz, *Bugaku: Japanese Court Dance*, Providence, R.I., 1971.

NŌ: J. R. Brandon, (ed.), *Nō and Kyōgen in the Contemporary World*, forthcoming; J. Goff, *Noh Drama and The Tale of Genji*, Princeton, N.J., 1991; T. B. Hare, *Zeami's Style: The Noh Plays of Zeami Motokiyo*, Stanford, Calif., 1986; D. Keene, *Nō: The Classical Theatre of Japan*, Palo Alto, Calif., 1966, and (ed.), *Twenty Plays of the Nō Theatre*, New York, 1970; K. Komparu, *The Noh Theater: Principles and Perspectives*, Tokyo, 1983; Nippon Gakujutsu Shinkokai (ed.), *Japanese Noh Drama*, 3 vols., Tokyo, 1955, 1959, 1960; P. G. O'Neill, *A Guide to Noh*, Tokyo, 1954, and *Early Nō Drama: Its Background, Character, and Development, 1300–1450*, London, 1959; E. de Poorter (tr.), *Zeami's Talks on Sarugaku*, Amsterdam, 1986; T. Rimer and M. Yamazaki (tr.), *On the Art of the Nō Drama: The Major Treatises of Zeami*, Princeton, N.J., 1984; R. Tyler, *Pining Wind: A Cycle of Nō Plays*, Ithaca, N.Y., 1978, and *Granny Mountains: A Second Cycle of Nō Plays*, Ithaca, N.Y., 1978; M. Ueda (tr.), *The Old Pine and Other Noh Plays*, Lincoln, Nebr., 1978; K. Yasuda, *Masterworks of the Nō Theater*, Bloomington, Ind., 1989.

KYŌGEN: D. Kenny, *A Guide to Kyogen*, Tokyo, 1968, and (comp.), *The Kyogen Book: An Anthology of Japanese Classical Comedies*, Tokyo, 1989; R. N. McKinnon (tr.), *Selected Plays of Kyogen*, Tokyo, 1968; S. Sakanishi, *Japanese Folk Plays: The Ink-Smeared Lady and Other Kyogen*, Rutland, Vt., 1960 (1938).

KABUKI: J. R. Brandon (ed.), *Chūshingura: Studies in Kabuki and the Puppet Theatre*, Honolulu, 1982, and (tr.), *Kabuki: Five Classic Plays*, Cambridge, Mass., 1975; J. R. Brandon, W. Malm, and D. Shively, *Studies in Kabuki: Its Acting, Music, and Historical Context*, Honolulu, 1978; J. R. Brandon and Tamako Niwa (tr.), *Two Kabuki Plays: 'The Subscription List' and 'The Zen Substitute'*, New York, 1966; E. Ernst, *The Kabuki Theatre*, Honolulu, 1974 (1956); M. Gunji, *Buyo: The Classical Dance*, New York, 1971, and *Kabuki*, Palo Alto, Calif., 1970; Z. Kincaid, *Kabuki, the Popular Stage of Japan*, New York, 1977 (1925); S. L. Leiter (tr.), *The Art of Kabuki: Famous Plays in Performance*, Berkeley, Calif., 1979 and *Kabuki Encyclopedia*, Westport, Conn., 1979; B. Powell, *Kabuki in Modern Japan: Mayama Seika and His Plays*, New York, 1990; A. C. Scott, *The Kabuki Theatre of Japan*, New York, 1966 (1955); R. Shaver, *Kabuki Costumes*, Rutland, Vt., 1966; Y. Toita, *Kabuki: The Popular Theatre*, New York, 1970; S. Tsubouchi and J. Yamamoto, *History and Characteristics of Kabuki: The Japanese Classical Drama*, Yokohama, 1960.

BUNRAKU: B. Adachi, *The Voices and Hands of Bunraku*, Tokyo, 1978; T. Ando, *Bunraku: The Puppet Theatre*, New York, 1970; D. Keene, *Bunraku: The Art of the Japanese Puppet Theatre*, Tokyo, 1965, and (tr.), *Major Plays of Chikamatsu*, New York, 1961; C. J. Dunn, *The Early Japanese Puppet Drama*, London, 1966; C. A. Gerstle, *Circles of Fantasy: Convention in the Plays of Chikamatsu*, Cambridge, Mass., 1986; C. A. Gerstle, K. Inobe and W. Malm, *Theater as Music: The Bunraku Play 'Mt. Imo and Mt. Se: An Exemplary Tale of Womanly Virtue'*, Ann Arbor, Mich., 1990; T. Izumo, *Chūshingura: The Treasury of Loyal Retainers*, tr. D. Keene, New York, 1971; S. H. Jones, Jr. (tr.), *Sugawara and the Secrets of Calligraphy*, New York, 1984; S. Saito, *et al.*, *Masterpieces of Japanese Puppetry: Sculptured Heads of the Bunraku Theater*, Rutland, Vt., 1958; A. C. Scott, *The Puppet Theatre of Japan*, Rutland, Vt. and Tokyo, 1963.

MODERN THEATRE: K. Abe, *Friends*, tr. Donald Keene, New York, 1969; D. G. Goodman (ed. and tr.), *After Apocalypse: Four Japanese Plays of Hiroshima and Nagasaki*, New York, 1986, *Japanese Drama and Culture in the 1960s: The Return of the Gods*, Armonk, N.Y., 1988, and 'Shingeki Under the Occupation' in *The Occupation of Japan: Arts and Culture*, Norfolk, Va., 1988; T. R. H. Havens. *Artist and Patron in Postwar Japan: Dance, Music, Theater, and the Visual Arts, 1955–1980*, Princeton, N.J., 1982; E. Hoffman and M. Holborn, *Butō: Dance of the Dark Soul*, New York, 1987; A. Horie-Webber, 'Modernisation of the Japanese Theatre: The Shingeki Movement', in *Modern Japan: Aspects of History, Literature, and Society*, ed. W. G. Beasley, Berkeley, Calif., 1977; J. Kinoshita, *Between God and Man: A Judgement on War Crimes; A Play in Two Parts*, tr. Eric J. Gangloff, Seattle, Wash., 1979; K. Kishida, *Five Plays by Kishida Kunio*, ed. D. G. Goodman, Ithaca, N.Y., 1989; S. Kubo, *Land of Volcanic Ash*, tr. D. G. Goodman, Ithaca, N.Y., 1986; Y. Mishima, *Five Modern Nō Plays*, tr. Donald Keene, New York, 1957; Y. Mishima, *Madame de Sade*, tr. Donald Keene, New York, 1967; B. Powell, 'Japan's First Modern Theatre: The Tsukiji Shōgekijō and Its Company, 1924–1926', in *Monumenta Nipponica*, 30, 1, 1975; J. T. Rimer, *Toward a Modern Japanese Theatre*, Princeton, N.Y., 1974; R. T. Rolf and J. K. Gillespie (eds.), *Alternative Japanese Drama: Ten Plays*, Honolulu, 1992; T. Suzuki, *The Way of Acting: The Theatre Writings of Tadashi Suzuki*, tr. J. T. Rimer, New York, 1986; T. T. Takaya, *Modern Japanese Drama: An Anthology*, New York, 1979; J. Viala and N. Masson-Sekine, *Butoh: Shades of Darkness*, Tokyo, 1988; M. Yamazaki, *Mask and Sword: Two Plays for the Contemporary Japanese Theatre*, tr. J. T. Rimer, New York, 1980.

KOREA

The peninsula of Korea, situated west of Japan and bordering on China and Russia on the north, is home to more than 60 million people speaking a single language and sharing one culture. Since 1948, the Korean people have been divided into two political states: the Republic of Korea with Seoul as its capital and the Democratic People's Republic of Korea with P'yongyang as its capital. For centuries folk theatre has existed in various geographical regions both in the North and in the South. During the successive rule of the three major kingdoms of Silla, Koryŏ and Chosŏn (or Yi), court forms of dance and masked play were patronized and encouraged. In the first part of this century, modern Western drama and theatrical realism were introduced. Before World War II, modern Korean theatre influenced by the West was limited in large part to Seoul, then capital of the whole country. Since 1948 modern theatre has been concentrated in the two capital cities, Seoul in the South and P'yongyang in the North. Regional theatre companies began to emerge in the South in the 1980s.

Folk theatre

The precise origin of Korean theatre is unknown. The beginning of Korean theatre may be traced back to ancient ceremonies, folk observances and shamanistic rites, some more than 2000 years old. Among civic observances that are believed to have included incidental theatrical elements are ch'ŏngun, much'ŏn and yŏngo. They were mainly performed for the purpose of worshipping heaven and appeasing ancestral spirits. Presumably these rituals required the performers to sing and dance as well as wear masks. During the 7th century, kiak, originally consisting of music and dance, was probably imported from China. This was performed at a Buddhist temple as a kind of simple didactic masked dance drama for a general audience. One theory suggests that kiak became the genesis of

today's folk masked dance drama, SANDAE-GŬK ('mountain performance', probably indicating a performance on a raised stage). Kiak was also taken to Japan where it was called gigaku.

During the long reign of the Silla Kingdom (57 BC–AD 935) kŏmmu, muaemu and ch'ŏyongmu were important dance forms containing theatrical elements. Kŏmmu was a masked sword dance, originating in the story of the death of a legendary young warrior who killed an enemy king. Muaemu was a dance performed without masks which promulgated Buddhism. Of these three, ch'ŏyongmu, based on the story of legendary Ch'ŏyong, a son of the Dragon King of the East Sea, was the most grotesque and pungent early type of masked dance of Korea.

During the strongly Buddhist Koryŏ period (918–1392) there were no important amusements other than religious festivals such as p'algwanhoe and yŏndŭnghoe. The former was primarily a midwinter festival offered in honour of the earthly deity, while the latter, held in the first lunar month, was a Buddhist mass. Although the purpose of the two events differed, preparations for both festivities were strikingly similar: numerous lanterns of different sizes and colours were hung, and a temporary high stage was constructed and adorned with bright colours. Programmes included somersaults, a tight-rope display, acrobatic dance on the top of a bamboo pole, puppet plays and various mixed forms of masked dance drama (sandae-japgŭk).

Another ritual of this period, narae, was performed to drive evil spirits out of the palace. Later the purpose of narae changed as it came to be performed for the public by professional male actors, kwangdae, probably the first actors in the history of Korean theatre to earn their living as performers. Some actors of this period belonged to the court, where they could be called upon to perform at any given time. Other actors maintained a livelihood entertaining wealthy and petty merchants. All actors were considered social outcasts and forced to reside in segregated areas, apart even from the residences of common people. When they were not performing, they engaged in such lowly professions as butcher, hunter and basket weaver.

In the following period of the Chosŏn court (1392–1910), cultural activities were heavily influenced by Confucianism. Popular literature, fine arts and theatre blossomed, gaining increasing support from commoners, particularly merchants and craftsmen. The Confucian court, strongly anti-Buddhistic, refused to sanction the Buddhist religious festivals of Koryŏ. From past dynasties, however, the inherited masked forms of *narae* and *sandae-japgŭk* continued, and contributed to the development of masked *sandae-gŭk*. Unmasked performances were also known. Some apparently were comic-satirical dramas in which perverse officials or tyrannical rulers were targets of ridicule. This type of theatre was referred to as *chaphŭi*, indicating plays performed by actors as distinguished from masked *sandae-gŭk* performed by dancers.

P'ANSORI, a solo narrative sung to drum accompaniment, was developed by professional *kwangdae* actors during the latter part of the Chosŏn period. The origin of this art is not clear. Some scholars trace it back to short songs sung by shamans in rituals of the early 8th century. As a kindred of shamans, the early *p'ansori* singer-actor belonged to the lowest class in society. If any member of that class was talented and possessed the necessary powerful quality of voice, he was given training to become a *p'ansori* singer-actor. A special hoarse vocal timbre was acquired after years of arduous training. In time *p'ansori* was taken over by itinerant professional *kwangdae* actors, in search of material with which to entertain their popular audiences. Probably they replaced the short lyrics with longer popular songs derived from well-known stories. In the 19th century, Shin Jae-hyo (1817–84) set down in writing the six stories of the repertoire which had existed until then in the oral tradition.

The performance of *p'ansori* requires no more than a singer-actor, a drummer and a small mat. This simplicity allows performances to be given anywhere, for any size audience and under almost any circumstance, and is responsible for *p'ansori* being one of the most popular entertainments for people of all classes during the past two centuries. Today *p'ansori* is frequently performed, not only live but also on television and radio reaching a mass audience.

Korean masked dance drama can be classified into two main types: village-festival plays (*purakje*) and various forms that derive from the court, collectively known as *sandae-gŭk*. Major village-festival masked forms include *HAHOE PYŎLSIN-GUT*, *kwanno*, *pŏm-gut* and *t'al-gut* of the east central region of the country. All other known forms of masked dance drama are related to court forms: *PYŎLSANDAE* plays of Yangju and Songp'a; *T'ALCH'UM* plays of

Folk masked dance: a lecherous monk dances with a prostitute.

Pongsan, Unyul, Haeju and Kangnyŏng; OGWANG-DAE plays of T'ongyŏng, Kosŏng and Kasan; and YARYU plays of Tongnae and Suyŏng. Whether originating in folk or court surroundings, it is notable that masked dance plays took root in many regions of the country.

Of the village-festival plays, Hahoe pyŏlsin-gut is the best known. Performance traditionally occurs once every ten years, on the 15th day of the first lunar month, as part of the Hahoe village festival. The play calls for twelve masks. Today, nine of the orginal wooden masks – the most refined among Korean theatre masks – remain. There is no record of the whereabouts of the other three. When they were not in use, the masks were traditionally kept in the village shrine. In Hahoe village the task of mask-making was supposedly accomplished only by a man instructed by divine message in a dream. The identity of the mask-maker and the date of carving the Hahoe masks are unknown today.

Village performers preserve and orally transmit knowledge of performance and the main action of the play without a written script. Rather than being built around a central plot, the play is made up of independent scenes held together by a common theme – satire of monks guilty of transgression, of corrupt aristocrats and of insensitive local officials.

During the early period of the Chosŏn dynasty, masked drama was organized at the royal court under the direction of a court official, the Master of Revels (sandae-togam). Performances served official functions – to entertain visiting Chinese envoys, to exorcise evil spirits, to welcome newly appointed provincial governors. However, in 1634 official support was withdrawn with the abolition of the Master of Revels position and during the last half of the Chosŏn period performers left the court and brought their theatre into the countryside. Different variations of masked drama were naturally developed in different regions, by village folk performers and by professional itinerant kwangdae troupes. This history explains why there are so many similarities as well as regional differences among the various masked drama forms in Korea.

Performance elements common to all sandae-gŭk forms include masking, dance, singing, music, pantomime, the exchange of witticisms and dialogue. Prime emphasis is placed on dancing, singing and music. Performance is held outdoors,

avoiding the need for stage settings. Grotesque masks and colourful costumes may be intensified by blazing torchlights at night. Dance movement patterns, numbering more than a dozen, are complicated and difficult to decipher. In the Yŏdaji dance, for example, the player moves forward, placing both hands on the upper front of his body and, extending them forward, pantomimes the opening of his chest while his feet kick forward. Some dances are used for a humorous purpose: for example, the Hŏrijapi dance, which requires lifting the player's leg while resting his hands on his waist, is designed to tease the other player.

With few exceptions, characters in sandae-gŭk are masked. The masks, made of dried gourds or paper, were traditionally burned at the end of each performance. Around the edge of the mask a dark cloth (t'alpo) is attached to cover the back of the head; dark strips of cloth are also used to tie the mask around the player's neck.

The musical ensemble generally consists of six instruments (samhyŏn-yukgak): a transverse flute (chŏtdae), two fifes (p'iri), a two-stringed fiddle (haegŭm), an hourglass-shaped drum (changgo) and a barrel drum (puk). A small gong (kkwaenggwari) may be added. Three tunes are played most frequently: 'Kutkŏri', 'T'aryŏng' and 'Yŏmbul'. 'Kutkori' is a flowing tune with a twelve-beat pattern, 'T'aryŏng' has a twelve-beat pattern with an accent on the ninth beat, and 'Yŏmbul' is a rhythmical six-beat pattern. The songs, which are interlaced with dance and dialogue, are mostly derived from popular folk songs and shamanistic incantations of the Chosŏn period. Because a song has come from a source outside the play, it may have no bearing on the plot at all.

The costumes make an important contribution to the theatrical spectacle. In particular, the costumes worn by the servants and the women of questionable morality are bright, even gaudy.

Being collaborative works and transmitted orally, the masked plays do not have identifiable authors. Only recently have performances been recorded and their texts transcribed and published. Each performance depends upon the village actors spontaneously improvising from a rough synopsis of the plot. The generally episodic nature of the plays can be illustrated by examples drawn from the masked play of Yangju (Yangju pyŏlsandae). Act I is about Sangjwa, a monk, while Act II consists of an exchange of nonsensical dialogue between two other characters. The transgressions of a second monk, unrelated to Sangjwa, are the subject of Act V. Characters introduced in one scene may not appear again. What is common to most of the masked plays is the satirical representation of four privileged character types: the corrupt local official who steals someone else's woman; the apostate Buddhist monk who engages in lascivious conduct with women; the aristocrat who blindly exercises his power; and the tyrannical husband who mistreats his wife. In the Confucian ethical system these male authority figures – monk, official, aristocrat, husband – should command total respect. The plays take the villagers' point of view, completely subverting the system by holding up their crudely excessive behaviour to contempt and ridicule. Dramatic language ranges from poetic expression in *Pongsan t'alch'um* to rough, bawdy vernacular in *Yangju pyŏlsandae*.

Dance of the Young Monk, in the Yangju Village masked play, performed in 1972 by young farmers adjacent to the village temple.

Traditionally, players are local farmers and petty town officials. In the past all performances took place at night and could last until dawn. Now, daytime performances are also given, sometimes in conjunction with a government cultural event or as a tourist performance.

Traditional puppet theatre, KKOKTU KAKSI, is believed to be the descendant of puppetry introduced into Korea during the 7th century by wandering players from the Asian continent. These groups of itinerant players, 'song-and-dance people' (*namsadang*), being nomads and social outcasts like *kwangdae*, never belonged to the mainstream of society, and developed and preserved puppetry in society's margins.

The Korean puppet, *kkoktu*, combines aspects of the hand puppet, the rod puppet and the marionette. The body of the puppet is held by the hand. The arms, somewhat like a marionette's, are manipulated by strings from below. And the stiff arm movements remind us of a rod puppet. During the performance a puppeteer manipulates a single puppet at a time, while delivering dialogue or singing songs to accompanying music.

A number of orally transmitted versions of the plays exist, ranging from seven to ten scenes. Although different in detail, they deal with a common pool of humorous subjects which are mercilessly ridiculed: the apostate monk; the triangular relationship between husband, wife and concubine; the unethical high official; the corrupt upper-class man. Generally, a different subject is treated in each scene. The structure of puppet plays is more tightly organized than masked plays because the main puppet character appears in each scene, serving as the narrator who links actions together.

Until the beginning of the 20th century, urban and rural audiences alike were greatly entertained by both the masked dance drama and puppet theatre. Modern audiences, however, find these art forms contain shortcomings: performance time is too long; because performances are outdoors lines often cannot be heard and, when delivered by the players behind their masks, are unintelligible; being entertained by masks and puppets seems old-fashioned. In addition, after 1910, these folk arts were faced by a stronger enemy, the occupying Japanese military who were determined to wipe out Korean culture and language completely. As part of its general cultural policy of forbidding Korean cultural expression, performances of masked dance drama and puppet theatre were banned by the Japanese colonial administration between 1930 and 1945.

Since the end of World War II, the folk theatre of Korea has not only been resurrected but also revitalized through performance, study and publication of the plays. The government of the Republic of Korea has designated these art forms as Important Intangible Cultural Properties. In contrast, the government of the Democratic People's Republic of Korea discourages the performance of folk theatre in its normal village environment. Traditional masked dance drama and the puppet theatre are considered not only backward but also not sufficiently revolutionary.

Modern theatre

At the beginning of the 20th century, two types of modern drama were introduced into Korea: *shinp'a*, an imitation of Western sentimental melodrama, and SHINGŬK, influenced by Western realistic drama. For a time, the folk theatre co-existed with these modern forms. But soon the popularity of the folk theatre began to decline.

The people of the folk theatre who were the first to respond to the influx of modern theatrical forms were *p'ansori* performers. They established the first modern, indoor theatre in Korea, the Hyŏpyul-sa theatre, in 1902, where they staged dramatized stories in *p'ansori* musical style. This reformed style of *p'ansori* was a kind of opera or music drama and was called *ch'anggŭk* ('song and drama'). The important difference between *p'ansori* and *ch'anggŭk* was that in the latter multiple singers enacted specific roles. The five basic stories of *p'ansori* make up the basic repertory, although other dramas are also written for *ch'anggŭk* staging. Despite the attempt at modernization, *ch'anggŭk* lost its popularity due to a limited repertoire. Occasional performances of the genre are seen today, mostly at the National Theatre. They appeal to the audience through sentimental lyrics and music.

Early Korean *shinp'a* artists were strongly influenced by the Japanese theatre of the same genre (see Japan, SHINPA). A prominent pioneer actor and leader of the Hyŏksin-dan troupe was Im Sŏng-gu (1887–1921). Some of Im's performances and pro-

ductions were extremely popular, but relying on third-rate touring Japanese troupes for his model and trusting to improvised dialogue, he was unable to raise the quality of *shinp'a* theatre. One of the artists most responsible for developing higher-quality plays and productions was PAK SUNG-HI, a prolific playwright and director, who led the noted Earth and Moon group (Towŏlhoe) for approximately 20 years. Pak was the first person to use completely developed play scripts for his productions.

Most plays were set in the present time and dealt with contemporary events in Korean life. There are three main types of plays: military plays, detective plays and domestic plays. In the military plays patriotic soldiers who defend the Korean nation against the invading enemy are glorified as national heroes. *The Battle in the Snow* (*Chinjungsol*, ?1908) portrays youthful patriotic soldiers fighting the invading enemy whose identity is not clearly defined, but vaguely suggests the Japanese military. Producing this type of play was still possible until a harsh censorship policy was enforced following the Samil Independence actions of March 1919. A very popular hero was the young policeman who relentlessly pursues the robber, disregarding personal wounds, to restore law and peace in the community in a detective play. Domestic plays, the soap operas of the time, deal with love, hatred, injustice, revenge, filial piety and the conflicts between legitimate and illegitimate children. Domestic plays became the predominant category in *shinp'a* and typically the Japanese occupation is shown to be the cause of inidividual and national suffering. In *Arirang Pass* (*Arirang-goge*), by Pak Sung-hi, the lovers are forced to part because of family bankruptcy due to Japanese exploitation. Korean audiences of the time responded enthusiastically to this theme because the misfortune of the dramatic characters in such plays reflected their own personal sufferings and their nation's tragedy.

In 1921, a group of Korean students studying in Tokyo formed the Society of Comradeship (Tongwuhoe) and performed first modern drama, or *shingŭk*. Under the leadership of KIM U-JIN, the group toured throughout Korea during the summer vacation, producing such important new plays as *The Death of Kim Yŏng-il* (*Kim yŏng-il ŭi chugŭm*) by Cho Myŏng-hi. The plays they chose dealt with the principle of self-determination and the freedom of man, ideas newly advocated by Woodrow Wilson after World War I. They staged plays by Ibsen, O'Neill, Capek and Pirandello, thus introducing European and American drama to Korean audiences. After 40 performances the group was ordered to dissolve by the Japanese police. Despite its short existence, the Society of Comradeship made significant contributions to Korean theatre: it pioneered serious modern drama in contrast to *shinp'a*; it forced other companies to raise their production quality; it demonstrated that modern drama could be an educational tool to teach new ideologies.

The Society of Comradeship had no immediate successors. A decade later, in 1931, a group of young intellectuals organized the Theatre Arts Research Society (Kŭgyesul Yŏnguhoe) devoted to popularizing the new realistic drama through staging performances, playwriting, criticism, audience education and the translation of foreign plays. They established an experimental stage, where they produced the plays of Chekhov, Ibsen, Gogol and Galsworthy. A number of notable young playwrights influenced by realism and naturalism emerged during the 1930s. Their plays exposed the true suffering Koreans endured under harsh Japanese military rule. *The Earthen Hut* (*T'omak*) by Yu CH'I-JIN depicts the misery of an aged farmer whose sole hope for regaining his farm ends in anguish when he learns that his only son, fighting for national independence, has been killed by the Japanese police.

During the 1930s modern Korean theatre was largely divided into two camps: popular commercial theatre represented by *shinp'a* and nationalistic, realistic *shingŭk*. Interestingly, some *shinp'a* artists were left-wing sympathizers who attempted to include Marxist ideas in their productions. Censorship and oppression directed against *shinguk* by the Japanese military, which began in the early 1920s, became harsher still. Artists active in nationalistic theatre were targets of arrest, torture and detention. In 1939 the Theatre Arts Research Society was finally ordered to dissolve by the Japanese. With the suppression of this group, Korean theatre was once again dominated by *shinp'a* for a short period until it too was suppressed. The Japanese military, seeing the possibility of using Korean theatre to serve their policies, proposed to form a single theatre organization in 1941 that would be under direct Japanese control. Nine troupes were allowed to join, and all other companies and individuals were banned from performing. Playwrights, too, were required to write plays glorifying Japanese military policy.

Korea's liberation from Japanese domination at the end of World War II resulted in the division of the nation into two parts, North and South, and the splitting of the theatre people into two vehemently opposing factions. For those in the leftist group, theatre became a tool for political propaganda. The majority of the left-wing theatre people came from the *shinp'a* troupes, while the right-wing theatre was organized by the nationalistic theatre people of *shingŭk*. When the governments of North and South Korea were separately established in 1948, a large number of the left-wing theatre people went to the North where they became the nucleus of theatre in the Democratic People's Republic of Korea. Since the end of World War II, the theatre of North Korea has been utilized to propagate official government policies and Communist ideology. Until 1950 the dominant subject of drama was the struggle during the 1930s against the Japanese led by General Kim Il-sung, leader of North Korea until his death in 1994. The plays of this period were written to proselytize Kim's political message, especially *juche*, placing man at the centre. During the 1950s, the so-called 'great revolutionary works' emerged, such as *The Great River is Flowing* (*Taeha-nŭn hŭnrŭnda*), *The Young Vanguards* (*Ch'ungnyŏn jŭnyu*) and *The Communist Guerrilla* (*Kongsan ppalchisan*). These spectacular productions were a modern version of *shinp'a*, devoted to political ideology.

Since the 1970s three types of theatre dominate the stage in North Korea: 'revolutionary opera'; 'music and dance drama'; and 'epic drama of music and dance'. The major characteristics of the 'revolutionary opera' are songs, chorus, music, exaggerated scenic settings and colourful costumes. The difference between this theatre and the 'music and dance drama' is that the latter places a heavier emphasis on dance. In 'epic drama of music and dance', a series of grand, epic scenes containing political messages are performed through dance, song, chorus and music. In the musical ensembles used in the theatre Western instruments predominate. Almost all the theatrical productions presented on the major stages in

P'yongyang today place great emphasis on spectacle with large casts, elaborate scenery, colourful costumes and dazzling lighting. To accommodate this type of production, the government has built large-scale theatres: P'yongyang's Mansudae stage can hold a cast of 5000. Because of tight ideological control, only a few approved themes may be used in the drama, and these occur again and again: the struggle against Japanese imperialism in the 1930s; the war against United States imperialism and the South Korean puppet government; commendation of Kim Il-sung; and praise for the glorious life under Communism. The collapse of Communist governments in Russia and eastern Europe, 1989–91, has had no effect on these themes in North Korea.

In the five years following World War II, theatre in South Korea was marked by two significant events: the founding of the Theatre Arts Association (Kŭgyesul Hyŏphoe) in 1947 and the establishment of the National Theatre in 1950. The former was organized by *shinguk* artists under the leadership of Yu Ch'i-jin to counter left-wing theatre. The National Theatre was created by the government to promote nationalistic theatre and to advance theatrical exchange with foreign nations. Two resident companies were attached to the National Theatre, the New Association (Shinhyŏp) and the Theatre Association (Kughyŏp). In two months 50,000 people attended the opening productions, *Wŏnsulrang* by Yu Ch'i-jin and *The Thunderstorm* by Cao Yu (see China, CAO YU), but this promising beginning was cut short by the outbreak of the Korean War. The staff of the National Theatre moved to Taegu and most theatrical groups barely continued. With the end of the war in 1953, the National Theatre returned to Seoul and resumed production. The Shinhyŏp troupe, now independent, achieved success in the war-ravaged capital staging recent works by Miller, Williams, Inge and Korean authors. Another notable event was the opening of the Wŏngaksa Theatre in 1958, a small theatre with 306 seats, constructed by the government to promote the little-theatre movement. Unfortunately this theatre burned down in 1960.

The 1960s were marked by the emergence of numerous new theatre troupes. In 1960 the Experimental Theatre (Silhŏm-kŭgchang) opened with a production of Ionesco's *The Bald Prima Donna*, an obvious rebellion against the dominance of Shinhyop and its realistic production style. The ambitious Drama Center, founded by Yu Ch'i-jin, opened in 1962 with the great expectation that it would stimulate a new Korean theatre and provide a home for new Korean plays. Built with initial funding from the Rockefeller Foundation, the Center contained a flexible theatre seating 450, classrooms for a theatre school, and a library. It did not meet these expectations, however, and five of its first six productions were foreign plays. Furthermore, audiences were increasingly drawn to American films and able theatre artists migrated to television.

If the 1950s were marked by the production of contemporary American drama, the 1960s were the period in which the plays of Durrenmatt, Frisch, Anouilh, Beckett and other modern European authors were introduced. A score of plays belonging to the Theatre of the Absurd were produced, often using the outmoded, and misunderstood, realism of the Stanislavski method. Young Korean playwrights began to treat new subjects: contemporary economic–political systems; the absurdity of modern society; and the problems of urban life. Notable authors of this period are O YŎNG-JIN, Ch'a Pom-sok (1924–), and Yi Kun-sam (1929–).

During the decade of the 1970s a return to Korean roots in playwriting and directing can be seen. Playwrights experimented with subject matter drawn, not from daily life, but from ancient legends, shamanistic rites, and classical literature. Others included traditional folk songs in plays on modern subjects. Authors in this period includes Yun Tae-sŏng, O T'ae-sŏk, Yi Jae-hyŏn, and Ch'oe In-hun (1936–). Energetic directors emerged such as Kim Chong-ok (1932–), Im Yŏng-ung and Yu Tŏk-hyong who attempted to apply the production techniques of total theatre.

Among many new initiatives of the 1980s have been: an experimentation with surrealism; updating the puppet theatre to meet the demands of today's audience; infusion of Brechtian epic theatre into playwriting; and modernizing the old theatre of exorcism (*gut*). Potentially the most significant is the creation of a new form of masked dance drama, *madang-gŭk*, or 'yard play', designed to be performed in the street or open field for a large popular audience. Plays deal with present-

Artists

Kim U-jin (1897–1927)

Early modern theatre director, producer and playwright. In 1921 he led, and was financially responsible for, the Society of Comradeship (Tongwuhoe) troupe which introduced Western realistic theatre to Korea. He was the first Korean playwright to be influenced by Western dramatic forms, writing five plays in which he experimented with realism, naturalism and expressionism. He wrote about the conflict between old ethics and new ideas, and the suffering of women in *Yi Yŏng-nyŏ* (1925), *The Shipwreck* (*Nanp'a*, 1926), and *The Boar* (*Santoeji*, 1926).

O Yŏng-jin (1916–74)

Playwright of SHINGŬK drama, active after World War II. Most of his 20 or so plays are satiric comedies that ridicule modern-day customs and behaviour. He took the subjects of his plays from folk sources, thus introducing traditional Korean culture into the modern Western form of *shingŭk*. His most successful play is *Wedding Day* (*Mengjinsadek Kyŏngsa*, 1969), in which he mercilessly exposed the cruelty of the old custom of marriage and the avariciousness of aristocrats (*yangban*).

Pak Sung-hi (1901–64)

Director, producer and playwright of *shinp'a*. As leader of the important Towŏlhoe Troupe he exhausted his inheritance. He was responsible for upgrading *shinp'a* by using fully-written play scripts, abandoning improvisations and demanding rigorous rehearsals of his casts. He is credited with writing or adapting 200 plays, most of which have not survived.

Yu Ch'i-jin (1905–74)

Playwright, director and producer of SHINGŬK modern drama. In 1931 he was a founding member of the Theatre Arts Research Society (Kŭgyesul Yŏnguhoe) group. His first successful play was *The Earthen Hut* (*T'omak*, 1932). In 30 plays he ranged from tragedy to comedy, becoming the most influential playwright of the 1930s and 40s. He was concerned with social and political issues, writing about the struggle against Japanese colonial policy, the struggle against occupying foreign military forces and the immorality of political feuds. In 1950 he was appointed the first director of the newly established National Theatre. In 1962 he established the Drama Center in Seoul. Representative plays are *The Cow* (*So*, 1935), *Prince Maui* (*Mauit'aeja*, 1936), *The Fatherland* (*Joguk*, 1946), *The Star* (*Pyŏl*, 1948) and *Wŏnsulrang* (1950).

day subject matter, especially social–political events, in satirical fashion, thus returning to the folk tradition of social satire in masked drama. It gained fashion among college students during the 1980s.

The Seoul Theatre Festival (originally the Korean Theatre Festival, begun in 1978) and the Regional Theatre Festival have been annual venues for supporting new productions and encouraging new plays. In an attempt to further encourage modern theatre, the Ministry of Culture proclaimed 1991 the 'Year of Theatre' and sponsored international and national conferences and performances. The objectives of the 'Year of Theatre' were to increase the audience; to exchange productions among domestic and foreign companies; to open new performing spaces. For Korean theatre, the 1980s were a decade of struggle to attract audiences in the South and to create new works in the North. The two governments are beginning to allow relations between the two Koreas, and in the distant future it may be possible again to speak of one Korean theatre. It is urged that theatre people in the South and the North cast aside ideological differences to exchange theatre productions. Recently troupes from eastern Europe have performed in Seoul (for example, in 1991 the Leningrad Bolshoi Drama Theatre and the Wybrzeze Theatre of Poland) and Seoul theatre artists welcomed the visit of a director of Korean descent from Kazakh in the USSR, a happy result of the lessening of political tensions in the world.

Genres

Hahoe pyŏlsin-gut

Literally, 'shamanic ritual of Hahoe'. The well-known folk masked play, formerly performed once every ten years as part of *pyŏlsin* ritual activities by farmers in Hahoe village, Kyŏngsangpukdo Province, South Korea. Its masks are refined in their carving and old for, unlike other forms of Korean masked dance drama, it was not required that the masks be burned at the end of each performance.

Kkoktu kaksi

Traditional puppet theatre which is largely humorous, dealing with the corruption of Buddhist monks, domestic problems and immoral officials. During the performance, a puppeteer manipulates a single puppet at a time as he delivers lines and sings songs to the music. The puppet, called *kkoktu*, is easy to construct. Into the carved wooden or papier-mâché head, the main stick of the puppet, a 1 x 2 in piece of light wood, is wedged. A rectangular main body frame of light wood is attached a few inches below the neck of the puppet. The upper horizontal bar of the frame forms the shoulders to which arm sticks are loosely fastened, enabling them to be manipulated from below by strings attached to the upper portion of the arms. Appropriate costumes are then fitted to the puppet. Traditionally, a puppet theatre company was made up of six or seven artists: three or four puppeteers and three musicians who played the small gong, an hourglass-shaped drum and a Korean oboe. Three melodies are associated with the puppet play: 'Kutkŏri', 'T'aryŏng', and 'Yŏmbul'.

Kkoktu kaksi, traditional Korean puppet theatre.

Ogwangdae

Literally, 'five performers'. The generic term for several traditional masked dance plays (*SANDAE-GŬK*) unique to Kyŏngsang-namdo province in the southwest of South Korea, especially the towns of T'ongyŏng, Kasan and Kosŏng. The term probably refers to ritual performance to the deities in 'the five directions'. The plays are generally made up of five scenes.

P'ansori

A one-person, folk, sung narrative, often called an 'operetta' in English translation. The solo performer, originally a man but often a woman today, is accompanied by a seated drummer (*kosu*) who plays the double-headed barrel drum (*pug*). The singer-actor's performance includes three theatrical elements: singing (*sori*), dialogue and narration (*aniri*), and acting and pantomime expressing joy (*ballim*). The performer may also employ gestures (*ch'umsae*). Of these elements, singing is the most important. The narrative is so composed that dialogue alternates with songs, so that the singer-actor need not sing continuously. The professional's voice is notably hoarse, a quality that is aesthetically desired and is the result of years of training and performing. Performers memorize scripts and performance can last several hours. *P'ansori* is still popular today.

Pyŏlsandae

Those traditional masked dance plays (*SANDAE-GŬK*) that are performed in villages of central Korea, near Seoul. Literally, 'separate stage performance', the term indicates folk performances 'separated' from the original, now defunct, masked plays of the Seoul court. The *pyŏlsandae* from Yangju town, about 15 miles northeast of Seoul, is one of Korea's major cultural treasures. Performances are given several times a year; that celebrating Buddha's birthday on the 8th day of the fourth lunar month is the most splendid. The entire town is lit up with colourful lanterns and the nighttime performance lit by torches lasts until dawn. The playing area is an open field at the foot of a hill, with the costume room (*kaebokch'ŭng*) installed at one side. Musicians playing transverse flute, two-stringed fiddle, hourglass-shaped drum, barrel drum and two fifes, take positions at one end of the circular playing area while the audience stands or sits at the other end. Actors make their entrances and exits through two doors in the costume rooms. A momentary pause in the action indicates a change of scene. The language is frank, the down-to-earth colloquial conversation of country people. Actors perform more than a dozen types of dances: including 'Yodaji', 'Kopsawi', and 'Kkaeki' dances. The faces of the masks are made of curved sections of large, dried gourds. Exaggerated features are glued and painted to the surface. No old masks of this theatre exist since they are burned as part of the religious ceremonies marking the end of each performance.

Sandae-gŭk

The literal meaning, 'mountain or hillside ritual', may be interpreted as indicating either a formal performance, that is, one given on a high stage, or a folk performance that uses a mound of earth for a stage. Now a term which broadly includes most forms of traditional masked dance drama in Korea (none today are performed on a built stage, however). They are folk forms preserved by local performers through oral tradition, and performed as a rule for ritual and ceremonial occasions specific to each village or area. Important regional varieties of masked drama are: OGWANG-DAE, PYŎLSANDAE, T'ALCH'UM and YARYU.

Shingŭk

Literally, 'new performance', in contrast to traditional theatre, within the context of South Korean theatre (the term is not used to describe North Korean theatre, although perhaps it could be). In general, all theatre that is recognizably cast in the mode of Western 'literary' or high theatre. This includes Western 'literary' plays (classic and modern) in Korean translation, plays by Korean authors written under the influence of Ibsen, Shaw, Beckett or other Western models, Stanislavskian and Brechtian acting styles, as well as proscenium theatre buildings and an audience of educated elite. Ideologically, shingŭk implies modernity and Western values (democracy, individualism, socialism and so on), as well as Korean nationalism. Most new theatre and drama is created today in Korea within this theatrical milieu.

T'alch'um

Literally, 'masked dance', the generic term for traditional masked dance plays (SANDAE-GŬK) originating in the towns of Pongsan, Haeju and Kangnyŏng in the northwest, presently in North Korea. Pongsan t'alch'um is especially noted for its poetry, songs, witty dialogue and punning. Pongsan masks are relatively small and portray grotesque faces. No longer performed in the North, this theatre has been preserved in South Korea by performers who escaped to the South during the Korean War (1950–53).

Yaryu

Literally, 'field play'. Masked plays performed in towns in South Kyŏngsang province near Pusan are called yaryu, referring to the outdoor nature of the performance. Like OGWANGDAE, the plays are short with four or five scenes. An example is the four-scene yaryu play performed at Suyŏng village. Performance consists of two parts, a procession followed by the mask play. The procession involves singing, dancing and exorcistic ceremonies. Both players and villager audience march together from the village well to the performing area. Eleven masks were employed for the performance of Suyŏng yaryu.

Bibliography

Oh-kon Cho, Korean Puppet Theatre: Kkoktu Kaksi, East Lansing, Mich., 1979, and Traditional Korean Theatre, Berkeley, Calif., 1988; Hae-ch'un Ch'oe, Sandae, Pusan, 1988; Sang-su Choe, A Study of Korean Puppet Play, Seoul, 1961; J. Kardoss, An Outline History of Korean Drama, New York, 1966; Korean ITI (ed.), The Korean Theatre: Past & Present, Seoul, 1981; Korean National Commission for UNESCO (ed.), Korean Dance, Theatre, and Cinema, Seoul, 1983, Traditional Performing Arts of Korea, Seoul, 1974, and Wedding Day and Other Korean Plays, Seoul, 1983; C. H. Kullman and W. C. Young (eds.), 'Korea', in Theatre Companies of the World, vol. 1, Westport, Conn., 1986; C. Mackerras, 'Theatre in the Democratic People's Republic of Korea,' Asian Theatre Journal 1, 1, Spring 1984; Ministry of Culture and Information (ed.), Masks of Korea, Seoul, 1981; In-sob Zong (ed.), Plays From Korea, Seoul, 1968.

LAOS

The population of this Southeast Asian country bordering on Thailand, Cambodia, Burma and Vietnam is comprised primarily of Lao peoples who are closely related to the Thai. The artistic traditions of the four million national Lao are shared by the 13 million Lao living in northern Thailand. Three kinds of performance are important: (1) proto-theatrical, indigenous forms; (2) court forms which since their 14th-century inception have emulated Khmer-Thai models; and (3) modern, popular genres created during the 20th century by combining folk forms with elements from popular Thai theatre, especially *LIKAY*.

Proto-theatrical, indigenous forms

These forms can be divided into three categories according to the functions they serve: (1) storytelling; (2) courting; and (3) curing. The format of the performance and the personnel needed devolve from the function.

Sung storytelling, *lum pun*, is an old, now rare tradition in which a male chanter, accompanied by a *kaen* (bamboo panpipe) musician, sings *Jataka* (tales of Buddha's previous lives), local epics or historical tales. One popular story is the defeat of the Lao kingdom of Wiangjun by the Thai in 1827. The stories, told over one to three nights, are in *glawn*, a verse form with four lines to a stanza, seven or more syllables to a line, and using specific tones from the tonal Lao language for set words. The singer is called *MAWLUM* (*maw* 'expert'; *lum* 'melody derived from word tones'). In *lum luang* the singer acts out all the parts, changing his costume and movement for each character. Other performance forms which relate to storytelling are *an nungsu* ('reading a book') in which men read tales from palm-leaf manuscripts during wakes and the sung recitation of *Jataka* tales or the delivery by Buddhist priests of sermons, *tet*. All are solo, male genres which tell a story.

It takes two to flirt; hence, the forms that relate to courting customs involve a male–female dialogue. *Pa-nyah* is a courting game in which boys and girls engage in a sung poetic dialogue, testing each other's wit and skill. A more theatrical form which alternates a male and female voice is the popular *lum glawn* presented at temple festivals and family celebrations. *Kaen* playing accompanies two professional singers who use memorized passages of poetry, improvising the order according to the needs of the presentation, or compose new verses in performance guided by the constraints of the poetic tradition. Performance begins about 9 p.m. with the male singer praising the beauty of the woman. It intensifies as she admits a reciprocal attraction, but fears betrayal, and concludes shortly before dawn when the pair sorrowfully part. Rhythm and musical scale as well as content of the poetry help create the different moods of the 'affair', and dance interludes (*fawn*) break up the singing. The charismatic singers may address the suggestive verses to audience members of the opposite sex, rather than their partner. Courting poems (*glawn gio*) have contributed heavily to the theatrical repertoire of *lum glawn*.

Performers customarily learn their art by studying music and poetry with a *mawlum* or a Buddhist monk. Many performers come from families that have a tradition of singing. The form may be called by a different name in each area of the country, but the pattern and personnel are constant. *Lum ching choo* ('competing for a lover') is a related courting form in which two males seek the hand of one lady. The courting forms customarily involve a member of each sex, and a contest of wits characterizes the subtle, procreant struggle of the sexes.

Curing is the aim of *lum pee fah* ('sky spirit singing'), in which old women contact this powerful, benevolent spirit to counteract illnesses caused by lesser sprites. Ecstatic dance, spirit possession and oracular statements about the identity of the disease-producing spirit are customary.

Predominance of females in this form may be evidence of the importance of women as spirit mediums in pre-Buddhist, indigenous ritual, a pattern repeated in Burma in *nat kadaw* (literally, 'spirit wife', that is female medium). In Laos, men are the storytellers, but women dance divination, healing and spirit rites.

Court forms

Court forms of dance theatre were established as Lao kings copied customs of powerful neighbouring monarchs. Tradition holds that Cambodian (Khmer) court dance, along with the *Ramayana* and *Jataka* repertoire were introduced to Laos by Prince Fa Nguan in 1353. During the 14th century the Lao kingdom of Lan Sang ('Million Elephants') was established and in this time the Khmer monarchs with their troupe of female wives-dancers were the epitome of potent kingship in the region. Keeping up with the Khmer meant establishing female court dance with movement and repertoire modelled on Khmer practice. The Lao kings were never as rich as the rulers of Angkor. Nor could the Lao compete later in the 15th century with Thai rulers who, first at Ayutthaya and later in Bangkok, emulated Khmer practice (see Cambodia and Thailand). Just as Lan Sang in the early period aped Ankgor, the small courts established by partition in 1700 – Luang Prabang, Wiangjun and Chapassak – imitated Thai models: Thai female court dance LAKON FAI NAI, male masked dance drama KHON and shadow play NANG yai were taught and performed at court. The Lao chose not to alter the forms: the Royal Lao Ballet of the 1960s in Luang Prabang included only female dancers, the best of whom had trained in Bangkok. Rather than staging full dance dramas like the Thai and Cambodians, this smaller court favoured solo and small-group dances.

Modern, popular forms

Drama which involves multiple performers playing characters in an extended narrative is largely a phenomenon of the last sixty years, occurring first in Lao-speaking areas which are a part of Thailand. Thai LIKAY troupes began touring to these northern provinces in the 1920s, and soon local Lao groups started mixing *likay* features with indigenous ideas. From *likay* came flashy costumes, wing-and-drop scenery, repertoire and stock character types;

from *lum pun* came *kaen* playing and *mawlum*-style singing. This mixed genre came to be called by different names, including *likay lao* ('Lao-style *likay*') , *mawlum moo* ('group *mawlum*'), *mawlum plun* ('spontaneous *mawlum*'), *lum moo* ('group singing'), and *lum luang* ('sung story').

Miller found two variants developed in the 1950s most popular during his fieldwork in the 1970s. *Mawlum moo* was more comic and added lute and Western drums to the *kaen*, while *mawlum plun* performance was more serious in tone and traditional in musical accompaniment. The staging, musical focus and repertoire, consisting of *Jataka* stories, Thai legends and Lao historical tales, were common to both forms.

Performances generally take place on temporary outdoor stages about 30 x 15 ft. Electric bulbs hang above the wooden stage providing light for the nightlong performance. Scenery mounted on bamboo poles represents general locales such as a court, a forest or a town. Immovable microphones, which make the singing audible to the audience standing or sitting in the open air, are the focal points of the performance and the slight staging of action that is attempted never takes the actors far from one.

A troupe averages twenty or so members. Thousands of performers are part of such troupes in Laos and northeast Thailand. Since the 1970s these forms have increasingly shown the impact of Western popular culture – rock music and miniskirted go-go girls becoming standard.

A form of Thai shadow theatre, NANG talung, has been adapted by Lao living in Thailand to create NANG DALOONG. This shadow theatre appeared in the north as early as 1926, when amateurs began performing the Thai version of the *Ramayana* to the accompaniment of xylophones, finger cymbals and drums. Currently troupes perform Lao tales as well as stories from the Thai repertoire and they incorporate *kaen* playing and *mawlum*-style singing to win local audiences.

Laos proper tends to be more conservative than the Lao-speaking area of Thailand to the south. Here proto-theatrical, folk forms prevail, and theatre proper is less developed. The court forms evolved with Khmer and Thai influence. It is in the areas where Lao arts have freely interacted with Thai theatrical stimuli that a unique Lao-speaking theatre has emerged in the last fifty years.

Everywhere singing skill remains the prime requisite for a good performer, and acoustics, rather than dramatic factors, govern the staging. What is heard, not what is seen, matters most to Lao theatre-goers.

Genres

Mawlum

The term, which means 'expert singer', is applied to at least eighteen different types of song forms, epic recitations and dramatic genres of Laos and northeast Thailand. One of the oldest genres, *lum pun*, consisted of the singing of a *Jataka* story by a male singer to *kaen* (panpipe) accompaniment. The dramatization of other stories borrowed the instrumentation and singing style of this form. Proliferation of dramatic forms using *mawlum* singing has taken place in the last fifty years under the influence of Thai LIKAY. Professional (as well as amateur) troupes enact stories drawn from the *Jataka* repertory or Thai and Lao legends. Actor-singers perform on a raised stage before a painted backdrop. In modernized versions drums and electric guitars may mix with *kaen* accompaniment. Actors specialize in a line of business. Major roles include: a hero (*pra ek*) and heroine (*nang ek*), secondary male and female characters (*pra rawung, nang rawung*), a king-father (*paw payah*), a queen-mother (*mae payah*), a villain (*poo rai*) and clown (*dua dalok*). Servants, monkeys, ogres, hermits, soldiers and ghosts are added as the particular plot demands. Costuming mixes traditional garb with more modern dress.

Nang daloong

A shadow-puppet theatre that plays stories drawn from the *Ramayana* or Thai and Lao legends to musicial accompaniment that mixes *kaen* and other percussion instruments with MAWLUM singing. Small leather puppets are moved before a cloth screen. Although the form ultimately derives from the WAYANG tradition of Malaysia and Indonesia, multiple manipulators have replaced the single puppet master of *wayang* and the ritual import of the theatre is gone.

Bibliography

R. de Berval, *Kingdom of Laos*, Saigon, 1959; J. R. Brandon, *Theatre in Southeast Asia*, Cambridge, Mass., 1967; C. Compton, *Courting Poetry in Laos*, DeKalb, 1979; T. Miller, 'Kaen Playing and Mawlum Singing in Northeast Thailand', PhD diss., Indiana University, 1977, and, "Laos", in *New Grove Dictionary of Music and Musicians*, ed., S. Sadie, New York, 1980; S. J. Tambiah, *Buddhism and Spirit Cults in Northeastern Thailand*, London, 1970.

MALAYSIA

This Southeast Asian nation has a population of 18 million people of Malay, Chinese, Indian and Negrito heritage. The small Negrito population has music, dance and trance performance. The Malays have had a lively performance tradition for at least the last 500 years, and their theatre shows a distinctive reworking of pan-Southeast-Asian patterns. The Malay genres, discussed here, fall into four categories: (1) proto-theatrical customs; (2) Hindu–Islamic folk and court genres; (3) popular, urban theatre of the last century; and (4) modern drama developed since World War II. The overseas communities from China and India largely transplanted practices from their homelands after British colonial rule began in 1824, and the many performances of these groups may be better understood in the context of those cultures. Notable genres found among the Chinese community are glove- and shadow-puppet plays; Hokkien, Teochew and Cantonese opera; and spirit mediumship. Common genres of the South Indian community include *bharata natyam* dance, Karnatic music and the yearly Thaipusam festival, in which Hindu devotees pierce their bodies with metal skewers and dance in processions.

Proto-theatrical customs

As throughout Southeast Asia, proto-theatrical customs, including epic recitation, poetry games and spirit mediumship, contributed much to Malay theatrical development. The singing of epics, *penglipur lara*, is still found. Stories are based on the *Ramayana* or Malay legends (*hikayat*). In a variant called AWANG batil, the performer accompanies himself on a brass bowl. Early storytelling traditions, like this, may have paved the way for the shadow-puppet tradition.

Songs and games that involve dialogues provide a base for folk theatricals. *Pantun* singing is poetry in which singers present memorized or newly composed octosyllabic lines in quatrains. The first two lines create a sound pattern and the final lines reveal the true message. Similar poetry is associated with courting games throughout the Malay world.

Call and response singing forms another base for Muslim theatricals. For example, *dikir barat* is a village entertainment, originally based on Sufi chanting (compare Thailand, LIKAY and Indonesia, DIKIR). Two teams of men present improvised texts: a leader inaugurates the song, and the group repeats his line. Verses can be satiric or ribald, and mimed interludes are included. *Boria* is a comic sketch followed by a call and response processional.

Though epic and poetic traditions may generate the techniques, the deep need for theatre may rise from the employment of performance to communicate with spirits. Music, dance, and drama are generally practised in the context of seasonal ceremonies and rites of passage when spirits must be placated, and, hence, performances of all types normally open with mantras addressed to the spirits. Clear links with spirits occur in trances in which dancers become the medium for spirits. In ULEK bandul, danced by seven girls and two boys, the featured female dancer communicates with the rice spirit; in *ulek meyang*, a man holding an areca-nut root enters into a trance to the chant of a male chorus; in *tari labi labi* a turtle spirit enters the dancer. *Kuda kepang* is a possession rite in the states of Johore and Selangor in which men possessed by horse spirits perform amazing feats: fire-walking or eating glass, fire or hay. And in *dabus* performers may dance *silat*, the martial-arts dance, then pierce their skin with knives, without pain or lasting wounds. The later two forms may be related to genres found in Indonesia.

Probably the most important of these trance-related forms is *main puteri*, which supposedly receives its name – 'play of the princess' – from the legend that it was first established to cure a melancholic princess. In performances, which are found in Kelantan and Trengganu states, two male curers (*bomoh*), using trance dances, diagnose and then treat patients, usually females. Since illnesses are believed to be caused by spirits, the main shaman, *to'puteri*, allows the spirits to enter his body. His assistant, *to'mindok*, plays a *rebab* to facilitate his trance. The assistant converses with the spirits who speak through the *to'puteri* to reveal the cause of illness. Clownish, refined and rough spirits may alternately possess the medium's body making the form a lively entertainment. Once the illness is identified the cure may be effected by a performance of the related female dance drama, MAK YONG, discussed below.

Likewise, major celebrations required performances to keep good relations with the spirits. *Puja pantai* ('ritual of the shore') is a three-day ceremony involving various performances meant to placate sea spirits. *Berjamu* are exorcisms whereby those in danger of angering spirits could regain their favour. For example, puppetmasters in the WAYANG siam ('shadow theatre') or *mak yong* dancers require such rituals every few years. Such ceremonies are focused at a spirit audience, but also entertain human audiences.

Folk and court theatricals

Some early folk or court theatre forms developed in old Malay states, like Patani, that are now part of Thailand. Hindu and Buddhist thought emanating from Indian and Indonesian sources affected this area, hence the *Ramayana* and *Jataka* (Buddhist birth tales) are standard stories. Indonesian influences seem to be especially important for understanding theatrical developments in Malaysia. Currently scholars hypothesize that the similarities in story patterns and theatre genres in island and mainland Southeast Asia and the variance of these from standard Indian models is due to the influence of the Indonesian Sriwijaya kingdom over both areas during the 7th–13th centuries. Sriwijaya's power declined, but its arts including female dance and puppet theatre prevailed in the courts of the new mainland states emerging in what is now Malaysia and southern Thailand. Islamicized re-interpretations of dance and puppetry may have again flowed from Indonesia in the 15th–16th century, carried by a network of Muslim traders and Sufi mystics. More recent emigration from Indonesia has established Javanese,

Sumatran and Buginese communities in Malaysia with their arts intact. Many centuries of intercommunication have created similar, but distinctive theatre genres in Indonesia and Malaysia today.

The puppet tradition and the female dance drama remain relatively strong in the northern part of Malaysia in states that bordered on the former Malay kingdom of Patani. NANG talung, shadow-puppet theatre of southern Thailand, and NORA, the masked dance drama, developed in the Patani area, perhaps as early as the 12th century. A tradition of female court dance was extant in 1611–13, when the European traveller Peter Flores visited there. From Patani *wayang siam* shadow theatre was supposedly brought to neighbouring Kelantan state by a female *dalang* ('puppetmaster'), about 400 years ago, and court dance and female dance drama in Kelantan and Trengganu states developed under Patani influence as well.

Wayang siam (see also Indonesia, WAYANG) of the east coast is probably the oldest of the three puppet genres currently found in Malaysia. The most important traditional theatre of the country, it depends on a solo puppetmaster (*dalang*) who controls all the puppets, speaks the dialogue and delivers the narration. He also regulates the accompanying musicians. This puppet art, which has strong ritual and exorcistic aspects, focuses on *Ramayana* material and was very popular on the east coast prior to this generation. Of special significance is the clown puppet, Pak Dogol, a local variant of the pan-Southeast-Asian god-clown. Legends hold that Pak Dogol first brought the shadow play to men from heaven, and puppeteers treat this figure with special ceremony.

Traditions are changing in current *wayang siam*. Puppets, traditionally made of water-buffalo hide, may now be fashioned of translucent plastic. Performances that traditionally took place all night, now generally last from only 8.30 p.m. to 12.30 a.m. Kerosene or electric lamps have largely replaced the flickering flames of old. Formerly, performances were given in the context of life-cycle ceremonies and were paid for by a single sponsor, but most current performances are played for a paying audience that comes specifically to attend the show. The added importance of clowning is highlighted in the proliferation of new clown characters in current performances. Wright noted two major groupings of *dalang* in the late 1970s – those who tend toward more traditional practice, as represented by Hassan Omar and Ghani Jambul, and those who incorporate new clown characters, puppets in modern dress and tunes from pop music, as represented by Abdullah Baju Merah and his emulators.

Wayang malayu, a more recent import to Mayalsia, is a variant on the *wayang kulit purwa* of Central Java, and was created by Javanese who have settled in Malaysia. Meanwhile *wayang gedek* is a variation on the *nang talung* tradition of Thailand, and also a recent import. All these puppet genres face significant competition from modern media and puppeteers face considerable odds in keeping their sponsors and audiences.

Scholars debate the age and origin of the female dance drama *mak yong* which thrived in the Kelantan palace in the first quarter of this century. It appears that the form originated in the folk tradition, was elevated to a court art by a princely patron, and returned after his death with newly acquired polish to the folk sphere. From 1912 to the 1920s the prince in Kota Baru, Temenggong Ghaffar, supported a *mak yong* troupe which carried out performances as we currently know them. The largely female troupe adds two male clowns, who serve shaman-like functions. The women performed opening dances and stories in dance-drama style playing all the refined male and female roles while the males played the clown roles. The three major roles are the refined hero, the heroine and the clown.

The form corresponds to female dance drama of Thailand, Indonesia and Cambodia. Three sources probably contributed to its genesis: *nora*, female court dance, and trance medium rites. The Thai *nora* thrived in Patani and is still found to some extent in Kelantan. Though *nora* supposedly began as a three-person male genre, similar stories, character types and auras of magic power animate it and *mak yong*. Likewise, *mak yong* relates to the female court dance adopted by Malay kingdoms, perhaps in emulation of ritual court dancers of the Indonesian archipelago. *Asik*, the graceful female dance of the Patani palace, shared movement, costume and dance features with *mak yong*. *Mak yong*'s clearest connection is with trance-medium forms: *ulek bandel*, like *mak yong* calls for a configuration of seven women and two men, and *main puteri* creates business for *mak yong* troupes. Current *mak*

A female shaman dances the role of Prince Suton in an exorcistic performance of *nora*, in Kedah state, Malaysia.

yong clowns often double as the shaman-like *bomoh* of *main puteri*. At the conclusion of a seance they will recommend that as a cure the patient play out the hero's part in a *mak yong* story with the assistance of experienced actresses.

Perhaps drama therapy is the original impulse behind many Southeast Asian female dance drama forms. Women who had healed themselves under the guidance of *bomoh*-clowns, turned their experience to curing and entertaining others. Since the forms were ways of communicating with powerful spirits, aristocrats might have desired groups of medium-wives who could maintain a firm connection with the other world. Such a model may lie behind these forms and explain the evolution of female drama in Burma, Cambodia and Thailand.

Popular theatre

Modern genres are developments of the more economically developed, urban west coast of Malaysia where traditional theatre forms have largely been abandoned. *BANGSAWAN* developed at the end of the 19th century in emulation of touring Indian

Parsi troupes that performed Indian, Arabian and Shakespearian tales in the 1870s. By 1885 Mohammed Pushi had created the first local Malaysian *bangsawan* company in Penang. *Bangsawan* played for commercial audiences, and actresses and actors mingled freely on the stage. Groups found audiences everywhere in the Malay-speaking world, touring to Java, Sumatra and Borneo (Kalimantan) in Indonesia and influencing Thai theatre. The troupes were actress-centred, used Western-influenced drop-and-wing sets and bright costumes, and created orchestras comprising both indigenous and Western instruments. Troupes improvised stories to enthusiastic audiences. *Bangsawan* flourished until World War II, but then declined; fighting with communist insurgents in the postwar period prevented groups from reforming. In 1972 a government-sponsored troupe was recreated, and later PESBANA (National Bangsawan Art Organization) was founded.

As *bangsawan* passed, a new more Westernized theatre appeared. SANDIWARA, popular into the 1950s, for the first time used a written script, amateur actors and a director. Arising first in schools, it appealed to Westernized, educated viewers. Authors treated historical and contemporary themes. Though *sandiwara* plays still appeared on a mixed bill with dance dramas and pantomimes, the productions were more realistic than *bangsawan* offerings. *Sandiwari* represents a transitional link between popular *bangsawan* and present-day modern drama.

Courses in drama are offered at a new national school for the arts in Kuala Lumpur, where contemporary theatre director-critic Krishen Jit and traditional theatre scholar Gulam-Sarwar Yousof are professors, and at Malaysia's two major universities – the University of Malaysia and the University of Science in Penang. Government support of performance includes competition prizes and sponsorship of festivals.

Modern drama

Who wrote the first scripted Malay spoken drama and when, are questions yet to be resolved. But the consensus is that the schoolteacher and playwright-director, Shahrom Hussain, was among the pioneers of the early modern-drama period (1940s to early 1960s). All but two of his plays are *purbawara*: plays based on the exploits and achievements of historical and mythical personages. Written mostly by students, teachers and journalists with a literary bent, *purbawara* plays re-enacted the glory and might of the Malay sultanate on stage. Offstage, however, Malay power had been progressively dissipated by British colonial rule. By highlighting the contrast between ideal and reality, *purbawara* plays contributed to post-World-War-II Malay nationalism.

Immediately after independence in 1957, some *purbawara* playwrights reversed course, and critically scrutinized the orthodox feudal values glorified by their predecessors. The spirit of rational inquiry was manifested, for example, in Shahrom's later works, particularly in his emblematic play, *The Hunchback of Tanjung Puteri* (*Si Bongkok Tanjung Puteri*, 1961), which introduced the blatantly ugly, aggressive but probing anti-hero, Si Bongkok. The poet, playwright and journalist Usman Awang elicited the modern rebel, garbed in the guise of the 15th-century warrior-'traitor', Hang Jebat, in the intense and compact verse drama *The Death of a Warrior* (*Matinya Seorang Pahlawan*, 1964; trans. 1988). Usman's Jebat, presented in the play as the champion of truth and justice, was repeatedly resurrected as the archetypal rebel in the 1970s theatre.

In 1963, Mustapha Kamil Yassin, a teachers'-training-college lecturer and later a university professor, pronounced that, thematically and aesthetically, poetic dramas clung too much to the past. In the next decade he launched a vigorous campaign promoting the 'dynamic', Western-influenced realistic drama, called *drama moden*, 'modern drama'. His mostly comic plays, of which the best is *Brick House, Nipa House* (*Atap Genting Atap Rembia*, 1963) are crowded with social types and reconcile conflicting forces in post-independent Malaysian society: rural versus urban values, old versus young generation, Malay versus Chinese. Mustapha and his colleagues, Usman Awang, Awang Had Salleh, Aziz Jahpin and A. Samad Said, drew the newly urbanized Malay literati towards acceptance of *drama moden*.

The ethnic riots of May 1969, which gripped the major cities of peninsular Malaysia, undermined the optimist themes of current *drama moden*. The profound impact of this event justifies recognition of a 'post-1969' perspective on the arts, including theatre. Some Malay playwright-directors set about

Chinese scarf dance in Kuala Lumpur.

reviewing the Malaysian past, in order to better understand the distrubing present. Significantly, political trauma did not provoke Malay theatre practitioners to take a radical course as they did elsewhere in the region. One of the earliest results of these steps towards 'self-apprehension' was Noordin Hassan's *It is Not the Tall Grass that is Blown by the Wind* (*Bukan Lalang Di Tiup Angin*, 1970), partly allegorical and replete with oblique references to May 1969. Nonlinear and surreal, it uncovered the ironies and ambiguities that lurk behind the mask of harmony, peaceful co-existence and progress in multi-ethnic Malaysian society. Through an inter-action between traditional and Western-modern performance modes and aesthetics, the piece strove to mediate between past and present in Malay experience. Audiences thought the play con-fusing and out of a deep need to communicate to the many, Noordin simplified his next two plays,

Five Braided Pillars (*Tiang Seri Tegak Berlima*, 1973) and *Door* (*Pintu*, 1976) without compromising on his multichannelled approach to performance, nor on his mission to inculcate a Malaysian identity.

What was to be called *teater kontemporari*, assumed the proportions of a movement by the mid 1970s, with the rise of playwright-directors Syed Alwi, Dinsman, Bidin Subari, Johan Jaafar and Hatta Azad Khan, a performing arts graduate of the Malaysian University of Science in Penang. Syed's *Tok Perak* (1975), the first multimedia event in Malaysian theatre – and arguably the best play of the era – juxtaposed folk theatre events, images from film and slides, and an intricately textured realistic theatre. The mixed-means performance was an analogue of the protagonist's condition: the middle-aged street medicine seller, Tok Perak, is trapped in the transition between tradition and modernity, in the end choosing the latter.

The troubled and ruminating self was also exalted in sensational theatrical images by the University of Malaya graduate, Dinsman, the only genuine cult figure of 1970s theatre. Dinsman created startling personae – Jebat in *Jebat* (1973), Adam in *Not Suicide* (*Bukan Bunuh Diri*, 1974), and Ana in *Ana* (1976) – who echoed a young generation restive with traditional values, but uncertain about the modern persuasion. Dinsman's partially absurdist performances, found the measure of the post-book television generation, and were frequently performed in the 1970s.

Nevertheless, the unceasing experimental zeal of contemporary theatre began to wear down the audience. Simultaneously, a resurgent Islam in Malaysia caught contemporary theatre practitioners unawares and defenceless against attacks that they were harbouring the sins of polytheism and nihilism in their plays. For most of the 1980s, the Malay avant-garde attack was blunted and transferred to local English drama, as demonstrated by the performances of K. S. Maniam's *The Cord* (1984) and *The Sandpit* (1991), Kee Thuan Chye's politically controversial *1984 – Here and Now* (1985), and Leow Puay Tin's *Three Children* (1988). Noordin Hassan continued to experiment, exploring an Islamic mode of theatre in *1400* (1981), and *Don't Kill the Butterflies* (*Jangan Bunuh Rama-Rama*, 1983).

Stirred by the threat of Malay political and religious divisiveness, other Malay-language theatre practitioners have turned to the presumably exemplary period of nationalist struggle of the 1940s and show a self-conscious empathy with popular *bangsawan* performers who also fought for race and country. This nostalgia is directly depicted in Normah Nordin-Najib Nor's musical, *My Nostalgic Song* (*Nostalgia Laguku*, 1989) and in Zakaria Arifin's *Opera Players* (*Pemain Opera*, 1989). Popular theatre, including *boria*, is resurrected by Noordin Hassan in *Son of Penang* (*Anak Tanjung*, 1987) and Sayed Alwi in *The Servant of God* (*Hamba Allah*, 1989). Perhaps unexpectedly, some of the deepest and most troubling questions about the Malay psyche in political and moral crisis are posed by these senior playwrights.

Genres

Awang

Narratives related by a storyteller (*penglipur lara*) include *awang batil* in which the performer adds

musical accompaniment by playing on a brass bowl and *awang selampit* where he plays a bowed lute. In other genres different types of drums (*kendang, rebana*) may be used. *Awang* corresponds to accompanied storytelling genres in other Southeast Asian countries, such as Vietnam and Indonesia.

Bangsawan

The most important commercial Malay theatre of the past hundred years. *Bangsa*, 'race', and *wan*, 'noble', suggest court connections, although this is a theatre of the commoner. In *bangsawan* the female star (*seri pangung*) was featured, though hero (*orang muda*), clown (*ahli lawak*), queen (*permaisuri*), king (*raja*) and villainous genie (*jin arfit*) were also important roles in the 30- to 60-member troupe. Islamic tales of Amir Hamzah were popular in the early period. Eventually stories drawn from Indian, Arabian, Western, Chinese and contemporary or historical Malay sources were played. Performances might contain 20 acts and could last all night or be shown in shorter segments over several evenings. The refined hero would triumph by the play's end, and the wicked genie inspired by Islamic popular culture would be vanquished. For accompaniment, indigenous musical ensembles combined with piano and saxophone. Proscenium stages with wing-and-drop sets and spectacular effects were the norm. The clever improvisations of actors (especially clowns) from the scenario, the lavish costumes and interludes by lovely female dancers packed houses. *Bangsawan*'s decline after World War II is attributed to the rise of films, which attracted audiences with similar story material. *Bangsawan* inspired other Southeast Asian popular theatres, such as Thai *LIKAY* and Indonesian *SANDIWARA*.

Mak yong

A female dance drama, popularized in Kota Baru in Kelantan state in the early part of this century, executed by female performers and two clowns. The major roles are the *mak yong* (queen), *mak yong muda* (princess), *pak yong* (king) and the *pak yong muda* (prince). Ogres, hermits and attendants round out the tale. Presentations start with opening rituals (*buka panggung*), followed by a tune for the lead actress, which culminates in the first dance ('Honouring the Rebab'). Then a scene in a palace will define the problem which takes the hero questing in the wilds. Among the traditional 12 plays performed in *mak yong* are *Dewa Muda* and *Dewa Pechil*, named after their heroes, and the Thai *The Conch Shell Prince*, called in Malaysia *The Child of Raja Godang*. The orchestra includes the featured *rebab*, two *gendang* drums, gong (*tetawak*), and sometimes oboe (*serunai*) and horizontal gongs (*canang*). About 30 tunes are found in the repertoire, associated with specific types of character or action. Dialogue is improvised within set constraints. Though lacking its former glory, *mak yong* is currently preserved by troupes like Seri Temenggong, named after the princely founder of the art. The form can be compared to Cambodian LAKON KABACH BORAN, Indonesian BEDAYA and LEGONG, and Thai LAKON FAI NAI.

Sandiwara

A theatre genre popular from the 1930s through to the 1960s. It shows its Western antecedents in its dependence on a written script and use of a director. It rose in Malay schools and colleges and often took historical incidents as its theme. Actors were amateurs who were guided in the melodramatic performance style on a proscenium stage by a director. *How Kassim Was Cured* (1938), which lauds the benefits of modern medicine, may have been the first scripted Malay *sandiwara*. Shahrom Husain was a major author of the category of historical (*purbawara*) plays. His *Hunchback of Tanjong Puteri* (1956) is about a pirate who opposed the British takeover of the country. Contemporary plays are a second category, and scripts often deal with evils of the urban modernization. An example is Kalam Hamidy's *To Keep Alive the Maize in London before Cooking the Rice*, considering intercultural problems of a Malay student in love with an English girl. Mustafa Kamil Yassin was another major writer of this genre. A literary approach to script and Shakespearean and Greek models are apparent.

Ulek

Trance dances of Malaysia include *ulek bandul* (*bandar*) in which an entranced girl encircled by seven girls and two boys communicates with the rice spirit. In *ulek meyang* a male enters trance to the chant of a male chorus. Such forms have comparable features to SANGHYANG and *sintren* in Indonesia.

Wayang

A general term for puppet performance. Three types of shadow-puppet performance are found in

Malaysian *wayang siam* figures sporting modern dress.

Malaysia today: *wayang siam*, *wayang malayu* (or *jawa*), and *wayang gedek*. *Wayang siam*, despite its Siamese name and origin, is the unique Malay tradition: with about 350 *dalang* (puppetmasters) currently performing in Kelantan, it is probably the most important traditional theatre genre in the country. *Wayang malayu* is a local variant of Javanese WAYANG *kulit purwa* of Indonesia, and *wayang gedek* is a Malay variant of NANG *talung* shadow theatre of Thailand. These last two genres have more limited appeal.

Wayang siam is a shadow form in which a single performer manipulates all the puppets, presents the dialogue and controls a *gamelan* orchestra composed of musicians playing six drums (two *gedang*, two *gedombak*, two *geduk*), two large hanging gongs (*tetawak*), two small horizontal gongs (*canang*), oboe (*serunai*) and metal clappers (*kesi*). Performances are based on Southeast Asian versions of the *Ramayana*, called *Cerita Maharaja Wana* (*The Story of Maharaja Ravana*) in Malaysia. But most performances will be invented episodes, called 'branch stories', that improvise new events around the givens of this central story. Tales from the Panji epic and local histories are sometimes presented. The Thai headdresses worn by major characters and opening incantations containing mixed Javanese–Thai–Malay vocabulary recapitulate the apparent migration of the form. The troupe performs inside an enclosed stagehouse while the audience watches the front of the screen. Puppets are stuck into a banana log resting along the screen bottom when not dancing or fighting. The performance opens with a musical prelude, then come the set scenes of the *dalang muda* ('young dalang') section which allow apprentice performers to gain needed expertise. The student will also need to gain magical skills to attract audiences before his master initiates

him. Fully trained *dalang* perform the later part of the performance, where the story of the evening is improvised within the structural requirements of the genre. In recent years performers, challenged by modern media have attempted various innovations, shortening the performance, using electric light and sound equipment, and putting additional emphasis on clown characters. The rise of Islamic fundamentalism has led to a ban on *wayang* and all theatre in some parts of the country which *wayang*, as other traditional theatres, must face if it is to survive.

Bibliography

Usman Awang, 'The Death of a Warrior', tr. Rahmah Hj. Bujang, *Asian Theatre Journal*, 5, 2, Fall 1988; L. Fernando (ed.), *New Drama One: Edward Dorall, K. Das, Lee Joo For*, Kuala Lumpur, 1972, and *New Drama Two: Patrick Yeoh, Lee Joo For, Edward Dorall*, Kuala Lumpur, 1972; K. Jit, 'Toward an Islamic Theatre for Malaysia: Noordin Hassan and *Don't Kill the Butterflies*', in *Asian Theatre Journal*, 1, 2, 1984, and 'Malaysia', in *New Grove Dictionary of Music and Musicians*, ed. S. Sadie, New York, 1980; N. Nanney (Nur Nina Zuhra), An Analysis of Modern Malaysian Drama, Shah Alam, 1992, and 'Evolution of a Hero: The Hang Tuah/Hang Jebat Tale in Malay Drama', *Asian Theatre Journal*, 5, 2, Fall 1988; M. T. Osman (ed.), *Traditional Drama and Music of Southeast Asia*, Kuala Lumpur, 1974; M. Sheppard, *Taman Indera*, Kuala Lumpur, 1972; P. L. A. Sweeney, *The Ramayana and the Malay Shadow Play*, Kuala Lumpur, 1972, and 'Professional Malay Storytelling', in *Studies in Malaysian Oral and Musical Traditions* 8, Ann Arbor, Mich., 1974; Tan Sooi Bing, 'Bangsawan of Malaysia', in *RIMA*, 23, 1989; B. Wright, 'Wayang Siam', PhD diss., Yale Univ., 1980; Gulam-Sawar Yousof, 'The Kelantan Mak Yong Dance Theatre', PhD diss., Univ. of Hawaii, 1976.

NEPAL

The kingdom of Nepal, with a relatively small population compared to its two great neighbours, India and China, can boast of the *mani-rimdu*, a fascinating form of dance drama.

Mani-rimdu is a form of dance drama popular among the Sherpa. It is acted by Buddhist monks as a seasonal three-day ritual held in the confines of Buddhist monasteries, such as Thami and Tengpoche, in the Khumbu valley of northeastern Nepal. Spectators assemble from nearby villages to participate in the ceremony.

The main purpose of *mani-rimdu* is to reinforce traditionally held beliefs in Buddhism and to depict the superiority of the religion over the ancient Bon religion, the tenets of which are denigrated in numerous ways in the performance. Performances are held in the month of May at Thami and in November at Tengpoche.

Mani-rimdu is a colourful outdoor spectacle which is remarkable for the grandeur of its backdrop, Mount Everest and the high valleys and peaks which surround it. It is thought to have had its origins in Tibet, which is considered to be the ancient homeland of the Sherpas, and may have been inspired by *cham* and *lha-ma* dance dramas, relatively obscure forms of performance of that remote region.

The open space of the courtyard (*cham-ra*) which is about 30 ft square, located in front of the temple (*gomba*), is used for the acting area. A flagpole with ritual objects at its base stands at the centre of the area. Dignitaries and ecclesiastical authorities are provided with special seats apart from the laity. The temple and monastic buildings are used for the dressing room and for entrances and exits.

The first day of performance is known as the 'Life-Consecration' rite and is intended to bless the entire ceremony. The festivities of the opening ceremony begin around 1p.m. Ritual acts and prayers are accompanied by special music and activities which have symbolic significance but little entertainment value.

The second day is regarded as the most enjoyable and significant part of the drama and laymen-spectators dress in their finest apparel for the occasion. The performance is divided into 13 separate units consisting of simple group dances and two short improvised comic dramas. The events are punctuated by the distribution of ritual foods and rice beer. Usually each of the events lasts approximately 20 minutes, partially because of the breathlessness of the dancers who tire easily under the strain of wearing heavy masks and costumes. The second day begins around 10 a.m. and continues until early evening. At the end on the second day the spectators gather in the courtyard to dance and sing folk songs until the early hours of the morning.

On the third day, rituals are performed to symbolize the final destruction of evil forces in the Khumbu valley. The chief abbot of the monastery presides over the rituals and his presence helps to ensure the sanctity of the *mani-rimdu* and to symbolize the supremacy of Buddhism as a means of protecting the laity from harm during the coming months until the next public festival.

The monks who dance and act *mani-rimdu* wear a variety of colourfully painted and designed masks representing deities, mythological characters and human beings. The masks are larger than life-size and weigh about five pounds each. The colour and cut of the costumes have symbolic meaning. The language of the performance is somewhat obscure which enhances the otherworldly quality of the event.

Musicians accompany the performers and play an important role in the progress of the action. Depending on the structure of the monastery, the musicians sit near the acting area or on the balcony above it. 10-ft-long brass horns are among the more unique musical instruments. A trumpet fashioned from a human thigh bone, brass trumpets, cymbals and drums are also part of the musical ensemble.

Modern theatre and drama in Nepal is primarily confined to Kathmandu, the capital. Little is known or has been written about the subject. Given Nepal's small middle class, modern theatre and drama are not likely to become a driving force in this remote region.

Bibliography

M. H. Duncan, *Harvest Festival Dramas of Tibet*, Hong Kong, 1955; M. Fantin, *Mani Rimdu of Nepal, the Buddhist Dance Drama of Tengpochi*, New Delhi, 1976; L. G. Jerstad *Mani-Rimdu, Sherpa Dance-Drama*, Seattle and London, 1969; J. K. Manandhar, *Nepal, Legend and Drama*, Banepa Wankhya, 1982.

OCEANIA

The Pacific region is customarily divided into three groupings based on linguistic, ethnic and cultural features: Melanesia, Micronesia and Polynesia. At the same time certain features bind together performances of this area as a whole. Firstly, a combination of music, dance and poetry and improvised comic skits are, traditionally, significant arts – rather than theatrical pieces in which actors portray another persona in an extended narrative. Secondly, the expertise of artists is high, although few are full-time, professional specialists in these small, geographically isolated communities. Thirdly, much performance takes place in the context of festivals, life-cycle ceremonies or communal feasts which celebrate the social life of the community. Large groups of dancers, most often of a single sex, participate: hundreds of dancers may join in a running dance at a New Guinea sing-sing ('communal feast'), long lines of women or rows of men perform unison dance movement in a Fijian meke, a Hawaiian hula or an ur on the Micronesian island of Ifaluk. This tendency is not new: in the 1790s, just 16 years after the first European landfall, George Vancouver described a Hawaiian performance in which 200 women danced in astounding unison.

The talents of singing and dancing are traditionally thought to be common to all rather than reserved to a few. Precision and uniformity of the group are cultivated in preference to self-expression on the part of a solo performer. Songs are often thought to be the gift of the spirits, communicated in dream or vision to the composer-choreographer. Performance is an activation of group cohesiveness.

The social change wrought by contact with the West and Christianization in the 19th and early 20th centuries was profound. In almost every area arts as previously practised, were deprived of their social context and attacked as 'heathen' by early missionaries. In some cases the indigenous language was largely replaced by that of the colonial power and audiences lost the ability to understand both text and context of traditional performance. Only in the last 30 years have religious festivals and government holidays increasingly become a venue for traditional performance due to altered church policy and growing local political autonomy.

Current performances are reflections of contemporary culture, showing the changing tastes of the indigenous peoples and interplay with performance generated for tourist entertainments. Music, dance and dramatic performance clearly maintain traditional elements, but the adaptation of European musical instruments is common. Dance movements, once indigenous to a specific island, can be found throughout the region. Often performances have changed from outdoor, nightlong, torchlit entertainment at communal feasts, to two-hour presentations on electrically lit, proscenium stages. Current attempts to create 'professional' companies of full-time, paid performers that emphasize individual creativity or solo dancing, have come in the wake of Western influence and urbanization. Governments feel the need to articulate an ethnic image to both a national and an international audience, by creating a national company (Papua New Guinea, the Cook Islands and Fiji).

Though artists often state that their aim is to recapture the forms which existed prior to European contact, they recognize that the context is dramatically changed. What they seek is a re-affirmation of the arts as the arena for exploring and defining community values. In this context, current performance becomes a modern political statement documenting the search for indigenous alternatives to the pervasive pop culture and mass media of the First World. These exciting experiments show that dance and drama remain important modes of integrating the societies concerned.

A brief survey of the three major areas can help clarify some of the variations and reveal continuities or disjunctures with the past. Two strains of performance can be noted: first, forms which develop out of indigenous music, dance and mime traditions and, second, forms which derive from Western models. The former include traditional dances and dance mimes. The latter include religious plays presented by the Christian churches and modern drama which has been introduced through the schools. A growing tendency of religious and modern drama to reintegrate traditional music, dance and themes shows the current blending of these two strains.

Melanesia

Melanesia includes Papua New Guinea, Irian Jaya, Vanuatu (New Hebrides), New Caledonia and the Solomons. These islands are largely inhabited by people of considerable linguistic and cultural diversity who cultivate democratic societies in which leadership is achieved rather than inherited. Leaders, called 'big men' in Pidgin, traditionally held feasts involving mass killings of pigs (which represented wealth) with concomitant public donations to bind supporters to them. Performances of music, dance and clowning were a regular part of such feasts.

Dance mimes are common throughout the Melanesian area. While Micronesians and Polynesians often act out fishing or hunting from the human viewpoint, Melanesian performance tends to adopt the perspective of the prey. Masks are common throughout the region, and are often thought to represent spirits. Drama is thus an important mode of understanding the others, animal and spirit, that round out the world. This mimetic bias makes drama an important feature of Melanesian society to the present.

The relative autonomy and variety of ethnic groups have resulted in a wealth of distinctive artistic choices within Melanesian societies. This brief survey can only mention selected genres and hint at the creative usage of elements like time, space and costuming. Many of these performances, linked to previous religious beliefs, are now extinct.

One performance that used time expansively was documented by F. E. Williams in the 1930s. The Orokolo of Papua conducted a cycle of ceremonies that took decades to enact. The cycle culminated in dancing with huge masks from the men's club house to the sea amid general rejoicing. Modernization and social change has since then enervated the men's organizations by undercutting their myths, and this ceremonial cycle is now defunct. The performance systems of other Melanesian groups have been substantially altered by changes in religion and social practices that have ended or greatly modified initiation rites, traditional warfare and secret societies.

The elaborate feather headdresses, penis coverings, leaf or tapa coverings, body painting and tattooing that are found in Melanesian performance show the human body in unique splendour. Masks of wood, gourds, bark-cloth and other natural materials are often presented in performance and ritual. The spatial usage is often striking: societies which use trees as stages (as in a New Ireland form of women's song) and allow masked images suddenly to materialize in front of a hut from the surrounding jungle (as in duk-duk dances of the Tolai of New Britain) show impressive use of the environment. On Vanuatu's Pentecost Island men dive from high platforms only to be caught by vines attached to their feet, a performance which is said to commemorate how a woman foiled a persistent suitor by sending him plummeting to death while she saved herself by this ruse.

The entire village can be involved in a performance, blurring the line between audience and performers. In a Papua New Guinea sing-sing, the whole community may join in the nightlong dancing. Perhaps as a result of this, the dance steps tend to be simple, consisting of a running hop-step or a side-to-side swing for women. Nevertheless some divisions between performers are significant. Men and women often dance in separate groups, reaffirming the importance of sex differentiation, and only a few performers tend to take central roles, often by wearing the masks that are the centrepieces of the event.

Exactly who takes the central roles varies significantly, but in New Guinea it is often initiated men. Many performance objects – bull-roarers, gongs, masks – are the property of a village men's club. Traditionally, boys learn the method of using these objects, said to represent spirits, as part of their initiation into manhood while separated from their mothers. Via performance, initiated men display their superior understanding of the spirit world to the audience of women and children.

In New Guinea performers may gain prime roles by making certain sacrifices. Gell noted that, among the Umeda, men who wore the main masks of a bowman and cassowary (a running bird) were required to undertake difficult fasts. In other areas, blood-letting ceremonies or beatings are inflicted on those learning songs or steps. Bought with pain, the songs and dances were apt to be remembered. Suffering has a part in the *gisaro* performance of the Papuan Kaluli peoples: singers try to make the audience members cry by making songs that remind people of their dead. The emotionally aroused audience members then seize torches and brand the singer, and the skilled performer is known by his wealth of burns the morning after a presentation. Such performers who suffer can, perhaps, be compared to 'big men' within the political sphere. Performance is democratic in that it is open for all men to participate, but those who sacrifice more gain the admiration of the community.

Performance in Melanesia serves recognized social functions. The conical masks of the *duk-duk* society of New Britain's Tolai people are 'spirit' manifestations, worn by initiated members of the group to frighten and control those who flout social mores or gain members' anger. Currently they may appear in less charged situations like a government celebration. Funeral rites in New Ireland, the buying of a higher grade in a secret society in Vanuatu, the dedication of slit gongs in the Solomon Islands, or the marking of male initiation ceremonies or a killing in battle in traditional Papua New Guinea, all require performances. In each case, something irreversible happens and the performance notes the new status. Currently a wedding or local festival ceremony might be celebrated with dances borrowed from these older rites.

In this century church theatricals were introduced by missionaries. Since then they have absorbed some of the energy of earlier men's house mimesis. Plays about the martyrdom of early missionaries were common and choirs and marching bands were widely introduced. Current officials are more open to incorporating traditional dance and music in the context of church events.

Modern drama is an innovation dating from the late 1960s, introduced by European teachers and reworked by local artists to inculcate social change. Students at the University of Papua New Guinea studied creative writing and literature under Ulli Beier, a German, in a programme aimed at creating political and cultural awareness. Students wrote plays which agitated for independence and portrayed the conflict between traditional values and those inculcated by Western education. An early play, Leo Hannet's *Ungrateful Daughter*, placed emphasis on text, and lent itself to realistic staging. It showed an adopted Papua New Guinea girl rejecting the values of her European parents in favour of indigenous standards. Produced in Port Moresby and abroad, this play advocated independence from colonial rule which was achieved in 1975. JOHN KASAIPWALOVA's *Kanaka* showed the problems a villager encounters returning to his hamlet from a sojourn in the city. John Kaniku's *Scattered By the Wind* dealt with the disruptions that Christianity, modern schooling and government regulations introduced into village life. Authors, a number of whom were subsequently to take prominent posts in the Papua New Guinea government, found writing was a way to make political statements with relative impunity.

In New Caledonia as well, modern drama was a seedbed for political activism. The first modern theatrical experiment was *Kanaka*, given at an exhibition entitled Melanesia 2000 in 1975. The text drew on pre-Christian ceremonies as recorded by the missionary-anthropologist, Maurice Leenhardt. The sound and light performance presented by actors-dancers moving to a prerecorded tape showed the invasion of the islands by missionaries, slavers and merchants as Kanak, local tribesmen, struggled to carry out death ceremonies for the old chief and prepare for the election of a new leader. The performance – created by Jean Marie Tjibaou, who spearheads anti-colonial activism, and George Dobbelaere – was a rehearsal for Kanak attempts to reassert control over the nickel-rich French colony.

As independence has come to some areas of Melanesia, more experimentation with traditional models has begun. Recent work in Papua New Guinea de-emphasizes text and initiates more lyrical, myth-based presentations which involve music, traditional dance and masks. These tendencies are evident in the plays of ARTHUR JAWADIMBORI, head of the Papua New Guinea National Theatre in Port Moresby, and the work of the Raun Raun Theatre in Garoka whose work has been influenced by GREG MURPHY, an Australian director. These troupes have been funded by the Papua New Guinea government since 1975. In 1980 the former group presented *Eberia*, a rock opera by William Takaku, and the latter a dance-mask play using visual and music elements of different ethnic groups to present John Kasaipwalova's *Sail the Midnight Sun*. Both performances were seen at the 1980 Pacific Arts Festival, a quadrennial event which since its inauguration in 1972 has prompted some of the best theatre productions in the pan-Pacific area. Both plays took indigenous myths and explored new theatrical avenues. The sound–movement emphasis of these productions may be a sign that the text-based modern drama of the 1970s is returning to more indigenous mime for a base.

Satire is a developing genre in Papua New Guinea. Indigenous clown traditions are evoked by the Raun Raun players who play improvised comedies in the open air at village gatherings. Political satire is exploited by NORA VARGI BRASH, author of *Which Way Big Man* (1977) which mocks the pretensions of the new government elite. Radio drama is another lively outlet for writers in Papua New Guinea, a leader in modern theatrical activity in the Pacific.

Micronesia

Micronesia is composed of the Federated States of Micronesia (Yap, Truk, Ponape and Kosrae – formerly the Carolines), the Mariana Islands, Marshall Islands, Beleu (Palau), Kiribati (formerly Gilbert Islands) and Nauru. The people are related to Malays and speak Austronesian languages. Societies acknowledge hereditary chiefs, in moderately hierarchical systems. Matrilineal patterns can be seen in traditional society and this may contribute to the importance of girls and women as performers. Research and documentation of the performing arts of this region is not extensive, but based on the information currently available, the following generalizations seem to hold true.

For Micronesians the beginning is the word: song texts are considered the most important element in a presentation. Songs are usually delivered in conjunction with group or solo dances, and most gestures are abstractly decorative. Mimetic role-playing exists, but is not emphasized. Poetry, as represented in the writings of Micronesian authors published in *Mana*, a journal of arts issued by the University of the South Pacific in Fiji, can be considered a livelier genre than mimetic drama.

Impersonation is found in: (1) representation of creatures, often a frigate bird or iguana; (2) mimes of fishing, canoeing, battling or lovemaking; and (3) possession trances in which a spirit enters a performer. Possession, *per se*, in performance is rare, yet the nature of some dance movements – the quivering movements of the frigate bird and the convulsive movements of the iguana – are possible evidence of a venerable link between possession and dance. Both animals are associated with old religious practice.

Dances are performed sitting or standing. Canoe paddles or sticks are used as props. Musical instruments are traditionally few and the human voice the major accompaniment. In group dances one or two dancers may parody the movements of the group, adopting a clown persona. Performances occur in village assembly halls or outdoors. Traditional contexts for performance include religious worship and female initiation rites, courting practices (including lovers' trysts) and group celebrations such as performance contests between villagers, entertainments at village feasts, and welcoming visitors from another island at the beach.

Islands such as Beleu, Guam and Ponape, which have served colonial governments as capitals, exhibit less of the traditional performance practices that were noted by early European visitors. Marching bands, church choirs, and 'Micronesian' dances of relatively recent vintage are common. More removed islands, like Ifaluk and Kiribati, have more conservative performance practice. On both islands danced poetry dealing with themes like the sea, spirits and love remains of great significance.

In Kiribati, traditionally, the composer-choreographer role has shamanic overtones, for he often receives songs from the spirit world in trance and then teaches these *ruoia* ('dance-songs') to villagers. One or two dancers may clown during performance, thereby distinguishing themselves from the group. A woman is often the dance leader. This practice may come from older sitting dances called

Artists

Beamer, Winona Kapuailohia (1923–)
Member of a large family devoted to preserving and extending Hawai'ian dance and music. She brought traditional hula to international attention after World War II and helped establish Hawai'ian hula and chant as legitimate academic subjects at Kamehameha Schools in Honolulu.

Brash, Nora Vargi
After studying at the University of Papua New Guinea she began writing plays, including *Which Way Big Man* (1977), a satirical examination of political pressures and Westernization in current government circles.

Jawadimbori, Arthur
Author of poetical plays like *Sun*, he was appointed head of the Papua New Guinea National Theatre in Port Moresby in the late 1970s.

Kasaipwalova, John
Playwright-author of Papua New Guinea. His epic poem tracing the allegorical genesis of the country, *Sail the Midnight Sun*, was dramatized by Raun Raun theatre for the 1980 Pacific Arts Festival. An earlier work, *Kanaka*, showed the problems a villager encounters returning to his hamlet from a sojourn in the city.

Murphy, Greg (1945–)
After teaching at Garoka Teacher's College he became the founding director of Raun Raun theatre leading the group 1975–84 and serving as a consultant in subsequent years.

Petelo
A popular *fa'aluma* comedian in Samoa. Admired for his ability to mimic human and animal traits, his perfect timing and unusual modesty. His talent in social satire is evident in his daring parody of Prince Philip, which he performed during the latter's visit to Samoa in 1970.

Topolinski, John R. Kaha'i
A leading young teacher of male Hawai'ian hula, and recipient of many prizes for his group's dynamic performances. He has been influenced by his studies under Mary Kawena Pukui, a leading figure in the renaissance of Hawai'ian chant and music after their languishing in the 1950s and 60s.

te bino, which feature a female and have movements said to be inspired by the flight of birds. In *ruoia* some performers will suddenly cease the group dance and emulate a frigate bird, associated with old religious belief. Small girls have prominence in some dances. The special status of pre-pubescent performers in societies as distant from each other as Bali (see Indonesia, SANGHYANG) and Kiribati may indicate this is an old practice common to Malayo-Polynesian groups.

On Ifaluk, Burrows reports old religious chant-dances. In *gapengpeng* the single-sex, seated chorus calls on the god to take possession of a dancer. In *ur*, a group standing dance done by either sex, dancers emerge from the group to 'become' a frigate bird. Women are also notable performers on Ifaluk. Their compositions, called *bwarux*, are primarily solo dance-songs meant for private performance by the female for her lover as sole audience. The association of these songs to female fertility may explain their traditional performance for female initiation ceremonies which mark a girl's first menstruation, rites honouring male visitors from other islands and ceremonies to welcome shoals of fish in the harbour.

Performance in Micronesia generally promotes group solidarity under the direction of the composer-choreographer, who may himself be thought to be directed by spirits. A performer may emerge from the group, primarily when the signs of the old god – possession or bird impersonation – occur. Traditionally performers do not seize the group focus for self-expression, but to act out the spirit world. Individual love songs, in theory at least, are for the ears of the loved one alone.

Polynesia

Polynesia is divided by specialists into two separate groups: West Polynesia includes Tonga, Samoa, Uvea (Wallis), Futuna, Niue, Tuvalu (Ellice), Tokelau, and Fiji; and East Polynesia includes the Society Islands (Tahiti), Marquesas Islands, Austral Islands, Mangareva, Tuamotu Islands, Cook Islands, Easter Island, New Zealand and Hawai'i. In the Eastern area, as Kaeppler notes, movement of the lower body, especially hips and knees, is a strong feature of dance, while this is not the case in the Western area. Performance in Polynesia traditionally involves music and dance interpretation of poetic texts that are rich in metaphor and allusion. Rather than decorative dance, as in Micronesia, the Polynesian tends to use the hands and arms to signify selected words of the text via an elaborate gestural language. Movements of the legs and hips are abstract and relate to the rhythm of the music. The dancer is a storyteller, delivering the narrative in his own persona and not by becoming the characters in the text. Mimetic interludes between these poetic dance-songs can include short skits. Men, or sometimes older women, improvise dialogue on pre-arranged themes, usually satirical in nature.

Polynesian societies were traditionally class-stratified and genealogy determined rank and power. Texts often were in praise of important individuals and presentations were at events that reiterated the power of the aristocracy. Solo chants were often reserved by and for the noted chanter who might him- or herself be a high aristocrat. Large-scale performances needed extensive resources. Performance specialists included composer-choreographers and dancers trained under them.

Kaeppler notes that performances were largely a re-affirmation of social structure: large groups of men, women or occasionally men and women might perform dances in unison with the choreography directed toward the most important viewers, that is the chief and his guests. Placement of dancers in the configuration might also reflect the hierarchy of rank and age, and obedience to the composer-choreographer was likewise strict. Satirical interludes seem to have served as a release from these customary constraints, and impromptu dialogue and the free use of space, language and subject matter delighted the audiences. A brief consideration of some Tahitian, Samoan, Hawai'ian and Fijian performance gives examples of traditional and contemporary performance in Polynesia.

Perhaps the most elaborate performance system reported by early European visitors was that of the *arioi* on Tahiti. This group worshipped Oro, the god of fertility, and as part of his service became specialists in dance-chant. Poetry was a major element in the performances of dramas enacting serious myths. Clowning and female actors are reported. Their 'lewd' dance which included much hip and pelvis articulation, the raising of skirts and facial contortions distressed Europeans. The sexual licence of members, who did not marry and were normally required to kill any children that they might bear, caused the missions effectively to outlaw the sect. It remains difficult to assess the parameters of pre-contact practice based on the fragmentary evidence remaining.

In current Tahitian practice as reported by Moulin, hip movement is still important. However churches now foster the dance as a mode of bringing congregations together. As in Hawai'i where the indigenous language has been largely replaced by a European tongue, the emphasis on poetry is greatly diminished and the gestural language is more limited. In contrast to the past group dances, virtuoso solo or couple dances receive focus. These are indications that the current societal values may vary significantly from former ones. Emphasis on decor and spectacle was noted by Victor Carrell in recent Bastille Day competitions. Since their inauguration at the end of the last century Bastille *fêtes* have become the major dance event in Tahiti, and the audience is apt to be treated to innovations such as that prepared by Coco, a major troupe leader, who had his dancers fall on their stomachs and mime swimming in the ocean in a 1985 piece that departed freely from traditional dance.

One group which presents a traditional version of dance is the Cook Islands National Theatre under Ota Joseph. The group is traditional in its preference for precision and group dancing. Still, theatricalization of folk culture is evident in their work. In addition to traditional group standing and sitting dances, the troupe stages mimes of kite-flying, coronation ceremonies, and dance dramas such as one exploring the coming of the Bible to the Cook Islands. These works, based on careful research, are conscious attempts to recycle traditional material in modes that will suit modern audiences.

Examples of how the comedy works in the total context of Polynesian traditional performance can be seen in Samoa. Performers of *fale aitu* ('house of the spirit') are called *fa'aluma*. Traditionally a chief might take along a pair of these clowns as part of his dance group when he went travelling to other islands. Supposedly, spirits (*aitu*) could be invoked by the best performers, and, under the protection of these ghosts, the *fa'aluma* might be allowed to mock the highest chief. The clown skits occurred between dance-chants by the larger ensemble of dancers. Performances that mix group dance by 50–200 performers and such clowning are now usually presented at church fairs. Skits show traditional comic figures, such as transvestites or homosexuals and Europeans, or explore Samoan economic difficulties. PETELO, from Western Samoa, is a noted exponent of this form.

In Samoa, church theatricals on religious themes are also popular, especially on children's day, White Sunday. Experiments in biblical opera, such as Ueta Solomona's *Jeptha* presented at the 1972 Pacific Arts Festival, are products of this tradition. In recent years there has been some experimentation in Samoa in modern spoken drama by authors like John Kneubuhl.

In Hawai'i the power of performance is in the poetry. Chant or *mele* was the single most important cultural expression, chronicling history, genealogy and emotion. *Mele* are divided into two categories: ones that have no musical accompaniment, are performed solo and may be on a religious theme (*mele oli*), and ones performed with dance movements, sometimes accompanied by musical instruments (*mele hula*). Divine inspiration was often considered the mode whereby the chanter (*kumu*) gained his songs. Male hula was associated with worship in the temples and martial-arts training (*lua*). Use of weapons and a strong physicality mark male style. Female hula was a more graceful art. Hips and feet elaborate the rhythm while the hands interpret the lyrics through mime and stylized gesture-language. Supported by the nobles, training took place under the teacher in a school (*halau*) which housed a temple to the goddess of dance, Laka. Students trained in religious dances, which were accompanied by the drum (*pahu*), and in dance that told the achievements of nobles, praised gods or recounted historical epics, and which were accompanied by the gourd (*ipu heke*). Comic dance and improvisa-

Chanters beating the ipu (gourd drum) accompany a hula in Hawai'i. Hula is widely popular among Hawai'i youth.

tion provided comic relief. In 1819 traditional religion was outlawed and public performance of hula largely discouraged, until King David Kalakaua (1836–91), a noted musician and patron of the arts, encouraged both revival of traditional chant-dance and innovations which incorporated Western instruments. Films, tourism, television and adopting English as the major language led to *hapa haole* ('half white') versions of hula in this century. Since the 1970s a strong revival of Hawai'ian chant and hula has been spearheaded by many Hawai'ian artists such as WINONA KAPUAILOHIA BEAMER.

Fiji lies on the border of Melanesia and Polynesia culturally and ethnically. It exhibits the strengths derived from each of these areas in its theatrical arts. Traditional dance and the highly formalized *kava* drinking ceremony are to be found at church fairs. The traditional *meke* (dance-songs) include war, club, spear, fan and other standing and sitting dances. The most important member of a group is the composer (*dau ni vucvu*) who may receive inspiration from the sprite-like *veli*, spirits who teach dances with quick unpredictable movement, or stillborn children, who teach more sedate songs. Other tunes are composed without such spirit helpers.

The Dance Theatre of Fiji is an innovative group under Manoa Rasignatale, a former pop star who began researching his island heritage after the 1972 Pacific Arts Festival. Performances of the company re-enact village life. Top-spinning contests or the spirit-inspired creation of a *meke* may be acted out. This theatrical presentation of indigenous practices is comparable to the choices of Cook Islands National Theatre and conforms to folkloric theatre-dance companies that have emerged in many Third World countries. The Dance Theatre has found popularity both at home and abroad.

Modern drama is written and presented at the University of the South Pacific in Fiji by Joe Nacola. In Hawai'i, too, university theatre programmes have resulted in a wealth of modern spoken drama and given rise to groups like the professional Honolulu Theatre for Youth, which plays to child audiences, and the Kuma Kahua players dedicated to the production of new plays by playwrights who live in Hawai'i.

It is notable that in Polynesia, as in Melanesia, spoken drama is being utilized to vent criticism of Western culture or remoulded to reflect the cultures that make up the multi-ethnic and multi-talented population of the Pacific basin. Film and television are becoming areas of experimentation. Films written and directed by Papua New Guineans are beginning to be made and the islands are experimenting with television programming. Pacific universities have distinctive features, including choirs that perform traditional dance-chant (University of the South Pacific) and give degrees for courses of study that focus on Asian Theatre or Pacific Dance (University of Hawai'i). The excitement that permeates the annual Merrie Monarch hula competition in Hawai'i, Bastille Day performances in Tahiti, and the pan-Pacific fervour that erupts as each island prepares to send dances and dramas to the South Pacific Arts Festival shows that the arts are changing, and remain vital to the peoples of Oceania.

Bibliography

U. Beier, *Voices of Independence: New Black Writing from Papua New Guinea*, New York, 1980; M. Browning, *Micronesian Heritage: Dance Perspectives*, 43, Autumn 1970; E. Burrows, *Flower in my Ear: Arts and Ethos of Ifaluk Atoll*, Seattle, Wash., 1963; B. Dean, *South Pacific Dance*, Sydney, 1978; N. Emerson, *Unwritten Literature of Hawaii: The Sacred Songs of the Hula*, Washington, 1909; A. Gell, *Metamorphosis of the Cassowaries: Umeda Society, Language and Ritual*, London, 1975; T. Henry, *Ancient Tahiti*, Honolulu, 1948; A. Kaeppler, 'Movement in the Performing Arts of the Pacific Islands', in *Theatrical Movement: a Bibliographical Anthology*, ed. R. Fleshman, London, 1986; G. Kanahele *Hawaiian Music and Musicians*, Honolulu, 1979; V. Kneubuhl, 'Traditional Performance in Samoan Culture', in *Asian Theatre Journal*, 4, 2, 1987; G. and S. Koch, 'Kultur der Gilbert Inseln', in *Encyclopaedia cinematographica*, Göttingen, 1969; J. Layard, *Stone Men of Malekula*, London, 1942; J. Moulin, *The Dance of Tahiti*, Papeete, 1979; D. Oliver, *A Solomon Island Society*, Cambridge, Mass., 1955; S. Sadie (ed.), *New Grove Dictionary of Music and Musicians*, New York, 1980, entries on 'Melanesia', 'Micronesia', 'Pacific Islands', 'Polynesia'; E. Schieffelin, *The Sorrow of the Lonely and the Burning of the Dancers*, New York, 1976; A. and M. Strathern, *Self-Decoration in Mount Hagan*, London, 1971; V. Tausie, *Art in the New Pacific*, Suva, 1980; C. Thompson, 'Fijian Music and Dance', in *Fijian Society Transactions and Proceedings*, 11; F. E. Williams, *The Drama of Orokolo*, Oxford, 1940; Sister Francis Xavier, 'Dancing and Singing in the Gilbert Islands', in *Mana*, 1, 2, December 1976.

PAKISTAN

The modern states of Pakistan and India were created in 1947. Pakistan's two parts, East Pakistan and West Pakistan, were separated by more than 1000 miles of Indian territory. In 1971 East Pakistan became the independent state of Bangladesh.

The history of the theatre of modern Pakistan is the history of the Urdu-language theatre which started in 1853 with the composition of Mirza Amanat's *Inder Sabha* performed at the court of Wajid Ali Shah of Oudh in the city of Lucknow in north central India. Pakistan is an Islamic state and like neighbouring countries of the Middle East has not, for religious reasons, condoned or encouraged the production of plays. It is not surprising that theatre in this region of the subcontinent has been relatively slow in developing and only recently became a part of the cultural heritage of the people. In Pakistan, there was no classical tradition on which a theatre could be built and what folk heritage there may have been is obscure, except for performances of the BHAND (see India) of the Punjab, recitation of dramatic poetry and the puppet theatre.

Inder Sabha was not intended to be a landmark production but was designed to satisfy the cravings of a lavish court ruled by an extravagant composer-king. The play is in verse and requires musical accompaniment, dance and elaborate costumes to be fully realized. In 1856 the kingdom of Oudh came to an abrupt end when the British deposed the Shah and exiled him to Calcutta. However, for at least two generations after that, actors and musicians of Oudh sang the songs of *Inder Sabha* and kept alive the potential of an Urdu-language theatre.

The next major dramatic activity in Urdu occurred in an entirely different region of the Indian subcontinent when some Parsi entrepreneurs of Bombay, motivated no doubt by economic gain, set about developing a form of theatre in Urdu which was to captivate the public imagination, not only in the whole of India but even in Sri Lanka and Malaysia, as well. Producers such as Pestonji Framji and Khurshidji Balliwalla developed a popular form of theatre known as the 'Parsi musical'. In 1870, assisted by several Muslim poets, they composed Urdu plays which were set to music. After 1880, Raunaq Banarsi, Mian Zarif, Vinayak Prasad Talib, Ahsan Lucknowi, Narain Prasad Betab and Agra Hashr Kashmiri are among the better known writers of Parsi musicals staged by the Victoria Theatrical Company, the Alfred Company and the New Alfred Company.

The plays were designed exclusively to entertain and thus satisfy the taste of audiences of the day. Themes of romantic love, chivalry and generosity, from a wide array of literary sources – Hindu and Muslim classics, history and legends – were elaborated upon in the plays. Even some Shakespearean plays were re-assembled and the characters provided with Indian names while the bard's dialogue was transformed to Urdu verse. Two distinct plot lines – one humorous and the other serious – were made to correlate and interweave in each play.

From the outset, dancing girls were a part of every show. This led to an expression of outrage in 1914 when the New Alfred Theatrical Company visited Lahore to stage Betab's *Mahabharata*, based on the Hindu epic of the same name. The audience reacted negatively to characters with religious names such as Rukmini and Draupadi when they were played by women whom they considered of questionable morals. As a consequence, the company refrained from presenting the show.

Some authors of the time demonstrated a social consciousness by attacking social evils of the day, such as child marriage and the rigidity of the purdah system. Others expressed an interest in political subject matter by addressing issues such as the controversy over the formation of Punjab state and border disputes.

With the development of the film industry in the 1930s, audiences quickly shifted their allegiance to the cinema and many of the most successful companies closed their doors for good and their personnel went into the film industry. Only the smaller groups and minor companies remained as a testament of an active past.

Scattered activity in modern theatre began in the western half of the country soon after independence in 1947 with the formation of dramatic clubs in colleges and universities. The dramatic club of the Government College of Lahore was managed by students under the supervision of interested staff members. At first both Urdu and English plays were presented. The Urdu plays were mostly translations from Western dramas. Some of the plays staged between 1951 and 1957 were *Swan Ran Ka Sapana*, a Punjabi version of Shakespeare's *A Midsummer Night's Dream*, an Urdu version of Gogol's *The Inspector General* and adaptations of one-act plays by Molière. Many of the students who were part of this early activity have since entered the professional field of films and television.

In 1956 the Pakistan Arts Council opened a small theatre in the council building and invited productions by Government College students. For the next three years the citizens of Lahore found an alternative theatre outside the college environment. Among the better-known productions were Priestley's *An Inspector Calls* and Ibsen's *A Doll's House*, both of which were presented in Urdu. After 1960 the production of comedies drew larger and more regular audiences.

In 1964 the Arts Council attempted to turn the Alahamra Theatre into a year-round theatre rather than an occasional place for performance. By 1966 plays were running on a regular basis and a campaign was begun to produce original plays in Urdu. In 1967 the theatre in Lahore was broad-based and had gained considerable momentum.

After independence, theatre in Karachi still clung to the old theatrical traditions inherited from Bombay and Calcutta. Then, in 1950–51, the Osmania University Old Boys produced Khwaja Moinuddin's *Zawal-e-Hydrabad*, a tense drama por-traying the conditions of the Kashmiris under Indian Army rule. The play had touching lyrics and music which helped make it a popular success. His *Naya Nishan* was produced in the same year and gained even greater public recognition; it was banned by the government for probing a sensitive political issue at the very time the Indian and Pakistan governments were attempting to negotiate a treaty over Kashmir.

In 1953 Moinuddin wrote *La Qile Se Lalukhet* which revolved around the trials of a family that had to migrate to Pakistan from India after partition. It was produced in the K. M. C. Stadium and the four-hour drama set a record attendance by drawing nearly 10,000 people. It was later staged in Karachi at the Katrak Hall and ran for 140 performances. Later it played in Lahore, Hyderabad and Mirpurkhas and was revived in 1956 in Karachi and Lahore.

Numerous productions were staged by various groups formed in Karachi between 1952 and 1955. Some of these were supported by the oil companies that encourage dramatic activity under their welfare programme for the benefit of employees. Throughout this entire period the British Amateur Society of Karachi, better known as the Clifton Players, produced a number of drawing-room comedies in English.

In 1956 the Karachi Theatre was formed. It was born of the Theatre Group of the Arts Council headed by Sigrid Nyberg Kahle, German wife of a diplomat, the playwright Khwaja Moinuddin and the actor Zia Mohyeddin, whose work in the film *A Passage to India* and the television series *The Jewel in the Crown*, later gained him world-wide recognition. Productions included Molière's *School for Wives*, *Gas Light*, *Our Town*, *Antigone* and Khwaja Moinuddin's *Lal Qile Se Lalukhet*, among others.

When Ms Kahle left the group to go abroad, the Avant Garde Arts Theatre came into being presenting Urdu versions of Gorky's *The Lower Depths*, Molière's *Perfect Gentleman*, Beckett's *Waiting for Godot* and Coward's *Hay Fever*. Much of the success of the group was due to the work of Meherji and Pervez Dastur, who later broke away from the AGAT and formed The Seekers.

In 1967–68 many of the theatre organizations in Pakistan's cities began to tour the country, much as groups do in India, in order to sustain their activities through revenues earned in the smaller towns of the countryside. During this period, theatre came to the attention of the central government when it exempted plays from paying a small but annoying entertainment tax. Similarly, state awards by the president of Pakistan helped to bring greater national recognition to theatre. Then, too, the period saw many plays published in Urdu, the formation of a number of small semiprofessional theatre companies, and an increase in the number of men and women interested and skilled in theatre, television and film.

Bibliography

M. Aslam Qureshi, *Wajid Ali Shah's Theatrical Genius*, Lahore, 1987.

PHILIPPINES

In this Southeast Asian island nation of 62 million, the tribes that follow indigenous religion retain performance traditions which probably were widespread in precolonial times. The 5 per cent of the population who are Muslim have traditions related to Malaysia and Indonesia, and the 90 per cent who are Christian have theatre forms developed under Hispanic and American colonial influence. The major performance categories are (1) proto-theatrical forms; (2) Islamic dances; (3) Hispanic-influenced theatre genres, and (4) American-influenced forms, including modern drama.

Proto-theatrical forms

In attempts to reconstruct the parameters of early Filipino entertainments, scholars have turned to the performance of the tribes that have not accepted the Christian or Islamic religion. Though performances themselves may have changed in the hundreds of years that Muslim and Christian influences have dominated lowland areas, their categories have probably remained stable. Spirit mediumship, epic recitation, dances and games involving improvised poetry, are widespread in Southeast Asia and part of the common heritage of Malay peoples, including inhabitants of the Philippines. The first European reports noted such forms in the 16th and 17th centuries.

Music and dance are traditionally used for curing, courting, entertainment and rites-of-passage ceremonies. Dances may be abstract or mimetic. Examples of the latter include the honey-gathering dance of the Negritos and the boar-hunting dance of the Igorots. Courting and war dances are widespread. The *pinanyo-wan* ('veiled'), for example, is a wedding dance of the Bontok, in which a boy and girl dance with the boy's foot movements emulating a cock attracting a hen. The *tchugas* ('exorcism') of the Kalinga is a victory dance over ghosts of a slain enemy in which two young men and a priestess re-enact a war dance, whereupon the priestess asks the ancestral spirits to give her the names of glorious headhunters.

Rituals were undertaken by local shamans, called *babaylan* among the Visayan peoples and *cat-alonan* among the Tagalog. Performances were frequently part of curing, and possession trance was common. A present-day example is the Tagbanwa female shaman who, dancing while in trance, communicates with spirits and may be possessed by them.

The singing of epics is found in all layers of Filipino culture, and it may be that Muslim and Hispanic variants are cultural adaptations that allowed older oral narrative practices to continue with a new content. Epics might be sung for one to three nights in celebration of a wedding, at gatherings for guests or as entertainment for villagers. Among the Mandaya, Mansaka and Bagobo, heroes like Agyu, Tuwaang and Ulahingan were praised. *Tutol* are epic songs treasured by the Muslim Magindanao. They tell of the exploits of heroes like Radya Indara Patra, a noble who flies to the palace of the clouds and fights mythical monsters to save his people. Epic singing may also be related to *pasyon*, a chanted narrative of the Passion and other biblical events sung during Lent, and to metrical romances, including the duodecasyllabic line *awit* and octosyllabic *corrido*. The latter are Filipino narratives, written in quatrains and published in the early 19th century. Based on European tales, they gave rise to corresponding folk theatricals.

Games involving dialogue between two or more voices are another indigenous theatrical impulse. In the *badiw* of the Ibaloi a singer improvises riddles in a strict verse form. The chorus repeats the last lines giving the singer a chance to compose the next verse. Performing during ceremonies for the dead, the singer might invite spirit relatives to drink rice wine, praise the host or comment on the properties of the deceased. In *kaharian*, a king (*hari*) makes an accusation – 'You stole the roses from my garden!' – and the accused must improvise a defence or accuse another in quatrains full of riddles and poetic devices. The player who fails to provide an acceptable response is found guilty as charged. Frequently the dialogue games involve a male and a female voice and may be part of old courting practices. As early as 1668 the Jesuit Alzina reported observing *bikal*, verbal jousts in song between boys and girls, each sex amusingly finding fault with the other. The rather functional *pamanhikan* asks for a girl's hand in marriage. One singer represents the groom and the answering voice sets out the demands of the girl. Although cast in game framework, this sung dialogue forms the substructure of indigenous drama, and shows that Filipino performance relates to a pan-Southeast Asian pattern of courting games between male and female groups, found in Cambodia, Laos and Indonesia.

Islamic dances

Muslim performance, believed to have come to the southern Philippines via Borneo, shows similarity to dance and music traditions of the Islamized peoples of Indonesia and Malaysia. Theatrical aspects, however, are little developed. Dances are generally performed in the *kulintang*, a gong-chime ensemble related to the Indonesian *gamelan*. The subtle grace of dancers who may impersonate princesses and slave girls and the curving gestures of the lower arm correspond to the movement of refined characters in Indonesian dance drama. There is some evidence that Muslim sword dances, probably related to Indonesia's horse-trance dance and *dabus*, contributed to the evolution of the Christian *moro-moro* folk theatricals. No evidence links the Filipino *carillo*, the shadow theatre using rough cardboard figures, with the intricately developed shadow theatre of the Malay world. Shadow puppetry in the Philippines, presented since 1879, emulated, perhaps, European experiments, which were themselves shadows of Asian models.

Hispanic-influenced genres

Major theatre traditions that developed during Spanish colonization and Christianization continue to the present. These include (1) religious spectacles; (2) KOMEDYA or *moro-moro*; and (3) ZARZUELA. Spanish and indigenous elements fuse in these forms.

Religious customs including dramatizations were introduced by the Spanish in an attempt to displace folk rituals. Popular performances intended to promote Christianity included the Lenten play (*senakulo*), Christmas theatricals (PANUNULUYAN), the digging for the true cross by St Helena (*tibag*), and the lives of the saints. *Senakulo*, for example, takes its name from the cenacle where the Last Supper took place. Produced during Holy Week all over the Philippines, these plays, which re-enact the death of Christ, may have evolved from the *pasyon* narrative singing. Plays are in verse, and major religious figures maintain slow, decorous movement and declamation. Peter, old and absent-minded, added comic touches, while Mary Magdalene, dancing and seducing her soldier, helped make the action more stimulating. Self-flagellations and real crucifixions of devotees, undertaken in fulfillment of vows, tableaux and processions made performances powerful events in community life. *Senakulo* performances continue to the present, especially in rural areas.

Komedya, the major genre of the 17th to the 20th centuries, is believed to have developed from religious plays based on Spanish models. In 1598 a priest, Vincente Puche, wrote a Latin play presented by schoolboys in Cebu. In 1609 the first play

An Easter-season *moriones*, or *pugatan* drama on Marinduque Island. Longinus is beheaded for his fealty to Christ.

in the vernacular concerning St Barbara reportedly prompted many religious conversions in Bohol. By 1619 there were five-day programmes presenting plays on Old and New Testament events and more recent themes, like the martyrs in Japan. The dramas were rehearsed for church celebrations by the sons of the native aristocracy.

The most famous play was supposedly written in 1637 to celebrate a victory of the local Christians over the Muslim leader Kudarat (Corralat). The event was probably first played out in Cavite province by boys, of whom the one playing the Muslim leader was actually wounded. Fr Jeronimo Perez saw the enactment and was inspired to write on this theme, creating the first play known as *moro-moro* or *komedya*. These are plays, affected by Spanish *comedia* models, centred on the struggle of Christians and Muslims resulting in the marriage of the hero with a princess. Open-air performance at festivals was common and inclusion of clown characters was standard.

Although most scholars trace the form to European models, some counterarguments should be noted. The fight of the boys inspiring the first author could have been a hobby-horse dance, related to the *KUDA KEPANG* trance dances of Indonesia that combine stylized battle with self-mutilation. This argument is strengthened by the fact that some sources cite furious battle dances by six Muslim soldiers at the baptism of a Sultan of Jolo in 1750 as the true source of *komedya*: such dances sound like *dabus*, martial dances still found in Sufi sects of the Malay area. Evidence becomes more convincing if we consider that plots which may involve princesses and heroes marrying after a ritual battle are commonly found after Muslim influence appears in areas as far apart as England, Spain, East Java and the Philippines. The persistence of the name – *moro-moro* ('play of the Moors'), morris dance, morisco – is notable. It is possible that Eurocentric biases are blinding scholars to a significant drama that grew from dances of Sufi mystics and entered the Philippines and other areas with Islamic, as well as Christian, influences.

Likewise, the use of set characters, stylized movement, the popularity of clown characters (*pusong*), the open-air production scheme, and the enactment in the context of a fiesta are features that relate to widespread Southeast Asian theatre practice, not just European models. The belief that

the omission of a *komedya* presentation might cause rain and trouble fits a Southeast Asian use of performance to placate supernatural powers. Perhaps even the puzzling lack of scripts prior to the 19th century may hint that like most Southeast Asian performance, scenario rather than text was the generative principle, and indigenous rhyming improvisation games paved the way for actors to create dialogue. JOSE DE LA CRUZ and his pupil FRANCISCO BALTAZAR were prolific *komedya* authors during the form's heyday.

Late-19th-century, middle-class educated Filipinos gave birth to a more literary theatre. Indoor proscenium theatres lit by gaslight appear from the beginning of the 1800s and become numerous around the end of the century. The Zorrilla theatre (1893) with 400 orchestra seats and 52 boxes was the most noted of these structures. Spanish genres, such as *entremés* ('interlude') and *sainete* (short comic piece written in octosyllabic verse), and Italian operas caught the audiences' attention.

In the 1880s a Spanish actor Alejandro Cubero, the 'Father of Spanish Theatre in the Philippines', and his mistress, actress Elisea Raguer, brought the Spanish-influenced *zarzuela* to the fore. These musical plays on contemporary themes first appeared in the mid 18th century. Spanish remained the language of performance until the United States took over the colony in 1898. By the turn of century *komedya* had retreated to the *barrios* as a folk performance, and Severino Reyes (1861–1942), a Tagalog playwright, wrote the satirical *zarzuela* play *R.I.P.* (*Requiescat in Pace*, 1902), showing actors burying the old *komedya* form and taking up the new, more 'realistic' musical genre.

Among the new musical plays came performances characterized by nationalistic fervour: Reyes' *Without a Wound* (*Walang Sugat*, 1902) was a stringent attack on Spanish dominance. Foreign heroes and locales were soon replaced with scenes of Filipino domestic life. Most plays were melodramatic entanglements where true love eventually triumphed, yet indigenous characters and scenes were considered a commitment to nationalism and realism. Wing-and-drop scenery and contemporary costuming were prized, and songs became hits of the period. ATANG DE LA RAMA was the most noted of performers in the first quarter of this century.

American-influenced genres

Vaudeville, called *bodabil* or *vodavil*, made its debut around American bases by 1916. Louis Borromeo, who arrived from the United States in 1921, made the genre important. Troupes included torch singers like the noted Katy de la Kruz, clowns like the Chaplinesque Canuplin, and rockette-like chorus girls. During the Japanese occupation in World War II *bodabil* shows, which had long included skits, expanded to include plays. The Barangay Theatre Guild under Lamberto Avellana, one of the foremost groups currently presenting modern drama, began working in this format. *Bodabil* itself later devolved into burlesque-like girlie shows.

Modern spoken drama, too, arose at the time of American intervention in the Philippines, although as early as 1878 the didactic domestic drama *The Ideal Woman* (*Ang Babaye nga Huaran*) was written by Cornelio Hilado in Iloilo vernacular. The first English-language play, *A Modern Filipina*, by Jesus Araullo and Lino Casillejo was written in 1915 and English was an important medium during American rule. In the 1970s the theatre returned to the vernacular: *komedya* and *zarzuela* texts were researched and performed and dance troupes like Bayanihan (founded 1958) and Filipinescas researched indigenous dances and rechoreographed them into dance dramas for modern, urban audiences. The importance of indigenous music, dance and folk arts in contemporary performance and the search for solutions to the dichotomy between young Filipinos' aspirations and reality, is exemplified in such productions as *Oath to Freedom* (*Panata Sa Kalayaan*) which the Peryante company opened on Human Rights Day, 10 December 1984. The injustice of the past (government corruption, unfair labour practices, education atuned to American rather than indigenous models) were explored through song, mime, choral recitation, and visual theatre. The piece demanded that the audience pledge to build a just and free nation that would break forever with the past. Further, the play has been done in several other countries, either touring or with local casts.

Modern Theatre

Contemporary Philippine theatre of the 1990s is the direct outgrowth of a century of struggle to shape an indigenous theatre out of the people's colonial past. The first scripted spoken dramas in all of Southeast Asia were written by Filipinos. The so-called 'seditious plays' of 1902–06 emerged while the Philippines was engaged in brutal guerilla warfare with the United States, and caused its creators to be harassed, if not imprisoned. These Tagalog dramas were written by *ilustrados* (elite) who regarded themselves as heirs to the committed literature tradition of Balagtas and Rizal. Couched in allegory, their inflammatory plays struck a responsive chord with the politicized Filipino populace. JUAN ABAD's 1902 play, *The Golden Chain* (*Tanikalang Guinto*), is considered typical of the genre. It tells of the persecution suffered by the damsel, Liwanang or 'Light' (the Philippines), at the hands of Maimbot or 'Greedy' (America), and the rescue attempt by her sweetheart, K'Ulayaw (Revolutionary Filipinos). Also suppressed were *I Am Not Dead* (*Hindi Aco Patay*) by Juan Matapang Cruz and *Yesterday, Today and Tomorrow* (*Kapahon, Ngayo, at Bukas*) by Aurelio Tolentino (?1867–1915) Despite its short duration, the revolutionary drama period left a legacy of allegorical theatre and 'people's art' that is vivid with Philippine contemporary theatre practitioners.

Once the fury of the Filipino Revolution had been contained by the Americans, spoken dramas and *zarzuela* sputtered into innocuity, and appeared in the 1920s as domestic tales of bourgeois romance and moral persuasion. The *ilustrados* switched their allegiance to the new rule, and with the coming of 'the second American occupation', that is the American education system, they also turned from the vernacular to English. The result was doldrums in modern Filipino drama. American-sponsored educators thought of drama as efficacious only for speech and moral training. The ensuing self-conscious literary homilies could hardly compete with the increasingly popular vaudeville (*bodabil*) and movies of the 1930s.

Even after the Philippines achieved independence in 1946, the urban Filipino elite continued to write their plays in English. Psychological and social realism was essayed by playwrights such as Wilfrido Ma Guerrero, Alberto Florentino, Severino Montano, Estrella D. Alfon, and NICK JOAQUIN who wrote mainly for magazines. Theatre was primarily based in schools, which staged Broadway musicals and Western classics. Theatre companies rose and fell with equal rapidity. By their Western-

Reynaldo Alejandro, a scholar-artist of Filipino dance, presenting a theatrical version of an indigenous tribal dance.

influenced standards, the indigenous product was found wanting. The introduction of playwriting competitions did not make a substantial dent in these attitudes, and plays languished while 'in search of a stage'. However, Joaquin's play, *The Portrait of the Artist as Filipino* (1952) became the most popular English-language play of the 1950s and 60s. While flawed by overwriting, the tragicomic paean to a lost Hispanic-Filipino age of nobility and to human compassion is often lyrical. The presence of the narrator-character, and (to the audience) unseen painting looming in spiritual potency during the course of the play, were clever and innovative images for its time.

Apart from Guerrero, who was the leader of the University of the Philippines Dramatic Club for three decades, and Joaquin, the work of only a few theatre directors, particularly that of Rolando Tinio, lent lustre to a theatre era (1946–66) that Fernandez describes as 'short-lived, merely transitional, and with an unfortunate alienating effect'. The maverick director, Tinio, anticipated a new age of theatre with his unconventional staging of conventional Western plays.

Two features in Philippine theatre since 1966 set it apart from the other contemporary theatres of

Southeast Asia. The first difference is that metropolitan Filipinos had to make a traumatic language change in theatre, from English to Tagalog. This was the initial Filipino route to a 'self-apprehension' that everywhere in Southeast Asia has been the wellspring of decolonization in contemporary theatre. Secondly, the intense and prolonged politicization of contemporary Philippine theatre is also uncommon. The process began with the student demonstrations in the late 1960s, and accelerated with the imposition of Martial Law in 1972. Since then, there swelled a sense that, as Fernandez writes, 'The present has too much urgency. It pressed on the playwright's consciousness too insistently. He had to respond'.

These unique sensibilities were foreshadowed even before Martial Law was declared. Beginning in 1966, Manila audiences were 'shocked' by the 'bold' Tinio translations and adaptations of Arthur Miller, Tennessee Williams and Garcia Lorca. In 1967, the Philippine Educational Theatre Association (PETA) inaugurated its 'national theatre' performances of indigenous and avant-garde foreign works in Tagalog vernacular. Theatre took to the streets and other open and crowded places in support of the students' demands for an end to 'American imperialism, feudal corruption, and bureaucratic capitalism'.

The exposure of injustice and the enactment on stage of kinship with the masses surfaced as persistent themes in contemporary Philippine theatre. By digging into themselves, Filipino playwrights and directors exhumed seemingly limitless theatre resources which they reshaped to suit their pressing needs. The resources excavated ranged from ur-dramas and epic plays of the pre-Hispanic period, to Spanish-influenced religious and secular dramas, and to the *zarzuela* musical and even its death knell, *bodabil*. One of the earliest deconstructions of indigenous and indigenized performance texts was the play *Monster* (*Halimaw*, 1971) written by Isagani Cruz and staged by PETA. Reviving traditional *zarzuela*, Cruz fused it with a variety of epic, absurd and Broadway-musical devices to convey his dire warning on tyrannical power. Passion plays (*senakulo*) were also refashioned for contemporary purposes by the revival-conscious Babaylan Theatre in the 1970s. This company's *senakulo* series was climaxed in 1977 with the appearance of a radical Christ taking up arms against his imperi-

One of several international productions of the group-developed *Oath to Freedom* satirizing the ills of Philippine society under Ferdinand and Imelda Marcos. This English production at the University of Hawai'i was directed by Chris Millardo in 1989.

alist persecutors. A Mass calling on the Filipino clergy to join 'the life-and-death struggles of the nation' was written by Bonifacio Ilagan. Called *The Nation's Worship (Pagsambang Bayan)*, it was reconstructed street theatre, persuading the audience into communion through the rituals of collection, readings and singing. The performance led to investigation of the playwright by the Martial Law authorities, and detention (for a second time) for the director, Behn Cervantes.

Conventional Western forms were not entirely rejected, instead they were selectively borrowed to serve indigenous ends. The constraints of Martial Law impelled naturalistic playwrights to camouflage their true intentions by 'sticking to the facts'. One of the best-received plays of this genre was Orlando Nadres's *Square Paradise (Paraisong Parisukat*, 1974) about a female shoe-store employee. Rediscoveries of neglected and hitherto maligned personalities of the Filipino past, provoked a spate of history-based dramas.

In the quest for effective and directly communicable forms of theatre, the University of the Philippines Repertory Company, led by Cervantes, created the 'play-poem' (*dula-tula*). Asian in its suppleness, minimalism and strategies of transformation, this didactic form requires only three performers: a narrator, principal actor and a 'common man' playing multiple roles. Amelia Lapeña

Bonifacio in her *The Journeying of Sisa (Aug Paglalakbay ni Sisa*, 1976) grafted Japanese *nō* drama techniques to *pasyon*, or 'passion', style chanting to poetically express the anguish of Sisa, a character taken from José Rizal's famous 1886 novel, *Touch Me Not (Noli Me Tangere)*.

The spirit of the age is perhaps best encapsulated by PETA. A polyfunctional and private theatre organization, it is unique in Southeast Asia. PETA is a performing company and a training centre reaching out to the provinces and to some other Asian countries. As a political action group, PETA is intent on creating political awareness among the masses. Founded and guided by Cecile Guidote, PETA in 1967 built a challenging 'environmental' theatre, the Raha Sulayman, encompassing the ruins of Manila's Fort Santiago. PETA's recent 'nuclear' rock operas sum up its means and ends. *Nukleyar I* (1983) and *Nukleyar II* (1984), performed in song, dance and mime, blended indigenous and empathetic Western dramaturgies, particularly the anti-bourgeois mischief of surrealism, the grotesque of the absurd, and the 'learning' devices of Brecht. The outcome was exhilarating theatre designed to transform the audience into active participants in the anti-nuclear cause.

Even before the Marcos regime ended in February 1986, disillusionment was expressed over the blatantly political theatre sponsored by

Artists

Abad, Juan (1872–1932)
A writer of *KOMEDYA* who became disillusioned with that genre. He wrote the 'seditious' play *Long Live the Philippines!* (*Mabuhay ang Filipinas!*, 1900), prompting his arrest by colonial authorities, which he followed by other nationalistic works. After being acquitted in 1907 he managed the Silanganan Company.

Baltazar, Francisco ('Balagtas') (1788–1862)
A *KOMEDYA* author credited with over 100 titles, he was a disciple of José DE LA CRUZ. Many of his works were staged at the Tondo Theatre including *Abdal and Miserena* (1859) and *Mahomet and Constanza*. In 1841 his *Almanzor and Rosalina* was staged for 12 consecutive days from 2.30 p.m. to dusk. He expressed anti-colonial sentiment in much of his work.

de la Cruz, José (1746–1829)
Prolific author of *KOMEDYA*. Known as Huseng Sisiw ('Chicken Joe'), supposedly because he charged a chicken for his services, he could create a *komedya* in a day. He is credited with such titles as *The Civil War of Granada* (*La Guerra Civil de Granada*) and *The Enchanted Queen or Forced Marriage* (*Reina encantada o casamiento de fuerza*). He was critic-censor of the *komedya* at the Tondo theatre. None of his many works are extant.

de la Rama, Atang
The 'queen of *ZARZUELA*' who was at the peak of her career in the 1920s–30s. She would open an operetta in Manila then tour throughout Luzon playing one-night stands. She was a noted singer and actress who excelled in the melodramatic material.

Joaquin, Nick (1917–)
The doyen of Filipino dramatists writing in the English language. He is best known for *The Portrait of the Artist as Filipino* (1952) which was aired first as a radio drama, ran 156 performances in Manila, and was translated to the screen by Manuel de Leon. It concentrates on the struggle of two unmarried sisters to keep their dignity in the streets and in the family home. *Tatarin, A Witches' Sabbath* is a comedy on the war between the sexes; *The Beatas* shows feminist militants battling against the church.

Cervantes and PETA, but more especially that of the latter's clones in the provinces. Beginning in 1984, influential detractors argued that while the radical theatre kept the issues and the struggle against Marcos alive, it had now reached a state of fossilization. They asserted that the politics of committed theatre people were too narrow, the dramas predictable, and the experiences they generated stale and counterproductive. The ending of the Marcos dictatorship found such issue-oriented theatres without a cause and ideologically leaderless.

On the other hand, the poetic voices of the best realistic and expressionist playwrights – Tony Perez, Paul Dumol, Rene Villaineuva, Jose Dalisay – and directors – Chris Millardo, Nonon Padilla – were discovering supporting echoes within Filipino theatre. One of the most evocative of Perez's works, staged in New York in 1986 and Singapore in 1991, is *Trip to the South* (*Biyahang Timog*) written in 1984. An existential drama, it subtly interweaves the real and metaphorical in exposing the debilitating effects of Filipino feudalism, as embodied by the power wielded by the dead father over his grown children journeying to his funeral.

After a short period of rejoicing and repose following the departure of Marcos, some theatre people were induced to delve deeper into the regional arts, in part so as to develop folkloric aptitude that could be applied to fusion performances. Theatre pieces that emerged veered toward dance drama, as exemplified by the confident works of the Mindanao group, Sinambayok, and PETA's production of Marilou Jacob's *Macli-ing* (1988) that expressed, with anguished rage, the continuing tragedy of the Cordillera people of the north.

Some of the inspiration and financial and moral support for the retrieval in living contemporary form of the regional folk arts, stemmed from the revamped Cultural Centre of the Philippines (CCP), artistically led since 1986 by the theatre scholar and playwright, Nicanor Tiongson. The shining emblem of elite Manila culture under the stewardship of Imelda Marcos, the CCP was restructured, after 1986, into a mini ministry of the the arts, leading the way toward the Filipinization, democratization and decentralization of the arts. The economic crisis of 1991–92 has forced retrenchment of these ambitions, neverthless, the CCP no longer functions as a 'First World institution in a Third World country'.

Genres

Komedya

Folk play performed on a saint's day showing the triumph of Christians over the Moors, so popularly called a *moro-moro*. Developed in the 17th century, performances were common in commercial theatres through the 19th century. The typical plot involves a Muslim prince or princess in love with a Christian ruler of the opposite sex. After love scenes, escapes, battles, magical episodes, some clowning, perhaps a death and a miraculous resurrection, the lovers unite upon the conversion of the Muslim partner. Alternatively, they are doomed to separation should death or different religions continue to divide them. Story material is related to the sung epics, the *corrido* and *awit*, and some see the genre as growing largely from these oral narratives. Today they are performed by local amateurs as an outdoor village entertainment for fiestas.

Speeches are in quatrains of 8-, 10- or 12-syllable lines. The style of the presentation is broad: bombastic speech and stylized battles using *arnis*, the martial-arts system. Open-air performances ran 3–5 hours a day for up to 30 days of the fiesta period; even today performances may last 2–3 days. A brass band plays three major pieces in variable tempi; dignified marches sound for Christians but double time is played for Moors. Rowdy audiences at Ilocano performances might even demand the repeat of favourite battle scenes or love encounters.

Panunuluyan

Also *pananapatan*, a Christmas pageant of the Philippines enacted on Christmas eve in Tagalog areas. It depicts Joseph and Mary seeking shelter in Bethlehem.

Zarzuela

Also *sarsuela*, a Filipino operetta modelled on Spanish performances introduced around 1878. Popular 1890–1930, plays concerned melodramatic domestic entanglements of the urban middle class, especially romantic love. Nationalism and realism reflected indigenous thought. Songs became hits of the period. The earliest *zarzuela* in a local language is *The Patcher* (*Ing Managpe*) by Mariano Proceso Pabalan in Pampanga language; it premiered 13 Sepember, 1900, opening the way for each language group to create in this tradition. Professional troupes usually opened a new play at the Zorilla Theatre in Manila, then would move to a smaller theatre and finally tour the countryside. A thriving theatre scene grew up to satisfy the audiences' unsatiable demand for plays of this genre. For the first time fully professional actors and actresses worked steadily in the genre while authors and composers were kept busy producing new works for the thriving scene.

Bibliography

R. Alejandro, 'Sayaw Silangan: Dance in the Philippines', in *Dance Perspective*, 51, 1972; R. Banas, *Philipino Music and Theatre*, Quezon City, 1969; D. G. Fernandez, *The Iloilo Zarzuela: 1903–1930*, Quezon City, 1978, 'From Ritual to Realism: Brief Historical Survey of Philippine Drama', in *Philippine Studies*, 28, 1980, 'Asian Theatre of Communion: A Look at Contemporary Philippine Theatre', in *Continuity and Change in South-East Asia: Papers of Distinguished Scholars Series: University of Hawaii*, Honolulu, 1982, 'Contemporary Philippine Drama: the Liveliest Voice', in *Philippine Studies*, 31, 1983, and 'Philippine Theatre after Martial Law', in *Asian Theatre Journal*, 4, 1, 1987; T. Hernandez, *The Emergence of Modern Drama in the Philippines (1898–1930)*, Philippine Studies Working Paper 1, Asian Studies Program, Univ. of Hawaii, 1976; N. Joaquin, *Tropical Baroque*, St Lucia, 1979; J. Maceda, L. Goquingco, L. Kasilag, 'Philippines' in *New Grove Dictionary of Music and Musicians*, ed. S. Sadie, New York, 1980; F. Mendoza, *The Comedia (Moro-Moro) Re-discovered*, Manila, 1976; L. Mendoza, 'Lenten Rituals and Practices: The Philippines', in *The Drama Review*, 21, 1977; T. Muoz, 'Notes on Theatre: Pre-Hispanic Philippines (Religion, Myth, Religious Ritual)', *Brown Heritage*, ed. Antonio Manuud, Quezon City, 1967.

SINGAPORE

Singapore has four official languages: Malay, Mandarin, Tamil and English. The plural linguistic–cultural system of Singapore has led to the formation of four separate enclaves or 'streams' of theatre. Until recently, rapprochement between streams was rare. Each stream looked to outside sources for inspiration and models to help shape its aesthetics and repertory: Mandarin theatre to China, Tamil to India, and English theatre to the West.

Singapore Malay theatre, however, was an integral and, occasionally, leading part of Malaysian Malay theatre until Singapore's separation from Malaysia in 1963. (Singapore was a part of The Federation of Malaysia for four years from the time of independence from the British in 1959, following more than a century of British rule.) For more than a decade after the Japanese occupation, Singapore was the virtual centre of Malay literary activities on both sides of the Causeway. The era spawned the durable Malay theatre company, Sriwana. Led by the idiosyncratic theatre professional, Kalam Hamidy, its eclectic performances encompassed *purbawara*, dramatized tales of legendary figures, and *drama moden*, realistic drama (see Malaysia). The separation from Malaysia in 1963 left Singapore Malays as a political and cultural minority in a Chinese-dominated society. Sriwana assumed the role of bastion of a beleaguered theatre culture. Recent efforts to encourage an experimental sensibility in the Sriwana troupe, particularly by Nadi Putra, Sriwana's leader, have so far been thwarted by the group's conservatism. Significantly, Nadi's contemporary vision of the legendary Malay rebel Jebat, *Ivory Tower* (*Menara Gading*, 1986), was staged by Teater Kemuning, a young theatre company drawn to Indonesian–Malaysian contemporary theatre. Directing the play was Lut Ali, an informal leader of the young-turk elements in Singapore Malay theatre.

Tamil theatre, also the product of a distinct cultural minority, turned from its traditional historical–mythological plays to a reformist realistic theatre in the 1950s. Since then, it has not felt any urgency radically to change its aesthetic direction, although of late Tamil audiences are responding to home-grown dramas.

The firm foundations of a Mandarin-based realistic theatre were laid by the teachers and journalists leading the Singapore Amateur Players in the early 1950s. Their painstaking groundwork was rudely shaken by the local reverberations of the Cultural Revolution in China (1966–76). What ensued was a Singapore version of the Cultural Revolution's militant non-realistic theatre of heroic gestures and images exalting the common man. KUO PAO KUN, a playwright-director trained in Australia's National Academy of Dramatic Arts, injected strong doses of professionalism and artistic responsibility into the revolutionary theatre. His epic-type plays, improvised and conceived collectively, demystified Mandarin playwriting in Singapore. Staged by the students, workers and clerks enrolled in the Practice Performing Arts School which he directed, his performances expounded on the social dislocations brought on by foreign investment and urban redevelopment in an increasingly corporate Singapore. In 1976 Kuo was detained during the government's massive anti-leftist drive. Upon his release in 1980, he immediately returned to the stage, disclosing a human and reflective dimension in his partially expressionist theatre. In 1985 he began the writing and directing of a successful series of Mandarin–English one-man theatre pieces, inspired by the Chinese oral storytelling tradition. Gently satirical and in convincing Singlish (Singapore English), *The Coffin is Too Big for the Hole* (1985), and *No Parking on Odd Days* (1986) rue the excessive homogenization and bureaucratization of contemporary Singapore society. These plays also gave witness to his new-found role as bridge-builder between the polarized theatre societies.

The early 1960s generation of Singapore playwrights in English was a politicized, nationalist-minded, university-trained literary elite, represented by Lim Chor Pee and Goh Poh Seng. The indifferent response to their pioneering plays was followed by a drought in local English drama, relieved only by the 1970s political plays of the poet and novelist Robert Yeo. At the end of the decade, an identity crisis was perceived by the theatre director and university lecturer, Max LeBlond, who lent his zest for the local *patois* of Singlish to resourceful adaptations of foreign works in the early 1980s. Along with Kuo's monodramas, LeBlond's staging of Stella Kon's *Emily of Emerald Hill* (1985) elevated the status of the Singapore English play in the national estimation. Kon's Asian treatment of time and space in her bitter-sweet eulogy of the disappearing culture of the local 'Straits-born Chinese' (peranakan) was a rare experience for the ethnically dispos-

Artists

Kuo Pao Kun (1939–)

Playwright, actor, director, teacher. The most influential person in present-day Singapore theatre. Born in Hebei Province, China, he came to Singapore to live when he was ten. He studied at the National Institute of Dramatic Art in Sydney (1963–65) and on his return to Singapore established the Practice Performing Arts School in 1965 with his wife, dance-choreographer, Goh Lay Kuan. In addition to writing, directing and acting in his own plays, three volumes of which have been published and which have been produced in China, Hong Kong and Malaysia, he has introduced plays from China, Taiwan and Hong Kong to Singapore and has done much to break away from Western theatre models. At the same time he has staged Brecht (1967) and Fugard (1985). Detained by the government for four years (1976–80) for political reasons, he also received that government's Cultural Medallion in 1989.

sessed middle-class audience. An alternative theatre, directly influenced by the Philippine Educational Theatre Association (PETA) (see Philippines) was proposed by Third Stage, which presented 'learning plays' on the ills of Singapore society to the young, 'high-rise' generation. The May 1987 detention of Third Stage leaders by the Singapore government has led to paralysis of the company.

If current trends prevail, English promises to be the dominant language of Singapore. Presently, the Singapore government has launched a rational support system for theatre, by way of providing physical infrastructure, grants and tax rebates, annual and biannual national and international festivals and playwriting competitions. The continually expanding middle class has responded by filling the theatres, causing the internationally-minded government and business agencies to be aggressive about sponsoring a 'cultural' Singapore.

One of the results of the expansionist drive was that in 1990 Kuo founded the Substation, a privately financed and managed all-purpose arts centre that acts as a channel for creative fellowship between ethnically and/or aesthetically diverse art forms and artists. In his own theatre, Kuo has been persuaded to take a deeper look at the usability of Asian dramaturgy. Indeed, the most concrete sign of the breakdown of audience resistance to presentational theatre was exposed by Kuo's performance of *Mama Looking for her Cat* (1988), a multilingual ensemble piece that aspired to bridge the generation gap.

Traditions of Asian theatre are also explored by William Teo's Asian Theatre Research Circus, unashamedly inspired by Peter Brook's intercultural performance methods. In 1988 the law graduate Ong Keng Sen took over artistic leadership of Theatreworks, Singapore's first professional theatre company, where he executed fusions of Chinese opera, tai chi and Western theatre in directing Leow Puay Tin's Malaysian play, *Three Children* (1988), David Hwang's *Dance and the Railroad* (1990) and Henry Ong's *Memories of Madame Mao* (1991). While also launching the first major Broadway-style musical, *Beauty World* (1988), written by Michael Chiang and Dick Lee, the 27-year-old Ong convened the first

'Retrospective of Singapore Plays in English' in 1990.

Singapore theatre is burgeoning and the idea and practice of the 'Singapore play' has gained momentum, so much so that the frequency of indigenous English drama performances from 1986 to the present is unprecedented. Even so, the new plays have not been able to match the moral resonance and/or the eclectic performance strategies of Kon's *Emily at Emerald Hill* or Kuo's *Coffin* and *Mama Looking for her Cat*. Also the pull of Asian theatrical images on the highly Westernized young generation remains uncertain.

Bibliography

Kuo Pao Kun, *The Coffin is Too Big For The Hole...and other plays*, Singapore, 1990; Lee Tsu Pheng (ed.), *Prize-Winning Plays*, vol. 3, Singapore, 1989; R. Yeo (ed.), *Prize-Winning Plays 1: Ronald Alcantra, S. Kon, Tan Sor Poh*, Singapore, 1980, (ed.), *Prize-Winning Plays 2: Koh Juan Toong, Elizabeth Su, Yeo Soh Choo*, Singapore, 1981, (ed.), *Prize-Winning Plays 3: Dorothy Jones, S. Kon*, Singapore, 1981, (ed.), *Prize-Winning Plays 4: S. Balaji, Lee Thien Wah*, Singapore, 1981, and (ed.), *Prize-Winning Plays*, vol. 4, Singapore, 1990.

SRI LANKA

Sri Lanka is an island nation inhabited primarily by Buddhist Sinhalese, with a large Hindu Tamil minority, the descendants of Indian immigrants. The theatre of Sri Lanka has originated in various rituals and ceremonies of folk religions that are practised throughout the island. Unlike their counterparts in India – the dominant culture of the region, which had a classical tradition of drama on which to build later dramatic forms – Sinhalese writers had no indigenous classical model, except that provided by the neighbouring Sanskrit tradition. A possible explanation for the absence of a classical tradition of drama in Sri Lanka is that Buddhist monks were the principal writers in ancient times and they considered drama a taboo art form and so confined their efforts to poetry and narrative stories.

The elaborate ceremonies connected with the worship and propitiation of numerous folk deities of the island seem to have inspired the dramatic impulse. In ritual form alone, a strong dramatic character is evident. For example, the *rata yakuma* ceremony, which is performed to ensure the safe delivery of a child, to protect the child in the womb, to ensure the health of the infant already born or to make a barren woman conceive, contains elements of mimesis and theatre. The ceremony begins with performance offerings of chanted invocatory stanzas, drumming and dancing before sacrificial altars dedicated to the Seven Barren Queens. Three exorcists dressed in female attire are questioned by the chief exorcist or a drummer in order to reveal the purpose of the ceremony. The exorcist chants the legend of the Seven Barren Queens, wraps a white cloth around his head and after chanting verses spreads the cloth on the altar and throws incense on the flames of a torch which causes the whole altar to seem to burst into flames. This is an enactment of the legend of the demons' birth. Then follows the Twelvefold Ritual in which the seven daughters present a cloth to the Dipankara Buddha and thus attain permission to cause illness to human beings. Eventually, through sacrificial offerings, they agree to relinquish their control.

At the conclusion of the Twelvefold Ritual, the exorcist depicts in mime how the Barren Queens wore a cloth to be offered to the Dipankara Buddha. During the action which follows a man comes forward and the exorcist leads him around the performance area and mimes the Origin of the Mat, a symbolic fertility rite. Through song and mime, the exorcist relates the birth and swaddling of a child. Eventually he symbolically places the child in the arms of the parent and pronounces blessings on the mother. In turn, he presents the child to relatives and to spectators who have gathered to watch the ceremony.

Ceremonies such as these often require either 'patient' or exorcist to dress in the supposed likeness of the 'afflictor'. He will be costumed, wear elaborate makeup or a mask and brandish various weapons. In the process of introduction, which may include dancing to musical accompaniment, the patient or exorcist may become possessed and speak in the voice of the demon when replying to the priest's numerous questions. These transitions, beginning and ending with rituals, closely resemble dramas in the structure of the acts that occur within the ritual framing elements. During the ceremonies, offerings are made to appease the demon, sometimes in the form of a cock whose blood is either symbolically or actually shed or in the form of human sacrifices depicted through effigies, dolls or their symbolic representations. Ceremonies usually begin in the evening and continue the entire night without reaching a conclusion until midday.

In some ritual events, dramatic interludes using mime and comic dialogue have been added for ritual purposes or to entertain an audience.

They break up the tedium of the long hours of the ceremonies and serve to entertain the participants.

Perhaps one of the most interesting and popular of these interludes is that of the 'Brahmins from the Port of Vadiga' which occurs in a ritual intended to dispel evil influence that may accrue to a person who is suspected of having evil charms performed against him. The interlude depicts the arrival in Sri Lanka of some Brahmins who are versed in the ritual. When they enter they see a ceremony being performed and begin to question what is going on. Because they cannot speak Sinhalese they have trouble communicating with the exorcist, a situation which results in a great deal of humour. Finally it is discovered that the Brahmins speak Pali, the Buddhist language of Sri Lanka, and a dialogue commences between them and one of the exorcists in a kind of pseudo-Pali which is considered very amusing. At the conclusion of the ritual, they dance, bless the patient and exit, allowing the ritual ceremonies to proceed.

Among the specific forms in which ritual and drama are almost equally balanced are masked SOKARI and KOLAM. Kolam's connection to religious ritual is clear in the structure of performance and is suggested by the fact that the large masks probably descended from ritual use. The date of their origin has not yet been determined. NADAGAMA is a full-scale form of folk theatre with a considerable body of dramatic literature. Its plays concerning royalty and fortune-telling were exceptionally popular during the late 18th and 19th centuries. Nadagama, in turn, became the source of RUKADA puppet theatre. In the late 19th century, PASKU, or the Passion play, was born and popularized among the Christian population.

Modern theatre

Modern drama, designed to appeal to urban audiences, began during the last decade of the 19th century in Colombo. It was inspired by the immense success of a touring Parsi musical troupe from Bombay – Baliwallas' Elphinstone Dramatic Company which appeared in the 1880s. The Parsi musical of that time appealed to audiences by combining popular Hindustani music with techniques borrowed from the amateur English theatre of India – proscenium-arch stages, painted changeable scenery, elaborate costumes, declamatory acting, Western-style auditorium seating and the permanent enclosed theatre designed exclusively for the purpose of performance. The popularity of the Parsi musical prompted Colombo writers to imitate the Parsi models, writing Sinhalese dialogue and lyrics for the Hindustani tunes. The resultant form was known as nurti, 'new drama', and it soon ousted nadagama as the city's most popular theatre.

Nurti became a popular medium of expression and low-cost play editions were published and widely sold. Among the best-known writers was John de Silva (1857–1922) whose popularity eventually led to the construction of a theatre named in his honour. He borrowed ideas from Indian classical Sanskrit drama and combined them with elements of Parsi musicals. His plays were staged by the Arya Subadha Natya Sabha and later by the Vijaya Ranga Sabha. The first Sinhalese nurti was C. Don Bastian's Romeo and Juliet staged in 1884 and published in 1885. It was based on an adaption of Shakespeare's work by D. J. Wijesingha.

Actresses performed in nurti, thus introducing women onto the stage for the first time. Educated middle class spectators of Colombo were therefore hesitant to patronize this theatre. Nurti's real popularity was realized among the working-class people of the smaller towns and cities and it is still preserved today by amateur theatrical organizations which present performances in these environs during major Buddhist religious festivals. Although these activities are not called nurti today, they maintain a similar amalgam of melodrama and comedy, song and declaimed dialogue and the same loose episodic structure. The performances are enacted during festival nights. In Colombo nurti declined and disappeared with the advent of the films in the 1930s. Symbolically, its death knell was sounded with the conversion of Colombo's Tower Hall Theatre to a cinema.

During the 1920s and 30s nurti was replaced by a brand of playwriting known by the name of an actor who made the plays successful – Eddie Jayamanna. Jayamanna plays satirized the middle and upper middle classes of Colombo. They maintained a pretence of using literary language and the characters sometimes burst into song. Besides the acting of Eddie Jayamanna, the plays are also remembered for the singing of Rukmini Devi. Eventually, *jayamanna* plays were adapted into films and have long since disappeared from the stage.

In the 1940s and 50s students of the Sinhalese Society of University College (now the University of Sri Lanka) in Colombo wrote straight plays in colloquial prose dialogue. These were Sinhalese translations and adaptations of Western dramatic classics by Molière, Wilde and Chekhov. They were written by the intelligentsia for the intelligentsia.

In 1956 Ediriweera Sarachchandra's dramatization of a Buddhist Jataka tale, entitled *Maname*, broke new ground by attempting to formulate an indigenous style of writing using *nadagama*, *sokari*, *thovil* and folk dance music coupled with a serious theme meant for intellectuals. This led to a split between those writers favouring realism and those favouring folk-related theatre. By the mid 1960s the paths of the writers began to converge.

Today, modern theatre in Sri Lanka is still a part-time occupation for most of those engaged in it. Short-term workshops and symposia provide the only training for practitioners outside of their own performances. By custom, playwrights usually serve as directors and producers, and groups of actors in urban centres generally disband after a show has been completed. Theatre facilities are minimal, except in Colombo. But a large and loyal following for modern theatre has developed outside the urban centres as a result of touring companies who carry their lighting equipment and scenery with them and who set up their shows in makeshift facilities in cinema houses and schools.

Interest in drama has been stimulated in the young by island-wide drama competitions which showcase young talent. They are sponsored by the Department of Cultural Affairs. Drama and theatre have recently been adapted as part of the school curriculum and the training of drama teachers has proved quite successful at the University of Sri Lanka.

Genres

Kolam

Kolam is a masked folk theatre once extremely popular along the southern coastal region. A dozen plays exist in this form. The word *kolam* in Sinhalese means appearance, impersonation or assumed guise, usually comic or exaggerated so as to provoke laughter. Full-face masks are used to identify at least 50 stock character types. Many are introduced through a ritual prologue and some assume importance in the dramatic action which follows. Among the characters that appear in the dramas are the king, the queen, the king's herald, his wife, a policeman, a washerman, the washerman's wife, a paramour, a village dignitary, celestial beings, demons and animals.

After ritual dances and chants in honour of the presiding deities, there is a colourful and elaborate ritual entrance of each character which is accompanied by the chanting of the verses of the musicians who outline the history of each character. The entrance of the characters is highlighted by dances appropriate to his or her station in life. The dramatic action of the play follows. The masks do not seem to have been designed for singing or speaking; therefore, in the dialogue portions of the play, masks are rarely worn.

Performances usually take place in any open space in a village, begin around nine in the evening and conclude about sunrise.

The origin of *kolam*, according to one of the dramas, is told in the story of a certain queen who, big with child, craved dances and amusements. The king ultimately satisfied her by ordering performances of *kolam*. This tale along with other stories dealing with fertility, suggests that *kolam* may well have arisen as an ancient pregnancy rite.

Nadagama

A form of folk theatre that is said to have been introduced to Sri Lanka by Catholic missionaries from south India in the early 19th century. Although its original intention seems to have been to proselytize the religion, it soon added non-religious stories to its repertory and thrived along the whole western coastal region of the island. The plays, many of which are available in script form, are long and episodic. They deal with the exploits of heroic characters who encounter numerous dramatic challenges in love and war. The Tamil and Sinhalese languages mix freely in the works indicating that they were particularly popular among the Tamil-speaking minority of the region.

Phillipu Sinno is regarded as the author of

many of the works and the legendary father of *nadagama*. Little is known about the man except that he was a popular versifier and a blacksmith born in Colombo in the late 18th century. No less than 13 plays are attributed to him.

Nadagama performances take place in a village and are acted on a semicircular raised platform. A roof shelters the acting area and painted scenery separates acting from dressing areas. No front curtain is used. Entrances are made from the side of the stage near which the Presenter (Pote Gura) stands and sings verses to introduce each character. The Presenter is joined by two other musicians who serve as a chorus, repeating each line of the song. Seated on the floor at the opposite side of the stage are two drummers, the *horana* and cymbal players. In recent times a violin and a harmonium have been added to the musical ensemble. A unique feature of the *nadagama* is the use of musical techniques adapted from south India and later from the more popular Hindustani music of north India. The audience gains entrance to the performance area by paying a small price for seating space on the ground or a slightly higher price to sit in a chair.

A performance begins when the Presenter chants introductory stanzas paying homage to the deities and asking their protection for a successful performance. Then he describes the plot of the story and craves the audience's indulgence. Next he introduces the stock characters, one by one, beginning with the jester. Punctuating the jester's dances, the Presenter asks questions which provoke humorous responses. The next character to be introduced is the Sellan Lama, a wise man who is learned in the 64 arts and sciences. Then come two Desanavadi, characters who foretell the future, and by doing so give insight into the story to be enacted. Next the drummers employed in the royal court enter and announce in a declamatory tone the arrival of the king. Last the king's criers enter making way for the king. He summons various characters of his court who make ceremonial entrances in dance and song. Finally the dramatic action gets underway.

A traditional *nadagama* play takes a week to enact, each night's episode lasting from about 9 p.m. until midnight.

Pasku

Pasku is a Roman Catholic Passion play which originated in the Catholic areas of Jaffna in northern Sri Lanka in the late 19th century. Soon after, it was performed in the Sinhalese-speaking Catholic regions of the western coastal region as well. The play began in Passion Week and lasted for the entire Holy Week. In some congregations, the actors are replaced by life-size statues depicting the central characters in the episodes of Christ's death and resurrection. The statues move and create stage pictures above and behind 6-ft-high temporary walls. Painted scenes ascend to nearly 20 ft behind the figures. A reciter stands between the audience seated on the ground and the statues, interpreting each scene of the well-known biblical stories. In some locales actors wear historical costumes of the period. Whether statues or live actors are used, performances incorporate Christian church music and sometimes Western musical instruments, such as the organ.

Several notable plays were written and produced by K. Lawrence Perera of Boralessa whose ambition was to imitate the famous Oberammergau Passion Play. He created the Shridhara Boralessa Passion Play in 1923 which drew together unschooled actors from among virtually every humble profession of the area. Over a hundred performers participated to create the epic. The stage consisted of five sections arranged like the RUKADA puppet theatre with a central acting area and side wings stretching out to the right and left. A sensation occurred in 1939 when it was announced that all the female roles would be played by women. The Archbishop of Colombo banned the performance on the grounds that women acting on the same stage as men would have violated the decorum of the country. Although they were not pleased, the actors gave in to church pressure and used only men.

Rukada

A doll-puppet theatre practised almost exclusively in the city of Ambalangoda on the southwestern coast. 3- to 4-ft-high puppets are manipulated by strings. Performances are presented on an acting area divided into three sections. The central area occupies the back of a raised platform. Side stages extend out towards the audience to the right and left. The centre stage symbolizes the audience chamber of the king. All three divisions have dark back curtains and drops. A front curtain is used to mask scene changes while action occurs in one of the other acting areas. Puppeteers stand on a ledge above the stage and manipulate the puppets below.

The orchestra is composed of harmonium player, violinist and *tabla* drummer who sit facing the stage with their backs to the audience. The form probably developed after NADAGAMA. *Rukada*'s songs and stories are derived from this live theatre form and puppeteers were former players of *nadagama*. The songs and stories are set to Hindustani tunes rather than in the more traditional Karnataka musical style of south India.

Sokari

Sokari, a devotional performance, may be the oldest form of theatre in Sri Lanka. It is staged after the Sinhalese New Year in the months of Vesak and Poson which end around September. It is performed as a votive offering to the goddess Pattini, chief among the deities who are worshipped through ritual with the object of blessing human undertakings and granting immunity from disaster. Performances are confined to remote hilly regions, and performers, who are all male peasants, undergo training by elder performers in preparation for their devotional duties. Any open spot in the village, usually the threshing ground, may be used for an all-night show. Dancing and music punctuate the lively events and full-face masks are often used by performers.

As in so many ritual performances, one story is enacted here, the story of Sokari. The story differs in various details from group to group and place to place, with some performers even integrating popular music to enliven the original story line.

In essence, the episodic events centre around the following story: Guru Hami, a north Indian, and Sokari, his wife, along with Paraya, their comic servant, are disenfranchised, build a boat and sail to Sri Lanka where they experience various comic adventures. Sokari, who is young and seductive, elopes with, or is seduced by, a local doctor who has been summoned to treat Guru Hami for a dog bite. Eventually Sokari returns and delivers a child. The ending, along with the recurrent sexual symbolism and ribaldry that appear throughout the performance, suggest that *sokari* may be a dramatic elaboration of an archaic fertility ritual.

Among its unique features, *sokari* makes elaborate use of mime in which the players depict various actions described in song.

Bibliography

J. Callaway, *Yakkum Nattanawa and Kolam Nattanawa*, London, 1829; B. de Zoete, *Dance and Magic Drama in Ceylon*, London, 1957; M. H. Goonatilleka, *Nadagama, the First Sri Lankan Theatre*, Delhi, 1984; A. J. Gunawardana, *Theatre in Sri Lanka*, Sri Lanka, 1976; E. R. Sarachchandra, *The Folk Drama of Ceylon*, Colombo, 1966, *Pemato Jayati Soko (Love is the Bringer of Sorrow)*, tr. D. M. de Silva, vol. 25 in *Poetic Drama and Poetic Theory*, ed. J. Hogg, Salzburg, 1976, and *The Sinhalese Folk Play and the Modern Stage*, Colombo, 1953; J. Tilakasiri, *Puppetry in Ceylon*, Colombo, 1961; P. Wirz, *Exorcism and the Art of Healing in Ceylon*, Leiden, 1954.

TAIWAN

Taiwan is a mountainous island of 13,885 square miles in the South China Sea, about 90 miles off the Chinese coast, with a population of some 19 million. The Chinese took control of Taiwan in the late 1600s and administered it as part of China until 1895 when Japan gained control of the island as a result of the first Sino-Japanese War. China regained Taiwan after World War II. In 1949 the Chinese Communists defeated Chiang Kai-shek's Nationalist forces and took control of the mainland. Chiang moved the government of the Republic of China to Taiwan in December of that year.

A major local theatre form is *GOZAI XI*, or Taiwanese opera, a regional Chinese drama that first flourished in the southern Fujian province. Taiwanese opera shares with Beijing opera (see China, *JINGXI*) basic patterns of staging such as movement, costumes, makeup and the percussive accompaniment, while musically the two forms are distinct. *Gozai xi* literally means 'drama of songs', indicating the singing element is the most important. At first *gozai xi* was performed at street corners or country fairs without a stage; later a makeshift, open-air stage came into use and finally performances moved into theatre structures with the added elements of scenery, lighting and special effects. During the Japanese occupation this Taiwanese-language form was banned by the authorities. After World War II it gradually regained its audiences, and today it is the most popular form of theatrical entertainment in Taiwan. A popular actress who has done much to revive audience interest today is YANG LI-HUA, who is the star of a widely seen television series featuring Taiwanese opera.

Other forms of Taiwanese theatre consist of the tribal dances of the Aborigines and puppet theatres of various kinds. Glove-puppet theatre, *BUDAI XI*, is especially popular among peasants and fishermen. The 1-ft-tall puppets can be highly expressive in the hands of skilled puppeteers who also provide the narration and the dialogue of the characters. The typical stage is a highly ornate, if makeshift, structure erected twelve feet above the ground in a market place or on a street corner. A performance is often hired or commissioned and the casual audience attends free. The most respected living puppeteer is Li T'ien-lu, whose Yi Wan Ran troupe celebrated its 60th anniversary in 1991.

Although mainland Chinese make up only one tenth of Taiwan's population, their theatrical taste – mainly the appreciation of the much refined Beijing opera – has affected theatre development in Taiwan for nearly a century. In 1909 a Beijing-opera company from Shanghai played for two weeks in Taipei, and ever since troupes from the mainland have toured the island with varying degrees of success. Especially the performances, beginning in 1948, of the talented young actress KU CHENG-CH'IU had a lasting effect on Taiwanese theatre. For four and a half years, she and her 60-member troupe performed at the Yung Lo Theatre in Taipei to an appreciative audience of wealthy mainlanders who had fled to the island to avoid the new Communist government. While Ku and her colleagues were forced to remain on the island, other Beijing-opera troupes also made their exodus to Taiwan. Some of these troupes were associated with the armed forces, most notably the Ta P'eng Troupe of the Chinese Air Force, personally initiated by Air Force Chief Wang Shu-min, an avid theatre-lover. For 40 years a training school attached to the troupe has nurtured many talented actors who are today mainstays of the stage.

Four major Beijing-opera troupes perform in Taiwan at present: the Ta P'eng troupe, the Lu Kuang troupe associated with the Army, the Hai Kuang troupe associated with the Navy, and the Fu Hsing troupe of the National Fu Hsing

Dramatic Arts Academy, the leading institution training Beijing-opera and Taiwanese-opera actors and musicians. They perform in Taipei at the Armed Forces Cultural Activities Centre, a modestly equipped 950-seat theatre devoted to traditional opera, and the newly constructed National Theatre. Both Beijing opera and Taiwanese opera are featured on television in a government effort to develop a wider audience for traditional theatre. Paid attendance at regular Beijing-opera performances, however, is declining steadily. In the late 1980s and early 90s, ambitious productions of Beijing opera were staged at the National Theatre using lavish scenery and based on newly created scripts. One example was a free adaptation of Shakepeare's *Macbeth*, which toured to the National Theatre in London in 1990. Among contemporary Beijing-opera performers, two of the most popular and important, in terms of their impact on the theatre, are Hsu Lu, a skilled performer of leading female roles with a superb singing voice, and KUO SHIAO-CHUANG, known for her creation of new-style Beijing operas favoured by young audience members. Both Hsu and Kuo are graduates of the Ta P'eng training school.

Modern theatre, *HUAJU* (see China), literally 'spoken drama', occupies a less important position than traditional theatre in Taiwan. The earliest performance activity can be traced to 1911 when a Japanese director came to stage several productions with local actors. Most of the actors recruited were ruffians in town, hence the term 'ruffian drama' (*langren ju*) for modern theatre. Over the next twenty years numerous local drama troupes were organized on an amateur basis and they staged works by well-known mainland playwrights and by local authors dealing with Taiwan themes. Influential was Chang Wei-hsien, who studied dramatic arts in Tokyo in the 1930s and then returned to become an innovative director and acting teacher. Spoken drama was given a major impetus by the influx of 1.5 million mainland refugees when Chiang Kai-shek's Nationalist government moved to Taiwan in 1949. Among the new arrivals were playwrights, directors and actors of modern spoken drama, most of whom were attached to the entertainment units of the armed forces. They mounted productions and

A *kunqu* actress, playing the role of a female warrior, gestures with long pheasant feathers while singing at the Great World Theatre, Taipei, in 1964.

trained the next generation of theatre workers. They also contributed to the development of the film and television industries. Prominent among them was the woman playwright and legislator Li Man-kuei, who promoted the Little Theatre Movement in the early 1960s. In 1962 she organized the Committee on Spoken Drama Appreciation, which became the major producing agency (120 productions between 1961 and 1969) of modern dramas. She and the Committee also started a World Drama Festival in 1967 to present foreign plays in the original languages performed by language students in local universities, and a Youth Drama Festival in 1968 to present plays by local playwrights, both of which continue to foster modern drama today.

Modern theatre in Taiwan is modest in scale and quality in comparison with neighbouring China, Japan, Korea or Hong Kong. The economics of performance do not support professional modern drama troupes; the active companies are either amateur or semiprofessional. Theatre facilities are scarce and the first adequately equipped theatre auditorium, Chung Hsing Hall in Taichung, was built in the mid 1970s. The theatre department of the University of Chinese Culture has long offered academic training in theatre, and since 1982 the National Institute of the Arts provides a full training programme in modern drama.

Among well-known spoken-drama groups in Taiwan are the Lan Ling Ensemble and Performance Workshop. The Lan Ling Ensemble, an experimental group, was founded in 1980 by Wu Chin-chi, a psychology professor who had worked at the La Mama Theatre in New York. Lan Ling productions are noted for their free adaptation of Chinese materials, simplicity of staging, and using the actor's voice and movement, rather than a dialogue text, as their chief means of communication. An early work, Ho Chu's New Match (Ho Chu xinpei, 1979), is a free adaptation of a Beijing opera in which conventions of the traditional theatre are used in hilarious, tongue-in-cheek fashion. This group disbanded in 1990 due to lack

Artists

Ku Cheng-ch'iu (?1928–)
A talented actress in Beijing opera (see China, JINGXI) who left mainland China for Taiwan in 1948. Her four-and-a-half-year run at the Yung Lo Theatre in Taipei marks a record in the history of the Chinese theatre. She and her colleagues became the main source of Beijing-opera performance and training in the immediate postwar years. Ku played the lead-female roles, and her singing voice was renowned among professionals. Since her retirement from the stage in the early 1950s, she has performed only on rare occasions such as the inauguration of a new President and the opening of the National Theatre.

Kuo Shiao-chuang (1951–)
Leading actress of Beijing opera (see China, JINGXI) on the Taiwan stage in the 1980s and early 90s, as well as a television and film star. In 1979 she formed the Ya Yin (Elegant Music) Opera Ensemble and began presenting Beijing operas in a contemporary spirit, utilizing modern stagecraft, sophisticated orchestration, well-written scripts and an arduous rehearsal period. The resulting productions achieved a polish and refinement adored by enthusiastic young audiences, including many who would not usually attend traditional theatre. Kuo and her company represent a new force to revive a fading interest in traditional theatre.

Lai Sheng-ch'uan (1954–)
Contemporary stage director, playwright, theatre-educator, and currently Head of Graduate Studies at the Theatre Department, National Institute of the Arts. He is the founder of the Performance Workshop (1984) which became the most successful modern theatre company on the island. He is known for his improvisation and group creation of scripts. His better-known productions are Secret Love for the Peach Blossom Spring (Anlien taohua yuan, 1986 and 1991), The Island and the Other Shore (Huitou shi biian, 1989), and Who's Playing Hsiang-sheng Tonight? (Jinyeh sheilai shuo xiangsheng?, 1989).

Yang Li-hua (?1945–)
The most popular of present-day Taiwanese-opera (GOZAI XI) actresses. She is especially known for her cross-gender portrayal of 'young male' roles, both civil and military, and widely known through her gozai xi portrayals on television. She heads a theatre company bearing her name and is instrumental in training young actors to sustain Taiwanese Opera traditions.

The performance workshop production of *Secret Love for the Peach Blossom Spring* in 1991, written and directed by Lai Sheng-ch'uan.

of leadership. The highly influential Performance Workshop was founded in 1984 by Berkeley-educated LAI SHENG-CH'UAN. Lai's company emphasizes improvisation and group creation of productions that deal with current political and social issues.

In the mid 1980s the government of Taiwan started ambitious projects to advance modern theatre. The National Theatre and National Concert Hall complex constructed in the heart of Taipei opened in 1987. It contains a 1524-seat main theatre and a 300-seat experimental theatre. Modern theatres that meet international standards are planned for other cities on the island as well. In 1982 the National Institute of the Arts was inaugurated, offering training in four departments: music, fine arts, theatre and dance. A well-equipped 400-seat theatre opened at its new campus in 1991.

Genres

Budai xi

Glove-puppet theatre in Taiwan originated from the Longxi district of Fujian province. The 1-ft-tall puppets are highly expressive in the hands of skilled puppeteers who also provide narrations and dialogues between characters. The acting style, character types, musical accompaniment and script format of *budai xi* are quite similar to those of the Beijing opera, but the narration and dialogues are native Taiwanese. The Taiwan version of *budai xi* puppetry remained basically

unchanged over the years, but the Fujian mother form has undergone considerable changes, making the puppets twice as large and the staging far more elaborate. The two puppeteers, originally seated, now stand, allowing the simultaneous presence of over twenty characters on a larger stage. The Taiwan version still keeps its casual, quaint atmosphere, entertaining a faithful audience consisting of native peasants and fishermen. The most respected living puppeteer is Li T'ien-lu, who has been featured in films and whose troupe the Yi Wan Ran celebrated its 60th anniversary in 1991.

Gozai xi

A regional Chinese theatre form that first flourished in southern Fujian province. It was introduced to Taiwan in 1662 when General Cheng Ch'en-kung and his followers made an exodus to the island refusing to be ruled by the Manchu invaders. The Fujian version of *gozai xi* adopted the ballad singing of Taiwan and the staging elements of Beijing opera. Over the years a new form emerged on the island, hence the name 'Taiwanese opera'. *Gozai xi* literally means 'the drama of songs', the singing element is therefore most important. The 'Wailing Tune' and 'Seven-Word Tune', both uniquely Taiwanese, are its most significant singing patterns. During the Japanese occupation this local theatre form was banned by the authorities. After 1945 it was revived and it is now the most popular form of theatrical entertainment in Taiwan. Yang Li-hua reigns supreme as the most celebrated actress, specializing in 'young male' roles.

Bibliography

J. R. Brandon, *Brandon's Guide to Theatre in Asia*, Honolulu, 1976; Huang Mei-shu, 'Taiwan huaju de huigu yu zhanwang' (The past and future of spoken drama in Taiwan), in *Muqien muhou, taishang taixia*, Taipei, 1980; C. H. Kullman and W. C. Young (eds.), 'Taiwan', in *Theatre Companies of the World*, vol. 1, Westport, Conn., 1986; Li Fu-sheng, *Zhonghua guoju shi* (History of the national opera), Taipei, 1969; Lu Su-shang, *Taiwan dienyin xiju shi* (A history of cinema and drama in Taiwan), Taipei, 1961; A. C. Scott, *Literature and the Arts in Twentieth Century China*, New York, 1963.

THAILAND

Thailand (formerly Siam) is a Southeast Asian country bordering on Malaysia, Burma, Laos and Cambodia. Its population is a mixture of hill tribes and lowlanders. Malays of the southern provinces have been significant in shaping Thai dramatic practice, while Lao peoples in the north-east and Chinese Thais enjoy performances comparable to those found in Laos and southern China respectively.

Theraveda Buddhism was adopted by the early Thai. Today this belief, mixed with indigenous animism and Brahmanism-Hinduism, is held by 95 per cent of the population. Dance and dramatic performances may first have evolved in conjunction with religious practice at the village level, and rural performances continue to be a regular part of religious festivals. The emergence of the Thai as a political force on the peninsula began in the 13th century, but artistic ascendency came only after the capture of the Khmer (Cambodian) kingdom of Angkor in 1431, an event which cemented the Thai predilection for adopting Khmer arts. Expertly trained musicians and harem wives-dancers of the Khmer king's household were carried into exile. This ready-made performance tradition was developed in Thailand over following generations, with many monarchs and princesses becoming accomplished poets or performers of dance-drama texts. This expanded tradition became, in turn, the model for the Burmese court theatre, when the Burmese seized the Thai court wives-dancers and musicians during the sack of Ayutthaya, the Thai capital, in 1767. Later the Thais returned the Cambodian loan of artistry with interest, for much of the repertoire which the Khmer court adopted in the 19th century seems borrowed from Thai court models of that time.

The current music, performance practice and repertoire of the Thai theatre are related to pan-Southeast-Asian patterns. The major theatre types are: (1) village animist-influenced performances; (2) court forms; (3) modern popular genres; and (4) modern spoken drama.

Village animist-influenced performances

Dance offerings to the spirits have probably been carried out from the early period of Thai history. Even in modern Bangkok one can find temples where dancers regularly carry out performances commissioned by donors as offerings for some boon granted. Dancers emulate the costume and dance style of the court forms. Pure dance is standard and occasionally dramatic episodes or whole plays may be presented. A mixture of animistic, Hindu and Buddhist influences seems to underlie these practices. Although most performances discussed hereafter are for audience entertainment rather than such ritual purposes, it is significant that much theatre continues to be presented in the context of temple festivals.

The earliest known drama in Thailand, NORA (also *manora*), may have originated in village performances connected with animist–Buddhist practice in the ethnically Malay south and around the 14th century. This early form is still extant in the area around Nakhon Sri Thammarat, the site of the old Malay Buddhist kingdom of Ligor, which became part of Thailand in the 14th century. The form seems to have evolved practices that affected later theatrical genres. The traditional all-male troupe included three actors: prince, princess and a clown who enacted the other roles, including ogres and monkeys, and often wore a mask for these characterizations. A performance included a musical prelude, an opening incantation, solo dances, songs, skits and finally a play.

The legendary origin of the form hints at a possible relationship with female spirit-mediums: a Thai princess, Nuensamli, was possessed by a god, and her crazed activity caused her family to cast her out. She gave birth to a son, who learned dance by watching *kinnari* (mythical bird-women); the son magically created a clown from a rock; and a god became incarnate to become the third performer of the genre. The Manora story, believed to be the only one presented in the early period of the form, may be further evidence of the relationship with spiritually empowered women. Manora is a bird-woman (*kinnari*), who takes off her wings to bathe and has them stolen by a hunter, Bun. He takes her to the prince, Suton, who marries her, but true love is complicated when a minister turns the people against her in the prince's absence. At the moment Manora is to be executed, she borrows her wings for one last dance, and thus escapes to her mountain home. Her faithful husband follows her there, proving his devotion.

This bird-woman story, seen in mainland Southeast Asia as a *Jataka* (tale of a previous life of the Buddha), is known in many cultures. Its pattern gains greater significance when seen in relation to later plots, such as *Rothasen*, in which a young prince strives to find a cure for his mother's blindness. He marries the stepdaughter of an ogress, who teaches him the cure, but then abandons the love-stricken maid to return home. She dies cursing him to be the lovelorn one when they meet in a future life.

Both plot patterns and the *nora* origin myth associate men with women who are possessed, powerful or semidivine. They may be evidence that *nora* was originally a male performance form that evolved from female-spirit-medium dances of divination. Such trance dances are still found in Burma, where two princes emulating female mediums in the 1400s are the alleged origin of Burmese drama. The two reports may be variants on a theme: female mediums' trance rites become the model for male artists' performance practice.

In times past *nora* was commonly called *lakon jatri*. *Lakon* means 'play' and *jatri* 'sorcerer'; troupe heads were felt to have great spiritual power and were called on for exorcisms, ordinations and other ceremonies. It is said these sorcerers would enchant their audiences so that viewers would follow from performance to performance. Though magic still creates an aura around the form,

A folk harvest dance in northern Thailand.

changes have occurred. Current performers may be of either sex, a troupe is larger than three actors and a vaudeville format prevails. By 1972 this genre had been transformed: singers in Western costume crooned romantic lyrics to Western band accompaniment and skits and comic routines abounded.

If the tradition dies out, it will be the end of an art which may explain patterns which underlie human drama in Thailand. The three-person configuration may be the source of the role types that dominate Thai theatre. The male (*phra*), the female (*nang*), ogre (*yak*) and monkey (*ling*) are the types into which all traditional roles are divided. The first two correspond to the hero and heroine of the *nora*, and the last two in court dance are always masked (resulting, perhaps, from the fact that in *nora* they were performed by a single person alternating masks). More research might clarify how *nora* relates to mask dance genres like Indonesia's *TOPENG* and how character types common to most theatres in the Southeast Asian region may be linked to these masked dance forms. The most important *nora* artist today is THONGBAI ROUNGNON.

A now defunct theatre form which developed out of the *nora* and pleased audiences through the first decades of this century is *lakon nok* (literally, 'play outside' [the palace]). It originated in the same southern area, and was introduced in the Bangkok region. An expanded cast and orchestra, and more secular emphasis, characterized the form. As in *nora*, dance and music were components, but in *lakon nok* the dialogue, action and comedy gained in significance.

Initially *lakon nok* troupes were all-male, but by the mid 19th century women began playing female roles as women from the palace tradition were allowed to perform in public. Eventually the *lakon nok* repertoire of Buddhist birth stories, local histories and legendary tales was emulated in court theatricals, and this expropriation has saved the form from complete extinction. Performances in *lakon-nok* style are occasionally staged by the National Theatre in Bangkok today, in a style style less lively and risqué than in the past.

Court forms

Court performance, consisting of *NANG yai* ('large leather puppets'), *KHON* ('mask dance drama'), and

LAKON FAI NAI ('female dance drama'), is derived from Cambodian court arts of the 15th century, but scholars debate the extent of Khmer impact. Cambodia currently boasts equivalents of all three forms, and origins of all Thai court genres might date from 1431, when the Thai captured Angkor. But many scholars feel that what was taken differed substantially from current practice, and that the close similarity of Thai and Khmer classical theatre in the current era results from Thai influence on Cambodian arts in the 19th century.

It seems reasonable to assume that the Khmer equivalent of *nang yai*, called *NANG SBEK THOM*, was already in existence. Although the 1458 Thai Palatine Law is the first extant reference to the mutually shared form, the Khmer had been influenced by Indonesia where shadow puppetry, masked dance and female non-dramatic dance were venerable court traditions.

Nang yai is a shadow and silhouette play performed with large, incised, two-dimensional leather puppets manipulated by dancing puppeteers who move in front of and behind a wide white screen 30 ft long and 10 ft high. Two narrators called *khon pak* recite an episode from the Thai version of the Ramayana (*Ramakien*) to the accompaniment of a *piphat* orchestra, composed minimally of a double reed (*pi*), xylophone (*ranat ek*), barrel drum (*klong that*), cymbals (*ching*), gong chime (*khong wong yai*) and another type of barrel drum called *taphon*. Eventually, other stories were presented using *nang yai* technique, but these stories did not rival the popularity of the Rama material, which was put into literary form by Thai kings, notably Rama I, who ruled 1782–1809.

The main outline of the story follows the Indian epic. Rama, an incarnation of the god Vishnu, with the assistance of monkey warriors wins back his wife Sita who has been kidnapped by the lustful demon king Ravana (Thai, Tosakanth). Variations from Indian material are apparent: for example, Sita is Ravana's daughter, abandoned as a child, and many new episodes are interpolated. Especially popular in the repertoire are dramatizations of these new episodes that deal with the amorous and martial exploits of Hanuman, Rama's monkey general. Typically Hanuman meets and marries a demon's beautiful daughter.

Similarities in story patterns may link *nang yai* to Indonesian *WAYANG* ('puppet theatre'). (Bengali versions of the *Ramayana* may be the ultimate source of the story materials used by both.) The centrality of a narrator or storyteller, the mode of introducing satire via the clowns, and the function of the orchestra within the performance are comparable as well. At the same time many techniques are unique to the Thai–Khmer court puppet tradition: the huge 4 ft x 5 ft puppets dwarf the 1 ft–3 ft puppets of Java. The depiction of multi-character scenes in a single puppet, and the need for multiple puppeteers who dance on both sides of the screen each carrying a single figure, are quite unlike the solo, stationary puppeteer mode of Indonesia and Malaysia, and lead some scholars to look for Indian models. In south India, puppet forms are found in which multi-character scenes are represented, and multiple puppeteers are common. However, the aesthetic which allows the dancing puppeteers to emerge from behind the screen has no known Indonesian or Indian precedent, and must be attributed to indigenous ingenuity.

The figures are impressive, being the largest shadow figures known in the world. The iconography of the puppets corresponds to images on temple walls, and most figures sport the distinctive crown-type headdress (*chada*) worn by classical dancers. The fine carving emulates the delicate patterns of the cloth of gold and jewel inlay of dance-drama costumes – outfits into which court dancers were sewn before each performance. The kings, including Rama I, Rama II and Rama IV, were responsible for writing the texts of the Rama story that were presented in the *nang* and masked dance. Unfortunately, performances of *nang yai* are rare today, but at least two temples maintain this tradition that fell into disarray when court support lapsed in the 1930s. The crown princess H.R.H. Mahachakri Sirinthorn has recently commissioned some new puppets.

Khon is a masked dance drama enacted by a male cast to the chanted narrative of a narrator (*khon pak*) accompanied by a *piphat* orchestra. Dancers mime the action of the text, normally excerpted from literary versions of the *Ramakien*. *Khon* was supposedly first presented in the Thai court in 1515 when King Rama Thibodi II celebrated his 25th birthday. The original dancers are said to have been manipulators of *nang yai*. The basic square, flat stance of the dancers, and the tendency in *khon*

to construct visual friezes as dancers assume poses, correlates well with the style of puppet manipulation aimed at enhancing the figure of the large puppet against a screen. Because of the puppet origin of the form, scripts are divided into 'sets' (*chut*), referring to sets of puppets used in *nang yai* episodes.

Khon luang ('royal *khon*') was supported by Thai rulers. Early court performances seem to have emphasized fight sequences and the recitation (*kampak*) of the narrator, making it close to the puppet theatre. In later periods, characters playing refined males and females have ceased to wear masks, and non-battle scenes and song have become more significant. The movement away from all-masked, martial theatre has probably come as a result of the popularity of the female dance-drama tradition, for females have increasingly taken over refined roles in which they do not wear masks.

The female dance tradition reportedly stems from 1431 when the Thai captured the Khmer court dancers. However, it seems likely that the Thai may have emulated the Khmer custom of coupling the role of queen or royal concubine and dancer prior to this date. Though it is difficult to pinpoint exactly when the custom originated and trace precisely when drama rather than abstract dance became the focus, the female court drama is clearly the most significant and innovative of Thai court arts. *Lakon fai nai* (literally, 'inner court play') is the most refined, poetic and slow-moving of the dance dramas. Female performers dance–act a story accompanied by a *piphat* orchestra and a chorus. The poetic texts are attributed to members of the nobility. Dialogue may be delivered by performers; much of the text is sung by offstage singers. Clowns who improvise their own dialogue are, traditionally, the only male performers.

The name of the form comes from the fact that it was performed by the ladies of court and, hence, only played inside the palace. Dancers would traditionally be under the direction of one of the queens and serve as performer and king's lady for the duration of a reign. Upon the death of a king, this group would disband, and the new monarch would appoint one of the former king's dancers to teach his own group. Provincial lords might emulate this practice, but few groups could compete with the training, grace, exquisite costuming and delicate singing of the king's troupe. Other terms for the form are *lakon nai* and *lakon phuying*.

Lakon fai nai evolved from the early, non-dramatic dances of the Khmer court ladies, which served a semiritual purpose of linking the ruler with chthonic forces of earth and fertility. In Javanese, Balinese and Malay court performances female dancers have an analogous function, and the Khmer may have been emulating the practice of these southern courts where tantric Hindu–Buddhist thinking laid the groundwork for the arts. The Thai secularized this ritual function, and allowed the form to become more dramatically oriented, often incorporating story material from the Malay regions of Thailand.

Thai court dancers were presenting drama in daylong performance episodes in the late 1600s when the Frenchman de la Loubère visited Thailand. Around 1760 two royal princesses learned from their Malay maidservant the Prince Panji story, called *Inao* in Thailand, and they wrote their own versions as a basis for a female court dance drama. Though the princesses' versions were later superseded by the version of Rama II, who reigned 1809–24, their choice of subject was apt. The amorous exploits of this Javanese prince, creeping unbeknownst to fathers and husbands into the bedchambers of his beloveds, must have had resonance for the ladies of the king's entourage, who were themselves given to forbidden affairs. It became the favoured subject of the dance drama and contributed to the dramatic enrichment of court dance.

The languorous, graceful dance style of the ladies fitted *lakon fai nai*'s emphasis on feminine concerns and characters. Some of the women were trained for the ogre and monkey roles needed for the *Ramakien* which was taken into its repertory, but episodes like 'Surpanakha's Pangs of Jealousy', which show the hopeless love of Ravanna's sister for Rama, and the 'Abduction of Sita', which depicts the helpless wife of Rama carried off by the ogre king, were preferred to the battles and monkey exploits presented in male-dominated mask and shadow plays. Other stories were introduced over time, including *Unaruth*, which tells of the loves of a grandson of Krishna. Rama II is said to have introduced six *lakon nok* stories, including the popular *Jataka* of *Sang Thong* about the prince born as a conch shell. The strange birth results in

mother and shell being cast out of the palace. The conch prince steals magic accoutrements from his adoptive mother, an ogress, and disguises himself as a negrito. Despite his disguise, a princess marries him, braving persecution by her mortified family. Another popular story from the south is *Suwanna-hongse*, which tells how Prince Suwanna-hongse climbs a kite-string to find the princess of his dreams, an ogre king's daughter, but is killed by her sisters. The princess disguises herself as a Brahmin and, with the aid of an oafish clown-ogre, restores the prince to life. This last tale seems to have come to the *lakon nok* from *nora*. Its presence in the repertoire may hint at some link with the female court dance drama of Malaysia, MAK YONG, for the story is a version of the most significant and sacred story in the MAK YONG repertoire, *Dewa Muda*, or *The Magic Kite*.

Both the Panji story and *lakon nok* tales come to the female dance drama from the Malay south. Further research into the past dramatic practice of the southern provinces might clarify whether the importance of women as actors in a court dance drama could have been stimulated by practices of this area as well, perhaps in the court of Patani where a visiting European, Peter Flores, attended a 1613 banquet given by the queen and saw, 'A commedye all by women, to the manner of Java, which were apparelled very antikly, very pleasant to beholde'.

Development and innovation in *khon* and *lakon fai nai* traditions continued through the last century, first under royal direction and then under the government Department of Fine Arts (Krom Silpakon). After the reign of Rama IV (King Mongkut) (r. 1851–68), division of the sexes in theatre forms disintegrated, as males were allowed to dance with the royal ladies and female dancers were allowed to perform and teach outside the court. Today women play in virtually all forms, often taking the refined male roles as well as female ones. Men customarily play ogres, clowns and monkeys and, perhaps, refined male roles. Clear distinctions between genres have blurred: *khon* has become more refined in its dance style and *lakon fai nai*, using males for ogre and monkey roles, probably lacks the delicate ambience of times past. The two forms are nowadays intermingled and the combined genre termed *khon* if masks are involved or *lakon ram* if masks are not.

Group dance in *lakon fai nai* style, Bangkok. Female dancers play male and female roles.

Extensive experimentation has characterized the 19th and 20th centuries. Performances of classical plays were given using three-dimensional puppets, *hun*. The form is probably inspired by Chinese rod- and string-puppet theatres. *Lakon dukdamban* (literally, 'ancient story') was an innovation during the reign of Rama V (King Chulalongkorn) (r. 1868–1910). Actors sang their own lines rather than merely pantomiming their parts, males played male roles, and the offstage chorus and descriptive passages characteristic of earlier court drama were eliminated. During the reign of RAMA VI (King Vajiravudh) (r. 1910–25) experiments proliferated. The king wrote examples of *lakon rong* (literally, 'a sung drama'), an all-female opera form developed in the 19th century. He also wrote spoken dramas, based on Western models. Meanwhile Prince Naradhip adapted plots from English musicals and European operas to present in Thai classical dance style.

Following the transition to a constitutional monarchy in 1932, sponsorship of theatrical activities was assumed by the government Department of Fine Arts, and expanded under the directorship of DHANIT YUPHO, 1956–68. In 1934 a training school for music and dance was founded under the department's direction, and this institution eventually became the College of Dance (Witthayalai Natasin). Since 1971 seven new branch Colleges of Dance, training students in *khon, lakon fai nai* and traditional music, have been established outside Bangkok. There students are groomed to play one of the four major roles, studying carefully the 66 gestures (sometimes said to be 68) of the classical dance technique which were codified in the reign of Rama I (1782–1809) in the *Text for the Training of Dancers*. Outstanding graduates may become members of the National Theatre Company at the National Theatre in Bangkok.

At the National Theatre thousands of ticket-buyers now can see the forms which a hundred years ago were played only to an invited few in a hall of the royal palace. The company presents most of the previously noted genres, *khon, lakon fai nai, lakon dukdamban, lakon nok* and *lakon phantang* (mixed-genre experiments). The latter form combines local legends from the *sebha*, a rhymed story-telling tradition, with classical dance presentation.

Few performers can maintain themselves by performing classical arts. Performers at the National Theatre receive token payment, and most turn to tourist performance for additional income. Thammasat and Chulalongkorn Universities stage student, amateur productions of classical dramas. The puppet performances, in particular, are extremely rare. *Nang yai* players are mostly aged, with few students to take over when they die. The last rod-puppet troupe retired in 1975, and only an amateur group under the Bangkok painter, Chakrapand, does occasional performances.

Popular forms

Thailand's most popular theatrical entertainments are NANG talung and LIKAY. Both trace their origins to the Malay south from whence *nora* and *lakon nok* came in generations past.

Little is known of the origin of *nang talung* (literally, 'shadow theatre of Pattalung province'). In its basic form it is related to the WAYANG *siam* of Malaysia and genres in Cambodia and Laos. A single performer, called a *nang nai*, manipulates translucent leather puppets whose iconography depicts the costumes of classical dance drama. Through dialogue and narration, the *nang nai* presents the story which may be based on *Ramakien*-derived stories, local histories or legends. Because it draws large rural audiences, in recent times it has been used for propaganda as well as mass-entertainment purposes.

Likay is a creation of the last hundred years. Remnants of court performance meet rock and roll in this popular, commercial drama that utilizes many elements of traditional forms (dance, singing and *piphat* music). All these elements fuse to suit the tastes of the middle-class housewives who form its prime audience. Actors are cast according to type. They improvise dialogue and song lyrics to play out the scenario. Stories are from the traditional repertoire and also modern inventions. Psuedo-classical dance melds with melodrama. If the female court dancer was the mistress in times past, the *likay* male lead, gigolo to his middle-aged patroness, is the man of the present. The tastes of the bourgeoisie, rather than the courtier, create the style.

The name *likay* is a variant of *dikay*, a form of

Islamic singing (see Indonesia, DIKIR) from the southern provinces, that originally preceded performance. Buddhist chanting for funerals, known as *suat phramalai*, may also have influenced the form in its early stages. As presently acted, it is far from these sources. In its combination of classical, rock and Indian popular singing and dancing it represents the mixture of influences that appeal to current audiences. Its popularity far surpasses the esoteric appeal of the court-derived and modern spoken drama (*lakon phut*) forms. It shows that drama which is sung and danced remains the preferred theatre of the Thai. Current actors such as SOMSAK PHAKDEE increase their popularity by performing on television and radio.

Other popular forms which exhibit some of the same flexibility as *likay* have maintained audiences outside Bangkok. *Mawlum luong* (see Laos, MAWLUM) in northeast Thailand uses Lao language for its Lao-speaking audience. Music is provided by a Lao mouth organ, called a *kaen*, rather than a *piphat*, while costumes, dancing and stories parallel *likay*. Some 3000 troupes were active in 1975. *Lakon saw* is found in northern Thailand: like *mawlum*, it is derived from a local storytelling tradition that has expanded into improvised theatre, perhaps in emulation of the *likay* model. Chinese operas performed by local troupes and by companies invited from Singapore and Hong Kong draw audiences from among the Chinese Thai population.

Different genres of Thai theatre enjoy varying popularity at present. In general, popular folk forms remain the most vigorous. Traditional mask dance and court dance drama retain an important place in government-supported training institutions and through the large-scale productions regularly produced at the National Theatre in Bangkok.

Spoken drama

For a number of reasons, modern spoken drama (*lakon phut*) remains a singularly elitist enterprise in Thailand and has yet to develop more than a tenuous hold on the Thai theatrical imagination. The earliest spoken dramas were staged by and for the Western-educated aristocracy. Prince Vajiravudh (King Rama VI) produced the first spoken drama in 1904 in a 100-seat theatre he had built upon his return from study in Europe. During his reign, 1910–25 he wrote more than 100 plays, romantic and didactic melodramas that swelled with national pride and exorted loyalty to the crown, such as *King Ruang* (*Phra Ruang*, ?1914), as well as Victorian-type farces, light romances and drawing-room comedies. M. L. Pin Malakul was another pioneer of Western-style drama.

Benefiting from the strong policy of Westernization pursued during the Phibul Songkram military government (1938–44), modern theatre re-emerged in the decades following King Rama VI's death and moved beyond aristocratic circles. At this time, chauvinist poet, novelist and playwright Luang Wichit Wathakorn 'modernized' Thai classical dance drama by grafting it with modern music, contemporary dialogue and historically accurate costumes (an attitude not confined to Thailand, but paralleled in China, Japan and other Asian countries).

Western and modern elements were exploited by professional theatre companies such as Chalerm Thai during and immediately following World War II. Their syncretic musical dramas recaptured the time-honoured practice of mischievously fusing foreign music and dance styles into indigenous theatre, proving more accessible to audiences than elitist spoken drama. This popular style went into premature decline with the rise of films and, after 1955, television.

Both Thai classical and modern Western theatre were introduced into the university system beginning in the 1960s. The programme at Chulalongkorn University, under the direction of UCLA-trained Sodsai Pantunkomal, has produced a generation of actors and directors trained in Western, and especially Stanislavskian, dramaturgy. Since the 1970s Mattani Rutnin has synthesized Thai, Asian and Western techniques in productions at Thammasat University. Formal campus theatre, however, remains remote from the national consciousness.

A new-wave theatre appeared in the 1970s in the context of the 'American Era' (1963–73) and the 'Democracy Period' (1973–76). Emerging from a middle class that had experienced a decade of unprecedented economic development, an intelligentsia sought 'self-apprehension' in an era of consolidation of militarism and bureaucratic capitalism. The modest surrealism and absurdism in the plays of Widhayakorn Chiengkul and Suthart Swardsri, leaders of the loose literary grouping,

Crescent Moon (Phrajan Siew), were a prelude to a politically radical theatre of the short-lived Democracy Period. Like its Filipino counterpart, this radical theatre was saturated with American counterculture and Maoist ideals. Kamron Kunadilok, a Crescent Moon adherent, married Western contemporary dramaturgies, particularly Brecht and Grotowski, and Thai folk rituals, fun and games, and popular *likay* theatre music in a trilogy, *Country I*, *Country II*, and *Country III*, produced in Chiengmai. These 'impoverished' theatre pieces told how a farmer, rendered impotent by tradition and feudal corruption, gained strength through fellowship in the urban workers' association. Agit-prop theatre groups, such as Shakdao and Thawanpleung, struck postures of a street parliament in their productions in Bangkok.

The radical theatre officially died in the right-wing coup of 1976, but the concerns of decolonializing theatre are continued by Santi Chitrachinda and Samsak Kanha in their mobile children's theatre company, MAYA, founded in 1981. Concerned with empowering children in city slums and the depressed countryside, MAYA performances infuse Thai folk arts with the contemporary lyricism of comics, cartoons and caricature. The same strategy was employed to provoke social and political consciousness among adult middle-class audiences in their productions of *Phlae Kan* (1991), inspired by the Thai folk classic *Siddharta*, and *Fifty Ways to Torture Children* (1991). Group 28 was initiated in 1986 by Suchart Sawardsri and other Crescent Moon alumni. Guided by artistic director Yale-educated Rassame Paolungtong, Group 28 has gained a tenaciously loyal following with thought-provoking productions of Brecht's *Galileo* (1986), Dürrenmatt's *The Visit* (1988) and Kafka's *The Fall* (1991).

Spoken drama is also performed for more popular audiences in commercial settings. The highest production values are achieved at the Montienthong Theatre in the Montien Hotel in Bangkok, whose audience comes from the prosperous upper middle class. Typically, the group's performers are well-known actors in television drama (*lakon toratat*) and Thai-language films and earn their living from these media. Playwrights, too, usually support themselves by other professions: Somopop Chandaraprapa, author of *Noresuan the Great* (1973), earns his living as an engineer. During

Artists

Phakdee, Somsak (?1960–)

A star of the *LIKAY* theatre who was honoured by the National Theatre in 1975 for the calibre of his work. Son of a *likay* actor, he debuted at age fourteen. In 1975 he moved his company to Bangkok. He has regular radio and television shows. He has developed the style of *likay* costuming and expanded the stage.

Rama VI (Prince Vajiravudh) (r. 1910–25)

This monarch initiated many theatrical experiments. Using traditional dance style he wrote and produced *Savitri*, the story of the faithful Indian wife who wins her husband back from death, as a *lakon rong* (literally, a 'sung drama'), an all-female opera form developed in the 19th century. He also wrote spoken dramas, based on Western models, and opened the first theatres for modern drama. Simultaneously he initiated modern scholarship on traditional dance and drama, identifying *lakon* and *khon* as classical genres, working to pereserve the shadow theatre, and identifying the link between palace forms and folk genres.

Roungnon, Thongbai (?1930–)

He took over the *NORA* troupe of his father, Phoon Roungnon, in 1976 upon the latter's death. He leads the group which includes over 100 performers, all of whom are relatives. Three troupes may be performing in different locales in a single day, usually at temples doing plays undertaken to fulfil a sponsor's vow. *Chaiyachet*, about the abduction of a baby prince of that name and the travails of his exiled mother, is the troupe's most popular piece.

Yupho, Dhanit

A major author of books on Thai theatre, he was director-general of the Fine Arts Department in Bangkok, 1956–68. He distinguished himself as head of the research section of the National Library in 1943 and director of the Division of Music and Drama in the Fine Arts Department from 1946–56. Under his direction the National Theatre was opened; it now provides the major venue for classical dance-drama performance.

---

the 1980s Montienthong productions tended toward locally written social satires. *Lady Amarapa* (*Khunying Amarapa*, 1986) showed a *noveau riche* woman trying to use her fortune to buy a title. *Sorry, No Name Card* (*Khotot tee, mai mee fun un ying yai*, 1988) dealt with the love between a high-born girl and a lower-class boy.

Group 28's disdain of indigenous plays is symptomatic of the larger issue that, with few exceptions such as the work of MAYA and Kunadilok's ensemble pieces, serious modern theatre is nearly synonymous with the staging of Western plays for the educated elite. It appears that a sense of Thai national identity is adequately fulfilled by the symbolic presence of the nationalized traditional performing arts.

Genres

Khon

Classical, court masked dance derived from puppetry (*NANG*) and presenting the *Ramakien* (the story of Prince Rama) or other tales. Male dancers dance–pantomine the chanted narrative of a storyteller accompanied by singers and *piphat* orchestra. The text consists of two literary styles: descriptive poetic verses (*kampak*) and dialogue in rhythmic prose (*ceraca*). The Rama texts are taken from compositions by Kings Rama I, Rama II, and Rama VI. Performers play one of four types: male, female, demon or monkey. An athletic, male style of movement is required of the performers, who engage in elaborate battle pantomimes. The iconography of the masks is strictly regulated: these are full head masks, unlike Japanese and Indonesian face masks. The colouring may be gilt, red, green, black, and 311 distinct masks may be used in the *Ramakein*. Currently women may perform, but in this case the dancer will be unmasked. Present performance occurs in five forms: outdoor performance emphasizing processions and battles without singing (*khon klang pleng*), informal performance indoors without singing (*khon rong nok*), performance danced before a white screen (*khon na co*), performance with singing in the court (*khon nang nai*), and performance with scenery on a modern stage (*khon chak*).

Lakon fai nai

The name means 'inner court play', and may also be called *lakon phuying* or *lakon nai*. The genre includes abstract group dances and dance dramas which, in the past, were performed by the wives and ladies of the king or an aristocrat. Troupes were organized under the artistic direction of a strong female of the court, a wife or sometimes a mother of the ruler. Clowns or a ritual specialist would be the only male performers. Dancers would specialize in a specific role (refined male, refined female, monkey or ogre). Texts, sung by a chorus to the pantomimed dance done to the *piphat* orchestra, were often written by the king or aristocracy. Performers, however, might sing some of their own speeches. Refined movement and fine singing are emphasized in actor training. Plays based on Inao (Prince Panji), the Rama story, local legends, and *Jataka* (stories of incarnations of the Buddha) are presented. The refined dance was derived from dances of Cambodia in the 15th century and later affected genres in Burma and Laos. In the last century training has continued under the government Department of Fine Arts, and performances are frequent in the National Theatre in Bangkok. Today, most performances mix the traditionally all-female dance with male genres like masked KHON.

Likay

Popular, commercial theatre that mixes elements of classical dance and costume, *piphat* and singing with modern music and dance influences, Western formal dress and costume jewelry, and melodramatic plot twists. The form developed as a popular, improvised genre in this century. Performances may be outside on simple temporary stages, in commercial theatre buildings or on permanent temple platforms. In the rainy season troupes may utilize an available cinema. Unlike the traditional theatre which uses no scenery, *likay* uses drops and wings. Typical sets will show throne-room and forest scenes. The

standard stage property is a bench (*tiang*) on which the characters may sit or make love. Prior to the show the troupe storyteller (*khonruang*) will outline the plot to actors, who must remember the order of events. The evening begins with an hour-long instrumental musical prelude during which offerings are made. Next comes an introductory song-and-dance salutation to the audience. Then the play begins. The backstage storyteller gives linking narration, then signals the orchestra to play the entrance or exit music for the characters. Main character types include the male (*phra*), father (*pho*), the female (*nang*), mother (*mae*), villain (*kong*) and clown (*chok*). Each actor improvises his own dialogue and song lyrics. The musical repertoire is drawn from sources as diverse as traditional *lakon* music and pop country music. The most frequent tune, called *Ranikloeng*, can be sung to express any emotion or explore any idea since the actor improvises the words. Plays, while improvised, have plots that follow stock patterns. Comedy, flashy costumes, clever improvisation and striking plot devices predominate. Modern stories as well as classical tales about the characters of *Khun Chaang and Khun Paen*, a romance of the Ayudhaya era, form the repertoire. The genre is sometimes called *yike* or *yeekay*.

Nang

Nang, literally 'leather' and by extension a shadow-puppet play, since figures are usually made of this material. By analogy movies came to be called *nang* since they are also 'shadows' that play on a screen. Puppets are made of hide soaked to soften the material before incising, then the figure may be coloured by natural dyes. Two major forms are found: *nang yai* and *nang talung*.

Nang yai (literally, 'leather' puppet play with 'big' figures) is a shadow play genre associated with court and temple performance that uses uniquely large hide figures. This form is related to Cambodian NANG SBEK THOM. Figures that carry magical properties or represent powerful spirits are made of select material: special hide for Shiva and Vishnu puppets, or tiger skin for the sage figure. Six types of puppets are used: a single character standing or praying, one walking, one flying, one or more characters in a palace setting, characters in battle scenes and special figures. Puppets are held by two poles and parts are not moveable. Figures are danced by puppeteers behind and before a large white screen while narrators sing. Ten dancers, two narrators and ten *piphat* musicians are needed for performances, which are still held for some temple festivals. Each performance begins with a ritual invocation, followed by a procession of puppets or a standard scene in which a pale and a dark monkey battle. Then the story will be enacted. A 17th century poem *Samudaghos* telling how a god incarnates in Prince Samudaghos and wins his wife was once performed, as were stories of the Javanese hero, Panji. Today only the Rama story is presented.

Nang talung ('leather' puppets of 'Pattalung') is the term for the shadow-play tradition of small puppets that is said to have originated in this southern city. The figures are manipulated by a *nang nai* (puppetmaster) who, accompanied by an orchestra of five musicians, performs on an enclosed stage set up for the occasion. Audience members watch, lounging and eating.

Performances of *nang talung* parallel Indonesian and Malay WAYANG in that they continue all night, are performed for festive occasions in the life of the individual or village, use 40–50 of the 200 puppets in the set in a single episode, feature the witty and obscene satire of the clown character, and combine entertainment and instruction.

Nora

Also called *manora*, *lakon jatri*, a seminal ritual-entertainment form of southern Thailand. A traditional troupe was composed of three actors – a hero-prince, a heroine-princess and a clown. The teacher of the dancers was the head of the troupe and the group was completed by an orchestra of musicians, who played a double reed (*pi*), two vase drums (*thon jatri*), a barrel drum (*klong jatri*) and a pair of small horizontal gongs (*khong khu*). Performance, as described in this century, began with a musical prelude, followed by a ritual incantation which described the origin of the *nora*. Then came a series of solo dances of the main characters, songs, skits and, finally, a play. The form, whose prime audience was believed to be spirits, takes its name from the ur-play of the genre: a *Jataka* tale which tells of a divine bird-woman (*kinnari*) named Manora who marries a human prince, then flies back to her home, only to be pursued by her spouse. Now, while the genre retains its roots in mysticism, it freely adapts to the popular tastes of its audiences in repertory, costuming and music. Today it is performed by either men or women and for either entertainment or ritual purposes.

Bibliography

J. R. Brandon, *Theatre in Southeast Asia*, Cambridge, Mass., 1967; Prince Dhaninivat, *Shadow Play (The Nang)*, Bangkok, 1968; Prince Dhaninivat and D. Yupho, *The Khon*, Bangkok, 1962; F. Ingersoll (tr.), *Sang Thong: A Dance Drama from Thailand*, Rutland, Vt., 1973; C. H. Kullman and W. C. Young (eds.), 'Thailand', in *Theatre Companies of the World*, vol. 1, Westport, Conn., 1986; D. Morton, *The Traditional Music of Thailand*, Berkeley, 1976; M. Rutnin (ed.), *The Siamese Theatre*, Bangkok, 1975, and 'The Development of Theatre Studies at the University Level', in *Journal of the National Research Council of Thailand*, 14, 2, July–Dec 1982; S. Virulrak, 'Likay: A Popular Theatre in Thailand', PhD diss., Univ. of Hawaii, 1980, and 'Theatre in Thailand Today', in *Asian Theatre Journal*, 7, 1, 1990; D. Yupho, *Khon Masks*, Bangkok, 1960, *The Khon and Lakon: Dance Dramas Presented by the Department of Fine Arts*, Bangkok, 1963, *The Preliminary Course of Training in Thai Theatrical Art*, Bangkok, 1955, and *Thai Musical Instruments*, Bangkok, 1960; X. Zarina, *Classical Dances of the Orient*, New York, 1967.

Vietnam

This Southeast Asian nation has a population of 66 million and borders on Cambodia, Laos and China. From the 1st to the 10th century the country was ruled by China: Mahayana Buddhism, Confucian values, and Taoist thought entered, while Chinese models influenced court performance. The Hindu kingdom of Champa was incorporated into the country in the 14th century and musical features of Indian origin, including the use of drum syllables, musical modes and improvisation technique, seem to have been borrowed for theatre music from that time. From 1862 to 1945 the country was a French colony: early experiments in staging translations of French playwrights led to a lively spoken-drama movement which continues to the present. Marxist socialist use of theatre as a tool of education and mass communication has helped raise the traditionally low status of performance in recent years. Four major kinds of theatre exist in Vietnam: (1) folk performance; (2) classical performance; (3) popular theatre; and (4) spoken drama.

Folk performance

Folk performance includes proto-theatrical forms (including possession-trance seances, courting songs and storytelling) and folk theatricals. Spirit mediums in Buddhist temples might take up in ecstatic dances the attribute (knives, clubs and so on) of the spirit they incarnated. Mediums' songs, *châu van* in the north, *hâu van* in the central region and *rôi bong* in the south, now dying out, flourished in times past. Courting songs were sung alternately by boys and girls in various areas. These dialogue songs, called *trông quân, quan ho* and other names according to the area, were popular folk performances that laid the groundwork for drama to develop. Storytelling, too, abounded: blind musicians (*xâm xoan*) travelled from village to village singing epic, historical, humorous and erotic songs. The courtesan singer (*a dao*), accompanied

by a musician on a lute (*dan day*), was another significant entertainer of the past.

Within the village environment a folk theatre, HAT CHEO, and water puppetry also emerged. The *hat cheo*, believed to have developed around the first century AD, remains in the northern part of the country. It was performed outside temples or *dinh*, places of worship for the tutelary god which simultaneously served as men's community houses. By the 10th century *hat cheo* included poetry, mime, singing and dancing. The rules of this form were laid down by theorist Luong The Vinh in 1501. Prior to the 20th century, performances were presented during the day in the forecourt of the community house, paid for by the communal fund or rich benefactors. Skits customarily showed the common man triumphing over greedy mandarins. These qualities endeared the form to the masses and eventually to the socialist government of the Democratic Republic of Vietnam which took over the northern part of the country after World War II. Several semi-professional troupes currently perform *hat cheo* in the Hanoi region.

Water puppetry, MUÁ RÔI NUOC, is another significant, and unique, folk theatre within the oral tradition. According to Dinh Gia Khanh, a stone inscription on a pillar in Nan Ninh province proves the form was well developed by AD 1121. Performances of short interludes, animals fighting and comic scenes, are staged on ponds via refined manipulation technique by manipulators hidden behind a staging house.

Classical performance

Vietnam's court-supported arts are strongly sinicized. Court dances, like Chinese forms, are divided into *van vu* ('civil dance') and *vo vu* ('military dance'). HAT BÔI (alternatively *hat tuông, tuông*) is a classical court theatre. Tradition holds that the form dates from 1285 when a Chinese actor, captured by a Vietnamese general, taught his art to the Vietnamese performers.

From the 13th to the 17th centuries the form served primarily as a court entertainment in Hanoi. The actor Dao Duy Tu (1572–1634) is credited with popularizing the form by introducing southern musical styles of Champa, an Indian-influenced kingdom. These poignant 'southern songs' (hat nam) were endearing to commoners and contrasted with the 'foreigners' songs' (hat khach) and patter songs (noi lôi, 'stylized speaking') already a part of this operatic form.

During the 18th and 19th centuries the form had the support of the Nguyen dynasty of Central Vietnam. Gia Long (1802–20) had the first theatre built in the imperial palace at Hue, the capital. Chinese influences were reinforced during the reign of Emperor Minh Mang (1820–41) when imported Chinese actors reworked the form. The current similarities between hat bôi and Cantonese opera in gestures, costumes and makeup probably result from this reform. However, distinctive Vietnamese sentiments in the scripts and musical and theatrical traits distinguish it from Chinese models.

An official court troupe, Phuong Nha Tro, operated until 1946 when court support faltered. Plays tend to exalt the emperor, and uphold Confucian ethics and feudal values. This content and Chinese features have alienated some recent audiences from hat bôi. Doan Quan Tan attempted a revision in the 1940s which involved the elimination of the falsetto voice and Chinese words. Up to the 1970s the form was still performed in Saigon, Hue and other areas, but lacked an enthusiastic audience.

Popular theatre

Vietnamese CAI LUONG ('reformed theatre') is a popular musical theatre. It reached a peak of popularity in the 1920s and continues today especially in the southern part of the country. Songs are the most significant feature of the performance. Tu dai, ballads in which one singer would perform a few lines and another sing a reply, form the base of cai luong. Around 1916 performers of one particular ballad 'The Song of Nguyet Nga' are said to have begun presenting the song in a more dramatic style. Travelling circuses began including this dramatic playlet in their programmes. The greater part of the performance was given to the singing of the songs. The clown who developed his own business and monologues soon became an important element in the performance. The falsetto voice of hat bôi was abandoned but, since many of the early performers were trained in the classical theatre, its southern songs were still used for sad scenes and some of the stirring, military songs were also incorporated. Diversity of subject matter was incorporated and the form remained popular until recently. The continuing political unrest after the partition of the country in 1954 was reflected in plays which criticized the French regime. Popular plays included modern domestic dramas and traditional stories, such as the The Story of Thuy Kieu, the story of a virtuous woman who becomes a courtesan against her will and finally is reunited with her first love.

In 1980, the government of Vietnam supported 16 professional hat cheo troupes, 13 cai luong troupes, 3 hat bôi troupes, 3 puppet troupes and a score of troupes devoted to contemporary spoken drama. Students are trained in all traditional genres at the Academy of Theatre and Film in Hanoi, which opened in 1980. Major cities have theatres which specialize in one or another form, or book in performances of various genres. Performers are paid a wage comparable to professionals in teaching or medicine, showing the respect the current government accords to the arts.

Modern spoken drama

The modern theatre journey of Vietnam up to 1954 took a course not too dissimilar from that traversed by many other Southeast Asian countries. From its beginnings at the opening of the 20th century, modern drama, or KICH NÔI, was an undertaking of a newly urbanized literary elite who reflected the influence of privileged Western education under the French colonial regime. The trek began with 'stilted' translations into the romanized 'national language' of Vietnam (quoc-ngug) of classical French dramas. Beginning with Molière's The Miser, staged in 1907, many plays by Molière and Corneille were translated and performed by Vietnamese actors. The first Vietnamese spoken drama was A Cup of Poison (Chen thuot doc), by Vu Dinh Long (1901–60), performed in Hanoi in 1921. It melodramatically depicts the impending downfall of a morally crippled civil servant, and his sudden and fortuitous rescue.

Most of the early spoken dramas, however, were

'brittle' Vietnamese versions of romantic drawing-room comedies, staged mainly by Western-oriented clubs and societies. An impressive exception to the milieu of insouciant 'amateur theatricals' were the dramatic forays of the advocate of 'new (or 'modernized') poetry', Pham Huy Thong, who briefly in the mid 1930s experimented with miniaturist verse tragedies.

The popular route to Westernization was taken by theatre practitioners convening informal marriages between the firmly ensconced and multifarious indigenous traditional theatre forms (for example, hat cheo and hat bôi) and Western staging techniques, costumes, music and, eventually, kitsch Western drama plots from the stage and screen. One of the most resilient and socially significant of the new theatre genres born of this unprepossessing fusion is the musical drama, cai luong, or 'reformed theatre', originating in Southern Vietnam around the time of World War I. Marr believes the mobile cai luong troupes 'undoubtedly played a major role in disseminating new ideas and language beyond the intelligentsia', holding sway over the Vietnamese dramatic imagination in the south until the advent of television in the 1960s and rendering impotent efforts of spoken-drama adherents to seriously pursue 'realism'.

The search for 'realistic' gestures by some spoken-drama writers coincided with the rise of Vietnamese nationalism. The consequence was passionately anti-colonial plays including Nam Xoung's The Annamite Frenchman (Ong tay An-nam, 1931), which in Molière fashion vilified the pretensions of francophile Vietnamese intellectuals. A differing strand of nationalism was explored by playwright NGYUEN HUY TUONG, who emerged as one of the most influential literary figures of his time. His historical play, Vu Nhu To (1943) about the dilemma of an imperial architect forced to choose between personal integrity and service to country, disclosed a visceral anti-establishment stance. Anticipating the appearance of a socialist direction in Vietnamese politics, Bac Son, that opened in Hanoi in 1945, pitted revolutionaries (heroic Bac Son guerilla fighters) against counter-revolutionaries (oppressive French).

The war with the French consumed the passions of the Vietnamese from the 1945 August Revolution to the 1954 Geneva Agreement that split the country into two parts. Although good plays were scarce, incendiary anti-French spoken dramas gained acceptance during this period. In areas the Vietnamese Communist Party gradually came to dominate, the seeds of 'socialist realism' in modern Vietnamese theatre were planted. In 1959 the Ecole Des Arts Théâtraux was established in Hanoi. The Maoist precept that writers and artists must identify with the masses both in life and art underlay official revival of folk theatre and adaptations of European dramas. Dissidence against the Party was not tolerated, as exposed by the 1956 crackdown on rebellious writers and poets. To a degree unmatched in Southeast Asia, theatre was resolutely wielded as a propaganda to uphold the socialist revolutionary system until 1975, when North and South Vietnam were reunified.

Especially after American entry into the conflict, South Vietnam's promotion of dramatic competitions and mobile theatre companies dispensing music, magic show and drama faced a mirror image in the arts campaign of the National Liberation Front. Following reunification, southern authors, who had enjoyed greater creative freedom, were charged with anti-communism, escapist erotica, spiritual demoralization of 'Americanized' society and existentialism. In Steinberg's view the intolerant and oppressive stance of the new Vietnamese government toward the remants of South Vietnamese 'critical middle-class intelligentsia...was a Vietnamese national disaster of incalculable proportions'. This provides a clue as to why, despite the government's agressive promotion and support of 23 professional kich nôi troupes, Vietnam lags behind in forging an innovative and nationally identifiable modern theatre.

Mackerras notes that in 1984 an anti-Chinese impulse dominated modern drama as a result of the Chinese invasion of Vietnam in 1979. However government policy was not so rigid as to disallow the exposure of 'serious social problems', as in Through the Night (Qua dem), which treats the re-education of a former Saigon supporter in the style of socialist realism. The contemporary comedy Once in a Lifetime (Doi chi co mot lan), staged in Ho Chi Minh City, unmasked conspicuous consumption at weddings and ubiquitous 'free marketeers' who dupe people into extravagance. The propaganda is light and there is an 'absence of class or foreign enemies'. Self-criticism is often tolerated so long as it does not fundamentally question the socialist system.

Vietnamese *glasnost* (*doi moi*, 'renovation') in 1986 opened the door to a new wave of theatre that focused on the conflict of generations and the bankruptcy of idealism, and spun parables about bureaucratic corruption. Writers such as Nguyen Huy Thiep and Pham Thi Hoa, in adopting a surrealistic mode, jousted with hegemonic socialist realism. In the late 1980s, troubled by the retreat of communism in eastern Europe and the Tiananmen revolt in China, the aging leaders of Vietnam appear to be backing off from *doi moi*. This has not stopped Thiep from writing a revisionist historical drama, *Love Remains* (*Con Lai Tinh Yeu*, 1990) featuring as hero the Kuomintang-like leader of the 1930s, Nguyen Thu Hoc, which was published in a well-known literary journal.

Deviations from the standard line can be explained in part by an 'anti-authoritarian' streak in Vietnamese character and the personalized nature of much of Southeast Asian politics. Important artists also hold prominent positions in official arts organizations that arbitrate on 'deviationist' practices. Thus, Dr Nguyen Dinh Quang, author, theatre director and drama professor, is Vice Minister of Culture and the Arts. If the moderating influences nurturing creative innovation are allowed breathing space in the febrile milieu of the politicized arts, the arrival of 'a truly distinct Vietnamese spoken drama' might not be too far away.

Genres

Cai luong

Literally, 'reformed theatre', a melodramatic, popular, sung drama of the south developed around 1916 from ballad-singing traditions which were then amalgamated with tunes and techniques of the classical HAT BÔI opera. Dang Thuc Lieng, a *hat bôi* performer, was instrumental in some of the early reforms as was actor-author Nam Chau. The popular tune 'Remembrances' ('Vong Cô') became an important part of the genre in the 1920s and figures prominently in every performance to the present. Different parts of this song will occur in different sections of the play. Musical accompaniment varies with the story performed, but frequently used instruments include

---

Artists

Dao Duy Tu (1572–1634)
Actor and author. He popularized courtly HAT BÔI by introducing the emotional musical styles of Champa. He authored the beloved *Fort of Son Hou*, which recounts how political intrigue prevails until the rightful heir is returned to the Vietnamese throne.

Ngyugen Huy Tuong (1912–60)
Author, film writer and playwright. He is esteemed for scripts like *Vu Nhu To* (1943), a historical play in five acts in which the title character, an architect commissioned to build a palace for a corrupt emperor, struggles with his conscience. The responsibility of an artist in a corrupt social order is skilfully explored. *Bac Son* (1945), named after a village, explores the evil nature of a collaborator. A Vietnamese in the service of the French kills his wife and father-in-law causing the villagers of Bac Son to rise against him.

---

a sixteen-string zither (*don tranh*), two-string violin (*don co*), two-string lute (*don nguyet*), wooden clappers, drums, cymbals, gongs and electric guitars. The form reached its zenith in the 1930s when French dances and tunes might be readily combined with more traditional stories. Plays could be on social themes depicting current Vietnamese life, Chinese or Western themes. During the 1930s troupes introduced innovations to lure audiences: Western plays such as Schiller's *Maria Stuart* and Shakespeare's *Hamlet* were adapted. Nam Phi introduced her version of Folies-Bergère dancing, and Hong Kong flying and sword-fighting techniques were introduced by the actor Mui Buu, giving rise to a new genre called 'flying plays'. Records of performances were released. The use of scenery and proscenium stage was introduced from the West, and Western instruments were incorporated into the orchestra. As television and film became established, much of this popular energy moved toward those genres. The most significant troupe of the 1950s and 60s was Kim Chung led by Nguyen Viet Long.

Hat bôi

Alternatively called *hat tuông* or *tuông*. Classical opera tradition developed in the courts from the 11th century under the influence of Chinese models and reaching its zenith during the reign of the Nguyen emperor Minh Mang (1820–41). The colour symbolism in painted-face characters corresponds closely, but not exactly, to Chinese practice. The falsetto voice, a bare stage with only a table and chairs to create the locale, stylized mimes for riding a horse or expressing emotion, costume practices and character types are related to Chinese models. Likewise, the division of the repertory into plays based on the history of China and Vietnam (*tuong thay*) and those dealing with commoners (*tuong do*) is related to Chinese categories of military and civil. The orchestral instrumentation and the Vietnamese language of the plays, replete with sinicized words and Chinese literary references, show borrowing too. But distinctive Vietnamese features are also apparent: many plays are strongly anti-Chinese; women have always played female roles; many plays deal with Vietnamese history and events and utilize Vietnamese dress; 'water sleeves' and the associated movement techniques characteristic of Chinese opera are lacking; and, of course, songs retain the distinctive Vietnamese musical flavour.

Song categories include southern songs (*hat nam*), which are considered emotionally evocative, *hat khach* or foreigners' songs which are stirring, and patter songs, *noi lôi*. The orchestra includes a small drum (*trong bat cau*), principal drum (*trong com*), war drum (*trong chien*), a two-string violin (*don co, don gao*), a three-chord lute (*dan tam*), a flute (*ong sao*), a reed instrument (*cay ken*), gong (*dong la*) and cymbals (*chap choa*).

Hat cheo

An old folk genre evolved from ceremonial entertainments and including dances, songs and skits. In the past the stage area was separated from the audience by a rope, and costumes hung in view of the audience. Performers were largely amateurs who showed skill at singing work-songs, but some risked the social opprobrium that was an actor's lot to join professional troupes in which they eked out an existence. The texts and songs were

A traditional *hat bôi* performance, televised from the studio in Ho Chi Minh City, 1970.

passed orally from one generation of performers to the next. The clown (*he*) improvised wittily during the graceful dance-and-song show of the actors. It has been supported since 1946 by the marxist government which found it a pliable form for government messages. It is taught at the National Film and Theatre Academy and is performed by semiprofessional troupes around Hanoi.

Kich nôi

Spoken drama developed in this century under the influence of Western models. The form, acted in realistic style and dealing with social issues, helped mould performance in cinema and television as these new genres evolved in this century. Strongly controlled under socialist artist policies,

249

it is more favoured, because of its relevance to contemporary society, than traditional genres. Since the 1980s it has become very popular with youthful audiences especially in Hanoi and Ho Chi Minh City (Saigon).

Muá rôi nuoc

A highly developed form of water puppetry has existed in Vietnam since at least the 12th century. A pond forms the stage and music accompanies the presentation. Puppets of about $1\frac{1}{2}$–3 ft are mounted on frames or attached to long poles that are submerged in the water out of view. Manipulators work behind a stage house constructed for the occasion. Animal battles, acrobatic feats, village activities and popular tales, such as that of the Trung sisters who opposed Chinese tyranny, are depicted. The puppet clown, Chu Teu, enlivens the performance with humour. Puppetry societies are village-based with admission to the group by consensus of the members.

Students at the National Film and Theatre Academy also learn to perform this genre.

Bibliography

J. R. Brandon, *Theatre in Southeast Asia*, Cambridge, Mass., 1967; M. Durand and Nguyen Tran Huan, *An Introduction to Vietnamese Literature*, tr. D. M. Hawke, New York, 1985; D. Hauch, 'The Cai Luong Theatre of Vietnam, 1915–1970', PhD diss., Southern Illinois University, 1972 (University Microfilms); Huynh Khac Dung, *Hat Bôi, Théâtre traditionnel du Viêt-nam*, Saigon, 1970; C. Mackerras, 'Theatre in Vietnam', in *Asian Theatre Journal*, 4, 1, Spring 1987; Song-Ban, *The Vietnamese Theatre*, Hanoi, 1960; Trân Van Khê, 'Vietnam', in *New Grove Dictionary of Music and Musicians*, ed. S. Sadie, New York, 1980, 'Vietnamese Water Puppets', in *Performing Arts Journal*, 9, 1, 1985, and 'Le théâtre vietnamien', in *Les théâtres d'Asie*, ed. J. Jacquot, Paris, 1968.

INDEX OF ARTISTS AND GENRES

The page references are to the main entries for artists and genres

Index

ILLUSTRATION ACKNOWLEDGEMENTS

The publishers gratefully acknowledge the following for supplying illustrations and granting permission for their use. We would like to thank especially those contributors who lent us original photographs from their own collection.

While every effort has been made to obtain permission to use photographs, we shall be pleased to make proper acknowledgements in future editions if any errors have been made.

3, 74, 75, 76, 77, 83 Farley Richmond; 5 Francis Haar; 7 James Araki; 10, 174 Shōchiku; 13, 149, 181 Asia Society; 16, 218 Photo: D. Linder, Asia Society; 21, 24, 152, 155, 160, 183, 231 James R. Brandon; ii, 28, 33, 35, 44, 45, 46, 54, 56 Colin Mackerras; 61 Office of Public Information, Hong Kong Urban Council; 71 Bahorupee; 84, 103 Sangeet Natak Akademi; 119, 122, 134 Rachel Cooper; 120 Kathy Foley; 125 Aislinn Scofield; 139, 199 Roger A. Long; 158 Mikoshiba Shigeru; 163 National Theatre of Japan; 176 University Theatre, University of Hawai'i; 188 Oh-kon Cho; 195 Ghulam-Sarwar Yousof; 197 Department of Information, Malaysia; 209 East–West Center; 215 Philippine Tourist and Travel Association; 219 Kennedy Theatre, University of Hawai'i; 233 Liu Cheng-hsiang; 235,239 Public Relations Department, Thailand; 249 Embassy of Vietnam.